W9-BBM-292

SOUTHERN LIVING® COOKBOOK

Casseroles

Contents

Library of Congress Catalog Card No: 67–30672

Introduction

Southern cooking has come down to us through three centuries—from early Jamestown in the 1600's to metropolitan today. In many cases, continental dishes have merged with native foods to produce our delectable Southern dishes. This is especially true of casseroles—those wonderful combinations of several foods cooked together until flavors blend and complement each other.

Southern homemakers, perhaps the busiest people anywhere, will find this Casseroles Edition of the Southern Living Cookbook a wonderful help to their meal planning.

Casseroles can be put together so quickly, they are the perfect answer to what to serve on busy days. And, no other jiffy dishes are as tasty and as nourishing. Add your salad, bread, beverage, and maybe a dessert, and you have a complete meal.

For party luncheons, after-the-game get-togethers, or any time you have friends over, you can be sure of a pretty, may-I-have-seconds dish with a casserole.

Casseroles always can be prepared in advance, then popped in the oven while you chat with your guests or prepare the rest of the meal. Soon, it's waiting—hot and tasty.

So-delicious breads are included in this edition, too. Add that something extra to your home-cooked meal with airy-light yeast breads, sweet breads and quick breads.

All of the casserole and bread recipes in this wonderful collection are favorites of homemakers throughout the South. They have been stamped with the approval of a Southern family, so you know you can use them confidently.

Under each recipe, you will find the name of the homemaker who submitted it. She has tried and tested the recipe in her own kitchen. Now she shares it with you.

Planning delicious and well balanced meals will become trouble-free with the recipes in this cookbook. There is a suitable casserole and bread recipe for every occasion, all designed to please Southern homemakers.

Lena Sturges, Foods Editor

Southern Living

Dishes With a History

Casserole cookery began over 200 years ago, originating in France about 1725. The term "casserole" developed from the "casse," a utensil used by European cooks for cooking stews and other large amounts of foods.

The original unglazed clay pot in which casseroles were cooked has not changed shape much since ancient times. It is squat, with bulging sides, easily grasped round handles and a slightly arched lid.

The whole idea of casseroles is to bring together main course foods, bind them with a sauce and seasonings and bake in the oven.

The ease with which casseroles are made seems to make them modern dishes. They save today's busy homemaker time, and keep the family budget in trim since casseroles are an excellent way to use leftovers.

Casseroles can be made from the very finest of ingredients—or from the lowly leftover. And they can be as simple or as elaborate as the homemaker wants.

Whether casseroles are served at a formal dinner party or a back-yard cook-out, they have a distinct advantage. They are easy to prepare.

Most casseroles are made by combining ingredients in a casserole dish and baking. There's no bother of mixing in several bowls before putting into the baking dish. Best of all, casseroles don't need to be watched during cooking.

Leftovers or any of the less-tender cuts of meat are ideal and economical for casserole cookery. The less-tender cuts, which are likewise less expensive, are perfectly adapted since casseroles usually are cooked for long periods at low temperatures.

As a real time saver, why not make two casseroles today, and freeze one for another meal? Many casseroles can be frozen right in the colorful containers in which they are cooked. Later, the casserole can be heated in the same container and taken right to the table.

Casseroles have the wonderful ability to expand and serve more people than you ever thought possible. If unexpected guests arrive for dinner, just take a casserole out of your freezer, heat it and serve.

For Spotless Containers

Clean your casserole containers thoroughly after each use. This makes it an easy job. Do not allow stains to accumulate because they will be hard to remove later. The container must be spotless when it is used as a serving dish.

GLASS—Containers of glass are cleaned by washing with soap and water. Stubborn stains can be removed by scouring with cleaning pads or a fine cleansing powder.

IRON—Probably the oldest material used in making cookware is iron. It must be kept seasoned to prevent rust. To season: grease with unsalted fat or oil, place in warm oven for several hours. Add more fat or oil when necessary, turn heat off, let container cool and remove excess oil with paper towel. Never let water stand in an iron container. It will begin to rust. In storing iron cookware, it's a good idea to turn it upside-down to make certain any water in it will drain.

PYROCERAM—This ceramic material is easy to clean. Just use soap and water. If steel wool or an abrasive is used on pyroceram, it will produce scratch marks. The best method of removing any stains is to soak the container for 10 minutes in 3 tablespoons of chlorine bleach to 1 quart of warm water.

TEFLON—Of all the materials used for containers, Teflon is probably the easiest to clean. Just wash in warm soapy water and rinse. There is no scouring necessary. A nylon pad will remove any particles you can't remove with a cloth. In storing Teflon containers, do not stack other utensils or dishes on them.

ENAMEL—Enamel can be cared for in the same manner as glass. It is formed by fusing glass on metal. Since enamel will chip and crack, it must be handled with care.

ALUMINUM—When aluminum turns dark from water, eggs or such, place 2 teaspoons of cream of tartar and 1 quart of water in a skillet or pan. Let this mixture boil for 10 minutes, then scrub lightly with a steel wool pad. Daily care of aluminum requires no more than the usual washing with soap and water.

CHROME—Utensils made of chrome can be cleaned by washing with soap and water, then polished with a soft dry cloth.

STEEL—Simply wash steel utensils with soap and water, being sure to dry thoroughly. Scour stubborn spots lightly. A household cleanser can be used to remove heat marks from steel containers.

Abbreviations in This Book

Cup	c.	Large	lge.
Tablespoon	tbsp.	Package	pkg.
Teaspoon	tsp.	Small	sm.
Pound	lb.	Dozen	doz.
Ounce	oz.	Pint	pt.

SUBSTITUTIONS

1 cup whole milk = ½ cup of evaporated milk plus ½ cup of water or 4 tablespoons of dry whole milk plus 1 cup of water.

1 cup skim milk = 3 to 4 tablespoons of nonfat dry milk plus 1 cup of water.

1 whole egg, for thickening or baking = 2 egg yolks or 2 tablespoons dried whole egg plus 2½ tablespoons water.

1 tablespoon flour, for thickening = ½ tablespoon cornstarch, potato starch, or rice starch.

1 cup cake flour, for baking = ⅞ cup all-purpose flour.

1 cup all-purpose flour, for baking breads = up to ½ cup bran, whole wheat flour or cornmeal mixed with enough all-purpose flour to fill a cup.

1 teaspoon baking powder = ⅓ teaspoon baking soda plus ½ teaspoon cream of tartar.

IN MEASURING, REMEMBER . . .

3 tsp. = 1 tbsp.
2 tbsp. = ⅛ c.
4 tbsp. = ¼ c.
8 tbsp. = ½ c.
16 tbsp. = 1 c.
5 tbsp. + 1 tsp. = ⅓ c.
12 tbsp. = ¾ c.
4 oz. = ½ c.
8 oz. = 1 c.
2 c. fat = 1 lb.
2 c. = 1 pt.
2 pt. = 1 qt.

1 qt. = 4 c.
2 c. sugar = 1 lb.
⅝ c. = ½ c. + 2 tbsp.
⅞ c. = ¾ c. + 2 tbsp.
5½ c. powdered sugar = 1 lb.
2¼ c. brown sugar = 1 lb.
4 c. sifted all-purpose flour = 1 lb.
4¾ c. sifted cake flour = 1 lb.
1 lb. butter = 2 c. or 4 sticks
A Few Grains = Less than ⅛ tsp.
Pinch is as much as can be taken between tip of finger and thumb.

Combine With Imagination

Experiment with casseroles. Let your imagination run rampant! With a dash of this and a bit of that, you can create casserole masterpieces. You'll find that casserole cookery is probably the easiest of all and may well be the most fun.

As with all cooking, you must have good ingredients. This means that the quality of the product must be good.

The basic ingredients for casseroles are meat, a combination of meat and vegetables, vegetables, cereals and pastas.

Begin with your basic recipe. Add to it until you have just the flavor you want. If you decide to use leftovers, be sure to use only enough for one meal. No leftover is so good that it can stand being left over for several meals.

Gravies or sauces add flavor to meat dishes. Canned creamed soups are convenient and add zest to most casseroles.

Cheese sprinkled over the top of almost any casserole adds color and nutritional value. But the cheese must only season the dish and not dominate it.

Hot cereals and pastas—cooked rice, spaghetti, noodles or macaroni—are economical extenders and make leftovers go further. Use equal amounts of ground, thinly sliced or diced meat with these starchy extenders to stretch your casserole. Perk up the flavors of these combinations with seasonings.

Speaking of seasonings . . . it's great fun to experiment with different ones. Mashed garlic, parsley, tomato paste, meat sauce, chili sauce, mustard or lemon juice . . . all give a delightful different flavor.

INGREDIENTS FOR CASSEROLES

BEGIN WITH	COMBINE WITH	BIND WITH	FINISH WITH
Meat	Rolled Oats	Crumbs	Pastry
Poultry	Rice	Sauce	Crumbs
Seafood	Eggs	Gravy	Biscuits
Cheese	Vegetables	Eggs	

BEGIN WITH	COMBINE WITH	BIND WITH
Spaghetti	Sauces	Crumbs
Macaroni	Meat	Eggs
Noodles	Cheese	Soups
Rice	Sour Cream	Sauce
Beans	Vegetables	Gravy
Cornmeal	Soups	

What They Mean

BAKE To cook foods in the oven at a set temperature.

BASTE To spread, brush or pour water, melted fat or other liquid over food.

BEAT To make a mixture smooth or to introduce air by using a brisk, regular motion that lifts the mixture over and over.

BEAT LIGHTLY To stir with a fork to mix. This process usually applies to mixing the whites of yolks of eggs.

BIND To hold foods together with a sauce or other ingredients.

BLANCH To boil in water for a short time, or to pour boiling water over food, then drain it almost immediately.

BLEND To combine two or more ingredients by mixing thoroughly.

BOIL To cook in boiling water or liquid.

BREAD To roll or coat with bread crumbs. Often the food is first dipped into beaten egg and then rolled in crumbs.

BRUSH To spread or brush with melted fat or other liquid to coat.

CHILL To cool in the refrigerator or other cold place.

CHOP To cut into small pieces with a sharp knife.

CREAM To work one or more foods until mixture is soft and creamy or fluffy.

CUBE To cut into small squares of equal size.

DICE To cut into small cubes.

DISJOINT To cut poultry into pieces at the joints.

DISSOLVE To completely mix dry ingredients with liquid until in solution.

DOT To scatter small pieces of butter or other fat over food before cooking.

DREDGE To coat or sprinkle lightly with flour, sugar, etc., until food is well covered.

DUST To sprinkle food lightly with a dry ingredient such as paprika.

FILLET	To cut a piece of meat or fish into desired shape, removing all bones.
FLAKE	To break into small pieces with a fork.
FOLD	To combine by using two motions, cutting vertically through the mixture and turning over and over by sliding the implement across the bottom of the mixing bowl with each turn.
GARNISH	To decorate foods, usually with other foods.
GLAZE	To brush or pour a shiny coating over foods.
GRATE	To cut food into minute particles by rubbing on a grater.
GRIND	To cut food into tiny particles by putting through a food grinder.
JULIENNE	Foods cut into match-thin strips.
KNEAD	To fold, turn and press down on dough with the hands until it becomes smooth and elastic.
MARINATE	To let food stand in an acid-oil mixture.
MELT	To liquefy by the addition of heat.
MINCE	To cut or chop into very small pieces.
MIX	To combine ingredients in any way that evenly distributes them.
PARBOIL	To partially cook food in boiling water before cooking completely by another method.
PARE	To cut off the outside covering.
PEEL	To strip off the outside covering.
PREHEAT	To heat oven to desired temperature before putting food in oven.
SAUTE	To cook in small amount of fat in skillet.
SCALD	To heat milk to just below the boiling point.
SCALLOP	To bake food in layers with a sauce.
SEAR	To brown surface quickly over high heat as in a hot skillet.
SHRED	To cut fine with a knife or sharp instrument.
SIFT	To put dry ingredients through a sieve or sifter.
SLIVER	To slice into long, thin strips.
STEW	To cook long and slowly in a liquid.
STIR	To mix foods with a circular motion for the purpose of blending or obtaining uniform consistency.
WHIP	To beat rapidly to produce expansion by incorporating air as applied to cream, egg and gelatin dishes.

The nutritional value of a meal is increased when a casserole that contains meat is served. Meat and vegetables that are combined to make a delicious main dish need only a salad, bread and beverage to make a meal complete. Bread may be omitted from the meal if a pastry topping is added to the casserole, or if a crisp crusty pastry shell is filled with casserole mixture.

The homemaker must recognize the need to buy meat wisely since meat is a relatively expensive item in the food budget. She must care for it properly and prepare it to retain the nutrients and develop the flavor.

FOR TOP-QUALITY MEATS

If the high quality of meat is to be maintained, it must be stored correctly. There are certain ways to store meat whether it is fresh, frozen, cooked or processed.

Fresh Meat—Wrap it loosely in waxed paper and store it in the coldest part of the refrigerator. The meat should not be stored in the market wrapper.

Frozen Meat—Use a paper that will keep out moisture and vapor. After packaging, store meat in a freezer at 0°F. or below. Check the chart below to find the maximum storage time for the meat. Carefully label each package with the date it was packaged and the kind of meat. Use the older packages first when you're cooking.

FREEZER STORAGE CHART

MEAT	MAXIMUM STORAGE TIME (Months)
Beef	6 to 12
Ground beef, veal and lamb	3 to 4
Lamb and veal	6 to 9
Pork	3 to 6
Ground pork	1 to 3
Variety meats	3 to 4

Cooked Meat—Cool quickly and store in the refrigerator either covered or wrapped.

Processed Meat—Store cured meats and ready-to-serve meats in the coldest part of the refrigerator. These meats should not be frozen. Ready-to-serve meats can be kept in the refrigerator about one week; cured meats can be kept one to two weeks.

Extra-Special Hamburger

Hamburger, the all-time national favorite, can be prepared in numerous ways for delicious dishes. When it is combined with other ingredients into a flavorful casserole, ground beef becomes fit for the king of your house.

The relative economy of ground beef, its nutrition, and the fact that just about everybody likes it make it most appealing.

FRESH GROUND BEEF

Look for a bright red color when you buy ground beef. This indicates it is fresh. Beef can be purchased as regular ground and lean ground. The two contain different amounts of fat. Ground lean should not contain more than 12% fat and regular ground beef should not contain more than 25%. The fat amounts are regulated by the United States Department of Agriculture.

Ground beef is usually bought pre-packaged. However, some homemakers still prefer to buy beef and have it ground to their order. Buy boned chuck for most economical, flavorful, juiciest ground beef. Then have it ground. The more beef is ground, the more compact it becomes. This compactness is fine if you plan to make meatballs or loaves. But, if you plan to use your ground beef for patties, have it ground coarsely only once.

Usually 1 pound of ground beef will make four generous servings. When you use rice, spaghetti or vegetables to stretch the meat, a pound of ground beef will probably serve five.

STORE IT IMMEDIATELY

If you plan to use your ground beef the day you buy it or the following day, wrap the meat loosely in waxed paper and refrigerate it immediately.

Freeze it the day you buy it if you plan to keep it longer. Remove the market wrapper and wrap in freezer paper or place it in an airtight plastic container. Ground beef stored in the freezer at 0°F. or below will keep for three to four months.

Easy Freezing

When you plan to make a casserole, prepare enough for two. It's just as easy to prepare enough to have one to serve and one to freeze! Think how wonderfully convenient it will be when unexpected guests come. While the casserole is in the oven heating, you will have time to sit and visit.

There are two ways of preparing a casserole for freezing. You can mix all the ingredients and freeze it uncooked. Or, you can bake the casserole and then freeze it. The wonderful thing about frozen cooked foods is they are ready to eat as soon as they are reheated. There's no time spent in preparing casseroles when you have so many other things to think of before mealtime.

Think how thrifty you can be when you use those leftovers in making delicious casseroles. Any time you have leftover meat it can be frozen for later use in casseroles. You will especially appreciate your freezer and the many casseroles you can prepare from leftover meat when you have food left from holidays.

REMEMBER WHEN FREEZING . . .

1. The smaller the pieces of meat you freeze, the more they will dry out in the freezer.
2. Most fried foods will lose their crispness when frozen.
3. Monosodium glutamate can be added to precooked foods during reheating to bring out the flavor of meats and vegetables.
4. A topping for a casserole should be added just before reheating.
5. Use only the best ingredients. You cannot expect a delicious casserole to develop from poor quality ingredients.
6. Do not completely cook the food in the casserole as some will become soft when reheated.
7. Add only small amounts of fat to food which will be frozen. It becomes rancid after about two months.
8. Garlic, cloves, pimiento and green pepper become strong after frozen. It is best to underseason your casseroles with these. Onions lose flavor.
9. Salad greens and other raw vegetables lose crispness and should not be frozen.
10. Diced potatoes should be added just before reheating casseroles. They will crumble if frozen with other ingredients.
11. Sauces and mayonnaise sometimes separate during freezing.
12. Egg whites which have been hard-cooked will become tough when frozen unless put through a sieve. Yolks of eggs can be put through a sieve or may be diced.

Package It Right

Casseroles can easily be frozen in the container in which they will be heated and served. There are other types of packaging materials for freezer use.

It is most important to package food properly before freezing. A freezer package must meet several requirements.

1. It must not hold moisture or vapor. A package that is moisture and vapor proof will keep the food from drying out.
2. The package should be tight to prevent darkening of food and rancidity.
3. It should be easy to pack in the freezer.
4. It must be sturdy and able to withstand freezing temperatures.
5. It must be odor free.
6. The package should be the proper size for the number of people it will serve.
7. The package should be of high quality but does not have to be the most expensive on the market.

In preparing a casserole, follow the recipe closely. If you plan to freeze it, the only change you will need to make is in amount of seasoning added to the dish.

As with any food which is to be frozen, it is important to work fast and prepare the food as quickly as possible. Take care not to overcook if the casserole is to be cooked before freezing. It is best to cook until almost done and then freeze. When reheated, the casserole will have to time to finish the cooking process.

The food should be chilled immediately by placing in a pan of ice water. Package food right away. After packaging, put the food in the freezer at once. Do not allow the casserole to remain at room temperature.

When reheating the dish, avoid overheating. Any food can cook for too long and lose some of its flavor.

The Basic Four

You need certain foods daily regardless of whether you're young or old. In planning meals, consider the food groups and the amount of each food needed daily. Certain foods in each group must be included every day for nutrition. The basic four food groups are meat, vegetables and fruits, cereals and breads, and milk.

1. MEAT—Two or more servings are needed daily. This group includes beef, pork, veal, lamb, variety meat, fish and shellfish, poultry and eggs. Meat substitutes such as dry beans, dry peas, peanuts, peanut butter, and lentils are in this group. About half of the protein needed daily is obtained from this group. Teenagers and pregnant women need more than two servings. A casserole prepared as the main dish for a meal must furnish a fourth of the protein needed daily.

A serving is 3 ounces of beef, poultry, pork or fish (without bone); 1 egg; or 1 cup of dried beans, peas or lentils. Iron and thiamine are found in this group.

2. BREADS AND CEREALS—Four or more servings are needed daily. All breads and cereals are in this group. These breads and cereals must be whole grain, enriched or restored.

These foods are important sources of several B vitamins, iron, protein, and food energy. A serving is a slice of bread or ½ to ¾ cup of cereal.

3. MILK—Adults need 2 or more glasses; children, 3 to 4 glasses; teen-agers and pregnant women, 4 or more glasses; and nursing mothers, 6 or more glasses. A glass is 8 ounces. This group includes milk (whole, skim, dry or buttermilk), cheese, cottage cheese, cream cheese, and ice cream. These foods are the best sources of calcium. They are also good sources of vitamin A, protein and riboflavin.

It is most important to include some amount of milk in the diet every day. Other foods may be substituted, but you will need to serve fluid milk at least once a day.

4. VEGETABLES AND FRUITS—Four or more servings are needed daily. All fruits and vegetables are included. These are good sources of vitamins A and C. Vitamin C is in the daily menu since it cannot be stored for any period of time in the body. One serving from this group must be high in vitamin A, which is needed daily or at least every other day. Other servings can be any fruits and vegetables.

A serving is ½ cup or a portion normally served, such as half a grapefruit, one banana or one orange.

SOURCES OF VITAMINS

VITAMIN A—Cream; egg yolk; butter; whole milk; yellow vegetables; green leafy vegetables; other green vegetables; apricot; tomato; liver; cod; halibut.

VITAMIN C OR ASCORBIC ACID—All citrus fruits; raw cabbage; strawberries; tomato (fresh or canned); peas; broccoli; raw green leafy vegetables; cantaloupe.

VITAMIN D—Cod liver oil and other fish liver oils; egg yolk; irradiated and other fortified foods.

NIACIN—Lean meat; kidney; liver; chicken breast; fish; peanuts; dried yeast.

RIBOFLAVIN—Milk; liver; egg; lean meat; kidney; green leafy vegetables; legumes; enriched white cereal; dark meat of poultry.

THIAMINE—Liver; kidney; lean meat; heart; pork; legumes; enriched white cereal; whole-grain products; bran, prepared; yeast; egg yolk; nuts; spinach; chard.

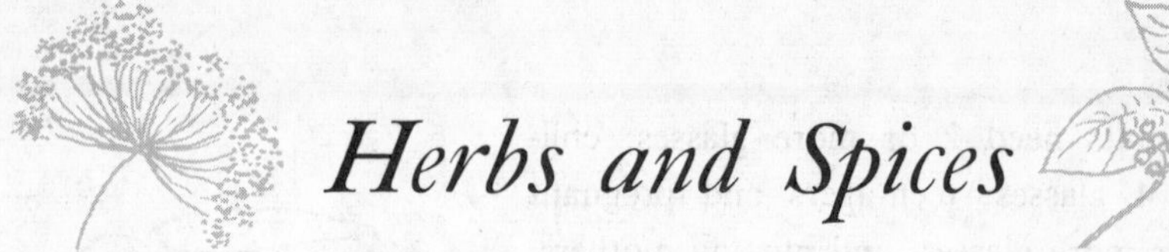

Herbs and Spices

FOR CASSEROLES AND BREADS

HERB OR SPICE	USE WITH
ALLSPICE	Vegetables, meat loaves, ham dishes, beef stew
ANISE SEED	Coffee cakes, rolls, sweet breads (especially the Scandinavian sweet breads), beef and veal stews
BASIL	Beef and veal, lamb, pork, seafood dishes, egg and cheese dishes, tomato dishes, peas, squash, string beans, potatoes, spinach
BAY LEAVES	Poultry, venison, beef and veal, lamb, fish stews, seafood dishes, tomatoes, onion, green beans, rice
CARAWAY SEED	Rolls, muffins, biscuits, bread, coffee cakes, vegetables, pork
CARDAMOM SEED	Coffee cakes, Danish pastry, bread, buns
CAYENNE	Meat and fish dishes
CELERY SEED	Fish dishes, meat dishes, rolls
CHILI POWDER	Stews, chili
CINNAMON	Buns, coffee cakes, muffins, sweet potatoes
CUMIN SEED	Chili, rice, meat loaf, fish, bread
CURRY POWDER	Poultry, fish and seafood, vegetables, rice, any leftovers
FENNEL	Bread, rolls, fish dishes
GINGER	Squash, sweet potatoes, carrots, spice cakes
MACE	Doughnuts, seafood stews
MARJORAM	Beef and veal, chicken, pork, lamb, duck, goose, omelets, souffles, vegetables, seafood dishes
MUSTARD	Cheese, egg and seafood dishes, baked beans, lima beans
NUTMEG	Coffee cakes, doughnuts
OREGANO	Tomato dishes, chilies, omelets, beef stews
PAPRIKA	Poultry, pork, fish, garnish for many dishes
POPPY SEED	Rolls, bread, coffee cakes
ROSEMARY	Fish and seafood dishes, stews, lamb, vegetables
SAGE	All pork dishes, tomato dishes, Brussels sprouts
SAFFRON	Bread, rolls, rice, buns, fish stews, chicken
SAVORY	Veal, lamb, fish, chicken, omelets, cabbage, peas
SESAME SEED	Rolls, bread, buns, coffee cakes
TARRAGON	Poultry, seafood, veal, cheese dishes, vegetables
THYME	Meat and fish, biscuits, tomatoes, egg and cheese dishes
TURMERIC	Fish and seafood, rice

Beef and Veal
Casseroles

RECIPE FOR VENETIAN VEAL ON PAGE 34

BEEF CASSEROLE

2 c. chuck beef, cubed
1 c. claret wine
2 lge. cans consomme
1 ½ tsp. salt
½ tsp. pepper
2 med. onions, diced or sliced
½ c. all-purpose flour, sifted
½ c. fine bread crumbs

Combine uncooked beef, wine, consomme, salt, pepper and onions. Put into a greased casserole. Mix flour with bread crumbs; stir into casserole mixture. Bake slowly at 300 degrees for 3 hours. Yield: 8 to 10 servings.

Maud Fearigo, Atlanta, Ga.

BEEF CASSEROLE

1 lge. onion
3 stalks celery
1 green pepper
2 c. leftover pot roast or
 1 lb. ground beef
2 tbsp. butter
1 10 ½-oz. can mushroom soup
½ c. water
½ tsp. salt
Dash of pepper
1 3-oz. can chow mein noodles

Preheat oven at 325 degrees. Cut onion, celery and green pepper coarsely. Chop leftover beef into small cubes. Cook beef in 1 tablespoon butter for several minutes; transfer to casserole. Put remaining butter in pan; toss in chopped vegetables and cook until limp. Stir in mushroom soup, water, salt and pepper; pour over beef and mix well. Cover and bake 30 minutes. Remove cover; sprinkle with chow mein noodles and bake 10 minutes.

Mrs. Lucille Jordan, Gary, N. C.

SHORT BEEF RIBS WITH YORKSHIRE PUDDING

6 short beef ribs
1 ½ tsp. salt
Black pepper
¾ c. water
1 c. sifted flour
1 tsp. salt
1 c. milk
2 eggs, well beaten
¼ c. drippings from roasting
 pan

Trim excess fat from ribs; sprinkle salt in hot skillet and brown ribs on all sides. Season with black pepper. Remove ribs to a pan that can be tightly covered. Add water to hot skillet and pour around ribs. Cover and bake at 250 to 300 degrees for 3 hours or until tender. Mix flour, salt, milk and eggs, beating until smooth. Place 1/4 cup beef rib drippings in 8-inch square pan. Bake at 350 degrees for 30 minutes. Serve hot. Yield: 6 servings.

Mrs. Ben H. Ray, Newport, Tenn.

CASSEROLE INTERNATIONAL

3 c. cooked prime rib roast,
 cut into large cubes
1 c. tomato juice
2 sm. cloves garlic, minced
½ tsp. fine herbs
1 tsp. curry powder
1 tsp. minced green pepper
1 pkg. frozen chow mein
1 c. cooked fettucine (macaroni)
½ c. cooking sherry
½ c. grated sharp cheddar
 cheese
2 tbsp. minced parsley

(Continued on next page)

Simmer cooked roast beef for 15 minutes in tomato juice with minced garlic, herbs, curry powder and green pepper. Add frozen chow mein; simmer until thawed and blended with other ingredients. Add cooked fettucine and cooking sherry, stirring all ingredients to distribute evenly. If more moisture is required, add tomato juice. Place in greased casserole dish; sprinkle top with grated cheese and parsley. Warm in 300-degree oven for about 15 minutes.

Mrs. Harry Ransom, Austin, Tex.

EGG NOODLE CASSEROLE

1 6-oz. pkg. egg noodles, cooked and drained
1 lb. stew beef, cooked
1 can mushroom soup
1 sm. onion, chopped
Salt and pepper to taste

Combine all ingredients in baking dish. Cover. Bake at 350 degrees for 45 minutes. Chicken may be substituted for beef.

Mrs. Wilma Snellgrove, North Augusta, S. C.

BEEF POTPIE

1 lb. beef chunks
1 c. diced carrots
1 c. diced celery
1 c. diced onions
3 to 4 potatoes, diced
Salt and pepper
1 biscuit recipe

Cook beef in water until almost tender; add carrots, celery, onions and potatoes. Season to taste. Cook until vegetables are tender. Pour into baking pan; top with thinly rolled biscuits. Bake at 450 degrees until brown. Yield: 3 servings.

Mrs. Gladys Hawks, Ettrick, Va.

CHUCK WAGON CASSEROLE

2 c. cooked beef, cubed
1 1-lb. can whole kernel corn, drained
1 10 ½-oz. can tomato soup
1 c. shredded cheddar cheese
1 tbsp. instant minced onion
1 tsp. chili powder
1 can refrigerator biscuits
2 tbsp. melted butter
¼ c. yellow cornmeal

Mix all ingredients except biscuits, butter and cornmeal. Place in shallow 2 1/2-quart casserole. Bake at 400 degrees for 10 minutes. Dip biscuits into melted butter, then into cornmeal. Arrange on casserole. Bake for 20 to 25 minutes longer or until biscuits are golden brown. Yield: 4-6 servings.

Mrs. Harold Lee Howdyshell, Staunton, Va.

CORNISH PASTIES

6 oz. potatoes, peeled and diced
¾ lb. lean steak, diced
2 tbsp. chopped onion
Salt and pepper
2 to 3 tbsp. cold water
1 lb. pie pastry
1 egg, beaten

(Continued on next page)

Combine potatoes, meat, onion, seasoning and water. Roll pastry into thin rounds the size of saucers. Wet edges of pastry rounds. Fill each with 2 tablespoonfuls meat mixture. Fold edges of pastry together; press and flute with fingers. Stand pasties upright on baking sheet; brush with egg. Bake at 450 degrees until pastry begins to brown. Reduce heat to 350 degrees; continue cooking until meat is tender. Total cooking time is 1 hour. Milk may be substituted for egg when brushing pastry.

Susan Williams, Augusta, Ga.

CORNISH PASTY

1 lb. stew beef, cut in sm. pieces
4 med. Irish potatoes, sliced ⅛ in. thick
2 med. carrots, sliced ⅛ in. thick
1 med. onion, sliced ⅛ in. thick
Pastry for double-crust 9-in. pie

Alternate layers of meat, potatoes, carrots and onion in pastry-lined pie pan; cover with top crust. Bake in preheated 250-degree oven for 1 hour and 30 minutes.

Evelyn Bryson, Greenville, S. C.

HOT TAMALE PIE

1 ½ lb. boneless chuck roast
½ c. suet
½ c. water
Salt
2 lge. onions, ground
¼ tsp. garlic salt
¼ tsp. paprika
1 1-oz. pkg. foil-wrapped chili powder
2 c. white cornmeal

Put beef and suet in large kettle. Cover with water; salt to taste. Cook until tender. Remove meat from stock; reserve. Grind meat and onions together; add garlic salt, paprika and chili powder. Mix well; set aside. Add cornmeal to beef stock; cook slowly for 10 minutes. Line ungreased 2-quart pan with cornmeal mush; add a layer of meat mixture over mush. Continue layers topping with cornmeal. Cover pan tightly with foil; steam 3 hours at 325 degrees. Yield: 10 servings.

Arline M. Bobson, Miami, Fla.

LAZY DAY BEEF PIE

1 ½ lb. stew beef, cut in sm. pieces
Flour
Salt and pepper
½ onion, cut up
2 c. canned peas and carrots
1 pkg. corn bread mix

(Continued on next page)

Dredge beef with flour, salt and pepper. Slowly cook meat and onion in water for 1 hour and 30 minutes to 2 hours until done. Add peas and carrots. Place in baking dish. Prepare corn bread, mixing according to package directions; spread over casserole. Bake at 425 degrees for 20 minutes. Yield: 6 servings.

Mrs. Arthur Cross, Clayton, Ala.

MEAT PIE WITH CORN BREAD TOP

- 3 c. chopped leftover beef
- Beef gravy
- 1 c. cooked carrots
- 1 c. green peas
- Few drops hot sauce (opt.)
- 1 c. cornmeal
- 1 egg
- ½ c. milk
- 2 tbsp. shortening
- 2 tsp. baking powder
- 2 tbsp. flour
- ½ tsp. salt

Combine beef, gravy, carrots, peas and hot sauce; mix well. Place in 2-quart casserole; let stand in oven while preparing topping. Combine remaining ingredients; mix well and spoon on top of casserole. Bake at 425 degrees until thoroughly heated and brown on top. Yield: 4 servings.

Mrs. Henry M. Ford, Gainesville, Tex.

MONDAY MEAT PIE

- 2 c. cubed cooked roast
- 1 ½ c. cooked diced potatoes
- 1 c. cooked diced carrots
- 1 tbsp. chopped pimento
- 1 c. grated mild cheese
- ½ c. chopped onions
- ¾ c. salad dressing
- 1 c. boiling water
- 1 c. cornmeal
- ½ c. milk
- 1 tbsp. melted butter
- 2 eggs, well beaten

Combine meat, vegetables, pimento, cheese, onions and salad dressing; heat until cheese melts. Pour into well-greased casserole. Pour water over cornmeal; mix well. Add remaining ingredients. Pour mixture over meat filling. Bake at 400 degrees for 40 minutes. Yield: 6 servings.

Mrs. Ruby Lee Henry, Ft. Worth, Tex.

SMOTHERED STEAK CASSEROLE

1 lb. round steak, cut in pieces
2 tsp. salt
Pepper
Flour
6 tbsp. shortening
2 med. potatoes, sliced
1 lge. onion, sliced
1 can biscuits

Season steak with salt and pepper; dredge in flour. Brown on both sides in shortening. Place half of steak in casserole. Add a layer of potatoes and a layer of onion; season to taste. Repeat layers. Sprinkle 2 tablespoons flour over all. Cover with water. Bake at 300 degrees for 1 hour and 30 minutes. Increase heat to 375 degrees. Arrange biscuits on top of casserole and bake until biscuits are brown. Yield: 4 servings.

Mrs. Vernon Gustin, Dalhart, Tex.

STEAK AND ONION PIE

1 c. sliced onions
1 lb. round steak, cut into small pieces
¼ c. flour
2 tsp. salt
⅛ tsp. pepper
½ tsp. paprika
Dash of ginger
Dash of allspice
¼ c. shortening
2 ½ c. boiling water
2 c. diced raw potatoes
1 pie shell

Cook onions slowly in melted margarine until onions are yellow. Remove onions from pan. Roll meat in mixture of flour, seasonings, and spices. Brown in hot shortening; add boiling water. Cover. Simmer for 1 hour or until meat is tender. Add potatoes; cook for 10 minutes longer. Pour into greased 8-inch casserole. Lay cooked onions on top. Fit pie shell over top; seal edge. Bake at 450 degrees for 25 minutes. Yield: 6 servings.

Mrs. Gertrude Pyles, Lewisville, Tex.

VENETIAN BEEF PIE

CRUST:

1 ½ c. flour
1 tsp. garlic powder
1 tsp. leaf oregano
¼ c. grated Parmesan or Romano cheese
½ c. butter
4 to 5 tbsp. cold water

Sift flour with garlic; add oregano and grated cheese. Cut in butter until crumbly. Sprinkle water over mixture, stirring with fork until dough holds together. Roll out 2/3 of dough onto floured surface to an 11-inch circle; fit into pan.

MEAT FILLING:

1 lb. round steak, cubed
½ c. flour
¼ c. butter
2 c. tomato sauce
¼ c. chopped onion
3 tbsp. grated Parmesan or Romano cheese
1 tbsp. sugar
1 tsp. sweet basil
½ tsp. salt
½ tsp. oregano
½ tsp. garlic
⅛ tsp. pepper
4 slices cheddar cheese

(Continued on next page)

Coat steak with flour; brown in butter. Stir in all remaining ingredients except cheddar cheese; cover. Simmer for 30 minutes or until meat is tender. Turn into pastry-lined pan; top with cheese slices. Roll out remaining dough 1/8 inch thick. Cut into 2-inch rounds; place on cheese overlapping slightly. Flute edges. Bake at 400 degrees for 30 to 40 minutes or until golden brown. Yield: 6-8 servings.

Mrs. Jeanette Knox, Decatur, Ala.

MEXICAN BEEF CASSEROLE

2 lb. round steak, ½ in. thick
Salt and pepper
Chili powder
Prepared mustard
1 lge. onion, chopped
3 tbsp. salad oil
¾ lb. long-grain rice
⅛ tsp. garlic
1 No. 2 can tomatoes
1 can kidney beans, drained
½ tsp. oregano
Ground cumin
10 ripe olives, sliced
2 c. bouillon

Rub steak with salt, pepper and 1 tablespoonful chili powder. Spread with thin layer of mustard; cut into 1-inch squares. Cook onion in oil in skillet until golden. Add rice; cook until brown, stirring constantly. Add garlic. Combine tomatoes and beans; season with oregano and cumin. Layer meat, rice and tomato mixture in oiled deep casserole. Sprinkle with chili powder and olives. Repeat layers until dish is 2/3 full, ending with tomatoes and olives. Fill casserole almost to the top with bouillon. Cover; bake at 350 degrees for 1 hour and 30 minutes or until rice is done. Yield: 4 servings.

Marvin A. McGuire, Jr., Richlands, Va.

MONDAY NIGHT ROAST DISH

1 c. uncooked rice
1 c. broth
1 c. cream of mushroom soup
1 c. chopped onions
1 c. cut-up celery
2 c. leftover meat
Salt and pepper to taste
Grated cheese

Combine all ingredients except cheese. Bake at 350 degrees for 35 minutes. Cover with grated cheese. Bake for 10 minutes longer.

Pat Burton, Marble Falls, Tex.

ROUND STEAK AND RICE CASSEROLE

1 c. rice, cooked
¼ c. flour
2 tsp. salt
⅛ tsp. pepper
2 lb. round steak, cut in thin slices
¼ c. salad oil
1 c. chopped onions
½ c. diced green pepper
1 clove garlic, minced
2 tbsp. butter
1 4-oz. can sliced mushrooms, drained
2 8-oz. cans tomato sauce
1 can water or liquid from mushrooms
½ tsp. basil

(Continued on next page)

Place rice in shallow 9 x 13-inch baking dish. Mix flour, salt and pepper; dredge meat in mixture. Brown steak quickly in oil; drain. Arrange steak slices over rice. Saute onions, green pepper and garlic in butter until onions are transparent. Add mushrooms and cook until lightly browned. Add tomato sauce, water and basil. Bring to a boil; pour over steak and rice. Cover with foil and bake at 350 degrees for 45 to 60 minutes, or until meat is tender. Remove foil for last 15 minutes of baking. Yield: 6-8 servings.

Mrs. W. M. Martin, Greenville, Miss.

SIRLOIN SUPREME

1 med. sirloin steak
2 onions
Salt and pepper to taste
2 cans cream of mushroom soup
1 c. rice

Place steak in roasting pan or Dutch oven. Slice onions over meat. Season to taste. Pour soup over all; cover. Bake at 250 to 300 degrees for 1 hour. Add rice, mixing well into soup. Cover; continue baking for 1 hour or until rice is tender.

Shelley Graham, Kilgore, Tex.

STEAK 'N' RICE

1 2-lb. cubed steak
¾ c. flour
½ c. cooking oil
Salt and pepper to taste
1 c. uncooked rice
1 10-oz. can beef bouillon
1 10-oz. can beef consomme
2 consomme cans water

Roll steak in flour. Brown on both sides in hot oil. Add salt and pepper while cooking. Pour rice into 3-quart casserole. Add bouillon and consomme mixed with water. Sprinkle with 1 teaspoonful salt. Arrange steak on top. Cover. Bake at 300 degrees for 45 minutes. Yield: 4-5 servings.

Mrs. Winfield K. Sharp, Walhalla, S. C.

SHORT RIBS OF BEEF

3 lb. short ribs
2 tbsp. prepared mustard
2 tsp. salt
½ tsp. pepper
½ tsp. chili powder
½ tsp. sugar
1 tbsp. lemon juice
6 tbsp. olive oil
1 clove garlic, crushed
7 onions, sliced
1 ½ c. water
1 tbsp. cornstarch

Place ribs in casserole or Dutch oven. Combine mustard, salt, pepper, chili powder, sugar, lemon juice, olive oil, garlic, few slices of onion and 1/2 cup water. Pour over ribs. Cook at 400 degrees for 30 minutes or until brown. Add remaining onions; cook, covered, at 325 degrees for 2 hours to 2 hours and 30 minutes or until meat is tender. Remove meat from casserole. Combine water and cornstarch; cook cornstarch in gravy from ribs. Yield: 4 servings.

Mrs. Ed Bishop, Fayetteville, Ark.

BEEF CASSEROLE

2 lb. round steak, cut into 1-in. cubes
3 tbsp. shortening
1 No. 2 can tomatoes
6 potatoes
6 lge. carrots
6 sm. onions
3 tbsp. flour
1 tsp. salt
¼ tsp. pepper
1 tsp. Worcestershire sauce

Brown steak in shortening; place in 3-quart casserole. Drain tomatoes, reserving liquid. Arrange potatoes, carrots, onions and tomatoes over meat in casserole. Add flour, salt, pepper and Worcestershire sauce to drippings. Add water to tomato liquid to make 1 cup liquid, if needed. Add to drippings. Pour over vegetables; cover. Bake at 350 degrees for 1 hour. Yield: 6 servings.

D. D. Varner, Beeville, Tex.

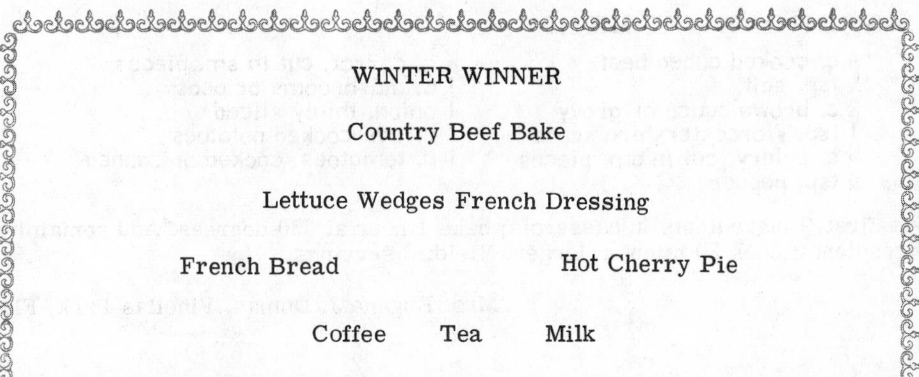

WINTER WINNER

Country Beef Bake

Lettuce Wedges French Dressing

French Bread Hot Cherry Pie

Coffee Tea Milk

COUNTRY BEEF BAKE

2 lb. beef chuck, cut into 1-in. cubes
¼ c. flour
2 ½ c. tomato juice
2 beef bouillon cubes
1 ½ tbsp. corn syrup
¼ c. finely chopped parsley
2 cloves of garlic, minced
3 tsp. salt
¼ tsp. pepper
4 med. turnips or potatoes, thinly sliced
8 sm. onions, peeled and quartered
1 acorn squash, split and seeded
2 tbsp. butter or margarine

Trim fat from beef; coat with flour. Combine tomato juice, bouillon cubes and syrup in saucepan; heat just to boiling. Dissolve bouillon cubes quickly. Combine parsley, garlic, salt and pepper in cup. Arrange half of turnips in 12-cup deep baking dish. Sprinkle with salt mixture. Top with a layer of half the onions; sprinkle with salt mixture. Add a layer of beef. Repeat with remaining turnips, onions, beef and seasoning mixture. Slice each squash half into 6 pieces; pare and arrange over beef casserole. Pour hot tomato juice mixture over all; dot with butter. Cover; bake at 350 degrees for 3 hours or until beef is tender. Yield 6-8 servings.

Reginald Scott, Jr., Live Oak, Fla.

BEEF PIE

1 lb. boneless stew meat, cut in pieces
Salt and pepper to taste
2 tbsp. flour
2 tbsp. cooking oil or bacon fat
1 can chicken soup
½ soup can water
1 can green peas
Celery salt to taste
Pastry
2 hard-cooked eggs, sliced

Season meat with salt and pepper; dredge in flour. Cook in oil until brown over medium heat, stirring constantly; add soup, water, peas and celery salt. Line 8 x 12-inch baking dish with half of pastry; roll remaining pastry to fit top. Pour meat mixture into crust; dot with egg slices. Top with pastry; bake at 350 degrees for 35 minutes or until brown. Yield: 6 servings.

Mrs. Clyde A. Smith, Vidalia, La.

CASSEROLE OF BEEF

4 c. cooked cubed beef
½ tsp. salt
2 c. brown sauce or gravy
1 tsp. Worcestershire sauce
½ c. celery, cut in sm. pieces
½ tsp. pepper
½ c. carrot, cut in sm. pieces
1 c. mushrooms or peas
1 onion, thinly sliced
1 c. sm. cooked potatoes
1 c. tomatoes, cooked or canned

Put first 9 ingredients in casserole; bake 1 hour at 350 degrees. Add remaining ingredients; cook 30 minutes longer. Yield: 8 servings.

Mrs. Eugene J. Dumas, Pinellas Park, Fla.

ONE-DISH MEAL

1 lb. lean chuck cubes
Oil or margarine
1 can condensed tomato soup
1 soup can water
2 or 3 carrots
2 or 3 med. potatoes
1 med. onion
1 tbsp. salt
1 tsp. pepper
1 tsp. sugar

Brown beef in skillet with oil. Remove to deep baking dish or heavy skillet; add remaining ingredients. Cover. Bake at 300 degrees for about 2 hours. Some water may be added during the last hour of cooking time. Yield: 2 servings.

Mrs. Alton W. Langley, Avondale Estates, Ga.

FAVORITE BEEF PIE

1 ½ lb. boneless beef stew meat
¼ c. flour
1 tsp. salt
⅛ tsp. pepper
3 tbsp. fat or oil
1 c. water
1 c. canned tomatoes
2 tsp. Worcestershire sauce
6 carrots, peeled
12 sm. onions, peeled
3 c. mashed potatoes
⅓ c. process cheese spread
Butter or margarine, melted

(Continued on next page)

Cut meat into 1 1/2-inch cubes. Mix flour, salt and pepper; roll meat in mixture to coat all sides. Brown meat well in hot fat; add water, tomatoes and Worcestershire sauce. Cut carrots into 1-inch crosswise slices; add with onions to meat. Cover tightly; simmer 2 hours, stirring occasionally. Pour into buttered 2-quart casserole. Blend together potatoes and cheese spread with mixer. Drop by spoonfuls around rim of casserole; brush with butter. Bake until bubbly at 375 degrees, about 30 minutes. Serve hot. Yield: 6-8 servings.

Mrs. M. Otis Couch, Houston, Tex.

PACKAGE STEAK SUPPER

1 1 ½-lb. chuck steak, 1 in. thick
1 pkg. dry onion soup mix
1 tsp. steak sauce
3 med. carrots, quartered
2 stalks celery, cut in sticks
2 to 3 med. potatoes, halved
2 tbsp. butter or margarine
½ tsp. salt

Place meat in center of a large piece of foil; sprinkle with onion soup mix and steak sauce. Cover steak with vegetables; dot with butter and sprinkle with salt. Fold foil over meat and seal securely. Bake at 400 degrees for 1 hour to 1 hour and 30 minutes or until done. Yield: 4 servings.

Mrs. Dean Wilson, Sarasota, Fla.

QUICK BEEF CASSEROLE

1 pkg. frozen peas and carrots
1 can or 2 c. sm. cooked potatoes
1 can or 2 c. sm. white onions
¼ tsp. thyme
1 tsp. salt
¼ tsp. pepper
1 lge. can or 2 to 3 c. roast beef and gravy
2 c. canned tomatoes

Cook peas and carrots for 5 minutes. Butter a 2 1/2 x 8 x 12-inch baking dish. Add peas and carrots, potatoes, onions and seasonings. Mix beef, gravy and tomatoes; pour over vegetables. Bake at 375 degrees for 20 to 30 minutes. Yield: 6 servings.

Mrs. W. O. Tune, Vernon Hill, Va.

ROAST BEEF CASSEROLE

½ c. cubed cooked potatoes
3 tbsp. butter
3 tbsp. chopped onion
1 tsp. salt
6 tbsp. flour
1 can beef-noodle soup
1 ½ c. milk
1 c. chopped roast beef
½ c. grated cheese

Combine all ingredients, except cheese, in a greased casserole. Bake at 350 degrees for 30 minutes. Top with cheese. Bake until cheese is melted. Yield: 6 servings.

Mrs. Wayne Tekell, Tahoka, Tex.

RICH BROWN STEAK DINNER

1 2-lb. round steak, 1 inch thick, cut in servings
2 tsp. salt
½ tsp. pepper
Flour
6 med. onions, sliced
¼ c. shortening
3 lge. potatoes, halved
1 bay leaf
1 can condensed tomato soup
1 pkg. frozen French-cut green beans

Season meat with salt and pepper; roll in flour. Cook onions in hot fat, until tender, but not brown; remove onions and brown meat slowly on both sides. Place meat in 3-quart casserole; add onions, potatoes, and bay leaf; pour soup over. Cover. Bake at 350 degrees 1 hour and 45 minutes, or until meat is tender. Add beans; cook 10 to 15 minutes longer.

Patricia A. Harrell, Colonial Heights, Va.

ROAST AND VEGETABLE CASSEROLE

1 2-lb. beef roast
2 tbsp. shortening
4 potatoes
4 carrots
2 onions
2 stalks celery
1 can tomato soup
½ tsp. salt
¼ tsp. pepper

Cook roast until almost done; place in baking dish with shortening. Arrange potatoes, carrots, onions and celery around roast; pour tomato soup over casserole. Season with salt and pepper. Cover and bake at 350 degrees for 45 minutes to 1 hour. Yield: 4-6 servings.

Mrs. Worth Stratton, Tellico Plains, Tenn.

ROLLED POT ROAST

1 4 to 5-lb. beef roast, rolled chuck or rump
1 clove garlic, cut
3 tbsp. flour
2 tsp. salt
2 tbsp. fat
1 c. water
6 potatoes, peeled
6 to 8 carrots
6 onions, peeled

Rub meat with garlic and flour; sprinkle with salt. Heat fat in deep heavy pan or fryer; brown beef on all sides 15 to 20 minutes. Place meat on rack. Add water; cover tightly and bake at 350 degrees for 1 hour per pound. Add vegetables 1 hour before roast is done. Yield: 8-10 servings.

Pauline Gooch, Huntingdon, Tenn.

SHEPHERD'S PIE

1 sm. onion, minced
1 tbsp. shortening
1 10¾-oz. can beef gravy
1 ½ c. cooked peas
2 c. seasoned mashed instant potatoes

Cook onion in shortening in skillet until tender. Combine with gravy, beef and peas. Pour into 1 1/2-quart casserole. Spoon potatoes on top. Bake at 450 degrees for 25 minutes or until potatoes are lightly browned. Yield: 4-6 servings.

Mrs. J. L. Skinner, Sr., Whitakens, N. C.

SHEPHERD'S PIE

1 tbsp. butter or fat
1 lge. onion, sliced
2 c. chopped leftover meat
2 c. tomatoes
½ tsp. pepper
½ tsp. salt
2 c. mashed potatoes

Melt butter; add onion and brown. Add meat, tomatoes and seasoning; simmer for 10 minutes. Place a layer of potatoes in greased baking dish. Add meat mixture; cover with remaining potatoes. Bake at 350 degrees for 30 minutes. Yield: 6 servings.

Mrs. Delbert Foster, High Point, N. C.

SHEPHERD'S PIE

2 14-oz. pkg. frozen whipped potatoes
½ c. shredded sharp cheddar cheese
½ c. milk
2 tbsp. butter or margarine
¼ tsp. thyme leaves, crumbled
1 tsp. salt
¼ tsp. ground black pepper
4 6-oz. pkg. frozen beef with onions in red wine sauce
1 10-oz. pkg. or 1 c. loose-pack frozen peas and carrots

Cook frozen potatoes according to package directions until thawed. Stir in cheese, milk, butter, thyme, salt and pepper. Heat frozen prepared beef according to package directions until thawed. Pour contents from package into mixing bowl. Add peas and carrots, defrosting if necessary to separate. Line bottom and sides of a shallow baking dish with about 1/3 of potato mixture. Spoon beef-vegetable mixture over potatoes. Drop remaining potatoes by spoonfuls around outside edge of casserole or put through a pastry tube. Bake in a preheated 350-degree oven about 20 minutes or until heated. Yield: 6 servings.

Photograph for this recipe on cover.

STUFFED FLANK STEAK

1 c. bread crumbs
2 tbsp. butter, melted
2 tbsp. chopped parsley
2 tbsp. chopped celery
1 tsp. salt
⅛ tsp. paprika
1 1-lb. flank steak
1 onion, sliced
¼ c. cubed carrots
2 slices suet
2 beef bouillon cubes
1 c. boiling water

Combine bread crumbs, butter, parsley, celery, salt and paprika; spread stuffing on steak. Roll and tie meat; place in casserole. Place onion and carrots around steak; top with suet. Dissolve bouillon cubes in water; pour over meat and vegetables. Cover and bake at 425 degrees for 20 minutes. Uncover and continue cooking for 30 minutes.

Mrs. Mary Thrasher, Chattanooga, Tenn.

STEAK 'N' POTATO CASSEROLE

6 tbsp. butter or margarine
1 c. sliced onions
4 cube steaks
¼ c. flour
1 ½ tsp. salt
¼ tsp. pepper
¼ tsp. dry mustard
2 c. buttermilk
1 2-oz. can mushrooms, drained
2 tbsp. chopped parsley
4 c. sliced potatoes

(Continued on next page)

In a large skillet melt butter; saute onions until tender. Remove onions from skillet; brown meat. Remove from skillet. To drippings in skillet, add flour, salt, pepper and mustard. Remove from heat; gradually stir in buttermilk. Cook over medium heat, stirring constantly, until thickened. Cook 2 additional minutes. Stir in mushrooms and parsley. In a buttered 2-quart shallow casserole, layer potatoes, then onions and steaks; pour sauce over all. Cover with aluminum foil. Bake at 350 degrees 1 hour and 15 minutes or until potatoes are tender. Yield: 4 servings.

Mrs. Iona C. O'Brien, St. Petersburg, Fla.

SWISS STEAK IN ONION SOUP

¼ c. flour
1 1-lb. round steak, ½ in. thick
2 tbsp. shortening
1 can onion soup
½ soup can water
4 carrots, cut into 2-in. pieces
4 potatoes, halved
Parsley (opt.)

Pound flour into steak; brown in shortening in ovenproof skillet. Add soup, water, carrots and potatoes. Cover; bake 1 hour and 15 minutes at 350 degrees. Uncover; bake 15 minutes. Top with parsley, if desired. Yield: 4 servings.

Mrs. Wm. E. Foster, Monroe, Ga.

GRANDMOTHER'S VEAL PIE

1 ½ lb. veal, cubed
3 tbsp. shortening
1 med. onion, chopped
1 carrot, sliced
1 med. potato, cubed
2 c. water
1 tsp. salt
⅛ tsp. pepper
3 tbsp. flour
2 hard-cooked eggs, chopped
½ tsp. sage
1 recipe pastry
Milk

Brown veal in shortening; add onion, carrot, potato, water, seasonings and flour. Cook over medium heat until thick. Place half of veal and vegetable mixture in a 10 x 6 1/2-inch glass baking dish. Cover with eggs; sprinkle with sage. Top with pastry and brush with milk. Bake at 350 degrees for 1 hour and 20 minutes. Yield: 6-8 servings.

Mrs. Delphine S. Hooker, Durham, N. C.

HOLIDAY CASSEROLE

2 lb. ground veal or hamburger
1 tsp. shortening
2 c. sliced celery
½ c. finely chopped green pepper
3 tbsp. grated onion
½ c. sliced blanched almonds
1 tsp. salt
½ tsp. pepper
3 tbsp. lemon juice
1 c. mayonnaise
¾ c. grated process cheese
¾ c. crushed potato chips

Brown veal in shortening; pour off drippings. Combine veal, celery, green pepper, onion, almonds, salt, pepper, lemon juice and mayonnaise. Place in greased 2-quart casserole; cover with grated cheese. Sprinkle potato chips around edge. Bake, uncovered, at 350 degrees for 40 minutes. Yield: 6 to 8 servings.

Mrs. J. Jolly, Hale Center, Tex.

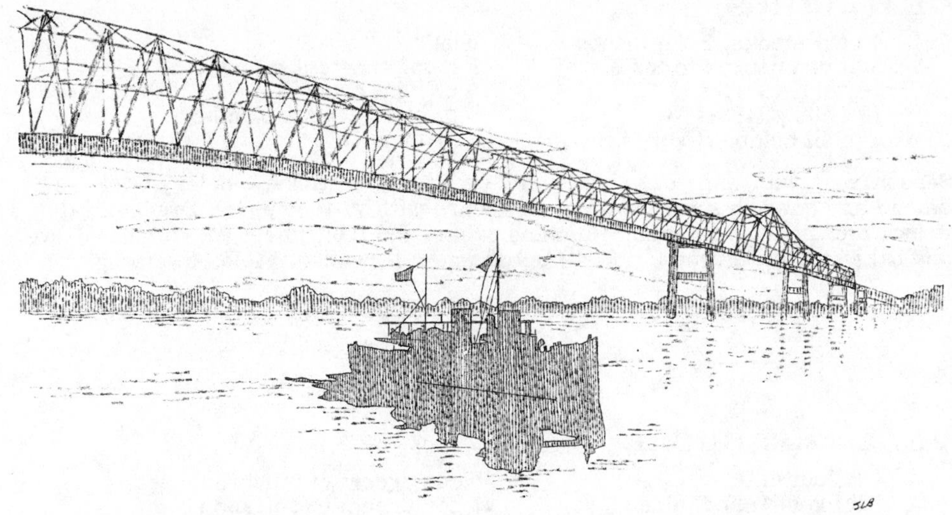

Greater New Orleans Bridge is world's longest cantilevered bridge.

STUFFED VEAL ROLLS

- 4 veal steaks, ½ inch thick
- ¼ tsp. salt
- 2 tbsp. butter or margarine
- 1 3-oz. can chopped mushrooms
- 1 tbsp. grated onion
- 4 slices day-old bread, broken into small pieces
- 2 tbsp. finely chopped parsley
- Dash of pepper
- Flour
- 4 tbsp. melted fat
- Mushroom sauce

Pound meat very thin. Salt lightly. Melt butter; saute mushrooms and onion. Combine with bread and seasonings. Place part of stuffing on each piece of meat; roll up and fasten with toothpick or tie with a string. Flour veal rolls; brown in melted fat. Add mushroom sauce. Cover; bake at 350 degrees for 30 to 40 minutes. Yield: 4 servings.

Jamie Morgan, Star City, Ark.

VEAL BREAST-RICE STUFFING

- 1 3 to 5-lb. veal breast
- 2 tbsp. grated onion
- 2 tbsp. lard or drippings
- ¾ c. rice
- 2 c. stock or water
- 1 ½ tsp. salt
- 1 tsp. poultry seasoning
- 1 egg, slightly beaten
- 1 sm. can mushroom pieces
- 4 slices bacon (opt.)

Cut pocket from end of veal breast. Brown onion in hot lard; add rice, stirring until golden brown. Add stock and seasonings; cover. Simmer for 40 minutes, or until rice is tender. Remove from heat; add egg and mushrooms. Fill veal pocket with rice stuffing; sew or skewer edges together. Place on rack in open pan; season. Place bacon slices over meat. Roast at 300 degrees for 2 hours or until done. Yield: 6-10 servings.

Mrs. Wm. E. Scholze, San Antonio, Tex.

VEAL BIRDS

4 veal steaks, 2 x 4 inches
Salt and pepper to taste
12 carrot sticks
12 celery sticks
½ med. onion, slivered
Flour
2 tbsp. shortening or oil
½ c. light cream
½ c. orange juice or other fruit juice

Season veal with salt and pepper. Place 3 carrot sticks, 3 celery sticks and 1 onion slice on each steak; roll up and secure with wooden picks. Dredge in flour; brown slowly in shortening. Combine cream and fruit juice; add to meat. Cover and bake at 350 degrees for 1 hour. Add water if needed. Yield: 4 servings.

Mrs. Ruth E. Bell, Eau Gallie, Fla.

VEAL CASSEROLE

¼ lb. butter
1 lb. veal round, diced
1 lge. onion, chopped
1 c. celery, diced
¾ c. uncooked rice
1 can cream of mushroom soup
1 can cream of chicken soup
1 c. water
1 8-oz. can button mushrooms
1 c. salted cashew nuts

Put butter into a skillet; add cubed veal, chopped onion and celery. Cook slowly until onion is clear, but not brown. Cover rice with water; let set for 20 minutes. Mix together soups, water and mushrooms. Drain rice; add to soup mixture. Add meat, celery and onions. Put into a large buttered casserole; cover. Bake for 1 hour and 30 minutes in a 325-degree oven. Fifteen minutes before end of cooking, remove cover; add cashews. Mix; cook the remaining 15 minutes uncovered. Yield: 8 servings.

Mrs. A. H. Magie, Pine Bluff, Ark.

VEAL CUTLET SUPREME

1 lb. veal steak, ½ inch thick
1 c. sifted bread crumbs
1 egg, beaten
1 tbsp. water
1 med. onion, sliced
¼ c. shortening
1 tsp. paprika
1 ½ tsp. salt
¼ tsp. pepper
1 c. sour cream

Cut veal into 6 serving pieces. Dip in crumbs, then in egg and water mixture and again in crumbs. Cook onion in shortening until yellow, stirring occasionally. Remove from skillet. Place veal in skillet and brown on both sides. Place veal and onion in greased 2-quart casserole. Combine remaining ingredients; pour over veal. Cover tightly; bake at 325 degrees for 45 to 50 minutes. Yield: 6 servings.

Mrs. John G. Wallace, Warner Robins, Ga.

VEAL FIESTA

1 2 to 2 ½-lb. veal steak
1 onion, chopped
½ c. chopped celery
1 No. 2 can tomatoes
1 tbsp. sugar
1 lb. macaroni
American cheese, grated

(Continued on next page)

Sear steak on both sides; add onion, celery and tomatoes. Simmer for 1 hour. Add sugar. Boil macaroni for 10 minutes; drain. Pour into baking dish; put steak on top. Sprinkle with cheese. Pour gravy from skillet over cheese. Bake at 300 to 325 degrees for 30 minutes. Yield: 6 to 8 servings.

Mrs. Albert Trigg, Hattiesburg, Miss.

VEAL HOT DISH

1 lb. veal, cubed
1 onion, diced
1 tbsp. fat
1 c. chopped celery
1 can mushroom soup
1 can cream of chicken soup
2 c. water
½ c. uncooked rice
1 ½ tbsp. soy sauce
Salt and pepper

Brown veal and onion in fat; cook celery in 1/2 cup water. Combine and add remaining ingredients; bake 2 hours at 350 degrees. Yield: 4 servings.

Mrs. Robert Chesbrough, Vero Beach, Fla.

VEAL PARMESAN

Salt and pepper
1 lb. thin veal steak, cut into serving pieces
1 egg
⅓ c. Parmesan cheese
⅓ c. bread crumbs
¼ c. oil
1 onion, chopped
2 tbsp. butter
1 6-oz. can tomato paste
2 c. hot water
½ tsp. marjoram
½ lb. mozzarella cheese, sliced

Salt and pepper veal. Beat egg with 2 teaspoonfuls water. Dip veal into egg; roll in cheese and crumb mixture. Fry until brown on each side in oil in heavy skillet. Lay veal in shallow baking pan. Cook onion in butter in skillet until soft; add tomato paste mixed with hot water, marjoram and 1/2 teaspoonful salt. Boil for a few minutes. Pour three-fourths of sauce over veal; top with cheese slices. Pour remaining sauce on top. Bake at 350 degrees for 30 minutes. Yield: 4 servings.

Eveleine Robertson, Jackson, Tenn.

VEAL POTPIE

Pastry
1 sm. onion, chopped
2 tbsp. butter or margarine
2 tbsp. flour
3 c. veal, cooked and cubed
2 c. broth
½ c. peas
½ c. cooked diced carrots
½ c. cooked diced potatoes
½ c. chopped green pepper
1 tsp. celery seed
1 ½ tsp. salt
¼ tsp. black pepper

Line baking dish with pastry; reserve some for top of baking dish. Brown onion in butter; stir in flour. Add remaining ingredients and bring to boil; pour into pastry shell and cover with pastry. Bake at 450 degrees for 15 minutes; lower heat to 325 degrees and continue baking for 30 minutes. Beef or lamb may be substituted for veal. Yield: 6 servings.

Mrs. Roy H. Meade, Johnson City, Tenn.

VEAL SUPREME

2 lb. veal steak or rump
1 sm. onion, cut up
2 tbsp. butter
1 can cream of mushroom soup
1 can mushrooms
1 c. sour cream
1 8-oz. pkg. noodles
2 c. shredded sharp cheese
1 green pepper, diced
¼ c. buttered bread crumbs

Cut veal in thin strips, 2 to 3 inches long and 1/2 inch wide. Brown onion in butter. Brown veal; add small amount of water and simmer for 1 hour or until tender. Add mushroom soup, mushrooms and sour cream; blend well. Boil noodles until tender. Place alternate layers of veal, mushroom soup mixture, shredded sharp cheese, green pepper and noodles. Cover mixture with buttered bread crumbs. Bake at 350 degrees for 45 minutes. Yield: 6-8 servings.

Mrs. George McClain, Arlington, Va.

VEAL SUPREME

1 sm. can mushrooms
6 tbsp. butter
¼ c. flour
¾ c. milk
1 c. cream
Salt and pepper to taste
2 ½ lb. veal steak, cut into small pieces
Fat
1 c. soft bread crumbs

Drain mushrooms, saving juice. Melt 3 tablespoons butter; add flour and blend. Slowly add milk, cream and juice from mushrooms. Simmer until thick, stirring constantly. Season with salt and pepper. Brown veal in hot fat; add to thickened mixture with mushrooms. Pour mixture into buttered baking dish. Mix bread crumbs with 3 tablespoons butter; sprinkle over top of meat mixture. Bake at 350 degrees until veal is done. Yield: 6-8 servings.

Estha Williams, Port Lavaca, Tex.

VENETIAN VEAL

1 1-lb. veal steak, ½ in. thick
½ c. butter
½ c. chopped celery
¼ c. chopped onion
¼ c. chopped carrots
1 4-oz. can sliced mushrooms, drained
2 tbsp. flour
½ tsp. salt
⅛ tsp. pepper
1 c. milk
¼ tsp. thyme
¼ tsp. basil
⅛ tsp. marjoram
2 tbsp. parsley
1 6-oz. can tomato paste

Brown veal in 1/4 cup butter in a skillet; remove from pan. Cut into 4 serving portions and remove bone. Place in bottom of buttered 1 1/4-quart casserole; set aside. Add 1/4 cup butter drippings into skillet. Saute celery, onions, carrots and mushrooms in skillet. Remove with slotted spoon; place over veal in casserole. Pour off remaining butter in skillet; measure 2 tablespoons and add back to skillet. Stir in flour, salt and pepper. Gradually add milk, stirring until smooth and slightly thickened. Add remaining ingredients; stir until blended. Pour over vegetables in casserole. Bake in preheated 350-degree oven for 1 hour. Serve over noodles. Yield: 4 servings.

Photograph for this recipe on page 17.

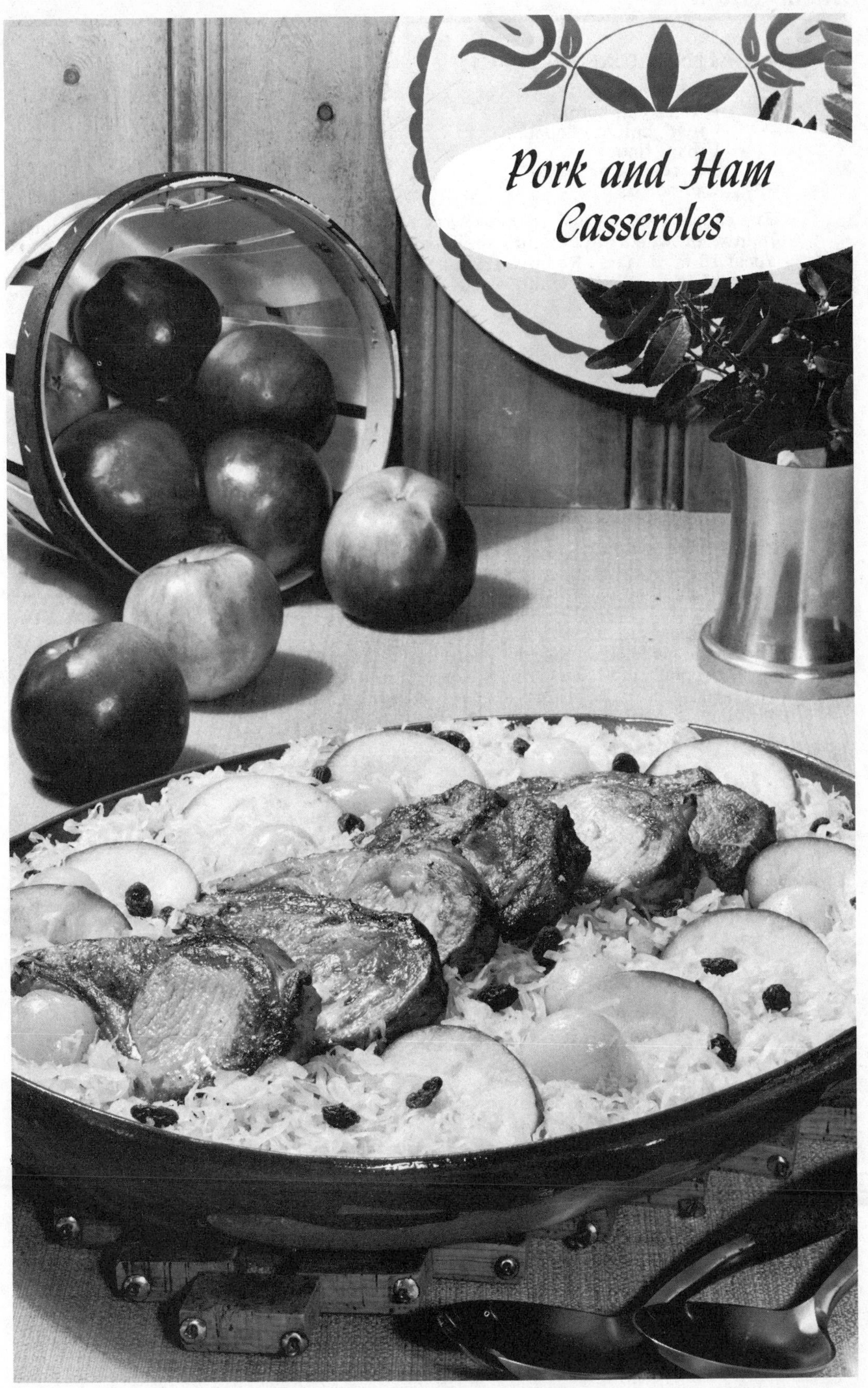
Pork and Ham
Casseroles

RECIPE FOR KRAUT, CHOPS AND APPLES ON PAGE 44

HOMINY CASSEROLE

1 ½ lb. bacon
1 No. 2 can hominy
1 med. onion, chopped
1 tbsp. flour
2 c. canned or fresh tomatoes
Salt and pepper to taste
1 tsp. chili powder
¼ lb. mild cheese, grated

Fry bacon; remove and crumble. Fry hominy and onion in 1/2 cup bacon fat until lightly browned. Add flour, tomatoes and seasonings; cook over medium heat about 15 minutes. Remove from heat; add crumbled bacon. Pour into bacon-greased casserole; sprinkle with grated cheese. Bake at 350 degrees 30 minutes. Yield: 6 servings.

Mrs. T. C. Holland, Huntsville, Ala.

MEXICAN TAMALIO

2 med. green peppers
1 8-oz. pkg. elbow macaroni
½ lb. sliced bacon
¼ c. butter or margarine
¾ glass Old English cheese
½ c. flour
3 c. milk

Cut peppers in small pieces; boil in water 15 minutes. Drain and set aside. Cook macaroni as directed on package; drain and set aside. Fry part of bacon until crisp and golden brown; break up into small pieces and set aside. Melt butter and cheese in top of double boiler; remove from heat and add flour all at once. Stir in milk slowly; return to heat and cook until thick as a white sauce consistency, stirring constantly. Place in alternate layers in buttered baking dish, macaroni, corn, peppers and bacon. Add sauce and mix in easy. Place remaining raw bacon slices on top. Bake at 350 degrees until bacon strips are nicely browned, about 35 minutes. Yield: 4-6 servings.

Mrs. John F. McCloskey, Sanford, Fla.

FAMILY CASSEROLE

2 to 3 c. diced cooked or canned ham
6 hard-cooked eggs, sliced
1 6-oz. can mushroom crowns, drained
1 can cream of celery soup
½ c. milk
2 c. grated American cheese
2 tsp. Worcestershire sauce
5 or 6 drops Tabasco sauce
¾ c. dry bread crumbs
3 tbsp. melted butter or margarine

Alternate layers of ham, eggs and mushrooms in a 2-quart casserole, starting and ending with ham. Combine soup and milk; add cheese, Worcestershire sauce and Tabasco sauce. Heat, stirring until cheese melts; pour over casserole. Mix crumbs and butter; sprinkle over top. Bake at 375 degrees for 25 minutes. Yield: 6 servings.

Mrs. Hubert Hiers, West Palm Beach, Fla.

HAM 'N' CHEESE

3 tbsp. flour
1 tsp. salt
2 tsp. dry mustard
1 lb. cheddar cheese, shredded
1 tbsp. butter
12 oz. (can or bottle) beer
1 8-oz. pkg. noodles, cooked and drained
1 ½ c. diced cooked ham

Mix flour and seasonings; stir in shredded cheese. Melt butter in saucepan; add cheese mixture and stir over low heat until cheese is melted and mixture is smooth. Stir in beer gradually and continue stirring over low heat until blended. Add noodles and ham; pour into a 2-quart casserole. Bake in 350-degree oven for 30 minutes. Yield: 6 servings.

Mrs. W. A. Thornburg, Long Beach, Miss.

HAM AND CHEESE FONDUE

6 slices bread
3 tbsp. butter or margarine
6 slices cheddar cheese
3 slices boiled ham
1 tbsp. prepared mustard
3 eggs, slightly beaten
2 c. milk
1 tsp. salt
¼ tsp. pepper

Spread three slices of bread with butter; top each with a slice of cheese. Add slice of ham and another of cheese. Spread remaining bread slices with mustard and place on cheese to make sandwiches. Cut each into nine 1-inch cubes; place in a well-greased 2-quart casserole. Beat eggs, milk, salt and pepper; pour over bread cubes. Set casserole in pan of hot water. Bake at 350 degrees for 1 hour, or until a knife inserted in center comes out clean and top is brown. Yield: 6 servings.

Mrs. Walter Dilworth, Booneville, Miss.

HAM AND EGG CASSEROLE

2 hard-boiled eggs, sliced
1 c. boiled ham, cut up
⅓ c. water
2 tbsp. chopped onions
2 c. potato chips, crushed
1 can mushroom soup

Line baking dish with eggs, then ham, water, onions and chips. Pour soup over all. Put a few chips on top. Bake 30 minutes at 350 degrees.

Mrs. J. W. Morse, Laurens, S. C.

HAM AND EGG PIE

Pastry for 2-crust pie
1 c. chopped cooked ham
6 eggs, slightly beaten
6 tbsp. top milk or cream
1 tbsp. minced chives or parsley
½ tsp. salt
¼ tsp. pepper

(Continued on next page)

Line deep 8-inch pie pan with pastry. Arrange ham in pan. Top with remaining ingredients. Cover with top crust. Bake at 425 degrees for 20 to 25 minutes or until nicely browned. Serve hot. Yield: 6 servings.

Mrs. Milton Hawkins, Walnut Cove, N. C.

HAM LUNCHEON PIE

1 stack-pack crushed crackers
⅓ c. margarine
1 lb. ground ham
1 med. chopped onion
1 c. cooked rice
1 c. milk
3 eggs, beaten
2 tbsp. chopped green pepper
½ lb. cheese, grated

Blend cracker crumbs and softened margarine. Reserve 2/3 cup crumb mixture for topping. Firmly press remainder against bottom of baking dish. Combine ham, onion and rice in baking dish. Add milk to eggs. Stir in green pepper and cheese. Pour over mixture and sprinkle with remaining crumbs. Bake at 350 degrees for 45 minutes. Yield: 6 servings.

Nancy Simonton, Greenville, S. C.

HAM AND NOODLE CASSEROLE

¾ c. diced onions
½ c. diced green pepper
2 tsp. salad oil
½ lb. broad noodles
1 ¾ c. canned tomatoes
1 c. water
1 c. (or more) diced ham
1 tsp. salt
¼ tsp. pepper
½ tsp. paprika
½ lb. cheddar cheese

Cook onions and green pepper slowly in oil until transparent but not brown. Add noodles, tomatoes, water, ham, salt, pepper and paprika; simmer for 10 minutes. Stir in cheese. Turn into a greased 2-quart casserole. Bake in 350-degree oven for 40 to 45 minutes.

Mrs. Frank J. Lesslie, Decatur, Ga.

HAM SOUFFLE

16 slices white sandwich bread
8 slices sharp cheese
2 c. ground baked ham
6 eggs
3 c. milk
½ tsp. mustard
1 tsp. seasoned salt
½ c. butter
2 c. cornflakes

Cut crust from bread; fit 8 slices in bottom of baking pan. Cover with slices of cheese. Top cheese with layer of ham. Beat eggs; add milk, mustard and salt. Place remaining slices of bread on top of ham; pour milk and eggs over all. Place in refrigerator overnight. Before baking, melt butter; add cornflakes and spread on top. Bake at 350 degrees 1 hour and 30 minutes. Serve plain or with cream of mushroom soup across top. Yield: 8 servings.

Mrs. Charles William Nipson, West Palm Beach, Fla.

World famous Cumberland Falls in Kentucky.

HAM AND CHEESE CASSEROLE

4 eggs, separated
1 c. ground cooked ham
1 c. cubed American cheese
1 tbsp. chopped parsley
1 tsp. onion juice
1 tsp. salt
½ tsp. Worcestershire sauce
1 ½ c. macaroni, cooked
1 c. milk
½ c. grated cheese

Mix egg yolks with ham, American cheese and seasonings; add macaroni and blend well. Fold in stiffly beaten egg whites. Place in greased 2-quart baking dish. Pour milk over mixture; sprinkle grated cheese on top. Bake at 350 degrees for 40 to 45 minutes. Yield: 6 servings.

Mrs. Jack Mullikin, Tollesboro, Ky.

HAM AND CHEESE CASSEROLE

1 c. macaroni
1 can tomato soup
½ soup can water
1 c. diced leftover ham
Cheese slices

Cook macaroni; drain. Heat soup and water. Pour a third of the macaroni in baking dish. Sprinkle half the ham over macaroni; cover with cheese. Repeat layers. Top with remaining third of macaroni. Pour soup over all. Bake at 350 degrees for 30 minutes or till bubbly. Yield: 2 servings.

Mrs. James J. Elder, North Miami, Fla.

HAM, MACARONI AND CHEESE FAMILY-STYLE

½ c. ground or finely chopped ham
¼ c. chopped onion
2 tbsp. butter or margarine
1 10 ½-oz. can condensed cream of mushroom soup
½ c. milk
1 c. shredded sharp cheddar cheese
2 c. cooked macaroni
2 tbsp. buttered bread crumbs

(Continued on next page)

Lightly brown ham and onion in butter. Stir in soup, milk and 3/4 cup cheese; heat until cheese melts. Blend sauce with macaroni; pour into buttered 1 1/2-quart casserole. Sprinkle remaining cheese and crumbs on top. Bake at 350 degrees about 30 minutes, or until nicely browned and bubbling.

Marolyn Westbrook, Leesburg, Ga.

HAM AND MACARONI CASSEROLE

4 oz. cooked elbow or twist macaroni
2 c. cubed smoked ham
2 tbsp. each chopped onion, green pepper and celery
1 crushed clove of garlic (opt.)
2 c. canned tomatoes
Salt and pepper to taste
1 c. grated sharp cheese
4 tbsp. Italian-style bread crumbs or buttered crumbs
Butter

Cook macaroni as directed on box; drain and return to same pan. Add all ingredients except cheese, bread crumbs and butter. Mix well; pour into 2-quart flat casserole dish. Cover with cheese, then bread crumbs; dot with butter. Bake, uncovered, for 35 minutes in 350-degree oven. Yield: 4 servings.

Mrs. Katherine M. Thompson, Falls Church, Va.

HAM AND RICE CASSEROLE

2 10 ½-oz. cans cream of celery soup
1 c. light cream
1 c. grated sharp cheddar cheese
½ c. grated Parmesan cheese
1 ½ tbsp. minced onion
1 tbsp. prepared mustard
⅛ tsp. pepper
4 c. cooked rice
4 c. cubed cooked ham
1 10-oz. pkg. frozen green peas
1 3 ½-oz. can French-fried onion rings

Combine celery soup and cream in saucepan; stir until smooth. Heat over low heat until hot. Do not boil. Stir in cheeses. Blend in onion, mustard and pepper. Remove from heat. Combine sauce with rice and cubed ham. Alternate layers of ham and rice mixture with green peas in 3-quart casserole, ending with ham and rice mixture on top. Sprinkle top with French-fried onion rings. Bake, uncovered, at 350 degrees for 15 to 20 minutes. Divide into 2 casseroles and freeze one for a later meal. Yield: 10 servings.

Mrs. Martha Jo Bredemyer, Lancaster, Tex.

HAM RICEWICH

½ c. uncooked rice
1 tbsp. fat
1 ½ tbsp. minced onion
1 can consomme
½ c. water
1 tsp. salt
½ tsp. poultry seasoning
1 tsp. mustard
2 slices of ham, ¼ inch thick

(Continued on next page)

Brown rice in fat. Add onion and cook until tender. Add consomme, water and seasonings; cover and steam for 20 minutes. Spread mustard on one side of a slice of ham; cover with rice. Top with second piece of ham. Place in a greased casserole. Cover and bake at 350 degrees for 1 hour and 30 minutes. Yield: 4-6 servings.

Winifred A. Rogers, Englewood, Tex.

HAM-A-LAY-A

- 1 can condensed cream of mushroom soup
- 1 ¼ c. water or milk
- ¼ c. chopped onion
- ½ tsp. salt
- Dash of pepper
- 1 ½ c. instant rice
- 1 ½ c. diced cooked ham
- 1 c. cooked green beans
- Grated cheese (opt.)
- Paprika (opt.)

Combine soup, water, onion, salt and pepper in saucepan; mix well. Bring to a boil over medium heat, stirring occasionally. Pour about half the soup mixture into a greased 1 1/2-quart casserole. Pour rice into casserole. Combine ham and beans; pour into casserole. Top with remaining soup. Sprinkle with grated cheese and paprika if desired. Cover and bake at 375 degrees for 20 minutes. Yield: 4-6 servings.

Mrs. Hubert Roper, Decatur, Ga.

BAKED BEANS AND HAM CASSEROLE

- 1 med. onion, peeled and chopped
- ¼ c. chopped green pepper
- 1 c. cooked ham, cut in julienne strips
- 2 tbsp. butter or margarine
- ½ c. tomato paste
- ½ c. water
- 1 tbsp. wine vinegar
- ½ tsp. salt
- 1 1-lb. can baked beans
- 4 slices bacon

Saute onion, green pepper and ham in butter. Add tomato paste, water, vinegar and salt; simmer about 5 minutes. Add beans; turn into 1-quart casserole. Arrange bacon on top. Bake at 350 degrees for 30 minutes or until bubbly and browned. Yield: 4-6 servings.

Mrs. Carol Ann Young, Swannanoa, N. C.

CHEESE STRATA

- 12 slices white bread
- ¾ lb. sharp American cheese, sliced
- 1 10-oz. pkg. frozen chopped broccoli (opt.)
- 2 c. finely diced cooked or canned ham or other cooked meat
- 3 ½ c. milk
- 2 tbsp. instant minced onion
- ½ tsp. salt
- ¼ tsp. dry mustard

(Continued on next page)

Cut doughnut shapes from bread and set aside. Fit scraps of bread, top and crust removed, in bottom of 13 x 9 x 2-inch baking dish. Place cheese in layer over bread, add layer of broccoli, then ham. Arrange bread doughnuts and holes on top. Combine remaining ingredients; pour over bread. Cover and refrigerate at least 6 hours or overnight. Bake, uncovered, at 325 degrees for 55 minutes. Sprinkle with shredded cheese 5 minutes before end of baking time, if desired. Let stand 10 minutes to firm; cut into squares. Yield: 12 servings.

Mrs. C. J. Cates, Birmingham, Ala.

BAKED HAM CASSEROLE

4 slices pineapple
3 lge. sweet potatoes
3 red apples
1 ham slice, 1 inch thick
1 c. pineapple juice
2 tbsp. brown sugar
2 tbsp. butter

Cover bottom of a casserole with pineapple slices. Peel and slice sweet potatoes lengthwise; place on pineapple. Core and slice apples crosswise; place on potatoes. Place ham slice on top. Pour pineapple juice over all. Bake, covered, at 300 degrees for 2 hours. Remove from oven; sprinkle with brown sugar and dot with butter. Broil until browned. Yield: 4 servings.

Zora Coleman, Printer, Ky.

DIXIE CASSEROLE

6 hard-cooked eggs
½ lb. sliced boiled ham
1 ½ c. cooked or canned whole kernel corn
2 c. med. white sauce
1 c. soft bread crumbs
Butter or margarine

Slice eggs; place 1/2 the eggs and 1/2 the ham in bottom of casserole. Add corn; cover with 1 cup white sauce. Add remaining eggs, ham, corn and sauce. Top with crumbs; dot with butter. Bake at 400 degrees 15 minutes. Yield: 4 servings.

MEDIUM WHITE SAUCE:

2 tbsp. butter or margarine
2 tbsp. flour
1 c. milk
½ tsp. salt
Few grains pepper

Melt butter; blend in flour. Gradually add milk. Cook over hot water, stirring constantly, until thick. Add salt and pepper. Cook 5 minutes, stirring occasionally. Yield: 1 cup.

Mrs. Alberta E. Veith, Louisville, Ky.

GREEN BEANS AND HAM

1 c. cubed cooked ham
1 c. cooked diced potatoes
1 c. cooked chopped green beans
Salt and pepper to taste
¾ c. thin white sauce
Buttered bread crumbs

(Continued on next page)

Arrange alternate layers of ham, potatoes and beans in a casserole; season to taste. Add white sauce; sprinkle with buttered crumbs. Bake at 375 degrees for 25 to 30 minutes. Yield: 6 servings.

Mrs. H. R. Perdue, Natchez, Miss.

HAM AND POTATO CASSEROLE

1 lb. leftover boiled or baked ham
5 sticks celery
1 med. onion
2 tbsp. butter
½ tsp. parsley flakes
2 med. potatoes
1 can mushroom soup

Grind ham and set aside. Dice celery and onion; saute in butter. Add 1 cup water and parsley flakes. Cover and cook over low heat until tender. Peel potatoes; slice thick as for scalloped potatoes. Cook in salted water until about half done; drain. Combine celery and onion mixture with ham; place half the mixture in a casserole dish. Mix soup with 1/2 soup can water; pour 1/2 of soup over ham. Place sliced potatoes over ham; cover with remaining ham. Pour remaining soup over all. Cover and bake for 35 minutes at 300 degrees. Cold roast pork may be substituted for ham. Yield: 4 servings.

Mrs. C. R. Bendy, Houston, Tex.

HAWAIIAN HAM

2 slices ham, 1 inch thick
Prepared mustard
6 slices canned pineapple
3 cooked or canned sweet potatoes, halved
¼ c. brown sugar

Cut each ham slice into 3 pieces; spread with mustard and place in greased baking dish. Top each slice with pineapple and a half potato. Pour pineapple syrup over top and sprinkle with brown sugar. Bake, uncovered, at 325 degrees for 1 hour. Yield: 6 servings.

Mrs. W. R. Atwood, Shelbyville, Tenn.

SWEET POTATO AND APPLE CASSEROLE

6 fresh sweet potatoes
3 apples, peeled, cored and sliced thin
1 c. brown sugar
3 tbsp. butter or oleo
Dash of salt
1 c. water
1 slice of ham or 4 pork chops, trimmed of all fat

Wash potatoes; boil with jackets on. Cook until tender; drain. Peel and cut into 1/2-inch slices. Arrange potato and apple slices alternately in casserole. Make a light syrup of brown sugar, butter, salt and water, stirring constantly. Pour over potatoes and apples. Put ham on top. Bake at 350 degrees until ham is well done and apples are tender.

Mrs. J. Norris Hanning, New Orleans, La.

APPLE STUFFED PORK CHOPS

6 lge. pork chops
1 c. chopped apples
1 ½ c. bread crumbs
¼ c. chopped onion
¼ c. chopped celery
1 tsp. salt
½ tsp. pepper
1 tbsp. sugar
2 to 3 tbsp. milk

Cut through lean portion of each chop to form pocket. Combine apples, bread crumbs, onion, celery, salt, pepper and sugar. Add only enough milk to moisten. Use dressing to stuff pockets in chops. Place chops in shallow baking pan. Bake at 350 degrees for 1 hour and 30 minutes. Baste occasionally with drippings. Cover during last 30 minutes of baking time. Yield: 6 servings.

Mrs. Warner Lowe, Carlisle, Ky.

BAKED PORK CHOPS AND STUFFING

4 pork chops
3 c. soft bread crumbs
2 tbsp. chopped onion
¼ c. melted butter or margarine
Water
Pepper to taste
1 10 ½-oz. can cream of mushroom soup

Brown pork chops on both sides; place in shallow baking dish. Lightly mix bread crumbs, onion, butter, 1/4 cup water and pepper. Place a mound of stuffing on each chop. Blend soup and 1/3 cup water; pour over all. Bake at 350 degrees for 1 hour, or until meat is tender. Yield: 4 servings.

Mrs. Dale McLemore, Roxie, Miss.

KRAUT-CHOPS AND APPLES

6 loin pork chops
12 sm. white onions
2 med. apples, quartered
½ c. seedless raisins
1 tbsp. brown sugar
2 c. undrained sauerkraut
1 tsp. salt
¼ tsp. pepper

Brown pork chops. Mix together onions, apples, raisins, brown sugar and kraut with half the salt and pepper. Arrange in 2-quart casserole. Top with chops; sprinkle on remaining salt and pepper. Cover and bake in 350-degree oven for 1 hour and 15 minutes or until pork is tender.

Photograph for this recipe on page 35.

PORK CASSEROLE DELUXE

½ c. bread crumbs
1 ½ tsp. salt
6 slices pork tenderloin
1 egg, beaten
3 tbsp. drippings
3 tart med. apples, peeled and sliced ½ inch thick
4 med. yams, peeled and sliced ½ inch thick
⅛ tsp. pepper
½ tsp. cinnamon
3 tbsp. brown sugar
⅓ c. water

(Continued on next page)

Mix together bread crumbs and 1/2 teaspoon salt. Dip tenderloins into egg and then into seasoned crumbs. Brown lightly in drippings. Place 1/2 the apples in a greased 2-quart casserole; top with 1/2 the yams. Repeat layers. Combine 1 teaspoon salt, pepper, cinnamon, brown sugar and water; bring to a boil. Pour sauce over apples and yams; top with tenderloins. Cover with aluminum foil. Bake at 350 degrees for 45 minutes or until meat is done. Yield: 4-6 servings.

Mrs. James C. Slavik, St. Petersburg, Fla.

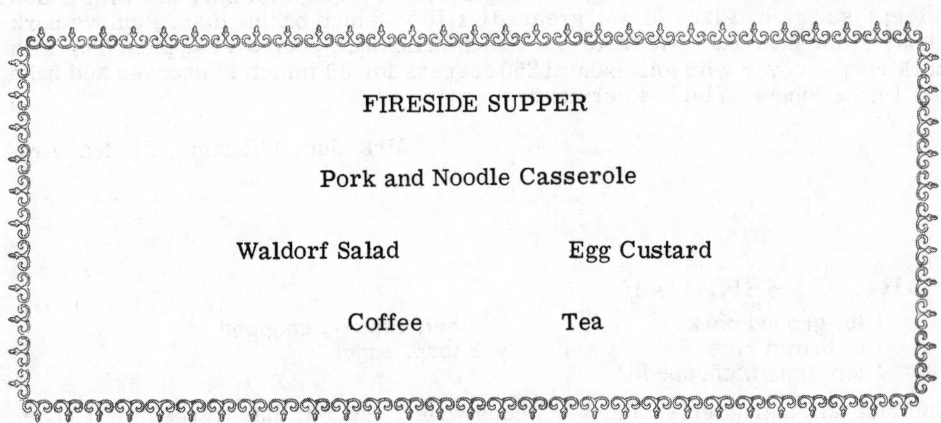

FIRESIDE SUPPER

Pork and Noodle Casserole

Waldorf Salad — Egg Custard

Coffee — Tea

PORK AND NOODLE CASSEROLE

- 1 8-oz. pkg. noodles
- ¼ lb. sharp cheese, grated
- 1 ½ lb. ground lean pork
- 1 onion, chopped
- 1 c. canned tomato soup
- 1 tsp. salt
- ½ tsp. pepper
- ½ tsp. paprika

Cook noodles according to package directions; drain. Add cheese, stirring until melted. Brown meat and onion; pour soup over meat. Combine all ingredients. Bake at 350 degrees for 30 minutes. Yield: 8 servings.

Mrs. Elsie Speegle, Monteagle, Tenn.

PORK CHOPS WITH DRESSING

- 4 slices bread, cut into cubes
- 1 sm. onion, chopped
- 1 stalk celery, chopped
- ¼ c. butter
- ⅛ tsp. savory
- ½ tsp. salt
- ⅛ tsp. thyme
- ½ c. water
- 4 pork chops
- 1 tbsp. shortening
- ¼ tsp. paprika

Place bread cubes on cookie sheet; toast until golden brown. Saute onion and celery in butter until tender but not brown. Add savory, salt, thyme and water. Mix with bread cubes; pour into 2-quart casserole. Brown chops in shortening on both sides. Place on top of dressing. Sprinkle with paprika. Cover; bake at 350 degrees for 45 minutes. Remove cover; continue baking for 10 minutes. Yield: 4 servings.

Mrs. Bennie Ricks, Moultrie, Ga.

PORK AND APPLE CASSEROLE

4 pork loin chops
1 ½ tsp. Kitchen Bouquet
1 tbsp. cooking oil
1 tsp. salt
1 qt. diced tart red apples
½ c. seedless raisins
2 tbsp. brown sugar
½ tsp. basil
⅛ tsp. ground cloves
3 tbsp. lemon juice
3 tbsp. water

Brush entire surface of pork chops with Kitchen Bouquet. Brown in oil in heavy skillet over moderate heat; sprinkle with salt. Place diced apples and raisins in mixing bowl. Sprinkle with sugar and spices, tossing lightly. Sprinkle with lemon juice; toss again. Place in well greased 6 x 10 x 2-inch baking dish. Remove pork chops from pan. Add water to pork chop drippings; pour over apples. Top with pork chops; cover with foil. Bake at 350 degrees for 30 minutes; uncover and bake for 1 hour longer. Yield: 4 servings.

Mrs. June Williams, Clinton, Ark.

PORK CASSEROLE

1 lb. ground pork
1 c. brown rice
1 sm. onion, chopped
½ bell pepper, chopped
2 tbsp. sugar

Combine all ingredients; add 2 1/2 cups water. Bake at 350 degrees for 1 hour. Yield: 4-5 servings.

Mrs. G. C. Lewis, Petal, Miss.

PORK CHOP BAKE

4 thick pork chops
1 tbsp. cooking oil
1 c. rice
2 ½ c. water
1 pkg. dehydrated onion soup mix
Onion or garlic salt
Pepper

Brown chops in oil on both sides in frying pan; remove and set aside. Stir rice into drippings in pan. Add water and onion soup; mix well. Pour into casserole. Arrange chops on top of rice mixture. Sprinkle with onion salt and pepper. Cover. Bake 1 hour in 325-degree oven. Yield: 4 servings.

Mrs. Donald E. Tryk, North Palm Beach, Fla.

PORK CHOP CASSEROLE

6 pork chops
1 c. rice
½ green pepper, cut up
2 tbsp. grated onion
1 ½ tsp. salt
¼ tsp. pepper
3 c. tomatoes

Brown chops in their own fat. Remove chops; add rice and brown slightly. Combine rice with green pepper, onion and seasonings in casserole; add tomatoes. Place chops on top. Bake, covered, at 350 degrees for 1 hour and 30 minutes. Add water if needed.

William E. Robbins, High Point, N. C.

PORK CHOP CASSEROLE

¾ c. uncooked rice
4 pork chops
1 onion, sliced
1 fresh tomato, sliced
1 bell pepper, sliced
1 can beef bouillon soup

Place rice in casserole dish. Brown chops in skillet; arrange on top of rice. Place slice of onion, tomato and pepper on top of each chop. Pour soup over all. Cover. Bake at 350 degrees for 1 hour. Yield: 4 servings.

Mrs. Sam Burns, Natchez, Miss.

PORK CHOPS AND RICE

4 lean loin pork chops
¼ c. raw rice
4 thick slices Bermuda onion
4 thick slices fresh tomato
4 thick rings green pepper
1 c. beef bouillon
¼ tsp. thyme
½ tsp. marjoram
Salt and pepper

Saute chops; place in shallow buttered casserole. Place 1 tablespoon rice, 1 onion slice, 1 slice tomato and 1 green pepper ring on each chop. Pour bouillon over all; sprinkle with seasonings. Bake, covered, at 350 degrees about 1 hour.

Mrs. Ruth Morris, Durham, N. C.

PORK HASH IN CASSEROLE

2 med. onions, finely chopped
Pork drippings or butter
1 c. diced cooked pork
1 c. tomato juice
1 tsp. salt
Pepper to taste
1 ½ c. cooked rice
½ tsp. Worcestershire sauce
Boiling water

Saute onions in drippings or butter. Add pork, tomato juice, salt, pepper, rice and Worcestershire sauce. Turn into greased baking dish; cover with boiling water. Bake at 300 degrees for 1 hour and 30 minutes.

Mrs. L. K. Halsey, Piney Creek, N. C.

RICE CASSEROLE

⅔ c. whole grain rice
1 ½ lb. lean pork loin, cut in sm. pieces
1 lge. onion, sliced
½ tsp. mixed herbs
Salt and pepper to taste
1 sm. bay leaf
1 8-oz. can tomato sauce
⅔ c. water

In a large baking dish, alternate layers of rice, pork and onion slices. Sprinkle herbs, salt and pepper on each layer; place bay leaf in center. Pour tomato sauce mixed with water over all. Cover and bake in 325-degree oven about 1 hour.

Mrs. Hugo A. Puls, Sr., Falkville, Ala.

TAMALE CASSEROLE

½ c. minced onions
1 c. ground or finely chopped cooked pork
1 tbsp. chili powder
⅛ tsp. garlic powder
2 c. corn bread crumbs
Salt and pepper to taste
2 c. broth

Grease casserole with oil. Combine all ingredients except broth in mixing bowl; mix well. Add broth and mix lightly. Pour into casserole. Bake, covered, for 30 minutes at 350 degrees; uncover and brown slightly. Yield: 6 servings.

Mrs. Jim R. Bell, Deatsville, Ala.

APPLE-CHOP CASSEROLE

6 pork chops
Fat
1 tsp. salt
⅛ tsp. pepper
4 med. apples, peeled and sliced
4 med. sweet potatoes, peeled and sliced
1 med. onion, chopped
1 c. water
1 tsp. Worcestershire sauce

Brown chops in fat. Place in casserole. Sprinkle with one-half of salt and pepper. Place apples and potatoes in layers on chops; sprinkle with remaining salt and pepper. Saute onion in fat used for chops. Add water and Worcestershire sauce; mix well. Pour over top. Cover. Bake at 375 degrees for about 1 hour and 30 minutes. Yield: 6 servings.

Mrs. Edna Head, Bynum, Ala.

CHOPS AND POTATOES CASSEROLE

4 pork chops
1 can cream mushroom soup
½ c. sour cream
¼ c. water
2 tbsp. chopped parsley
4 c. thinly sliced potatoes
Salt and pepper

Brown chops. Blend soup, sour cream, water and parsley. Arrange sliced potatoes, sprinkled with salt and pepper, in 2-quart casserole dish. Alternate layer of potatoes and sauce; top with chops. Cover and bake in a 375-degree oven 1 hour and 15 minutes. Yield: 4 servings.

Mrs. Thomas L. Williams, Mobile, Ala.

BAKED PORK CHOPS

4 pork chops, ½ in. thick
2 tbsp. fat
¼ c. diced onion
1 c. cream of celery soup
½ c. milk
1 ½ tsp. salt
⅛ tsp. pepper
3 med. potatoes, peeled and sliced
1 lb. cabbage, shredded
¼ c. flour

(Continued on next page)

Brown chops in hot fat in heavy fry pan; remove chops. Add onion, soup, milk, salt and pepper to fat in pan; blend well. Alternate layers of potatoes and cabbage in a 2-quart casserole or 8 x 8 x 2-inch cake pan. Sprinkle each layer with flour; pour soup mixture over each layer. Place chops on top; cover casserole or use aluminum foil to cover pan. Bake at 350 degrees for 1 hour and 15 minutes. Yield: 4 servings.

Mrs. George Hemingway, Blairsville, Ga.

PORK CASSEROLE

1 lb. pork steak, diced
Flour
1 tbsp. shortening
1 c. raw peas
1 c. raw carrots, diced
1 c. raw potatoes, diced
Salt and pepper
1 c. water
6 cloves

Roll pork in flour; brown in shortening. Remove meat from skillet; mix with vegetables and seasonings. Turn into casserole. Add water to drippings in skillet; heat. Pour over meat and vegetable mixture. Add cloves. Bake at 350 degrees for at least 1 hour. Mixture should be consistency of scalloped potatoes. Yield: 6 servings.

Mrs. Mae Caris, Pineview, Ga.

PORK CHOP CASSEROLE

6 pork chops
1 can cream of celery soup
¼ c. milk
Dash of thyme
2 10-oz. pkg. frozen cut green beans, thawed
¼ tsp. salt
⅛ tsp. pepper

Trim excess fat from chops. Brown in rendered fat on both sides in an ovenproof skillet. Pour off drippings. Combine soup, milk and thyme; stir in beans. Place in skillet, arranging chops on top. Sprinkle with salt and pepper. Cover and bake at 350 degrees for 45 minutes or until chops are tender. Remove cover and bake 5 to 10 minutes longer. Serve immediately. Four cups canned green beans may be substituted for frozen ones. Yield: 6 servings.

Mrs. Noah Elam, Index, Ky.

PORK CHOP CASSEROLE

3 lge. potatoes
3 lge. onions
Salt and pepper
6 pork chops, ½ in. thick
1 can condensed cream of mushroom soup

Peel and slice potatoes and onions into 9 x 13-inch pan. Sprinkle salt and pepper on both sides of chops; lay on top of sliced vegetables. Spoon soup onto chops and potatoes. Bake at 350 degrees for 1 hour and 30 minutes or until done.

Mrs. Irene B. Harrell, Wilson, N. C.

PORK CHOP CASSEROLE

4 lean pork chops
4 baking potatoes, cut into ½-in. slices
1 lge. onion, sliced
1 sm. bell pepper
1 can tomato soup
1 soup can water

Brown pork chops. Place potatoes in bottom of square baking dish. Add sliced onion. Slice pepper in strips; place on top of onion. Put browned chops on top; add soup, which has been diluted with water. Cover with foil. Bake at 450 degrees until potatoes are done, approximately 30 minutes. Yield: 4 servings.

Mrs. George Fox, Miami, Fla.

PORK CHOPS EN CASSEROLE

6 sweet potatoes, sliced crosswise
½ tsp. salt
¼ tsp. pepper
½ c. brown sugar
1 to 2 c. milk, heated
6 pork chops

Place layer of sweet potatoes in large greased casserole; dust with salt, pepper and a little brown sugar. Repeat layers until casserole is about 2/3 full. Pour enough milk over potatoes to just cover. Place chops on top. Cover and bake at 350 degrees for 1 hour; remove cover and cook until chops are tender and nicely browned on top. Four tart apples, pared, cored and cut in eighths may be used in place of sweet potatoes. Yield: 6 servings.

Mrs. Gladys Mason, Roanoke, Va.

PORK CHOPS AND SAUERKRAUT

4 thick pork chops
Salt to taste
Flour
3 tbsp. fat
1 onion, sliced
2 ½ c. sauerkraut
Mashed potatoes

Season chops with salt and dredge lightly in flour. Brown in hot fat. Pour fat into baking dish; add onion. Cover onion with sauerkraut. Place chops on top of kraut. Cover dish tightly. Bake at 300 degrees for 1 hour and 30 minutes to 2 hours. Cover chops with generous layer of fluffy mashed potatoes. Bake at 400 degrees until potatoes are lightly browned. Water may be added if kraut is not juicy, or is too salty. Yield: 4 servings.

Mrs. George Hill, Edwards, Miss.

SPARERIB BEAN BAKE

4 lb. spareribs, cut into 2-rib pieces
1 13 ½-oz. can pineapple chunks
2 tbsp. brown sugar
1 ½ tsp. salt
Ground cloves
Ground ginger
1 tbsp. Worcestershire sauce
½ tsp. onion salt
3 16-oz. cans pork and beans

(Continued on next page)

Arrange spareribs in 13 x 9-inch baking dish. Drain pineapple; reserve syrup. Combine brown sugar, salt, 1/4 teaspoonful cloves 1/4 teaspoonful ginger, Worcestershire sauce and reserved syrup. Brush ribs with one-half of mixture. Sprinkle ribs with onion salt. Bake, uncovered, at 350 degrees for 1 hour, basting with drippings every 15 minutes. Remove spareribs from baking dish; set aside. Pour off drippings from baking dish. Combine pork and beans, pineapple chunks, 1/8 teaspoonful cloves and 1/8 teaspoonful ginger in baking dish. Arrange spareribs on top of bean mixture. Spoon remaining basting mixture over ribs. Return to oven; bake, uncovered, for 1 hour longer or until beans are hot and spareribs brown. Yield: 6 servings.

Mrs. Browning Graham, Morgan City, La.

BRIDGE NIGHT CASSEROLE

1 lb. pork sausage links
3 c. cooked noodles
1 c. applesauce
2 tsp. lemon juice
¼ tsp. nutmeg
¼ tsp. cinnamon
½ c. grated cheese

Bake sausage in shallow pan for 25 minutes at 400 degrees. Turn sausage once. Place layer of noodles in casserole; dribble 4 tablespoons sausage drippings over top. Add applesauce, lemon juice and spices, then another layer of noodles. Place sausages on top and sprinkle grated cheese over all. Bake at 350 degrees for 10 minutes.

Kathryn S. Johnson, St. Petersburg, Fla.

GRITS CASSEROLE

1 c. grits
½ tsp. salt
2 c. boiling water
½ stick butter or oleo
4 eggs, beaten
1 c. milk
¼ c. grated cheese
½ c. pork sausage

Cook grits in salted boiling water until thickened. Add butter, eggs, milk, cheese and sausage; stir thoroughly. Pour into a casserole, greased with bacon grease. Bake at 350 degrees for 30 minutes. Yield: 4-6 servings.

Mrs. Jessie Lester, Alexandria, Va.

AMARILLO SAUSAGE BAKE

1 lb. country-style bulk sausage, plain or hot
¾ c. uncooked rice
1 can chicken gumbo soup
1 c. water
Salt and pepper to taste
¼ tsp. oregano

Break up sausage meat into small bits; brown well in heavy frying pan. Drain off fat. Mix in remaining ingredients; pour into casserole. Cover. Bake at 350 degrees for 35 to 45 minutes. Yield: 3-4 servings.

Mrs. Donald Tryk, North Palm Beach, Fla.

RICE AND PORK CASSEROLE

1 lb. pork sausage hot or regular
½ green pepper, chopped
1 bud crushed garlic
½ c. chopped celery
1 sm. onion, chopped
4 ½ c. water
1 envelope dry chicken-noodle soup
1 c. regular rice
½ c. slivered almonds (opt.)

Cook sausage, green pepper, garlic, celery and onion in skillet. Heat water in in large saucepan; bring to a boil. Add soup and rice; cook for 10 minutes. Combine all ingredients; mix well. Place in baking dish. Bake, covered, at 350 degrees for 45 minutes; uncover and bake 15 minutes longer. Yield: 6-8 servings.

Mrs. Ernest T. Olson, Taylor, Tex.

RICE AND SAUSAGE CASSEROLE

1 lb. lean mild sausage
1 onion, chopped
1 green pepper, chopped
3 stalks celery, chopped
Salt and pepper
1 c. regular rice
1 can cream of chicken soup
1 qt. chicken broth made from bouillon cubes
1 pkg. almonds, sliced

Brown and drain sausage. Brown onion, pepper and celery in sausage drippings. Add all ingredients except almonds. Put in greased casserole and refrigerate overnight. Add almonds. Bake at 325 degrees for 1 hour and 30 minutes. Stir every 20 minutes during cooking period. Yield: 8-10 servings.

Mrs. Eunice Jackson, Morgan, Ga.

RICE AND SAUSAGE CASSEROLE

1 lb. pkg. sausage
1 lge. onion, chopped
1 ½ c. celery, chopped
1 c. raw rice
5 ½ c. water
5 oz. blanched almonds, chopped
¼ tsp. sugar
1 pkg. dry chicken-noodle soup
1 can mushroom soup

(Continued on next page)

Brown sausage, which has been crumbled, in heavy skillet, stirring constantly. Drain; reserving 1/3 of grease. Saute chopped onion and celery in grease. Combine sausage, onion, celery, rice, water, almonds, sugar and chicken-noodle soup. Mix together in casserole. Bake for 1 hour in 350-degree oven. Combine mushroom soup and 1 soup can water; pour over casserole and continue cooking for 1 hour longer. Yield: 10 servings.

Mrs. Beatrice Wooden, Mobile, Ala.

SAUSAGE CASSEROLE

1 ½ lb. sausage
2 stalks celery, chopped
2 pkg. chicken-noodle soup mix
4 ½ c. water
1 sm. can water chestnuts, cut up
5 green onions, chopped
1 green pepper, chopped
1 c. cooked brown or wild rice

Fry sausage until crumbly and brown. Drain off all fat. Add all remaining ingredients; mix well. Simmer 15 minutes. Place in casserole. Bake, covered, at 350 degrees for 1 hour and 30 minutes. May be frozen.

Mrs. J. W. Williams, Concord, Tenn.

SAUSAGE CASSEROLE

½ lb. lean pork sausage
4 or 5 spring onions and tops, chopped
1 med. bunch celery and 3 tender leaves
1 lge green pepper, chopped
2 pkg. chicken-noodle soup
4 ½ c. boiling water
1 c. brown rice
1 can water chestnuts, sliced and drained
Salt and pepper
¼ c. slivered almonds (about)

Cook sausage until crumbly; remove from fat and reserve. Pour off all but 2 or 3 tablespoons of fat. Saute onions, celery and green pepper. Salt and pepper to taste. Cook soup and rice in boiling water about 7 minutes. Add water chestnuts. Mix all ingredients together; place in large casserole. Sprinkle with almonds. Cover. Bake in 350-degree oven for 1 hour and 30 minutes to 2 hours. Remove cover last 30 minutes of baking. Yield: 10-12 servings.

Mrs. B. S. Jones, Leaksville, N. C.

SAUSAGE PILAF

1 lb. bulk sausage
1 c. chopped celery
½ c. chopped onion
½ c. green pepper
¼ c. chopped pimento
1 can cream of mushroom soup
1 ¼ c. milk
½ c. rice
½ tsp. rubbed sage
¼ tsp. salt
2 tbsp. melted butter
1 c. soft bread crumbs

(Continued on next page)

Brown sausage; drain off excess fat. Add celery, onion and green pepper; cook until tender, but not brown. Stir in pimento, soup, milk, rice and seasonings. Pour into an ungreased 1 1/2-quart casserole. Bake, covered, at 350 degrees for 50 minutes, stirring occasionally. Mix butter and crumbs; sprinkle over casserole. Bake for 20 minutes, uncovered. Recipe may be used as stuffing for green peppers. Yield: 6 servings.

Mary Ann Templeton, Starksville, Miss.

SAUSAGE-RICE CASSEROLE

1 lb. pork sausage
¾ c. uncooked rice
2 c. canned tomatoes
¾ c. finely chopped onion
1 tsp. salt
1 tsp. chili powder
2 c. hot water
½ c. grated sharp cheese

Break sausage into pieces in a cold skillet; fry slowly for 12 to 15 minutes until evenly browned, pouring off fat as it accumulates. Remove sausage. Pour off all but 1/4 cup fat. Add rice to fat in skillet. Cook and stir over low heat until rice is lightly browned. Stir in tomatoes, onion, salt, chili powder, hot water and sausage. Pour into baking dish. Bake, uncovered, at 350 degrees for 45 minutes. Sprinkle cheese on top and bake for an additional 10 minutes. Yield: 6-8 servings.

Lynda Hunter Black, Bartow, Fla.

SAUSAGE-NOODLE CASSEROLE

1 lb. bulk pork sausage
1 c. chopped onions
1 8-oz. pkg. wide noodles, cooked
½ tsp. salt
1 No. 303 can tomatoes
2 tsp. salt
1 tsp. chili powder
1 c. sour cream (opt.)
1 tbsp. sugar
1 c. grated sharp cheese

Cook sausage and onions until meat is brown; drain off excess fat. Add all remaining ingredients except cheese; pour into a casserole. Top with grated cheese. Bake at 350 degrees for 30 minutes. Yield: 8-10 servings.

Hazel Herring, Evergreen, Ala.

SAUSAGE-CORN BREAD

1 lb. bulk pork sausage
1 c. sifted flour
¼ c. sugar
4 tsp. baking powder
¾ tsp. salt
1 c. yellow cornmeal
2 eggs
1 c. milk
¼ c. soft shortening
2 tbsp. chopped green pepper
Onion Cream Gravy

Brown sausage in skillet; drain, reserving 3 tablespoons of drippings for gravy. Place crumbled sausage in bottom of 9-inch square pan. Sift flour, sugar, baking powder and salt together; stir in cornmeal. Add eggs, milk, shortening and green pepper; beat just until mixed, about 1 minute and pour over sausage. Bake at 425 degrees for 20 to 25 minutes. Serve with Onion Cream Gravy.

(Continued on next page)

ONION CREAM GRAVY:

3 tbsp. chopped onion
4 tbsp. flour
Salt and pepper to taste
2 c. milk
½ tsp. Worcestershire sauce.

Cook onion in reserved pan drippings. Blend in flour, salt and pepper to taste and milk; cook until thick. Stir in Worcestershire sauce.

Mrs. C. M. Mize, Lakeland, Fla.

SAUSAGE-NOODLE CASSEROLE

1 lb. bulk sausage
1 c. chopped onions
1 8-oz. pkg. wide noodles
2 ½ tsp. salt
1 No. 303 can tomatoes
1 tbsp. sugar
1 tsp. chili powder
1 c. sour cream (opt.)
1 c. grated sharp cheese

Cook sausage and onions in skillet until meat is brown; drain off excess fat. Cook noodles in water with 1/2 teaspoonful salt for 10 to 12 minutes or until tender; drain. Add cooked noodles, tomatoes, sugar, remaining salt and chili powder to meat mixture; mix well. Cool. Add sour cream. Bake in 2 1/2-quart casserole at 350 degrees for 30 minutes or until bubbly hot. Add cheese just before serving. Dish may be frozen up to four weeks if packaged for freezing before baking. Thaw in refrigerator for 5 to 7 hours or until completely thawed. Yield: 6 servings.

Mrs. W. Hodges Dial, Sumterville, Ala.

SOUTHERN SAUSAGE CASSEROLE

½ lb. pork sausage
1 c. chopped celery
¼ c. chopped onion
¼ c. chopped green pepper
2 tbsp. minced parsley
¼ tsp. salt
¾ c. tomato paste
¾ c. water
1 c. cooked kidney beans

Brown sausage in heavy skillet; add uncooked vegetables. Brown lightly; drain off excess fat. Season with salt. Combine tomato paste and water; add to meat mixture. Add beans; mix well. Cover; simmer for 10 minutes. Pour mixture into 1 1/2-quart casserole.

CHEESE PUFFS:

1 c. sifted flour
1 ½ tsp. baking powder
½ tsp. salt
2 tbsp. shortening
½ c. shredded American cheese
½ c. milk

Sift flour with baking powder and salt. Cut in shortening until mixture is crumbly. Add cheese. Add milk, mixing only until flour is moistened. Drop cheese puff mixture by spoonfuls over top of sausage casserole. Bake at 425 degrees for 20 minutes. Yield: 6 servings.

Mrs. James Elms, Jamestown, Ark.

SPAGHETTI-SAUSAGE CASSEROLE

½ lb. sausage links
6 oz. spaghetti
2 hard-cooked eggs
1 tbsp. salad dressing
½ tsp. prepared mustard
¼ tsp. salt
Dash of pepper
1 10 ½-oz. can mushroom soup
½ c. milk

Brown sausages in heavy skillet. Cook spaghetti in boiling water 7 minutes. Drain and rinse. Cut eggs in half. Put yolks through a sieve; add salad dressing, mustard, salt and pepper. Fill whites with mixture. Combine soup and milk; stir until smooth. Fold into spaghetti; pour into a greased 1 1/2-quart casserole. Arrange sausage and eggs on top. Bake at 350 degrees for 20 minutes. Yield: 4-6 servings.

Mrs. Jack Mollenbour, Sharon, Tenn.

BROCCOLI CASSEROLE

½ lb. sausage
½ c. minced onion
3 tbsp. milk or cream
3 eggs, beaten
2 pkg. chopped cooked broccoli
1 ½ tsp. salt
¼ tsp. nutmeg
¼ c. bread crumbs

Roll sausage into small balls; brown with onion. Add milk and eggs. Add broccoli, salt and nutmeg; pour into casserole. Top with bread crumbs. Bake at 350 degrees for 30 minutes or until bread crumbs are browned. Serve with cheese sauce if preferred. Yield: 6-8 servings.

Mrs. Andrew J. Hillman, Fordyce, Ark.

CORN AND SAUSAGE CASSEROLE

¾ lb. sausage
1 egg, beaten
1 c. cracker crumbs
1 ¼ c. milk, heated
1 c. cream-style corn
1 sm. green pepper, chopped
1 can tomato sauce

Cook sausage until almost done. Combine sausage, egg, crumbs, 1 cup milk, corn and green pepper. Pour into greased casserole dish. Pour tomato sauce and remaining 1/4 cup milk over all. Bake at 350 degrees for 1 hour. Top with slices of cheese if desired.

Mrs. Hubert Garrett, Bolivar, Tenn.

MERRY ANN CASSEROLE

½ lb. sausage
1 can red kidney beans
1 diced apple, unpeeled
¼ c. brown sugar
1 lge. diced onion
1 button garlic
½ c. tomato juice
2 tsp. salt
½ tsp. pepper
½ tsp. chili powder

(Continued on next page)

Cook sausage and drain grease off. Combine all ingredients in casserole. Bake at 325 degrees for 1 hour and 30 minutes. Yield: 8 servings.

Mrs. Johnnie Fincher, Fairfield, Ala.

POTATO AND SAUSAGE CASSEROLE

3 or 4 Irish potatoes, sliced
1 or 2 onions, sliced
1 lb. sausage, cooked
1 can mushroom soup
⅓ c. water

Place layer of potatoes in greased casserole; add layer of onions, then layer of sausage. Repeat layers until all ingredients are used. Dilute soup with water; pour over casserole. Bake at 300 degrees for 1 hour and 30 minutes. Yield: 4-6 servings.

Mrs. George Brooks, Meridian, Tex.

QUICK TAMALE PIE

SAUSAGE BASE:

1 lb. pork sausage links
½ c. chopped onion
¼ c. chopped green pepper
2 c. cooked lima beans, drained
½ c. chili sauce
2 ½ c. tomatoes
1 tsp. salt

Brown sausage in frying pan; remove sausage. Drain off all but a few tablespoons fat. Add onion and green pepper; cook until brown. Cut sausage into pieces; add with remaining ingredients to onion and green pepper. Cover; simmer 30 minutes. Pour into 2-quart casserole.

CORN BREAD TOPPING:

¾ c. cornmeal
1 tbsp. flour
½ tsp. salt
1 ½ tsp. baking powder
1 egg
⅓ c. milk
1 tbsp. shortening, soft

(Continued on next page)

Sift dry ingredients into bowl. Add egg, milk and shortening. Beat with rotary beater until smooth, about 1 minute. Do not overbeat. Drop batter onto hot meat mixture. Batter will sink but rise during baking to form topping. Bake at 425 degrees about 20 minutes. Yield: 6 servings.

Mrs. C. C. Weigh, Lubbock, Tex.

QUICKIE CASSEROLE

1 lb. sausage links
3 c. thinly sliced raw potatoes
1 c. thinly sliced onions
½ tsp. salt
½ c. milk
1 1-lb. 1-oz. can cream-style corn
6 to 8 green pepper rings

Preheat oven to 375 degrees. Cook sausage as label directs; drain. Place potatoes in 10 x 2-inch baking dish; cover with onions and sprinkle with salt. Pour milk over all. Spread corn over casserole. Top with green pepper rings and sausage links. Cover with foil. Bake for 1 hour. Yield: 4 servings.

Mrs. William C. Kitchens, San Antonio, Tex.

SAUSAGE AND BEAN MEDLEY

1 lb. mild sausage
1 c. water
2 envelopes chicken-noodle soup mix
3 c. dried bread crumbs
1 green pepper, diced
2 1-lb. cans green beans, with liquid
1 onion, finely diced
1 c. sliced almonds
Paprika or parsley or both

Brown sausage; remove grease. Boil water and add chicken soup. Pour over sausage, crumbs, green pepper, beans and onion in casserole. Sprinkle almonds thickly over all and sprinkle with paprika. Bake at 350 degrees for 1 hour. Yield: 8-10 servings.

Mrs. Gloria Baker, Orlando, Fla.

VEGETABLE-SAUSAGE LOAF

1 lge. carrot
6 med. raw potatoes
1 med. onion
4 stalks celery
1 egg, beaten
¼ c. bread crumbs
⅛ tsp. sage
¼ tsp. pepper
1 tsp. salt
¼ c. milk
½ lb. pork sausage

Grind vegetables using medium blade of chopper. Add remaining ingredients. Shape into loaf and bake at 350 degrees for 1 hour. Yield: 6 servings.

Mrs. James Devotie, Parrottsville, Tenn.

Fish and Shellfish
Casseroles

RECIPE FOR SCALLOP CASSEROLE ON PAGE 82

FISH CASSEROLE

1 green pepper, cut fine
3 tbsp. butter
2 tbsp. flour
1 ½ c. cream or top milk
1 c. flaked cooked fish
1 c. soft buttered bread crumbs
Salt and pepper
Sherry to taste

Saute pepper in butter; add flour. Blend until smooth; stir in cream. Stir until thick and smooth. Add fish, 1/2 cup crumbs and seasonings to taste. Pour in baking dish; cover with remaining crumbs. Bake at 375 degrees until brown. Yield: 4 servings.

Mrs. Griffis Meek, Grenada, Miss.

FISH AND SPAGHETTI CASSEROLE

¼ lb. spaghetti
3 tbsp. chopped onion
⅓ c. diced celery
2 c. canned tomatoes
½ tsp. salt
Pepper
1 c. flaked cooked fish
¼ c. bread crumbs

Cook spaghetti, onion and celery in boiling salted water; drain. Heat tomatoes, salt and pepper. Place in a casserole; alternate layers of spaghetti, tomatoes and fish. Top with bread crumbs. Bake at 350 degrees until mixture is heated through and top is brown, about 20 minutes. Yield: 4 servings.

Mrs. M. Wokurka, Forest Park, Ga.

ASPARAGUS-SALMON RIVIERA

2 pkg. frozen asparagus spears
4 tbsp. butter
3 tbsp. flour
2 c. milk
1 6-oz. can salmon, drained and flaked
Salt and pepper
¼ c. Parmesan cheese

Cook asparagus according to package instructions; drain and place in buttered baking dish. Melt butter; blend in flour. Stir in milk; cook, stirring, until thick. Stir in salmon and seasonings. Pour over asparagus. Top with Parmesan cheese. Bake at 350 degrees for 15 to 20 minutes. Garnish with lemon and parsley. Yield: 8-10 servings.

Mrs. S. L. Norrell, Cleburne, Tex.

BAKED SALMON CASSEROLE

1 sm. onion
½ green pepper
Butter
1 can pink salmon
1 lge. can evaporated milk
2 pieces toasted bread
Salt and pepper to taste

Cook onion and green pepper in butter and little water for about 10 minutes. Break up salmon; add milk, broken pieces of toast, pepper, onion, salt and pepper to taste. Mix; put in greased baking dish. Bake at 400 degrees for 30 minutes.

Mrs. Evelyn Garber, Harrisonburg, Va.

FISH 'N' GRITS LOAF

- 2 tbsp. chopped celery
- 2 tbsp. chopped white onion
- 1 tbsp. butter
- 1 c. cold cooked grits
- 1 No. 2 can salmon
- 2 tbsp. cream
- 1 egg, beaten
- ½ tsp. salt
- Pepper to taste

Cook celery and onion lightly in butter. Break up and mix cold grits and salmon, including juice. Add celery and onion. Mix well; add remaining ingredients. Turn into greased baking dish. Bake 30 to 40 minutes at 300 degrees.

Mrs. Charlotte Corley, South Miami, Fla.

SAUCY SALMON

- 1 can cream of celery soup
- ½ c. milk
- 1 8-oz. can salmon, drained and flaked
- 1 ¼ c. crushed potato chips
- 1 c. unsalted cooked green peas, drained

Preheat oven to 375 degrees. Place soup into 1-quart casserole. Add milk; mix thoroughly. Add salmon, 1 cup potato chips and peas; stir well. Sprinkle top with remaining potato chips. Bake for 25 minutes or until heated through.

Mrs. G. C. Thompson, Franklin, Tenn.

RICE AND SALMON CASSEROLE

- 1 ¾ c. water
- 1 ¾ tsp. salt
- 1 ½ c. instant rice
- 1 7 ¾-oz. can salmon
- 1 c. canned peas
- 2 tbsp. butter
- 2 tbsp. flour
- Dash of pepper
- 2 c. milk
- ½ c. grated American cheese

Bring to a boil water and salt. Stir in rice. Cover; remove from heat. Let stand for 5 minutes. Drain salmon and peas. Arrange rice, flaked salmon and peas in alternate layers in a greased 1 1/2-quart casserole. Repeat until all is used. Set aside. Melt butter or margarine. Blend in flour, salt and pepper. Gradually add milk. Cook over medium heat, stirring constantly, until thickened. Pour over layers in casserole. Sprinkle with cheese. Bake at 350 degrees until cheese is melted, about 20 minutes.

Mrs. Gladys Mason, Roanoke, Va.

SALMON CASSEROLE

- ½ stick margarine
- 2 tbsp. flour
- 1 ½ c. milk
- ½ lb. Velveeta cheese
- 1 can salmon
- 1 can refrigerator biscuits

(Continued on next page)

Melt margarine in double boiler; mix in flour and milk. Cut cheese into small pieces; drop into milk mixture. Stir until cheese is melted and sauce thickens slightly. Drain salmon; stir into sauce. Place biscuits in a ring in well-greased baking dish. Fill center of dish with sauce. Pour any remaining mixture over biscuits. Bake at 375 degrees until biscuits are browned.

Mrs. Maurice McNeel, Garland, Tex.

SALMON CASSEROLE

1 c. chopped celery
¼ c. chopped green pepper
⅓ c. chopped onion
1 c. sliced canned mushrooms
2 tbsp. butter
2 c. flaked salmon
1 ¼ c. canned whole kernel corn
2 ½ c. white sauce
¼ tsp. curry powder
Dash of pepper
6 or 8 unbaked biscuits

Fry celery, green pepper, onion and mushrooms in butter until tender. Add salmon and corn. Combine white sauce, curry powder and pepper. Add to salmon mixture; turn into 2-quart casserole. Arrange biscuits over salmon mixture. Bake at 425 degrees for 25 to 30 minutes. Yield: 6 servings.

Mrs. Robert A. Slater, Hanover, Va.

SALMON CASSEROLE

1 pkg. egg noodles, cooked
2 cans salmon
2 cans mushroom soup
Salt and pepper to taste
1 c. grated cheese

Into a greased casserole, alternate layers of noodles, salmon and mushroom soup until dish is filled. Season with salt and pepper. Cover with grated cheese. Bake at 350 degrees for 30 minutes. Yield: 6-8 servings.

Mrs. Cleon Sundby, Ft. Lauderdale, Fla.

SALMON CASSEROLE

4 oz. egg noodles, cooked and drained
1 med. onion, chopped
½ c. sliced pitted ripe olives
1 c. cheese soup
Salmon liquid
1 ½ tsp. Worcestershire sauce
1 1-lb. can salmon, drained and flaked
1 1-lb. can peas, drained

Combine noodles, chopped onion, ripe olives, cheese soup, oil and liquid drained from salmon and Worcestershire sauce. Lightly mix in salmon and peas. Put in a casserole. Bake at 350 degrees about 30 minutes or until heated through.

Mrs. J. M. Forbus, Hogansville, Ga.

SALMON CASSEROLE

1 c. chopped celery
½ c. chopped onion
1 can cream of chicken soup
1 egg, beaten
⅛ tsp. parsley
1 lge. can salmon
2 ½ c. crushed cornflakes

(Continued on next page)

Combine all ingredients in large bowl. Put in 1-quart casserole. Bake at 250 degrees for 1 hour or until brown. Yield: 6 servings.

Mrs. Helen Kendrick, Good Pine, La.

SALMON-CORN PIE

- 2 c. fresh grated corn
- 2 eggs, slightly beaten
- 1 tbsp. (heaping) butter
- ½ c. coffee cream
- 1 1-lb. can salmon
- Salt
- Freshly ground pepper to taste
- Dash of mace

Combine corn, eggs, butter, coffee cream, salmon and seasonings. Turn into a well-buttered casserole. Bake at 300 degrees until puffy and lightly browned. Yield: 4 servings.

Mrs. M. L. Shannon, Fairfield, Ala.

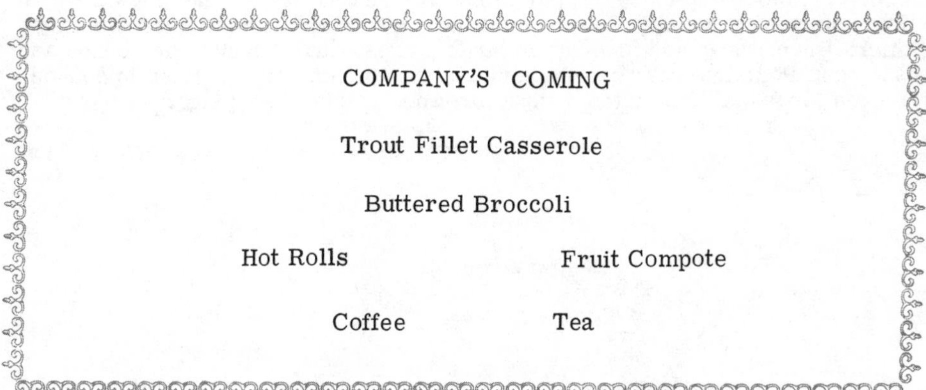

COMPANY'S COMING

Trout Fillet Casserole

Buttered Broccoli

Hot Rolls　　Fruit Compote

Coffee　　Tea

TROUT FILLET CASSEROLE

- 6 fillets of trout or other fish
- 4 slices bacon, partially cooked and drained
- 1 c. grated carrots
- 2 tbsp. chopped celery
- 1 c. chopped onions
- 1 c. chopped mushrooms
- 2 tbsp. minced parsley
- ½ tsp. thyme
- 2 tsp. salt
- ½ tsp. pepper
- ½ c. diced ham
- 1 c. white wine
- 3 tbsp. butter or margarine

Cut trout fillets into halves. Place partially cooked bacon in casserole. Mix together carrots, celery, onions, mushrooms, parsley, thyme, salt, pepper and ham. Spread half of mixture over bacon. Arrange fish fillets over vegetable mixture. Cover with remaining vegetable mixture. Pour wine over all. Dot with butter. Bake in preheated 375-degree oven for 50 minutes. Yield: 6 servings.

Mrs. John H. Kolek, Lakeland, Fla.

ASPARAGUS AND TUNA CASSEROLE

2 cans green asparagus
1 can chopped mushrooms
2 cans flaked tuna
2 cans mushroom soup
1 c. chopped toasted almonds
¾ c. Parmesan cheese

Drain asparagus; place in baking dish with mushrooms. Cover with tuna. Spread with mushroom soup. Sprinkle with almonds, cheese and paprika on top. Bake at 350 degrees for 30 minutes. Yield: 6 servings.

Mrs. H. C. Edgar, Edinburg, Tex.

DEVILED TUNA CASSEROLE

⅓ c. chopped celery
2 tbsp. minced onion
2 tbsp. chopped green pepper
3 tbsp. margarine
3 tbsp. flour
1 ½ c. milk
1 7-oz. can tuna
1 tbsp. chopped pimento
1 10 ½-oz. can lima beans
2 tsp. prepared mustard
½ tsp. salt
Dash of pepper
1 ½ tsp. Worcestershire sauce
2 drops Tabasco sauce
1 c. crushed potato chips

Cook celery, onion and green pepper in margarine until tender, not brown. Blend in flour; add milk gradually. Cook over low heat, stirring constantly, until mixture is thick. Drain tuna; add to sauce in large pieces. Add pimento, lima beans and seasonings. Pour into baking dish. Sprinkle potato chips on top. Bake in 400-degree oven for about 20 minutes or until browned. Yield: 4 servings.

Mrs. Joseph Basset, New Orleans, La.

MACARONI WITH TUNA AND CORN

1 pkg. elbow macaroni
2 tbsp. butter
2 tbsp. flour
2 c. milk
1 7-oz. can tuna
1 c. whole kernel corn
Salt and pepper
Paprika
1 c. grated cheese

Cook macaroni as directed on package; drain. Melt butter; stir in flour. Gradually add milk; stir over low heat until smooth and thick. Stir in tuna, corn, seasonings to taste and 1/2 the cheese. Arrange fish mixture in alternate layers with macaroni in a buttered baking dish. Sprinkle with remaining cheese. Bake at 350 degrees until brown.

Mary Lou Campbell, Honea Path, S. C.

MEETING-NIGHT TUNA CASSEROLE

1 3-oz. pkg. potato chips, crushed
1 9-oz. can tuna
4 slices American cheese
1 can cream of mushroom soup

Place a layer of potato chips in casserole. Add 1/2 of tuna and 2 slices cheese; cover with 1/2 of soup. Repeat layers. Bake at 350 degrees for 25 to 30 minutes. Yield: 4 servings.

Mrs. Janet Hester, Lancaster, Tex.

PERFECT TUNA CASSEROLE

1 10 ¾-oz. can condensed cream of vegetable, celery, chicken, or mushroom soup
⅓ to ½ c. milk
1 7-oz. can tuna, drained and flaked
2 hard-cooked eggs, sliced
1 c. cooked peas
1 c. slightly crumbled potato chips

In 1-quart casserole, blend soup and milk; stir in tuna, eggs and peas. Top with chips. Bake at 350 degrees for 30 minutes.

Mrs. H. L. Deans, Durham, N. C.

RICE-TUNA CASSEROLE

1 No. 3 can green beans or peas
1 10 ½-oz. can cream of celery soup
1 7-oz. can tuna, drained
1 c. diced celery
2 c. cooked rice

Drain beans or peas, reserving liquid. Blend liquid from beans or peas with soup. Mix in beans and remaining ingredients. Bake in greased 1 3/4-quart casserole at 350 degrees about 30 minutes.

Martha Hallaway, Happy, Tex.

SCALLOPED TUNA

2 c. crushed cheese crackers or potato chips
2 7-oz. cans tuna, flaked into large pieces
3 c. med. white sauce
¾ c. sauteed mushrooms or 2 hard-cooked eggs, sliced

Arrange all ingredients in alternate layers in buttered 1 1/2-quart baking dish, beginning and ending with crackers. Bake in a preheated 350-degree oven for 35 minutes. Yield: 6 servings.

Nancy T. Martin, Roxboro, N. C.

SEVEN SEAS CASSEROLE

1 10 ½-oz. can condensed cream of celery soup
1 ⅓ c. water
¼ tsp. salt
¼ c. finely chopped onion
Dash of pepper
1 ⅓ c. raw instant rice
1 ½ c. cooked peas
1 7-oz. can tuna, drained and flaked
½ c. grated cheddar cheese
Pimento strips

In saucepan, combine soup, water, salt, onion and pepper. Bring to a boil, stirring occasionally. Pour 1/2 of mixture into greased 1 1/2-quart casserole. Make 3 layers in casserole, using raw instant rice, peas and tuna. Cover with remaining soup. Sprinkle with grated cheese. Bake, covered, at 375 degrees for 20 to 25 minutes. Cut through mixture with knife after 10 minutes of baking time. Garnish with pimento before serving, if desired. Yield: 4 servings.

Mrs. Evelyn Jones, Jackson, Tenn.

SPECIAL TUNA CASSEROLE

2 ¼ c. egg noodles, uncooked
4 tbsp. margarine
2 tbsp. flour
2 c. milk
½ tsp. salt
¼ tsp. white pepper
¼ tsp. monosodium glutamate
⅔ c. sharp cheese, grated
2 6 ½-oz. cans tuna, drained and flaked
1 No. 303 can English peas
Buttered cracker crumbs or crushed potato chips

Cook noodles in salted water until tender. Rinse in cold water and drain. Melt margarine in saucepan; add flour, stirring to prevent lumps forming. Add milk and then seasonings. Cook until sauce is of a medium consistency. Add cheese; stir until melted. Fold in noodles, tuna and peas. Pour into a 2-quart casserole; top with buttered cracker crumbs or crushed potato chips. Bake in 325-degree oven for 20 to 30 minutes. Yield: 6 servings.

Mrs. Robert E. Tanner, Atlanta, Ga.

SUNBURST TUNA CASSEROLE

1 6 ½-oz. can drained tuna
1 can cream of mushroom soup
¼ c. milk
1 ½ c. cooked drained peas
½ c. shredded cheese
Biscuits

Combine first 5 ingredients in 2-quart casserole. Arrange biscuits on top. Bake at 400 degrees for 25 minutes. Sprinkle with additional cheese. Bake 5 minutes longer.

Mrs. B. H. Cumnock, Chattanooga, Tenn.

TASTY TUNA CASSEROLE

1 can tuna or 1 6-oz. can frozen Alaska King crab meat, thawed
1 can condensed mushroom soup
2 egg yolks

(Continued on next page)

1 tbsp. Worcestershire sauce
1 can ripe olives, drained
½ c. water
Peanut oil
½ c. grated cheese
crumbs

If crab meat is desired, drain and break into small pieces. If tuna is used, flake into mixing bowl. Add mushroom soup, egg yolks, Worcestershire sauce and ripe olives to tuna or crab meat. Fold together lightly with water. Place in 4 x 9-inch baking dish greased with peanut oil. Sprinkle mixture of grated cheese and buttered bread crumbs over top. Bake at 375 degrees for 25 minutes until top is golden brown.

Mrs. Alta Yelvington Forbess, Pineville, N. C.

TUNA BAKE

1 can tuna
2 c. cooked noodles
1 can mushroom soup
½ soup can water
1 tsp. lemon juice
Salt and pepper to taste
2 hard-cooked eggs, sliced
1 can French-fried onions

Mix first 7 ingredients with 3/4 cup onions in buttered 1 1/2-quart casserole. Sprinkle remaining onions on top. Bake at 375 degrees about 20 minutes. Yield: 4 servings.

Mrs. Mabel B. Bywaters, Arlington, Va.

TUNA-CASHEW CASSEROLE

1 3-oz. can chow mein noodles
1 can mushroom soup
1 7-oz. can chunk tuna
1 c. finely diced celery
⅛ tsp. pepper
¼ c. minced onions
¼ c. water
½ c. cashew nuts
¼ tsp. salt

Combine all ingredients, reserving 1/2 cup noodles for topping. Toss lightly; place in casserole. Top with reserved noodles. Bake at 350 degrees for 50 minutes.

Mrs. C. C. Chamberlain, Louisville, Ky.

TUNA CASSEROLE

1 6-oz. pkg. egg noodles
1 can cream of mushroom soup
1 c. milk
1 c. American cheese, cubed
Dash of pepper
2 hard-boiled eggs, chopped
1 7-oz. can tuna, chicken or turkey
½ c. cereal crumbs, buttered

Cook noodles in boiling salted water until tender; drain. Place mushroom soup in saucepan; stir well. Add milk and heat. Add cheese; stir until cheese melts. Combine noodles, pepper, eggs and tuna with sauce. Put into a 2-quart greased casserole; sprinkle with buttered cereal crumbs. Bake at 350 degrees for 30 minutes. Yield: 8 servings.

Mrs. Robert Dulin, Memphis, Tenn.

TUNA CASSEROLE

2 cans white tuna
2 c. cream
2 bouillon cubes
¼ stick butter
2 tbsp. cornstarch
¼ c. sherry
Salt
Cayenne pepper
Wedges of toast
½ c. cornflakes

Drain tuna. Make a white sauce of cream, bouillon cubes and butter. Thicken with cornstarch. Add sherry; season with salt and pepper. Fold in flaked tuna; pour in casserole. Stand wedges of buttered toast around casserole. Top tuna with cornflakes. Bake in 400-degree oven for 8 to 10 minutes.

Mrs. Winthrop Rockefeller, Wife of Governor of Arkansas, Little Rock, Ark.

TUNA CASSEROLE

1 c. crushed potato chips
1 7-oz. can tuna
1 can cream of mushroom soup, not golden
½ soup can milk
½ tsp. salt

Spread 1/2 of potato chips in greased casserole. Drain oil from tuna; break into even-sized chunks. Spread over potato chips. Mix soup, milk and salt in small bowl. Pour over tuna. Top with remaining potato chips. Bake at 375 degrees for 25 to 30 minutes.

Mrs. Walter R. Payne, Jr., Belleview, Fla.

TUNA CASSEROLE

2 c. crushed potato chips
1 can tuna
1 can cream of mushroom or chicken soup
½ tsp. salt

In a 1-quart casserole, put 1 cup crushed potato chips on bottom, then a layer of tuna. Pour in 1/2 can soup. Repeat the layers; sprinkle with salt. Bake at 300 degrees for about 25 to 30 minutes. Yield: 4-6 servings.

Mrs. Helen Kendrick, Good Pine, La.

TUNA AND CHINESE NOODLES

1 5-oz. can fried noodles
1 10½-oz. can cream of mushroom soup
½ c. milk
1 c. celery, cut fine
1 7-oz. can white tuna
¼ c. cashew nuts

Put 1/2 of fried noodles in a buttered 1-quart casserole. Mix soup, milk, celery, tuna and nuts; spoon over noodles. Sprinkle remaining noodles over top. Bake, uncovered, at 350 degrees for 30 minutes. Yield: 4 servings.

Mrs. Hubert W. Morgan, Memphis, Tenn.

TUNA-MACARONI CASSEROLE

2 6 1/2-oz. cans tuna
2 c. cooked elbow macaroni
1 c. sour cream
3/4 c. chopped green pepper
1/2 c. sliced ripe or stuffed olives
3/4 c. sliced mushrooms
1 c. grated cheese

Combine all ingredients except cheese. Spoon into greased casserole. Sprinkle cheese on top. Bake at 350 degrees for 25 to 30 minutes. Yield: 4-5 servings.

Frances Garrison, Louisville, Ky.

TUNA-MACARONI CASSEROLE

1 c. macaroni
1 tsp. salt
1 6 1/2-oz. can tuna, flaked
1 can cream of mushroom or chicken soup
2 tsp. chopped onion or 1 tsp. instant minced onion
2 tsp. chopped green pepper (opt.)
American cheese

Cook macaroni and salt in boiling water for 15 minutes or until tender. Drain. Place a layer of macaroni in a 1-quart glass baking dish, then a layer of tuna. Sprinkle with 1 teaspoon chopped onion or 1/2 teaspoon instant minced onion and 1 teaspoon chopped green pepper. Top with slivers of cheese. Dilute soup with 1/2 cup water; pour half the soup over casserole. Repeat layers. Bake at 375 degrees for 20 minutes.

Mollie Gatrell, Ashland, Ky.

TUNA-NOODLE CASSEROLE

1 3 to 4-oz. can chow mein noodles
1/4 lb. salted cashew nuts, broken
1 can cream of mushroom soup
1/4 c. water
1 can (or more) white tuna, rinsed and drained
1 c. finely diced celery
1/4 c. chopped green onions and tops
Dash of salt and pepper

Set aside 1/2 cup crisp chow mein noodles and a few whole nuts to sprinkle on top of casserole. Combine remaining ingredients in casserole. Stir well. Sprinkle reserved noodles and nuts on top. Bake at 325 degrees for 25 to 40 minutes. Yield: 5-6 servings.

Mrs. Walter L. Gant, Virginia Beach, Va.

TUNA-POTATO CHIP CASSEROLE

1 can white tuna
Potato chips
2 tbsp. sherry
1 can condensed mushroom soup

Place alternate layers of tuna and potato chips in casserole ending with potato chips. Stir sherry into soup; pour into casserole. Bake at 350 degrees for 30 minutes.

Orlin R. Healy, Apopka, Fla.

TUNA-RICE PIE

1 1/3 c. instant rice
1 1/3 c. water
1 tsp. salt
1 1/2 tsp. butter
3 eggs
1 c. grated American cheese
1 7-oz. can tuna, drained
3/4 c. milk, scalded
1/8 tsp. nutmeg
1/8 tsp. pepper

Place rice in 9-inch pie pan. Combine water, 1/2 teaspoon salt and butter; bring to a boil. Stir into rice. Cover; let stand for 5 minutes. Beat 1 egg slightly; blend into rice. Press rice mixture against bottom and sides of pie pan. Sprinkle with 1/2 cup cheese. Top with 1/2 of tuna. Repeat layers of cheese and tuna. Blend remaining salt with remaining eggs, milk, nutmeg and pepper. Pour over tuna. Bake at 400 degrees for 25 minutes. Yield: 4 servings.

Susan Elrod, Plymouth, N. C.

TUNA SCALLOP

1 7-oz. can tuna
1 tbsp. grated onion
1 can mushroom soup
1 tbsp. chopped bell pepper
Salt and pepper to taste
3 med. potatoes, cooked and sliced

Combine first 5 ingredients. Cover bottom of a well-greased casserole with 1/2 of tuna mixture. Cover with 1/2 of thinly sliced potatoes. Add remainder of tuna mixture. Top with remaining potatoes. Bake at 350 degrees until brown and heated through, about 20 minutes.

Mrs. Dan Kyser, Birmingham, Ala.

TUNA SOUFFLE

1 onion, minced
1 tbsp. minced green pepper
2 tbsp. butter
2 tbsp. flour
1 c. milk
3 eggs, separated
1 can light tuna, drained and flaked
Salt and pepper

Saute onion and green pepper in butter. Blend in flour; add milk slowly. Remove from heat; stir in egg yolks. Add tuna. Beat egg whites until stiff; fold into tuna mixture. Add salt and pepper. Set casserole in pan of hot water. Bake at 350 degrees for 1 hour.

Mrs. William Guy Reed, Corbin, Ky.

UNUSUAL TUNA CASSEROLE

1 family-sized can tuna
2 cans cream of mushroom soup
2 cans Chinese noodles
1 sm. can cashew nuts
1 c. chopped celery
1 tsp. chopped onion

(Continued on next page)

Combine all ingredients, reserving part of Chinese noodles and nuts for top. Place in casserole. Sprinkle reserved noodles and nuts on top. Bake at 350 degrees for 1 hour. Yield: 8-10 servings.

Mrs. Rita M. Vestal, Annandale, Va.

CLAM AND EGGPLANT CASSEROLE

1 lge. eggplant, pared
Rind of ½ lemon
3 tbsp. minced onion
¼ c. chopped celery
Butter
¼ c. flour
½ tsp. salt
½ c. milk
2 7-oz. cans minced clams, undrained
1 egg, beaten
Soft bread crumbs
2 tbsp. Parmesan cheese

Heat oven to 375 degrees. Parboil eggplant in large saucepan in boiling water with lemon rind. Drain; discard lemon rind. Mash eggplant. Saute onion and celery in 1/4 cup butter or oleo in a medium saucepan until soft but not brown. Blend in flour and salt; stir until smooth. Remove from heat. Gradually add milk and clams. Cook over medium heat, stirring constantly, until mixture is thickened. Stir in beaten egg. Mix with eggplant. Pour mixture into buttered baking dish. Toss soft bread crumbs with 2 tablespoons of butter or oleo; sprinkle over eggplant mixture in baking dish. Sprinkle with Parmesan cheese. Bake 25 minutes or until bread crumbs are a delicate brown. Yield: 4 servings.

Maye Mefford, Longview, Tex.

BAKED CRAB

2 tbsp. flour
2 tbsp. butter
1 c. milk
Salt and pepper
2 tbsp. mayonnaise
1 lb. flaked crab meat
Bread or cracker crumbs
Butter

Make white sauce using flour, butter and milk. Remove from heat; season with salt and pepper. Stir in mayonnaise. Add flaked crab meat. Place in casserole; cover top with bread or cracker crumbs. Dot with butter. Brown under broiler.

Mrs. Charles Martin Peery, New Market, Va.

CASSEROLE WITH CRAB MEAT

2 7¾-oz. cans King crab meat
1 10½-oz. can mushroom soup
½ c. onion, chopped fine
1 c. celery, chopped fine
1 3-oz. can cashews, chopped fine
1 med. can chow mein noodles
⅓ c. cream

Combine all ingredients. Bake 30 minutes at 325 degrees. Yield: 8 servings.

Mrs. Paul A. Lindig, Avondale Estates, Ga.

CASSEROLE GEM

1 med. eggplant, peeled and cubed
Salt and pepper
Ground basil
½ tsp. seasoning salt
½ c. finely chopped onion
¼ c. finely chopped green pepper
⅔ c. sliced mushrooms, drained
4 tbsp. melted butter or margarine
1 8-oz. can tomato sauce
2 med. tomatoes, peeled and thinly sliced
¾ c. finely shredded cheddar cheese
1 ½ c. crab meat, drained and flaked
2 c. bite-sized shredded rice biscuits, crushed to 1 cup

Heat oven to 375 degrees. Butter a 2-quart baking dish. Cook eggplant in 1 cup water with 1/2 teaspoon salt, 1/4 teaspoon pepper, 1/4 teaspoon basil and seasoning salt until tender, about 15 minutes; drain. Cook onion, green pepper and mushrooms in 2 tablespoons butter until tender. Mix in 1/2 teaspoon salt, 1/8 teaspoon pepper and 1/4 teaspoon basil. Layer half of eggplant, tomato sauce, tomato slices and all of onion mixture in baking dish. Sprinkle with 1/2 cup cheese and crab meat. Repeat layers of eggplant, tomato sauce and tomato slices. Bake 35 to 40 minutes or until mixture begins to bubble. Combine cereal crumbs, 1/4 teaspoon basil, remaining butter and remaining cheese; sprinkle over casserole. Bake 1 hour longer or until well browned. Yield: 6 servings.

Mrs. Susan Toaz, Bradenton, Fla.

CRAB CASSEROLE

¼ c. chopped green pepper
2 tbsp. butter
3 tbsp. flour
2 7 ½-oz. cans crab, drained
1 c. evaporated milk
½ tsp. salt
½ tsp. chervil
½ c. slivered toasted almonds
1 can celery soup
¼ tsp. pepper
½ c. thinly sliced celery
2 tbsp. chopped pimento
½ c. cheese cracker crumbs

Saute pepper in butter; blend in flour. Add remaining ingredients except cracker crumbs; mix well. Pour into greased 11 x 7-inch casserole; top with crumbs. Bake at 350 degrees for 30 to 35 minutes. Parsley flakes may be substituted for chervil. Yield: 12-14 servings.

Mrs. Fred Roberson, Cookeville, Tenn.

CRAB CASSEROLE

1 lb. Alaskan King crab
1 c. half and half
1 c. mayonnaise
1 ½ c. soft white bread crumbs
6 hard-boiled eggs, cut up
1 tbsp. minced onion
2 tbsp. fresh chopped parsley
½ c. grated sharp cheese
Cornflakes

Mix first 7 ingredients, cutting crab and eggs into pieces. Add 1/4 cup cheese to mixture; put in buttered casserole. Crumble cornflakes on top; sprinkle with remaining cheese. Bake in 350-degree oven 45 minutes to 1 hour.

Mrs. W. H. Kuhrt, St. Petersburg, Fla.

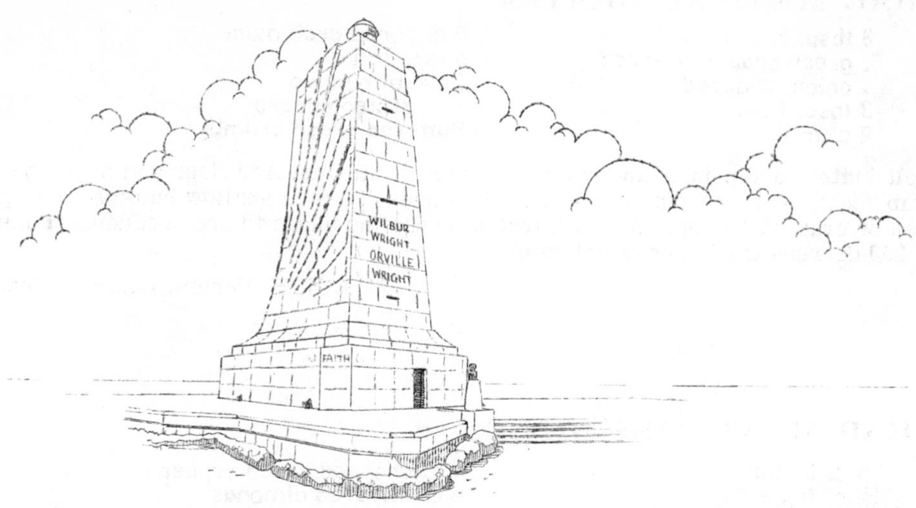

Memorial to the Wright brothers' first flight, Kitty Hawk, North Carolina.

CRAB CREOLE CASSEROLE

- 1 med. onion, finely chopped
- 1 tbsp. butter
- 2 tbsp. flour
- 4 med. tomatoes, peeled and cut into small pieces
- ¼ c. green olives, finely chopped
- Salt and pepper
- Pinch each of thyme leaves and mace
- 2 tsp. Worcestershire sauce
- 2 c. cooked crab meat
- Buttered bread crumbs

Cook onion in butter for 2 minutes, stirring constantly. Stir in flour; brown lightly. Add tomatoes and olives; mix thoroughly. Season to taste with salt, pepper, thyme and mace. Simmer gently for 10 minutes; stir in Worcestershire sauce and crab meat. Place mixture in oiled earthenware casserole. Sprinkle with bread crumbs. Bake in 350-degree oven for 15 to 20 minutes until crumbs are delicately browned.

Julia Dehan, Shreveport, La.

CRAB IMPERIAL

- 1 stick butter
- 2 tbsp. flour
- 1 c. milk
- 2 tbsp. lemon juice
- 1 tbsp. parsley flakes
- Salt and black pepper to taste
- Red pepper to taste
- Worcestershire sauce
- 1 lb. backfin crab meat
- Buttered bread crumbs or crushed potato chips

Melt butter in saucepan. Add flour; stir until smooth. Add milk; stir until thickened. Remove from heat. Season well with lemon juice, parsley flakes, salt, black and red pepper and Worcestershire sauce. Add crab meat; mix thoroughly. Place in casserole or individual baking dishes; top with buttered crumbs. Bake at 325 to 350 degrees until heated through and brown on top.

Mrs. V. G. Stewart, Wilson, N. C.

CRAB MEAT AU GRATIN

3 tbsp. butter
½ green pepper, minced
½ onion, chopped
3 tbsp. flour
2 c. milk
2 c. boned crab meat
½ tsp. salt
Dash of nutmeg
½ c. grated cheese
Buttered bread crumbs

Melt butter; add pepper and onion. Cook for 5 minutes. Add flour and milk, then crab meat, salt and nutmeg. Cook 10 minutes. Pour in shallow buttered baking dish or crab shells. Sprinkle with grated cheese and buttered bread crumbs. Bake at 350 degrees until cheese is brown.

Mrs. E. H. Denton, Denison, Tex.

CRAB MEAT CASSEROLE

½ c. butter
⅔ c. flour
2 ⅔ c. milk
2 6 ½-oz. cans crab meat
4 c. chopped celery
1 sm. jar pimentos, chopped
½ c. chopped green pepper
⅓ c. slivered almonds
4 hard-cooked eggs, chopped
2 tsp. salt
1 c. shredded cheddar cheese
Buttered bread crumbs

Melt butter in saucepan. Add flour and mix well. Remove from heat; slowly add milk. Return to heat; cook, stirring constantly, until thick. Add crab meat, celery, pimentos, green pepper, almonds, hard-cooked eggs and salt. Pour into a 2-quart casserole. Top with shredded cheese and buttered bread crumbs. Bake at 350 degrees for 45 minutes. Yield: 6 servings.

Mrs. G. R. Deakle, Grand Bay, Ala.

CRAB MEAT CASSEROLE

½ c. milk
¾ c. soft bread crumbs
1 7 ½-oz. can flaked cooked crab meat
3 hard-cooked eggs
¾ tsp. salt
⅛ tsp. dry mustard
Dash of cayenne pepper
3 tbsp. melted butter
Wheaties or buttered bread crumbs

Mix milk and bread crumbs. Gently stir in crab meat, diced egg whites and egg yolks. Blend in remaining ingredients. Place in buttered 9 x 5 x 3-inch loaf pan or 1 1/2-quart baking dish. Sprinkle with Wheaties or buttered crumbs. Bake in preheated 450-degree oven for 15 minutes. Yield: 3 servings.

Mrs. Jo Ann Kemp, Crestview, Fla.

CRAB MEAT CASSEROLE

1 7-oz. can crab meat
2 c. bread crumbs
1 egg
1 c. milk
2 hard-cooked eggs, mashed
1 ½ tsp. Worcestershire sauce
1 tbsp. chopped green pepper
2 tbsp. lemon juice
2 tbsp. salad dressing
⅔ c. melted butter
Salt and pepper to taste
Cayenne to taste

(Continued on next page)

Combine all ingredients. Place in greased casserole. Bake at 350 degrees for 45 minutes. Yield: 6-8 servings.

Mrs. Jimmy Barrett, Eudora, Ark.

CRAB MEAT CASSEROLE

- 2 minced shallots
- 2 pimentos, chopped
- 1 tbsp. mustard
- 2 tbsp. chopped celery and leaves
- 1 tbsp. minced parsley
- 2 eggs
- ½ c. mayonnaise
- ½ c. (or more) bread crumbs
- ¼ c. sherry
- Salt, pepper and garlic to taste
- Few drops of Tabasco (opt.)
- 2 c. fresh pickled crab meat
- Crushed potato chips

Mix together shallots, pimentos, mustard, celery and parsley. Combine with eggs, mayonnaise, bread crumbs and sherry. Season with salt, pepper, garlic and Tabasco. Add crab meat; mix well. Pour into well-buttered baking dish; top with potato chips. Bake in preheated 350-degree oven for 20 minutes. Yield: 4-6 servings.

Rosalie Carlson, Abbeville, La.

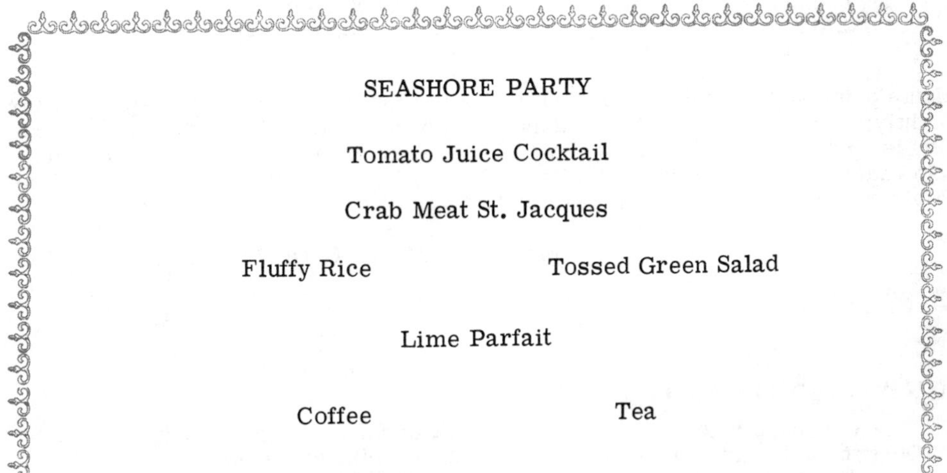

SEASHORE PARTY

Tomato Juice Cocktail

Crab Meat St. Jacques

Fluffy Rice

Tossed Green Salad

Lime Parfait

Coffee

Tea

CRAB MEAT ST. JACQUES

- ¼ onion, chopped
- ½ green pepper, chopped
- ½ c. mushrooms, finely chopped
- Butter
- 2 c. white sauce
- Salt and pepper
- Paprika
- 1 tsp. Worcestershire sauce
- 1 lb. canned crab meat
- Grated American cheese
- Buttered bread crumbs

Saute onion, pepper and mushrooms in a small amount of butter. Add white sauce seasoned with salt and pepper, a generous amount of paprika and Worcestershire sauce. Add crab meat; stir to mix. Put mixture into a buttered casserole; sprinkle top lightly with grated American cheese, buttered bread crumbs and paprika. Bake at 450 degrees for 15 minutes.

Mrs. John A. Bracey, Springfield, Tenn.

CRAB MEAT AND EGGPLANT CASSEROLE

1 lge. eggplant, peeled and diced
Juice of 1 lemon
1 lb. crab meat, flaked
6 med. ripe tomatoes, diced, seeded and drained or 2 cans tomato sauce
3 eggs, beaten
¼ c. bread crumbs
Salt and pepper to taste
3 tbsp. butter or margarine

Sprinkle diced eggplant with lemon juice. Cover with water; cook over medium heat until barely tender, about 10 minutes. Drain; put in baking dish. Add layer of crab meat; pour in tomatoes and beaten eggs. Sprinkle tops with bread crumbs, salt and pepper; dot with butter. Bake at 350 degrees for about 25 minutes. Yield: 4 servings.

Mrs. T. W. Nicholson, Eastman, Ga.

CRAB-RICE CASSEROLE

½ c. chopped onion
¼ c. pimento
2 tbsp. vegetable oil
2 7½-oz. cans crab meat, drained
½ c. halved olives (opt.)
½ tsp. salt
¼ tsp. pepper
2 8-oz. cans tomato sauce with cheese
1 c. evaporated milk
3 c. cooked rice
½ c. cracker crumbs

Saute onion and pimento in oil in skillet. Add crab, olives, salt and pepper. Saute lightly; remove from heat. Combine tomato sauce and milk with crab mixture. Place rice in bottom of shallow baking dish. Pour crab mixture over rice. Sprinkle cracker crumbs over top. Bake at 350 degrees for 25 minutes. Tuna, shrimp, lobster or any cooked fish may be substituted for crab. Yield: 6 servings.

Mrs. Walter J. G. Hays, Jr., Jacksonville, Fla.

CRAB AND RICE IN SEA SHELLS

1 c. cooked rice
1 6½-oz. can crab meat, flaked
2 hard-cooked eggs, chopped
3 tbsp. mayonnaise
½ tsp. salt
¼ tsp. cayenne pepper
Few grains of black pepper
1 tbsp. minced parsley
2 tsp. finely chopped onion
⅓ c. evaporated milk
½ c. finely shredded cheddar cheese

Combine rice, crab meat and eggs. Mix remaining ingredients except cheese; add to crab meat mixture, tossing well. Pour mixture into eight buttered shell-shaped ramekins or individual casseroles; sprinkle with cheese. Bake at 350 degrees for 25 minutes or until cheese is melted. Yield: 8 servings.

Mrs. Lloyd C. Emery, Paducah, Ky.

CRAB SUPREME

2 tbsp. flour
½ stick butter or margarine, melted
1 ½ c. milk
¼ tsp. salt
Juice of small onion

(Continued on next page)

Juice of ½ lemon
1 tsp. Worcestershire sauce
Dash of cayenne pepper
¼ tsp. celery salt
2 eggs, well beaten
2 cans crab meat
Buttered bread crumbs

Blend flour in melted butter; gradually add milk and cook until thick, stirring constantly. Add salt, onion juice, lemon juice, Worcestershire sauce, pepper and celery salt. Stir in eggs; heat but do not boil. Add crab meat. Place in buttered baking dish; cover with buttered crumbs. Bake at 350 degrees for 30 to 40 minutes. Yield: 6 servings.

Mrs. Jack U. Collex, Louisville, Ky.

DEVILED CRAB CASSEROLE

1 lb. crab claw meat
1 section saltine crackers, crumbled
½ bell pepper, chopped
½ med. onion, chopped
3 boiled eggs, grated
1 stick margarine, melted
1 tbsp. mayonnaise
1 tbsp. Worcestershire sauce
1 tsp. prepared mustard
½ bottle catsup
Dash of hot sauce
Dash of black pepper
Dash of garlic salt
1 tbsp. lemon juice
1 lge. can evaporated milk

Combine all ingredients; mixture will be soupy. Let set in refrigerator for 30 to 40 minutes. Bake at 400 degrees for 5 to 10 minutes. Reduce temperature to 350 degrees; bake for 25 minutes or longer.

Mrs. H. J. Jennings, Sylvester, Ga.

DEVILED CRAB CASSEROLE

Butter
1 lb. crab meat
½ tbsp. catsup
1 c. soft bread crumbs
1 egg
1 tbsp. Worcestershire sauce
Dry bread crumbs

Mix 2 1/2 tablespoons butter with crab, catsup, soft crumbs, egg and Worcestershire sauce; place in casserole. Top with dry bread crumbs; dot with butter. Bake at 350 degrees for 30 minutes. Yield: 6 servings.

Mrs. E. D. Caldwell, Charleston, S. C.

LOBSTER AND MUSHROOM CASSEROLE

1 lb. mushrooms
5 ½ tbsp. butter
3 tbsp. flour
1 tsp. salt
⅛ tsp. paprika
1 ½ c. milk
½ c. chicken bouillon or vegetable stock
2 c. diced fresh lobster meat
½ c. cream
2 egg yolks
½ c. cooking sherry
⅓ c. bread crumbs

(Continued on next page)

Slice mushrooms; saute 2 minutes in 4 tablespoons butter. Add flour, salt and paprika. Cook and stir over low heat for 5 minutes. Stir in the milk and stock. Cook and stir for 3 minutes. Add lobster. Beat in cream and egg yolks. Add sherry to taste. Pour into buttered casserole. Cover the top with bread crumbs and dot with remaining butter. Bake at 450 degrees for 10 minutes. Yield: 6 servings.

Mrs. William B. Jackson, Huntsville, Ala.

BAKED OYSTER AND SPAGHETTI CASSEROLE

1 c. soft bread crumbs
2 c. spaghetti, cooked
2 c. grated cheddar cheese
1 pt. oysters
Salt and pepper
Butter
Paprika
½ c. light cream, heated

Grease baking dish; sprinkle with part crumbs. Alternate layers of 1/2 of spaghetti, cheese and oysters. Season with salt and pepper. Dot generously with butter. Repeat ending with oysters and crumbs. Sprinkle with paprika. Add warm cream. Bake at 400 degrees for about 20 minutes. Yield: 8 servings.

Mrs. Michael J. Paytas, Emporia, Va.

BEST SCALLOPED OYSTERS

1 c. cracker crumbs
½ c. toast crumbs
½ c. melted butter
1 pt. oysters, drained
Liquid from oysters
¼ c. cream
1 tsp. Worcestershire sauce
2 tbsp. sherry
Dash of cayenne pepper
½ tsp. salt
¼ tsp. pepper
Paprika

Toss crumbs with melted butter. Place 1/3 of crumbs in greased baking dish; top with 1/2 of oysters. Mix oyster liquid with cream, Worcestershire, sherry and seasonings; pour 1/2 of sauce over oysters. Cover with 1/3 of crumbs, remaining oysters and remaining sauce. Top with remaining crumbs; dot with additional butter. Dust with paprika. Bake at 400 degrees for 20 minutes. Yield: 8 servings.

Mrs. W. P. Bryant, Springfield, Tenn.

MAMA BROWNE'S SCALLOPED OYSTERS

2 c. buttered bread crumbs
1 tsp. salt
1 tsp. black pepper
1 tsp. grated onion
1 clove of garlic, grated
1 stick butter, melted
1 qt. medium oysters
1 tsp. Worcestershire sauce
1 ½ c. milk

In baking dish, place part of bread crumbs, salt, pepper, onion and garlic; sprinkle butter over each layer. Cover with a layer of oysters. Repeat layers. Add Worcestershire sauce to milk; pour over layers. Sprinkle a few crumbs over top. Bake at 350 degrees for 25 minutes or until brown.

Mrs. Russell O. Behrens, Apalachicola, Fla.

EUNICE'S SCALLOPED OYSTERS

1 8-oz. can oysters
1 c. cream
1 c. milk
1 doz. crackers, crushed
3 eggs, beaten
Salt and pepper to taste

Combine oysters, cream, milk and crackers, mixing well. Stir in eggs, salt and pepper; pour into casserole. Bake at 350 degrees for 1 hour or until brown. Yield: 12 servings.

Eunice Robinson, Lynnville, Tenn.

MINCED OYSTERS

3 pt. oysters, finely chopped
Liquor from oysters
4 slices dry toasted bread, crushed
4 onions, finely chopped
½ green pepper, finely chopped
¾ c. diced celery
2 tbsp. chopped parsley
Bacon drippings
Salt and pepper
Juice of ½ lemon
Butter
Bread crumbs

Mix oysters and liquor with bread. Saute onions, pepper, celery and parsley in bacon drippings; add to oyster mixture. Season with salt and pepper; stir in lemon juice. Cook in frying pan until moisture is absorbed. Pour into greased baking dish; top with butter and crumbs. Bake at 350 degrees until browned. Yield: 6 servings.

Mrs. W. B. Franklin, LaGrange, Tenn.

OYSTER CASSEROLE

Coarse cracker crumbs
Oysters
Salt and pepper
Garlic salt to taste
Meat broth
1 tbsp. sherry
Butter or margarine

Alternate layers of cracker crumbs and oysters in casserole until 3/4 full; season with salt, pepper and garlic salt. Cover with broth mixed with sherry. Dot with butter. Bake at 350 degrees for 30 to 40 minutes.

Perry William B. England, Gastonia, N. C.

OYSTER CASSEROLE

4 tbsp. butter
1 c. sweet milk
½ tsp. salt
⅛ tsp. pepper
1 8-oz. can cove oysters
¾ c. condensed mushroom soup
Whole crackers

Combine butter, sweet milk, salt and pepper. Place drained oysters in casserole; add soup and milk mixture. Cover top with crackers. Bake in 350-degree oven for 30 minutes. Yield: 4 servings.

Mrs. Charles M. Campbell, Honea Path, S. C.

OYSTER AND MACARONI CASSEROLE

4 tbsp. butter
4 tbsp. flour
½ tsp. salt
2 c. milk
1 ½ tbsp. Worcestershire sauce
1 ½ c. finely chopped celery
4 tbsp. grated onion
2 doz. large oysters
1 ½ c. cooked macaroni
½ c. bread crumbs
½ c. grated cheese

Make white sauce with butter, flour, salt, milk and Worcestershire sauce; add celery, onion, oysters and macaroni. Place in casserole. Sprinkle bread crumbs and grated cheese. Bake 30 minutes at 350 degrees.

Mrs. Paul O. Morrison, Lighthouse Point, Fla.

OYSTER PIE

½ stick butter
½ tsp. pepper
½ tsp. salt
2 pt. oysters, drained
1 box oyster crackers
½ tsp. pepper

Heat milk to boiling; add butter, pepper and salt. Simmer oysters in milk for 5 minutes. Place a layer of oyster crackers in a greased casserole. Add a layer of oysters. Repeat layers, ending with crackers. Combine oyster liquid and warm milk; pour over casserole. Bake for 15 to 20 minutes at 370 degrees. Yield: 8 servings.

Mrs. George G. Townsend, Forest, Miss.

OYSTER-VEGETABLE CASSEROLE

1 med. onion, sliced
4 tbsp. butter
2 tbsp. flour
1 lge. can evaporated milk
6 slices cheese
1 pt. oysters
7 oz. noodles, cooked
1 can cut snap beans, drained
Salt and pepper to taste

Saute onion in butter; add flour, milk and cheese, stirring until cheese has melted. Line casserole with foil or grease with butter. Mix oysters, noodles and beans; season to taste. Place in greased casserole. Add onion sauce. Bake at 350 degrees until golden brown. Shrimp or tuna may be substituted for oysters. Yield: 6-8 servings.

Mrs. Ignace David, Abbeville, La.

RICE AND OYSTER CASSEROLE

3 tbsp. butter or margarine
½ c. minced onion
3 tbsp. minced fresh parsley
1 ½ tbsp. flour
2 10-oz. cans frozen condensed oyster stew soup, thawed and undiluted
Dash of cayenne pepper
3 c. hot cooked rice
5 hard-boiled eggs, sliced
½ to 1 c. fresh bread crumbs, buttered

(Continued on next page)

In a medium saucepan over low heat, melt butter; add onion and parsley. Cook and stir until onion wilts but not brown. Stir in flour, then the thawed undiluted oyster soup and cayenne. Cook and stir constantly until thickened. Turn hot cooked rice into a 1 1/2-quart shallow baking dish. Cover with sliced eggs. Pour sauce over rice and eggs. Sprinkle with buttered crumbs. Bake in a 350-degree oven until piping hot, about 20 minutes. Yield: 6 servings.

Mrs. Martin Lesley, Easley, S. C.

SCALLOPED OYSTERS

1 pt. oysters
12 saltine crackers, crushed
¼ stick butter
2 eggs, well beaten
1 c. milk
Salt and pepper to taste

Place a layer of oysters in buttered casserole; cover with cracker crumbs and dot with butter. Repeat layers, reserving crumbs for topping. Combine eggs, milk and seasonings; pour over casserole. Sprinkle reserved crumbs over top. Bake at 350 degrees for 15 to 20 minutes or until casserole is bubbly and oysters curled around the edges. Yield: 4 servings.

Mrs. Ethan L. Taylor, Meansville, Ga.

SCALLOPED OYSTERS

1 ¼ c. fine toasted bread crumbs
1 pt. oysters
1 ½ tsp. salt
1 tsp. black pepper
¼ tsp. red pepper
1 stick butter
2 c. milk

Alternate layers of crumbs and oysters in casserole; sprinkle each layer with salt and peppers. Dot with butter; pour milk over casserole. Place casserole in pan of water; bake at 350 degrees for 50 minutes. Yield: 10 servings.

Mrs. T. W. Bratton, Franklin, Tenn.

SCALLOPED OYSTERS

½ c. butter
½ c. flour
½ tsp. salt
¼ tsp. pepper
½ tsp. paprika
1 onion, minced
½ green pepper, minced
1 tsp. lemon juice
1 tbsp. Worcestershire sauce
1 qt. oysters
¼ c. cracker crumbs

Melt butter; add flour. Cook 5 minutes or until light brown. Add salt, pepper and paprika; cook 3 minutes. Add minced onion and green pepper. Cook slowly for 5 minutes. Remove from heat. Add lemon juice, Worcestershire sauce and oysters which have been heated in their own liquid. Pour in baking dish; sprinkle with crumbs. Bake at 400 degrees for 30 minutes. Yield: 8-10 servings.

Mrs. Ben B. Blaud, Richmond, Va.

SCALLOPED OYSTERS

½ c. dry bread crumbs
½ c. coarse cracker crumbs
3 tbsp. melted butter
½ tsp. salt
⅛ tsp. pepper
Dash of nutmeg
2 tbsp. chopped parsley (opt.)
¼ c. oyster liquid
¼ c. milk
1 pt. oysters

Combine bread crumbs and cracker crumbs with butter; combine next 6 ingredients. Alternate layers of oysters and milk mixture in casserole. Top with crumbs. Bake at 350 degrees for 1 hour. Canned cream of mushroom soup may be substituted for all of the liquid. Yield: 4 servings.

Mrs. Calvin A. Campbell, Birmingham, Ala.

SCALLOP CASSEROLE

¼ c. margarine
3 tbsp. cornstarch
2 ½ c. milk
1 pt. fresh sea scallops, washed and halved
½ c. sliced celery
¼ c. diced pimento
¼ tsp. salt
Dash of paprika
½ c. fine dry bread crumbs
2 tbsp. melted margarine
Lemon slices or wedges

Melt margarine in saucepan. Blend in cornstarch. Remove from heat. Gradually stir in milk, mixing until smooth. Cook over medium heat, stirring constantly, until sauce thickens and boils. Simmer for 1 minute. Mix in scallops, celery, pimento, salt and paprika. Pour into shallow 1 1/2-quart casserole or 10-inch pie plate. Mix bread crumbs and melted margarine. Spoon on top of scallop mixture to form 1-inch ring around edge. Bake in 350-degree oven until thoroughly heated, about 30 minutes. Garnish with lemon slices. Yield: 3-4 servings.

Photograph for this recipe on page 59.

CORN AND SHRIMP DELUXE

1 5-oz. can ready-to-eat shrimp, deveined and cooked
1 12-oz. can whole kernel corn
1 4-oz. can mushroom pieces
½ c. lge. egg noodles
1 envelope white sauce mix
⅔ c. grated American cheese
½ tsp. (scant) salt
Dash of pepper

Drain shrimp; discard liquid. Drain corn and mushrooms; reserve liquid. Cook noodles according to package directions in slightly salted water until tender. Make white sauce using liquid from corn and mushrooms plus enough milk to equal 1 1/3 cups. Remove from heat; when smooth, add half the grated cheese, stirring to melt. Stir in salt and pepper. Drain noodles; add corn, shrimp and mushrooms. Mix with cheese sauce. Pour into 13 x 9-inch casserole dish; sprinkle remaining grated cheese over top. Bake 30 to 40 minutes at 375 degrees. If cheese is not melted and golden, place under broiler for a moment. One and one-half tablespoons each butter and sifted flour mixed and cooked over medium flame may be substituted for white sauce mix. Yield: 6 servings.

Mrs. Kathy Brown, Abilene, Tex.

EGGPLANT AND SHRIMP CASSEROLE

1 lge. eggplant
2 tbsp. oleo
1 lge. onion, chopped
1 sm. bell pepper, chopped
2 pieces celery, chopped
1 lb. peeled shrimp
1 egg
Bread crumbs

Peel and boil eggplant; drain. Place oleo in a skillet; fry onion, bell pepper and celery until glossy. Add shrimp; cook on low heat for 15 minutes. Add egg. Place in casserole; sprinkle with bread crumbs. Put into 350-degree oven; bake until mixture is bubbly and crumbs are brown. Yield: 4-6 servings.

Mrs. Jean Williams, Lafayette, La.

EGGPLANT AND SHRIMP CASSEROLE

2 med. eggplants, boiled
1 lb. shelled deveined shrimp
1 c. wet, stale French bread
2 slices bacon
½ c. chopped green pepper
½ c. chopped parsley
¼ c. chopped celery
1 lge. onion, chopped fine
2 garlic cloves, chopped fine
Seasoning to taste
Bread crumbs
1 tbsp. margarine

Peel eggplant; mash in large mixing bowl. Cut shrimp in small pieces; add to eggplant. Squeeze bread dry. Break bacon in pieces. Add all ingredients to eggplant mixture except crumbs and margarine; mix well. Cook in large pot, using bacon grease. Stir often to keep from burning. Cook on low heat, about 30 minutes. Add 1 tablespoon margarine; stir well. Put in large casserole dish; top with bread crumbs and dot with margarine. Bake at 350 degrees about 20 minutes or until top is browned. Yield: 6 servings.

Mrs. Rose Singer, New Orleans, La.

SHRIMP-ARTICHOKE NEWBURG

2 9-oz. pkg. frozen artichoke hearts
2 12-oz. pkg. frozen shrimp newburg
¼ c. grated Parmesan cheese
1 tbsp. fine dry bread crumbs

Cook artichoke hearts according to package directions until almost tender; drain. Place in single layer in 4 individual shallow baking dishes. Heat shrimp newburg according to package directions until thawed; spoon evenly over artichoke hearts. Mix together cheese and bread crumbs; sprinkle evenly over casseroles. Bake in preheated 350-degree oven about 20 minutes or until heated. If desired, bake in 1 large casserole. This recipe may be varied by substituting frozen lobster or King crab newburg for the shrimp newburg. Yield: 4 servings.

Photograph for this recipe on cover.

OKRA-SHRIMP CASSEROLE

1 can cut okra
1 can shrimp
¼ can bread crumbs
Lemon juice
Shrimp stock
1 tsp. baking powder
1 tsp. chili powder
½ tsp. salt
1 tsp. all-purpose seasoning
1 tbsp. mayonnaise

(Continued on next page)

Place layer of okra on bottom of casserole; add shrimp. Cover with half the bread crumbs. Place remainder of okra on top of bread crumbs; add lemon juice, shrimp stock mixed with baking powder, chili powder, salt and seasoning. Dot with mayonnaise; sprinkle remainder of bread crumbs on top. Bake in 450-degree oven for 20 minutes.

Mrs. Carl Danley, Kreole, Miss.

SHRIMP CASSEROLE

¼ to ½ c. dry sherry wine
1 10-oz. can cheddar cheese soup
1 qt. cooked and peeled shrimp
1 c. buttered bread crumbs

Mix wine and soup; pour over shrimp. Place in 1 1/2-quart casserole; top with bread crumbs. Bake at 350 degrees for 30 minutes or until bubbly and browned.

Mrs. Jack Hayman, New Smyrna Beach, Fla.

SHRIMP CASSEROLE

2 c. macaroni
1 can frozen cream of shrimp soup
¼ c. milk
1 tbsp. catsup
1 tbsp. Worcestershire sauce
1 tbsp. parsley
¼ c. chopped onion
¼ c. slivered almonds
½ tsp. paprika
½ tsp. salt
Pepper
1 sm. can shrimp, drained
1 c. crushed potato chips

Cook macaroni as directed on package; drain. Blend soup, milk, catsup and Worcestershire sauce with parsley, onion, almonds, paprika, salt and pepper in saucepan. Stir in shrimp; heat over low heat for 5 minutes. Add macaroni; mix well. Remove from heat; pour into buttered casserole dish. Top with crushed potato chips. Bake at 375 degrees for 15 minutes. Yield: 4-6 servings.

Mrs. Ted G. Tudor, Port Neches, Tex.

SHRIMP CASSEROLE

3 strips bacon
1 sm. onion, chopped fine
1 sm. green pepper, chopped fine
1 4¼-oz. can deveined shrimp
1 1-pt. can tomato soup
½ can condensed chicken soup or mushroom soup
Bread crumbs

Fry or broil bacon; place on absorbent paper. Place remaining ingredients, except crumbs, in mixing bowl; mix well. Crumble bacon; sprinkle over top. Sprinkle bread crumbs over bacon. Place in preheated 350-degree oven; cook 20 minutes or until firm. Serve on cooked rice or spaghetti. Yield: 6 servings.

Mrs. W. H. Clark, Columbus, Ga.

SHRIMP AND DEVILED EGG CASSEROLE

8 deviled eggs
2 lb. cooked shrimp
2 cans mushroom soup
½ c. sharp cheddar cheese, grated
Garlic to taste
1 tbsp. catsup
1 tbsp. parsley, chopped
1 tbsp. Worcestershire sauce
1 tsp. salt
1 tsp. dry mustard
½ c. dry sherry
Buttered crumbs
2 cans chow mein noodles

Into greased oblong casserole put a layer of deviled eggs and a layer of shrimp. Mix and heat all other ingredients except crumbs and noodles. Pour over the egg and shrimp. Top with buttered crumbs. Bake 30 minutes in 350-degree oven. Serve over chow mein noodles.

Mrs. Marion H. Buchanan, Lake Wales, Fla.

SHRIMP AND MUSHROOM CASSEROLE

1 ½ tbsp. butter or margarine
Chopped onion
2 tsp. chopped green pepper
2 tbsp. flour
¾ c. half and half
¼ tsp. paprika
½ tsp. salt
½ c. grated cheese
1 6-oz. can mushrooms
1 lb. shrimp, boiled and cleaned
Buttered bread crumbs

Melt butter or margarine; add onion and green pepper. Cook until tender, but not brown. Blend in flour. Add remaining ingredients except bread crumbs; pour into a buttered casserole. Top with buttered bread crumbs. Bake at 350 degrees for 20 minutes. Yield: 4 servings.

Mrs. Ray DeLoney, Sebring, Fla.

SHRIMP SPICED RICE

1 lb. brown or pink shrimp, cleaned and split
Lemon juice
4 c. cooked rice
½ c. parsley
1 tsp. nutmeg
3 tbsp. butter

Shell, rinse and devein shrimp; sprinkle with lemon juice. Spoon cooked rice into buttered casserole; sprinkle with parsley sprigs. Place shrimp in center; sprinkle with nutmeg. Dot with butter. Bake 45 minutes in 350-degree oven.

Armenia Knox, Miami, Fla.

BAKED SEAFOOD CASSEROLE

1 can shrimp
1 can crab meat
½ c. chopped green pepper
2 tbsp. chopped onion
2 tbsp. chopped pimento
⅔ c. mayonnaise or salad dressing
1 tsp. Worcestershire sauce
Salt and pepper to taste
1 med. can chow mein noodles

(Continued on next page)

Mix all ingredients except noodles. Pour mixture into casserole; sprinkle noodles over top. Bake until warm at 325 degrees, about 30 minutes.

Mrs. G. L. Hearn, Forest Hill, La.

BAKED SEAFOOD CASSEROLE

2 6-oz. or 1 lge. can fresh crab meat
2 cans shrimp or 1 lb. fresh cooked shrimp
½ green pepper, chopped fine
½ c. finely chopped mild onion
½ can pimento, cut fine
1 c. chopped celery
1 4-oz. can (or more) mushroom stems and pieces
1 c. salad dressing or mayonnaise
½ tsp. salt
1 c. top milk or half and half
⅛ tsp. pepper
1 tbsp. Worcestershire sauce
½ to 1 c. raw rice, cooked
Dry bread crumbs

Mix first 7 ingredients. Mix together remaining ingredients except crumbs. Blend mixture together. Place in a 2-quart buttered casserole; sprinkle with dry bread crumbs. Bake 30 minutes at 375 degrees or until of desired texture. Any leftover casserole may be frozen and reheated to be served later. Yield: 8-10 servings.

Mrs. J. W. Kistler, Baton Rouge, La.

COMPANY SEAFOOD CASSEROLE

6 eggs
3 c. milk
3 c. soft bread cubes, without crusts
2 c. American cheese, coarsely grated
1 tsp. salt
¼ tsp. pepper
Dash of cayenne
½ tsp. dry mustard
1 tsp. onion juice
1 ½ tsp. Worcestershire sauce
2 drops Tabasco
1 c. cooked shrimp, sliced lengthwise in half
1 c. cooked lobster, cut in bite-sized chunks
Crab meat
2 tbsp. melted butter

Beat eggs slightly; add milk and bread cubes. Let set for a while. Stir in grated cheese and seasonings. Saute seafood lightly in melted butter; add to mixture. Pour into large casserole. Set inside pan; pour in hot water 1/2 inch deep. Bake in 350-degree oven until a knife inserted comes out clean, about 1 hour. Yield: 10-12 servings.

Mrs. John L. Clark, Jr., Arlington, Va.

CRAB-SHRIMP CASSEROLE

1 green pepper, diced
1 onion, diced
1 c. diced celery
3 c. crab meat
½ lb. shrimp, cooked or 3 hard-cooked eggs, sliced
½ tsp. salt
⅛ tsp. pepper
1 c. mayonnaise
1 tsp. Worcestershire sauce
1 c. buttered cracker crumbs

Mix all ingredients except cracker crumbs; place in baking dish. Sprinkle crumbs on top. Bake at 350 degrees for 30 minutes or until vegetables are tender and crumbs browned.

Mrs. Betty Smith, Jesup, Ga.

CRAB-SHRIMP CASSEROLE

1 lb. shelled shrimp
1 lb. crab meat
2 c. mayonnaise
1 green pepper, chopped
1 med. stalk celery, chopped
2 onions, chopped
Dash of cayenne
Bread crumbs
Butter

Mix all ingredients except crumbs and butter. Place in ungreased baking dish. Top with bread crumbs; dot with butter. Bake at 375 degrees until bubbly. Yield: 8-10 servings.

Jo Ann Durner, Burgan, N. C.

CRAB AND SHRIMP CASSEROLE

1 7 ½-oz. can crab meat, drained and flaked
1 6-oz. can shrimp
1 ½ c. chopped celery
¼ c. chopped green pepper
¼ c. chopped onion
⅛ c. pimento
¾ c. sour cream
¼ c. mayonnaise
1 tbsp. lemon juice
½ tsp. Worcestershire sauce
½ tsp. salt
Dash of black pepper
1 c. buttered bread crumbs

Combine meat and vegetables. Blend remaining ingredients except crumbs. Stir into meat and vegetable mixture. Spoon into baking dish. Cover with bread crumbs. Bake at 350 degrees for 20 to 25 minutes or until brown and bubbly. Yield: 4-6 servings.

Mrs. Wesley A. Parker, Pasadena, Tex.

EASY SHRIMP CASSEROLE

1 ½ tsp. prepared mustard
Dash of Worcestershire sauce
⅛ tsp. each salt and pepper
1 ¼ c. mayonnaise
1 1 to 1 ½-lb. pkg. frozen shrimp
2 cans white crab meat
½ c. chopped onion
½ c. chopped celery
½ c. chopped bell pepper
Ritz cracker crumbs

(Continued on next page)

Mix together first 4 ingredients; add remaining ingredients except crumbs. Place crumbs on top. Bake in 350-degree oven for 45 minutes.

Mrs. Charles R. May, Jr., Bennettsville, S. C.

LONG BEACH SEAFOOD

2 cans frozen shrimp soup
2 tbsp. sherry
2 sm. cans button mushrooms, drained
1 2 ½-oz. pkg. slivered almonds
½ lb. fresh crab meat
½ lb. sm. fresh shrimp
American cheese, sliced
Paprika

Melt soup according to directions on can; do not add milk or water. Place melted soup in a 2-quart casserole; stir in sherry, mushrooms and almonds. Gently fold in seafood. Cover with a layer of cheese; sprinkle paprika on top. Refrigerate until ready to bake. Bake at 300 degrees for 1 hour. Serve over rice. Frozen seafood may be used.

Dorothy Burritt, Sarasota, Fla.

OYSTERS BIENVILLE

4 tbsp. butter
8 sm. shallots, finely chopped
2 tbsp. flour
1 c. chicken broth or fish stock
1 c. finely chopped cooked shrimp
1 7-oz. can mushroom pieces, finely chopped
2 egg yolks
½ c. white wine
Salt and pepper to taste
2 doz. oysters on the half shell
Rock salt
½ c. bread crumbs
2 tbsp. grated Parmesan cheese
Paprika

Heat butter in saucepan; add shallots and saute until soft. Add flour; stir until lightly browned. Add chicken broth, stirring until blended. Add shrimp and mushrooms. Beat egg yolks with wine; add to shrimp mixture, stirring until blended and slightly thickened. Remove from heat; season to taste with salt and pepper. Remove oysters from shells and set aside. Scrub shells thoroughly. Arrange 6 shells on each of 4 pie pans that have been filled 1/2 full of rock salt. Heat in 450-degree oven for 10 minutes. Remove pans from oven. Place oysters in shells; top each with a spoonful of shrimp mixture. Combine bread crumbs and cheese; sprinkle on top of mixture. Lightly sprinkle with paprika. Bake at 450 degrees for 15 minutes or until tops are lightly browned. Serve with lemon wedges. Yield: 4 servings.

Mrs. Suzanne Grand, Hendersonville, Tenn.

SEAFOOD CASSEROLE

1 med. green pepper, chopped
1 med. onion, chopped
1 c. chopped celery
1 7 ½-oz. can crab meat
1 or 2 c. cooked shrimp
½ tsp. salt
½ tsp. pepper
1 tsp. Worcestershire sauce
1 c. mayonnaise
1 c. buttered bread crumbs

(Continued on next page)

Combine all ingredients except bread crumbs. Place in lightly buttered casserole; top with bread crumbs. Bake at 350 degrees until light brown, about 30 to 45 minutes. Yield: 6-8 servings.

Mrs. Karl Morrison, University, Miss.

SEAFOOD CASSEROLE

1 c. celery
1 diced green pepper
Butter
1 c. crab meat
1 c. shrimp
1 c. mayonnaise
2 diced pimentos
Paprika
Dash of Worcestershire sauce
Tabasco
Salt and pepper to taste
1 c. seasoned bread crumb mix

Saute celery and green pepper in butter until tender. Add remaining ingredients except bread crumb mix. Top with bread crumbs; dot with butter. Sprinkle with paprika. Bake 15 to 20 minutes at 350 degrees.

Mrs. H. T. Woodall, Huntsville, Ala.

SEAFOOD CASSEROLE

1 lb. crab meat
1 lb. shrimp
1 lb. scallops
½ c. chopped green pepper
½ c. chopped onion
1 tsp. salt
1 tbsp. Worcestershire sauce
1 c. mayonnaise
2 c. potato chips

Combine all ingredients except potato chips; pour in casserole. Top with chips. Bake in 400-degree oven for 20 minutes. Yield: 6-8 servings.

Mrs. W. P. Roper, Atlanta, Ga.

SEAFOOD CASSEROLE

1 lb. fresh or 2 cans canned shrimp
2 doz. lge. oysters, fresh or canned
6 mushrooms, sliced
½ green pepper, sliced
2 tbsp. butter
1 c. crab meat, cooked or canned
1 recipe med. cream sauce
½ c. chopped pimento
¾ c. buttered bread crumbs

Wash shrimp; drop into boiling water. Cook 20 minutes. Place in cold water; remove shell and black vein along back. Heat oysters in liquor 8 minutes or until edges curl. Saute mushrooms and green pepper in butter 3 minutes. Add shrimp, oysters, crab meat, cream sauce and pimento; pour into large casserole. Top with buttered crumbs. Bake in 400-degree oven 15 minutes or until crumbs are brown.

MEDIUM CREAM SAUCE:

4 tbsp. butter
4 tbsp. flour
2 c. light cream
½ tsp. salt
⅛ tsp. pepper

(Continued on next page)

Melt butter; stir in flour. Gradually stir in cream; stir until mixture boils and thickens. Cook about 5 minutes longer, stirring constantly. Add seasoning. Yield: 10-12 servings.

Mrs. John A. Laws, Memphis, Tenn.

SEAFOOD CASSEROLE

1 stick margarine
½ c. flour
1 pt. sweet milk
2 cans chicken broth
2 c. chopped onion
1 sm. can mushrooms
1 can lobster
1 can crab meat
1 lb. raw shrimp
1 c. grated sharp cheese

Melt margarine; add flour to make a smooth paste. Add milk and broth, then all other ingredients except cheese. Cook over medium heat, stirring constantly. When mixture begins to thicken, place in baking dish; top with cheese. Bake 45 minutes in 300-degree oven. Yield: 6 servings.

Mrs. H. C. Abraham, Tracy City, Tenn.

SEAFOOD CASSEROLE SUPREME

1 can lobster
1 can shrimp
1 med. green pepper, chopped
1 c. mayonnaise
1 can crab meat
1 med. onion, chopped
1 c. celery, chopped
Salt and pepper
Bread crumbs (opt.)
2 beaten eggs (opt.)

Combine all ingredients as listed. Bake at 350 degrees for 30 minutes. The beaten eggs may be added to increase servings and add lightness. Yield: 4-6 servings.

Mrs. Judith Preirte, Fairfax, Va.

SEAFOOD HIT

2 cans frozen shrimp soup, undiluted
2 tbsp. sherry
2 sm. cans button mushrooms, drained
1 2½-oz. pkg. slivered almonds
¾ lb. fresh sm. shrimp
½ lb. fresh crab meat
Sliced American cheese
Paprika

Melt soup according to directions on the can. Put melted soup in a 2-quart casserole; add sherry, mushrooms and almonds. Gently fold in seafood; cover with a layer of sliced cheese. Sprinkle paprika over top. Place in 300-degree oven, uncovered, for 1 hour. Serve over hot fluffy rice. Yield: 6 servings.

Mrs. Wilbur A. Smith, Texarkana, Tex.

SEAFOOD IN SHELLS

4 tbsp. butter or margarine
4 tbsp. flour
1 c. milk
¼ c. cooking sherry
2 c. cooked diced shrimp
1 c. cooked diced lobster
Parmesan cheese
Paprika

Melt butter; blend in flour. Gradually add milk; stir until thick. Add sherry, shrimp and lobster; place in 6 seafood casserole shells. Sprinkle generously with Parmesan cheese and paprika. Broil until lightly browned. Yield: 6 servings.

Mrs. William Oberg, Richmond, Va.

SHRIMP AND CRAB CASSEROLE

4 slices bread
½ lb. sharp cheese
1 c. water
Butter
½ med. green pepper, chopped
1 med. onion, chopped
1 pod garlic, chopped
½ c. celery, chopped
1 egg
1 sm. can crab meat
1 sm. can shrimp
Dash each of Tabasco and Worcestershire sauce
½ c. mayonnaise
1 c. water chestnuts (opt.)
Buttered bread crumbs

Soak bread and cheese in water; brown in butter. Add to green pepper, onion, garlic and celery. Add remaining ingredients except bread crumbs. Top with bread crumbs. Bake 30 minutes in 300 to 350-degree oven. This casserole freezes well. Yield: 6-8 servings.

Maidie Hilbun, Laurel, Miss.

SHRIMP-CRAB MEAT CASSEROLE

1 c. cooked shrimp, cut up
1 6 ½-oz. can crab meat
1 ½ c. cooked rice
¾ c. mayonnaise
Worcestershire sauce
1 tbsp. prepared mustard
Tabasco sauce
Salt
Milk
Crushed potato chips

Combine shrimp, crab meat, rice and mayonnaise. Season with Worcestershire sauce, mustard, Tabasco sauce and salt. Moisten with milk. Cover with crushed potato chips. Bake in 350 to 375-degree oven for 30 to 40 minutes.

Mrs. Louis Morris, Selma, Ala.

TASTY SEAFOOD CASSEROLE

1 c. or 7 ½-oz. can cooked shrimp
1 c. or 7 ½-oz. can crab meat
4 tbsp. chopped onion
1 c. chopped celery
½ c. chopped bell pepper
½ c. homemade mayonnaise
½ tsp. Worcestershire sauce
½ tsp. salt
Pinch of pepper
½ tsp. dry mustard
Buttered bread crumbs

Cut shrimp in half; mix with crab meat. Add all ingredients except bread crumbs; mix lightly. Put into greased casserole; top with buttered bread crumbs. Bake in

(Continued on next page)

350-degree oven until crumbs are lightly browned, about 25 to 35 minutes. If desired, onions, celery and green pepper may be sauteed in 2 tablespoons butter until tender before adding to other ingredients. Yield: 4 servings.

Mrs. William H. Richards, Nashville, Tenn.

TRITON'S TRIUMPH

1 c. mayonnaise
1 tsp. Worcestershire sauce
1 tbsp. prepared mustard
2 tsp. capers (opt.)
¼ c. sherry
Dash of cayenne pepper
¼ tsp. curry powder
1 tbsp. parsley flakes
½ c. finely chopped onion
½ c. finely chopped celery
1 ½ c. shredded bread
⅔ c. water
2 5 to 6-oz. cans crab meat
2 5 to 6-oz. cans jumbo shrimp
Salt

Combine mayonnaise, Worcestershire sauce, mustard, capers and wine. Add remaining ingredients and mix gently, seasoning with salt. Place in greased casserole. Bake at 350 degrees for about 30 minutes or until heated. Yield: 6 servings.

Claire Barnard, Fredericksburg, Va.

SEAFOOD CASSEROLE

1 6 ½ to 7-oz. can tuna, drained
1 6 ½ to 7-oz. can crab meat, drained
2 c. cooked rice
½ tsp. salt
¼ tsp. paprika
¼ tsp. dry mustard
3 tbsp. sherry
2 c. med. white sauce
½ c. grated cheddar cheese
½ c. buttered bread crumbs

Mix tuna and crab meat lightly with rice; add salt, paprika, dry mustard and sherry. Place in a 1 1/2-quart casserole; add white sauce. Top with grated cheese, then buttered bread crumbs. Place in a 350-degree oven; heat thoroughly until mixture is bubbly and cheese and bread crumbs well browned. Yield: 6 servings.

Mrs. Harvey Hamann, Aiken, S. C.

SEAFOOD SUPREME

1 can crab meat
1 can tuna, drained well
2 cans mushroom soup
½ c. milk
6 eggs, separated
⅛ tsp. salt
1 or 2 tbsp. cream
Dash of pepper

Combine crab meat, tuna, soup and milk in greased baking dish. Bake in 400-degree oven until heated thoroughly, about 12 minutes. Beat egg whites with salt until light and fluffy. Beat yolks well; add cream and pepper. Fold whites into yolks; pour mixture over hot seafood. Bake 15 minutes or until firm.

Mrs. Richard Hoodman Parks, Reynolds, Ga.

Lamb, Variety Meat
and Game Casseroles

RECIPE FOR CORNED BEEF CASSEROLE ON PAGE 97

BAKED LAMB STEW WITH CORNMEAL BISCUITS

1 ½ lb. cubed lamb shoulder
1 c. sliced onions
1 ½ c. sliced beets
1 ½ c. cut green beans
2 c. diced tomatoes
1 c. sliced mushrooms
3 c. stock or bouillon
Salt and pepper to taste
1 ½ c. biscuit mix
½ c. yellow cornmeal
½ c. milk

Combine lamb and onions; cook over low heat until lamb is browned on all sides. Add beets, green beans, tomatoes, mushrooms, stock and seasonings. Mix well; turn into 3-quart casserole. Cover and bake at 350 degrees for 1 hour. Combine biscuit mix and cornmeal. Add milk; mix lightly. Turn onto lightly floured surface; knead gently 10 times. Roll out 1/2 inch thick. Cut into 2 1/2-inch rounds, using floured cutter. Arrange biscuits over stew. Bake at 400 degrees for 15 minutes or until browned. Yield: 6 servings.

Mrs. Lou Massey, Camden, Ark.

LEFTOVER LAMB

2 c. cold diced lamb
1 c. lamb gravy
½ c. raw diced potatoes
½ med. onion, finely cut
1 green pepper, diced
1 can tomato sauce
1 sm. can pimento
½ tsp. paprika
1 tsp. Worcestershire sauce
½ tsp. salt
⅛ tsp. pepper
Grated Romano cheese
Butter

Cut lamb into small pieces; put into baking dish with gravy. Boil potatoes, onion and green pepper in salted water for about 10 minutes. Drain and add to meat and gravy. Add remaining ingredients except cheese and butter. Top with grated cheese; dot with butter. Bake at 350 degrees for 30 minutes or until brown. Yield: 6-8 servings.

Mrs. A. E. Soderholm, Hendersonville, N. C.

CHILI AND CORN CHIPS CASSEROLE

1 bag corn chips
1 can chili
1 8-oz. can tomato sauce
1 sm. onion, chopped
1 c. American or cheddar cheese, grated

Cover bottom of large casserole dish with corn chips; spread with chili. Pour tomato sauce and chopped onion on top. Sprinkle with corn chips; top with grated cheese. Bake in preheated 375-degree oven for 15 to 20 minutes. Yield: 5-7 servings.

Mrs. Clifford E. Hogue, Midland, Tex.

CHILI-TAMALE

3 cans tamales, cut in bite-sized pieces
2 cans chili with beans
1 ½ c. cheese, grated
1 pkg. corn chips

(Continued on next page)

Combine tamales and chili in baking dish. Rinse chili can with small amount of water; add to mixture. Stir in 1 cup grated cheese and 3/4 package crushed corn chips. Bake at 325 degrees for 30 minutes. Top with remaining cheese and whole corn chips; brown. Yield: 12 servings.

Peggy Jones, Athens, Ala.

CORN BREAD CASSEROLE

- 1 can chili
- 1 can Ranch Style beans
- 2 c. self-rising corn bread mix
- 1 ½ c. milk
- 1 egg
- 4 tbsp. shortening
- 2 tbsp. sugar (opt.)

Heat chili and beans together. Combine remaining ingredients for corn bread batter. Line bottom of well-greased casserole dish with 1/3 of corn bread batter. Add heated chili and bean mixture. Top with remaining corn bread batter. Bake at 450 degrees for 25 to 30 minutes. Yield: 4-6 servings.

Mrs. Dolores Kroll, Huntsville, Tex.

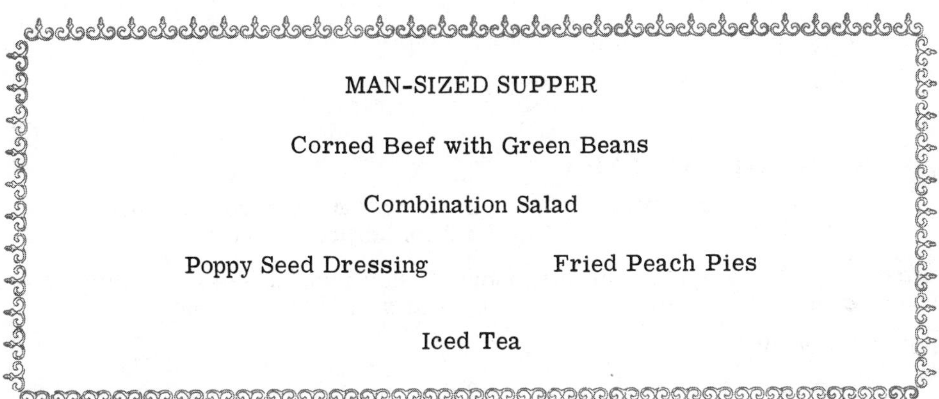

MAN-SIZED SUPPER

Corned Beef with Green Beans

Combination Salad

Poppy Seed Dressing

Fried Peach Pies

Iced Tea

CORNED BEEF WITH GREEN BEANS

- 6 hard-cooked eggs
- ¼ c. mayonnaise
- ½ tsp. salt
- Dash of pepper
- ¼ tsp. Worcestershire sauce
- ¼ c. margarine, melted
- ¼ c. flour
- 2 c. milk
- 1 c. grated cheddar cheese
- 1 1-lb. can cut green beans, drained
- 1 12-oz. can corned beef, flaked
- Buttered strips of bread

Cut eggs in half lengthwise. Remove yolks; mash with mayonnaise, salt, pepper and Worcestershire sauce. Fill egg whites with mixture. Arrange eggs in casserole. Blend margarine and flour in saucepan; gradually stir in milk. Cool, stirring constantly, until thickened. Stir in cheese, beans and beef. Pour over eggs. Overlap bread strips around edge of casserole. Bake at 350 degrees for 15 to 20 minutes.

Mrs. Hollis Jones, Liberty, Miss.

CORN CHIPS AND CHILI CASSEROLE

1 No. 2 can chili
1 No. 2 can tamales
1 onion, chopped finely
1 c. grated cheese
1 7-oz. bag corn chips

Arrange all ingredients in layers in casserole. Bake at 350 degrees for 30 minutes. Yield: 6 servings.

Mrs. Daniel L. Metts, Macon, Ga.

RICE RANCHERO

2 cans condensed chili-beef soup
1 ½ c. water
1 med. onion, chopped
1 ¼ c. precooked rice
1 c. shredded, sharp process cheddar cheese
1 c. coarsely crushed corn chips

Combine soup, water and onion in medium saucepan. Heat to boiling, stirring occasionally. Add rice. Pour into 2-quart casserole. Cover and bake at 375 degrees for 30 minutes. Uncover; fluff rice with fork. Top with shredded cheese. Bake, uncovered, 10 minutes more. Garnish with corn chips just before serving. Yield: 6-8 servings.

Susan Toaz, Bradenton, Fla.

CORN 'N' BEEF BAKE

1 tbsp. dry onion flakes
⅓ c. chili sauce
2 15-oz. cans corned beef hash
3 tbsp. barbecue sauce

Soften onion flakes in chili sauce. Combine hash, barbecue sauce and onion mixture in greased 2 1/2-quart casserole. Spread with following topping.

BISCUIT TOPPING:

¾ c. flour
¾ c. yellow cornmeal
1 tbsp. sugar
1 tsp. baking powder
½ tsp. salt
¾ c. milk
3 tbsp. melted shortening
1 egg, slightly beaten
1 12-oz. can whole kernel corn with sweet peppers, drained

Combine all ingredients except corn; stir until smooth. Add corn and mix well. Pour over casserole. Bake at 425 degrees for 40 to 45 minutes. Yield: 6-8 servings.

Edwin Foster, Jr., Bradenton, Fla.

CORNED BEEF CASSEROLE

⅔ pkg. shell macaroni
1 can corned beef
¾ c. cheese cubes
1 med. onion, chopped
1 can cream of chicken soup
½ c. milk
¼ tsp. black pepper
1 tbsp. butter
Cracker crumbs

(Continued on next page)

Cook macaroni in salted water; set aside. Flake beef into small pieces. Combine cheese, onion, soup and milk. Alternate layers of macaroni, beef and cheese mixture in large casserole. Sprinkle with pepper; dot with butter and cover top with crumbs. Bake at 300 degrees for 1 hour.

Mrs. J. Carl West, Memphis, Tenn.

CORNED BEEF CASSEROLE

2 12-oz. cans corned beef
2 ½ c. finely diced cooked potatoes
2 tbsp. butter or margarine, melted
1 med. onion, chopped
1 1-lb. can red kidney beans
Salt and pepper to taste

Break corned beef into chunks with a fork. Brown potatoes lightly in butter. Reserve 1/2 cup for topping. Add onion to fat and brown lightly. Stir in corned beef, beans and liquid. Mix well and place in 1 1/2-quart casserole. Spread reserved potato cubes over top. Sprinkle with salt and pepper. Bake at 375 degrees about 20 minutes. Yield: 6 servings.

Photograph for this recipe on page 93.

CORNED BEEF CASSEROLE

1 pkg. wide noodles
1 12-oz. can corned beef, diced
1 lge. can evaporated milk
1 can mushroom soup
½ lb. yellow cheddar cheese, grated

Cook noodles in boiling salted water until just tender. Add corned beef, milk and mushroom soup. Mix with cheese. Put into large casserole dish. Bake for 1 hour. Yield: 10 servings.

Mrs. Helen E. Ramsey, Bradenton Beach, Fla.

CORNED BEEF CASSEROLE

1 8-oz. pkg. elbow macaroni
1 12-oz. can corned beef
4 slices American cheese
1 sm. can evaporated milk
1 sm. onion, chopped
1 can cream of chicken soup
3 slices bread, crumbled and buttered

Cook macaroni in salted water; drain and rinse. Mix all ingredients except crumbs. Pour into greased casserole. Top with bread crumbs. Bake about 1 hour at 375 degrees. Yield: 8 servings.

Mrs. Rena Boyett, Montgomery, Ala.

CORNED BEEF CASSEROLE

1 can cream of mushroom soup
½ c. evaporated milk
1 12-oz. can corned beef, cut up
1 c. grated American cheese
⅓ c. finely cut onion
1 ½ c. cooked elbow macaroni or noodles
1 c. crushed potato chips

Mix all ingredients except potato chips. Place in greased 1 1/2-quart baking dish. Top with potato chips. Bake at 425 degrees for 20 minutes. Yield: 4 servings.

Mrs. Dudley Foreman, Lafayette, La.

CORNED BEEF AND CABBAGE

1 10 ½-oz. can condensed cream of celery soup
½ c. chopped onion
1 tsp. dry mustard
1 c. diced cooked corned beef
4 c. coarsely shredded cabbage

Mix all ingredients in a 1 1/2-quart casserole. Cover. Bake at 375 degrees for 45 minutes. Yield: 3-4 servings.

Susan Frugia, Venice, La.

CORNED BEEF NOODLES

¼ c. chopped onion
Margarine
1 can cream of mushroom soup
1 c. milk
1 can corned beef
1 5-oz. pkg. noodles, cooked
2 slices bread, crumbled
¼ lb. sharp cheddar cheese, grated

Cook onion in small amount of margarine; add soup, milk and meat. Mix with noodles. Place in greased baking dish; sprinkle with crumbs and cheese. Bake at 350 degrees for 30 minutes. Yield: 10 servings.

Mrs. J. L. Gibbons, Dallas, Tex.

CORNED BEEF-NOODLE CASSEROLE

1 8-oz. pkg. cooked egg noodles
1 can corned beef
1 can mushroom soup
1 can cream of chicken soup
1 c. evaporated milk
Bread or cracker crumbs

Combine all ingredients except cracker crumbs. Place in greased baking dish; sprinkle with crumbs. Bake at 350 degrees for 30 minutes. Yield: 8 servings.

Mrs. A. J. Kohl, Gassville, Ark.

HASH DIVAN

1 10-oz. pkg. frozen broccoli, cooked and drained
1 can corned beef hash, sliced ½ in. thick
1 can cream of chicken soup
½ c. milk

(Continued on next page)

Arrange broccoli in buttered shallow baking dish; top with corned beef hash. Blend soup and milk in small saucepan; cook over low heat until bubbly. Pour over hash and broccoli. Bake at 350 degrees for 15 to 30 minutes. Yield: 4 servings.

Vera Smith, Elizabethtown, Ky.

HASH DIVAN

1 pkg. frozen broccoli or Italian beans, partially cooked
1 can corned beef hash
1 can cream of chicken soup
Grated cheese

Layer all ingredients in order given in small casserole, sprinkling generously with cheese. Bake 40 minutes at 325 degrees. Yield: 4 servings.

Mrs. Ira C. Finn, Bradenton, Fla.

MACARONI AND CORNED BEEF LOAF

4 oz. macaroni
1 egg, beaten
1 8-oz. can tomato sauce
½ tsp. pepper
1 tbsp. brown sugar (opt.)
¼ c. bread crumbs
½ c. chopped onions
1 tsp. Worcestershire sauce
1 can corned beef, diced

Cook macaroni until tender; drain. Combine egg, tomato sauce, pepper, sugar, bread crumbs, onions, Worcestershire sauce and corned beef. Mix well; add macaroni. Place in baking dish. Bake at 350 degrees for 1 hour. Yield: 6-8 servings.

Janie Montgomery, Kingsport, Tenn.

EGGPLANT CASSEROLE

1 med. eggplant, peeled
1 can tomatoes
½ c. chopped celery
¼ c. chopped green pepper
¼ c. chopped onion
2 tbsp. butter
1 sm. can deviled ham
1 tsp. Worcestershire sauce
Salt and pepper to taste
1 egg, beaten
⅓ c. day-old corn bread crumbs

(Continued on next page)

Cook eggplant until tender. Steam tomatoes down low. Saute celery, green pepper and onion in butter until tender. Do not brown. Add eggplant, tomatoes, ham and Worcestershire sauce. Season to taste. Cook for 45 minutes. Remove from heat; add egg and mix well. Place in casserole; sprinkle with corn bread crumbs. Bake at 325 degrees for 20 minutes.

Mrs. Frances M. Watkins, Aberdeen, Miss.

EGGPLANT AND RICE MEDLEY

2 tbsp. butter
½ c. diced celery
2 c. cooked rice
1 4 ½-oz. can deviled ham
1 egg, beaten
¼ tsp. salt
Dash of black pepper
½ c. cheddar cheese, grated
Crumbled bacon

Melt butter in skillet; saute celery until tender, but not brown. Add rice, ham, egg, salt and pepper; heat thoroughly, stirring constantly. Pour into buttered casserole; top with cheese and bacon. Place under broiler only until cheese is melted. Yield: 4 servings.

Mrs. Jack Spears, Graceville, Fla.

BARBECUED FRANKFURTERS AND NOODLES

2 c. egg noodles
1 lb. frankfurters
¼ c. chopped onion
¼ c. salad oil
1 tbsp. Worcestershire sauce
1 tbsp. brown sugar
½ tsp. salt
¼ tsp. paprika
¼ c. lemon juice
½ c. water
1 c. chili sauce

Cook noodles according to package directions. Drain and put in shallow baking dish. Arrange frankfurters over noodles. Cook onion in oil over low heat for 10 minutes, stirring frequently. Add remaining ingredients; simmer for 15 minutes, stirring occasionally. Pour sauce over frankfurters. Bake at 375 degrees for 30 minutes. Yield: 4-6 servings.

Mrs. Woodrow Jasek, Columbus, Tex.

FRANK SNACK

1 12-oz. pkg. corn muffin mix
½ lb. frankfurters, sliced crosswise
Salted peanuts
Oregano and garlic salt
2 c. shredded process cheese

Prepare corn muffin mix according to directions. Spread in a greased 15 x 10 x 1-inch jelly roll pan. Arrange frankfurters over prepared mix. Top a third of the frankfurters with peanuts, a third with oregano and a third with garlic salt. Sprinkle shredded cheese on top. Bake at 400 degrees 15 to 20 minutes or until cheese browns. Cut into bars and serve hot. Yield: 30 pieces.

Mrs. P. L. Bradford, Memphis, Tenn.

BEANS AND FRANKS

1 lb. navy beans
1 tsp. salt
2 8-oz. cans tomato sauce
1 lb. frankfurters, thinly cut
5 tbsp. brown sugar

Wash beans. Cook in water with salt for 2 hours and 30 minutes or until done; remove from heat. Add tomato sauce, frankfurters and brown sugar. Place in oblong pan. Bake at 350 degrees for 1 hour. Yield: 20 servings.

Emily Mae Linenschmidt, Denton, Tex.

FRANKFURTER-BEAN FARE

2 1-lb. cans pork and beans
½ c. finely chopped onion
¼ c. molasses
¼ c. catsup
2 tsp. horseradish
1 tsp. dry mustard
6 frankfurters
1 tbsp. melted butter or margarine

Pour pork and beans into casserole; mix in onion. Top with mixture of molasses, catsup, horseradish and mustard. Arrange frankfurters over top of casserole. Brush frankfurters thoroughly with butter. Bake at 350 degrees 20 to 30 minutes, or until thoroughly heated. Yield: 6 servings.

Mrs. B. P. McCraw, Gaffney, S. C.

FRANKFURTER CROWN CASSEROLE

2 slices bacon
½ c. chopped onion
1 can cream of mushroom soup
½ c. water
½ tsp. salt
Dash of pepper
3 c. sliced cooked potatoes
1 c. cooked cut green beans
½ lb. frankfurters, split and cut in half

Cook bacon in skillet; remove and crumble. Cook onion in drippings. Stir in soup, water, salt and pepper. Add potatoes and beans; pour into 1 1/2-quart casserole. Stand frankfurters up around edge. Bake at 350 degrees for 30 minutes. Top with bacon. Yield: 4 servings.

Mrs. Allen M. Clark, Bradenton, Fla.

FRANKFURTERS IN CASSEROLE

3 c. potatoes, diced
1 sm. onion, diced
1 can tomato sauce
6 frankfurters, sliced into 1-in. pieces
1 ½ tsp. salt
Dash of pepper
½ green pepper, diced
½ c. water

Cook potatoes in salted water for 10 minutes; drain. Pour into casserole; add remaining ingredients. Bake at 350 degrees for 45 minutes or until done. Yield: 6-8 servings.

Laura Shutt, Advance, N. C.

FRANKFURTERS AND MACARONI

6 or 8 frankfurters, cut into ½-in. rounds
6 tbsp. shortening
1 sm. onion, finely chopped
1 stalk celery
1 can tomato paste
Salt to taste
Pepper (opt.)
1 tbsp. sugar or to taste
½ pkg. macaroni, cooked and drained

Slightly cook frankfurters in shortening; add onion and celery. Continue cooking until done, but not brown. Add tomato paste, seasonings, sugar and enough water to cover frankfurters; simmer for about 30 minutes. Combine macaroni and frankfurter mixture; serve.

Mrs. Alter Smith, Wesson, Miss.

FRANKFURTER SURPRISE

1 8-oz. pkg. shell macaroni
1 lb. frankfurters
1 c. cottage cheese
1 c. sour cream
1 tsp. dehydrated onion
½ tsp. garlic powder
2 tsp. parsley flakes

Cook macaroni according to directions on package. Cut frankfurters into 1-inch pieces. Combine macaroni, cottage cheese, sour cream, onion, garlic powder and parsley flakes. Add frankfurters. Place in a 2-quart casserole. Bake, uncovered, at 350 degrees for 30 minutes. Yield: 6 servings.

Mrs. Norma Day, Hanahan, S. C.

FRANKLY CORNY STRATA

6 slices day-old white bread
6 frankfurters (opt.)
4 slices American pimento cheese, quartered
2 eggs, slightly beaten
½ tsp. salt
½ c. milk
1 17-oz. can cooked yellow cream-style corn

Cut bread in 1/2-inch cubes; place half in bottom of greased 8-inch square casserole. Slice frankfurters in rings; arrange evenly over bread cubes. Top with cheese pieces and cover with remaining bread cubes. Combine eggs, salt, milk and corn; pour over all. Let stand 10 minutes. Bake at 375 degrees about 25 minutes. Yield: 4-6 servings.

Audrey Mathis, Gastonia, N. C.

FRANKS AND CORN PIE

6 frankfurters
2 c. whole kernel corn, drained
¼ c. chopped onion
¼ c. chopped green pepper (opt.)
½ tsp. caraway seed
½ tsp. salt
1 c. cracker crumbs
1 egg, slightly beaten
1 c. milk
2 tbsp. butter
¼ c. grated cheese

(Continued on next page)

Split franks lengthwise; cut in half crosswise. Combine corn, onion, green pepper, caraway seed and salt. Spread half of mixture in greased 1 1/2-quart shallow casserole. Cover corn mixture with half of cracker crumbs. Arrange layer of frankfurters, spoke fashion, on top of crackers. Repeat layers. Combine egg and milk; pour over casserole. Dot with butter; sprinkle cheese in center. Set casserole in shallow pan of water. Bake at 325 degrees for 45 to 50 minutes. Yield: 6 servings.

Mrs. C. E. Schooley, Nocona, Tex.

FRANKS AND CHEESE CASSEROLE

1 ⅔ c. evaporated milk
½ tsp. salt
2 c. grated cheese
4 c. cooked noodles
2 c. sliced frankfurters

Simmer evaporated milk and salt on low heat to just below boiling point. Add cheese and stir until melted. Pour over cooked noodles and franks in a buttered casserole. Bake at 350 degrees for 30 minutes. Yield: 4-6 servings.

Mrs. Ray Dickson, DeWitt, Ark.

FRANKS 'N' FRIES CASSEROLE

2 9-oz. pkg. frozen French fries
1 lb. frankfurters, cut in 1-in. slices
1 11-oz. can cheese soup
¼ c. milk
¼ c. chopped onion
¼ c. chopped pimento
¼ c. chopped green pepper

Place French fries on baking sheet; bake in 400-degree oven for 15 minutes. Combine frankfurters, cheese soup, milk, onion, pimento and green pepper. Arrange half the French fries in bottom of 1 1/2-quart casserole. Pour half the frankfurter mixture over French fries. Repeat layers. Bake in 400-degree oven 15 to 20 minutes. Yield: 4-6 servings.

Betty P. Simpson, Dobson, N. C.

SOUTHERN FRANKFURTER DINNER

1 med. onion, cut in rings
⅓ c. green pepper, diced
1 tbsp. shortening
½ lb. frankfurters, thinly sliced
2 c. canned tomatoes
Dash of salt and pepper
1 8 ½-oz. pkg. corn muffin mix

Fry onion rings and green pepper in shortening. Add frankfurters, tomatoes, salt and pepper. Pour into 8 x 8-inch baking dish. Prepare corn muffin batter as directed on package; spoon carefully over meat mixture. Bake at 400 degrees for 20 to 25 minutes or until golden brown. Yield: 4-6 servings.

Mrs. Charles A. Routh, Winston-Salem, N. C.

FRANKS AND MASHED POTATOES CASSEROLE

8 frankfurters
Mashed potatoes
1 c. grated cheese
Paprika

Line flat square baking dish with franks, sliced in half. Top with layer of mashed potatoes; sprinkle with grated cheese and paprika. Bake in 400-degree oven for 15 minutes. Yield: 8 servings.

Inez Hendrix, Greensboro, N. C.

WIENER-BEAN POT

2 1-lb. cans pork and beans
1 envelope dry onion soup mix
⅓ c. catsup
¼ c. water
2 tbsp. brown sugar
1 tbsp. prepared mustard
1 lb. frankfurters, sliced

Combine all ingredients in 2-quart casserole or bean pot. Bake, uncovered, at 350 degrees for 1 hour. Yield: 6-8 servings.

Mrs. Sandra Robinson, Selmer, Tenn.

WIENER CASSEROLE

4 tbsp. margarine
4 tbsp. flour
2 c. milk
6 c. cooked diced potatoes
8 to 10 wieners, sliced

Melt margarine; blend in flour, stirring until smooth. Gradually add milk, stirring constantly, until thickened. Combine potatoes and wieners in casserole dish. Pour sauce over mixture. Bake at 300 degrees for 1 hour.

Mrs. Robert W. Poirier, Virginia Beach, Va.

GOLDEN GRITS RING

2 c. cooked grits
2 tbsp. butter
1 sm. jar chipped beef
2 pkg. brown gravy mix
4 to 6 slices American cheese

Form grits into a ring in a greased 10-inch tube pan. Bake in 350-degree oven until firm. Remove ring when cold from tube pan. Cover chipped beef with boiling water; drain. Rinse beef with warm water; drain. Add 2 cups cold water to gravy mix. Simmer chipped beef and gravy mix together to make a sauce. Place ring in skillet. Cut cheese slices in triangular flaps and lay over top. Fill center of ring with chipped beef; place in warm oven to heat grits and melt cheese.

Mrs. John R. Taylor, Jr., Jonesboro, Tenn.

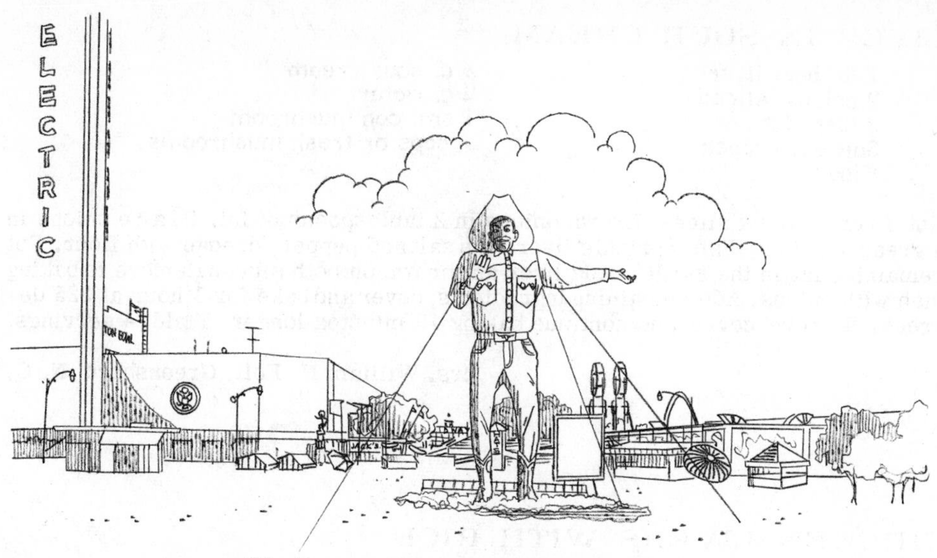

Big Tex presides over the Texas State Fair.

COLUMBUS CASSEROLE

1 c. elbow macaroni
4 slices bacon
½ lb. beef liver, cubed
2 tbsp. flour
1 tsp. salt
Chopped onion
1 can condensed cream of mushroom soup
¾ c. milk
1 ½ tbsp. bottled meat sauce
1 c. canned whole kernel corn
Chopped parsley

Cook macaroni as package directs; drain. Saute bacon until lightly browned; drain. Pour off all but 2 tablespoons drippings. Sprinkle liver with flour and salt; saute quickly in drippings until well browned. Add onion and cook until just tender. Pour soup into a 1 1/2-quart casserole; slowly stir in milk and meat sauce. Fold in macaroni, liver, onion and corn; top with bacon. Chill. Bake in preheated 350-degree oven about 50 minutes or until bubbly. Sprinkle with parsley before serving. Yield: 4 servings.

Mrs. A. H. Thielen, Gulfport, Fla.

LIVER AND ONION CASSEROLE

1 lb. liver, sliced
Flour
5 med. onions, thickly sliced
5 lge. potatoes, sliced thick
Salt and pepper to taste
1 can cream of mushroom soup
¾ soup can water
Bacon slices

Roll liver in flour and brown; place layer on bottom of casserole. Add layer of onions, then layer of potatoes. Season each layer. Repeat layers. Combine soup and water; pour over casserole. Top with bacon. Cover with lid or foil. Bake at 350 degrees for 1 hour; uncover and bake 15 minutes longer or until bacon is crisp.

Mrs. A. B. Fortson, North Little Rock, Ark.

LIVER IN SOUR CREAM

1 lb. beef liver
2 onions, sliced
3 tbsp. fat
Salt and pepper
Flour
½ c. sour cream
¼ c. water
1 sm. can mushroom caps or fresh mushrooms

Cut liver in thick slices. Brown onions in 2 tablespoons of fat. Place onions in a greased baking dish. Sprinkle liver with salt and pepper; dredge with flour. Put remaining fat in the skillet. Add liver and brown on both sides. Remove to baking dish with onions. Add remaining ingredients; cover and bake for 1 hour at 325 degrees. Remove cover and continue baking 15 minutes longer. Yield: 4 servings.

Mrs. William N. Felt, Greensboro, N. C.

CHICKEN LIVERS WITH RICE

3 tbsp. minced onion
¼ c. butter or oleo
5 oz. instant rice
Flour
Salt
Pepper
Paprika
Celery salt
Seasoned salt
½ lb. thawed frozen or fresh chicken livers
1 can condensed cream of chicken soup
½ c. milk
1 tbsp. chopped parsley
Pinch of dried basil

Cook finely chopped onion until tender in 1 tablespoon melted butter; add rice. Cook as package directs. Prepare seasoned flour by mixing flour with salt, pepper, paprika, celery salt and seasoned salt. Mix well; roll chicken livers in seasoned flour. Use a fork to separate pieces of liver. Brown livers in remaining butter over low heat; turn to brown well on all sides. Combine rice, livers and remaining ingredients. Turn into 1 1/2-quart casserole. Cover; bake in oven at 375 degrees about 30 minutes or until bubbly hot. Yield: 5 to 6 servings.

Mrs. David Pontius, Memphis, Tenn.

CHICKEN LIVERS IN PEACH WINE

1 lb. chicken livers
1 stick butter
1 lge. can whole mushrooms
1 can mushroom soup
¼ c. peach wine
Salt and pepper to taste

Saute livers in butter. Mix remaining ingredients; put into casserole with livers. Bake 30 minutes at 200 degrees. Yield: 4 servings.

Ruth M. Scoggins, Commerce, Ga.

MACARONI-BEEF BAKE

2 12-oz. pkg. frozen macaroni and cheese
1 5-oz. jar dried beef
8 cherry tomatoes

(Continued on next page)

Heat macaroni and cheese according to package directions until thawed. Cut beef into bite-sized pieces; place in 4 individual shallow baking dishes. Spoon macaroni mixture over beef. Cut tomatoes into quarters; arrange on tops of casseroles. Bake in preheated 350-degree oven about 20 minutes or until heated. Yield: 4 servings.

Photograph for this recipe on cover.

VIENNA SAUSAGE AND BROCCOLI CASSEROLE

- 1 tbsp. chopped onion
- 4 tbsp. oleo
- 2 tbsp. flour
- ½ tsp. salt
- 1 ½ c. milk
- ¼ c. grated cheddar cheese
- 1 10-oz. pkg. frozen broccoli, cooked
- 2 hard-cooked eggs, chopped
- 2 4-oz. cans Vienna sausage
- ½ c. bread crumbs

Cook onion in 4 tablespoons oleo till tender. Stir in flour and salt; add milk. Cook, stirring constantly, till thickened. Add cheese; cook till melted. Place cooked broccoli in bottom of greased 1 1/2-quart casserole. Sprinkle chopped eggs over broccoli; cover with layer of Vienna sausage. Pour cheese sauce over top. Mix bread crumbs with remaining melted oleo; arrange around edge of casserole. Bake for 30 minutes in 350-degree oven. Yield: 4 servings.

Mrs. George W. Kaupp, Buros, La.

DOVE AND DRESSING

- 12 dove breasts
- ½ c. light oil
- Salt
- 4 c. poultry stuffing mix
- 2 tsp. dried parsley leaves
- 1 tsp. pepper
- 1 tsp. minced garlic
- ½ tsp. ground thyme
- ½ c. melted butter
- 1 tsp. paprika

Wash dove breasts in cold water; dry thoroughly with paper towels. Rub each dove with oil and salt lightly. Mix stuffing mix with 1 teaspoonful salt and remaining ingredients. Place dove breasts in greased shallow casserole on layer of stuffing. Sprinkle remaining stuffing over doves. Bake at 350 degrees for 45 minutes. Cover with foil if casserole browns too fast. Yield: 6 servings.

Mrs. Arnold Witzke, Brunswick, Ga.

DOVE PIE

8 to 10 dove breasts
Tops and leaves of 6 stalks celery
1 stick butter or margarine
Salt and pepper to taste
2 c. sifted flour
4 tsp. baking powder
2 eggs
Milk
Pastry

Cover doves with water; add celery leaves and tops. Simmer until tender; remove doves and celery. Add margarine, salt and pepper to stock. Sift flour, baking powder and 1 teaspoon salt together 3 times. Break eggs in 1-cup measuring cup; add enough milk to fill cup. Beat well; stir into dry ingredients. Add additional milk if necessary; batter should be stiff. Thicken stock with flour. Moisten spoon with stock; fill with batter. Drop batter into stock. Continue until dumplings barely touch. Cover and simmer for 2 minutes. Line a baking dish with pastry; place doves on top. Add dumplings and stock. Cover top with pastry; make slits in top. Bake at 350 degrees until browned.

Mrs. Avery Burdette, Guntersville, Ala.

VENISON PARMIGIANA

1 ½ lb. venison or round steak, 1 ½ in. thick
1 egg, beaten
⅓ c. fine dry bread crumbs
⅓ c. grated Parmesan cheese
⅓ c. cooking oil
1 med. onion, minced
1 tsp. salt
¼ tsp. pepper
½ tsp. sugar
½ tsp. marjoram
1 6-oz. can tomato paste
2 c. hot water
½ lb. mozzarella or process cheese, sliced

Pound meat thin; cut into serving pieces. Dip meat into egg; roll in crumbs and Parmesan cheese. Brown in oil in skillet. Place meat in shallow, wide baking dish. Cook onion in remaining oil in skillet until soft; add salt, pepper, sugar, marjoram and tomato paste. Gradually add hot water. Boil for 5 minutes. Pour most of sauce over meat; top with cheese slices. Add remaining sauce. Bake at 350 degrees for 1 hour. Yield: 4-6 servings.

Mrs. Carl H. Panzer, Sweetwater, Tex.

VENISON WITH SOUR CREAM

2 lb. venison
¼ c. fat
1 clove garlic
1 c. diced celery
½ c. minced onion
1 c. diced carrots
1 tsp. salt
1 bay leaf
2 c. water
4 tbsp. butter
4 tbsp. flour
1 c. sour cream

Cut venison in pieces; melt fat in heavy frying pan. Add meat and garlic. Brown on all sides and arrange in dish. Put vegetables in remaining fat and cook for 2 minutes. Add salt, bay leaf and water. Pour over meat. Bake at 250 to 300 degrees until meat is tender. Melt butter in frying pan; stir in flour. Add water the meat was cooked in; boil until thick. Add sour cream and additional salt, if necessary. Pour over meat and vegetables. Serve with buttered noodles and currant jelly. Yield: 4-6 servings.

Mrs. Uyvonna C. Bell, Eatonton, Ga.

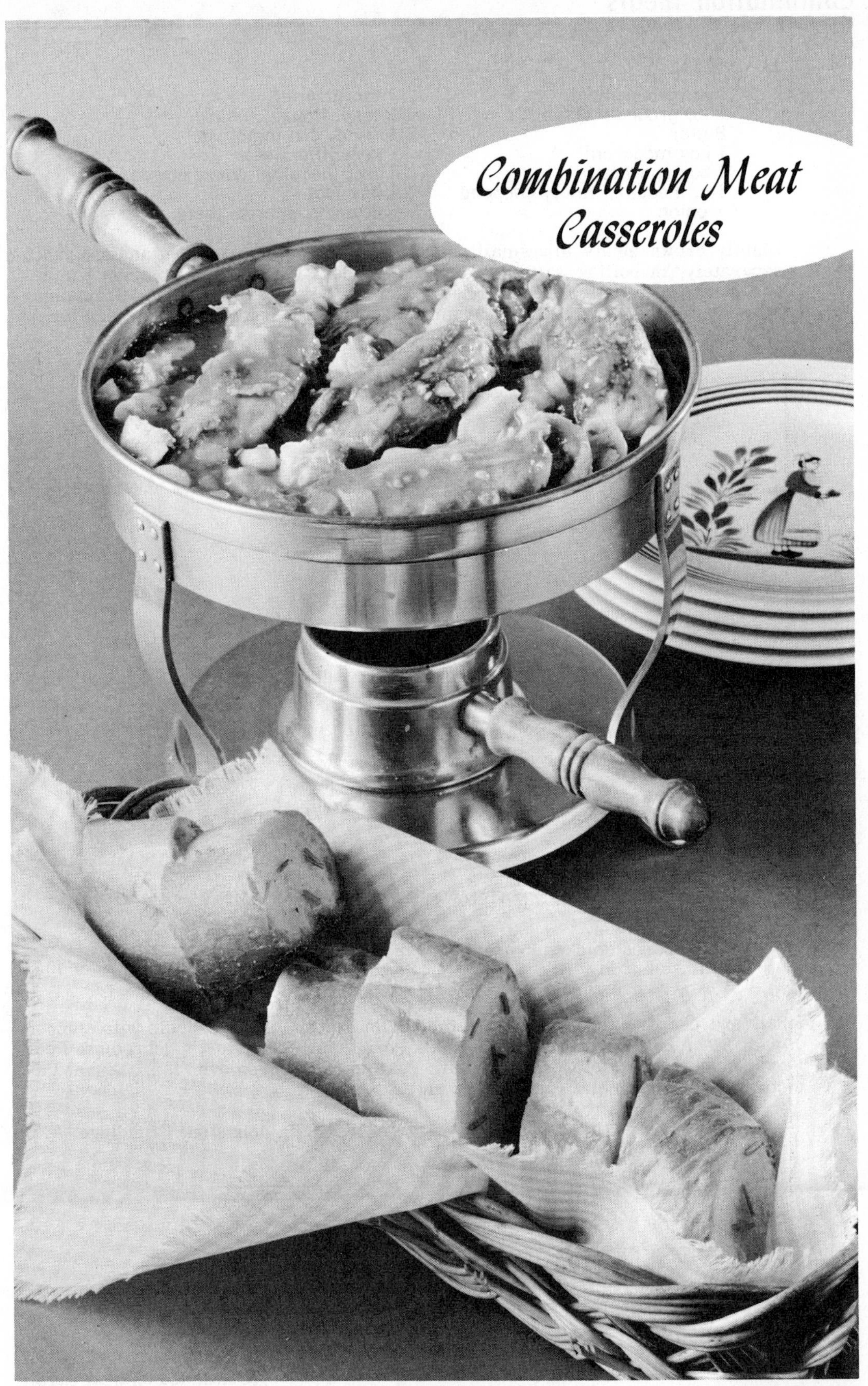
Combination Meat
Casseroles

RECIPE FOR CHICKEN MARENGO ON PAGE 111

BAMMI

1 lb. ground beef
1 lb. ground lean pork
Butter
1 box macaroni
1 box spaghetti
1 c. (heaping) finely chopped onion
1 tsp. thyme
2 tbsp. flour
1 1-qt. can tomatoes
1 c. boiling water
1 tsp. (heaping) curry powder
1 bay leaf
Salt and pepper to taste

Lightly brown meats in a small amount of butter. Cook macaroni and spaghetti, separately, in boiling salted water until tender. Drain each. Combine 1 tablespoon butter, onion, thyme and flour; cook until lightly browned. Add remaining ingredients; stir in meat, macaroni and spaghetti. Bake at 350 degrees for 45 minutes. Yield: 15 servings.

Mrs. S. Y. Stribling, Clarkesville, Ga.

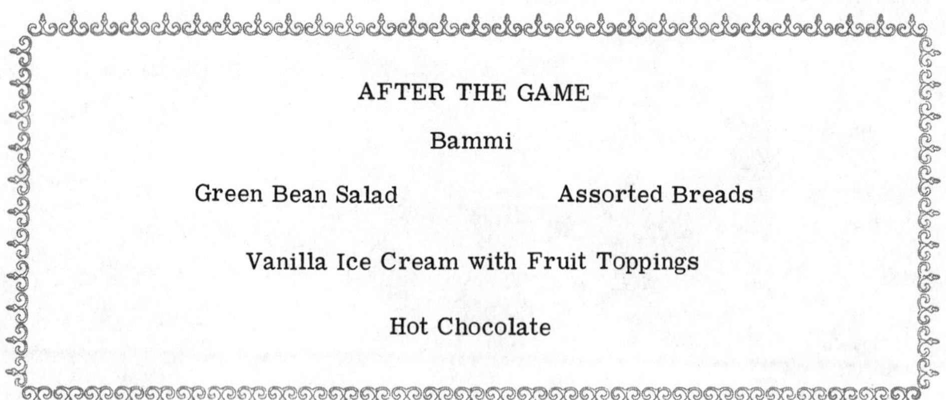

AFTER THE GAME

Bammi

Green Bean Salad | Assorted Breads

Vanilla Ice Cream with Fruit Toppings

Hot Chocolate

CHICKEN CASSEROLE

Salt and pepper
6 lge. boned chicken breasts
6 slices bacon
1 pkg. chipped beef
1 sm. can chopped mushrooms
1 carton sour cream
1 can cream of mushroom soup

Salt and pepper chicken. Wrap each piece in bacon. Line casserole with chipped beef. Place chicken breasts on top. Mix soup, sour cream and mushrooms. Pour over chicken breasts. Cover with foil. Bake in 300-degree oven for 2 hours. Uncover; bake 30 minutes. Serve over rice.

Mrs. J. D. Johnston, Brundidge, Ala.

CHICKEN CASSEROLE DIVINE

2 jars chipped beef
4 chicken breasts, boned and halved
8 strips bacon
1 can cream of mushroom soup
½ pt. sour cream
Slivered almonds, toasted

(Continued on next page)

Crumble beef into baking dish. Wrap each piece of chicken in bacon slice; place on beef. Combine soup and sour cream; pour over chicken. Sprinkle with almonds. Bake at 250 degrees for 4 hours. Yield: 8 servings.

Mrs. L. H. Rainwater, Birmingham, Ala.

CHICKEN MARENGO

2 1-lb. pkg. frozen chicken parts
1 9-oz. pkg. frozen rock lobster tails
Salt and pepper
3 tbsp. olive oil or vegetable oil
1 tbsp. butter
¾ c. frozen sliced mushrooms
¾ c. frozen chopped onions
2 tbsp. flour
½ c. dry white wine
1 8-oz. can tomato sauce
1 1-lb. can whole tomatoes
½ tsp. crumbled thyme

Partially defrost chicken and lobster tails in unopened packages, approximately 6 hours in refrigerator or 2 hours at room temperature. Remove skin from chicken breasts, if desired. Sprinkle with salt and pepper. Heat olive oil and butter in a heavy skillet. Add chicken and saute until golden brown on both sides. Remove from skillet and place in baking dish. Cover and bake in preheated 350-degree oven for 20 to 25 minutes or until tender. Add mushrooms and onions to the chicken drippings and saute until onions are soft but not browned. Blend in flour. Add wine, tomato sauce, tomatoes, 1 teaspoon salt and thyme. Cover and simmer for 15 minutes. Cook lobster tails according to package directions. Remove lobster meat from shells and cut into bite-sized pieces. Add to tomato sauce and simmer 5 minutes or until lobster is heated. Place chicken breasts in chafing dish or on a platter and pour sauce over them. Accompany with rice and crusty French bread. Yield: 6-8 servings.

Photograph for this recipe on page 109.

CHICKEN SUPREME

6 chicken breasts
1 can cream of mushroom soup
6 slices boiled ham
6 thick slices fresh tomatoes
Salt and pepper
1 c. crushed cornflakes

Place chicken breasts in baking pan. Mix soup as directed on can; pour over chicken. Cover and bake at 350 degrees for 45 minutes. Remove from oven; cover each piece chicken with a slice of ham. Top with tomato slice. Sprinkle generously with salt and pepper. Top with cornflakes. Bake, uncovered, for 45 minutes longer. Yield: 6 servings.

Hursie M. Stockstell, Millbrook, N. C.

JALAPENO-HAMBURGER PIE

1 lb. ground beef
½ lb. ground pork
1 tbsp. oil
1 c. chopped bell pepper
1 c. chopped celery
1 c. chopped onion
1 ½ tsp. salt
1 tbsp. parsley
2 tbsp. barbecue sauce
Dash of pepper

(Continued on next page)

Brown meats in oil; stir in remaining ingredients. Keep warm.

CORN BREAD TOPPINGS:

2 eggs, beaten
1 c. milk
1 ½ c. cornbread mix
¼ c. flour
¼ c. cooking oil
4 tsp. sugar
1 med. onion, chopped
1 c. grated sharp cheddar cheese
1 6-oz. can jalapeno peppers ground or finely, chopped
1 can cream-style corn

Combine all ingredients; blend well. Pour over meat mixture. Bake at 350 degrees for 1 hour. Yield: 8 servings.

Robin Ann Lester, Lewisville, Tex.

MEAT CASSEROLE

1 green pepper, chopped
1 onion, chopped
½ lb. beef
½ lb. pork
1 c. macaroni
1 can corn
1 can chicken rice soup
1 c. buttered bread crumbs

Cook pepper and onion until tender; add meat and brown. Cook macaroni according to package directions. Combine meat mixture, macaroni, corn and soup; pour into casserole. Cover with bread crumbs; bake at 375 degrees for 15 minutes or until bread crumbs are brown. Yield: 8-10 servings.

Mrs. Ermine Ritchie, Carlisle, Ky.

JOHNNY MARZETTI

2 c. chopped green peppers
1 c. chopped celery
1 c. chopped onions
1 lb. ground beef
1 lb. ground pork
1 c. margarine
2 tsp. salt
½ c. chopped stuffed olives
1 4-oz. can sliced mushrooms
1 10 ½-oz. can tomato soup
1 8-oz. can tomato sauce
1 8-oz. can meatless tomato-mushroom sauce
½ lb. med. noodles
2 c. grated American cheese

Saute green peppers, celery, onions and ground meats in hot margarine in a large skillet. Add salt. Reduce heat; cook for 5 minutes. Add olives, mushrooms and liquid, soup and sauces; mix well. Cook for 5 minutes. Cook noodles according to directions on box; drain. Place noodles in a 14 x 10 x 2-inch roasting pan; add sauce, stirring gently until well mixed. Sprinkle grated cheese on top. Bake at 350 degrees for 35 minutes. Yield: 10 servings.

Mrs. V. A. Coltes, Portsmouth, Va.

MEXICAN CASSEROLE

2 lb. ground steak
½ lb. cured ham, ground
2 cans tomato paste
1 can Shoe Peg corn
1 can mushrooms
1 can pimento
1 lge. onion, chopped
1 clove of garlic, minced
1 green pepper, chopped
¼ bottle hot sauce
1 lb. wide noodles
Grated cheddar cheese

(Continued on next page)

Simmer steak and ham in hot grease until brown. Cook all remaining ingredients, except noodles and cheese, until onion and pepper are done; add meat mixture. Cook noodles in salted water until tender. Drain. Place a layer of noodles in casserole; add a layer of sauce and a layer of grated cheese. Repeat layers. Heat at 350 degrees until heated through. Yield: 8 servings.

Mrs. Mildred B. Keener, Maiden, N. C.

LASAGNA EN CASSEROLE

2 tbsp. olive oil
½ lb. ground beef
½ lb. ground sausage
1 med. onion, chopped
1 clove of garlic, minced
1 tbsp. chopped parsley
1 ¼ c. tomato paste
¼ tsp. oregano
2 c. water
1 tsp. salt
14 wide lasagna strips
1 lb. mozzarella cheese, thinly sliced
¾ lb. ricotta cheese
4 tbsp. grated Parmesan cheese

Heat oil; add beef, sausage, onion, garlic and parsley. Stir and cook until meat is broken up in small pieces and browned. Add tomato paste, oregano, water and salt. Cover and simmer over low heat 1 hour and 30 minutes. Cook lasagna according to directions on package or until tender. Drain. Place alternate layers of lasagna, sauce, mozzarella cheese and ricotta cheese in a well-oiled 3-quart baking pan. Repeat 2 or 3 times. Sprinkle top with Parmesan cheese. Bake at 375 degrees 20 to 25 minutes or until the top is browned. Yield: 4-6 servings.

Mrs. J. V. Blankmeyer, Tampa, Fla.

MARZETTI

¾ c. finely chopped celery
½ c. melted butter or margarine
1 c. minced onions
¾ c. minced green pepper
1 lb. ground chuck
1 lb. ground pork
1 ½ tsp. salt
½ tsp. pepper
12 oz. noodles
1 4-oz. can sliced mushrooms, undrained
2 10 ½-oz. cans condensed tomato soup, undiluted
Grated Parmesan cheese

(Continued on next page)

In water to cover, cook celery until tender; drain and reserve. In 1/4 cup butter, saute onions, green pepper 5 minutes; stir in chuck, pork, salt and pepper. Cook, uncovered, until meat loses its red color. Cook noodles as package directs; drain and rinse. Turn into 3-quart casserole; toss with remaining butter; stir in meat mixture, celery, mushrooms and tomato soup; mix well. Sprinkle with Parmesan cheese; cover. Refrigerate for several hours. Bake, uncovered, at 400 degrees for 1 hour and 15 minutes.

Coby Thompson, Nashville, Tenn.

PORK AND BEEF CASSEROLE

- ½ lb. lean pork
- ½ lb. ground beef
- 1 lge. onion, chopped
- 1 clove garlic
- 1 sm. green pepper, finely chopped
- 1 No. 2 can tomatoes
- Salt and pepper to taste
- Chili powder to taste
- 1 lb. rat cheese, grated
- 1 8-oz. pkg. fine noodles, cooked

Brown meat, onion, garlic and green pepper; add tomatoes. Cook until done; add salt, pepper, chili powder and two-thirds of cheese. Pour noodles in buttered baking dish; top with meat mixture. Sprinkle with remaining cheese; let set 2 hours. Bake, covered, at 300 degrees for 45 minutes. Yield: 6 servings.

Mrs. Herman Whitson, Fort Smith, Ark.

PORK AND VEAL CASSEROLE

- 1 lb. pork, cubed
- 1 lb. veal, cubed
- 1 sm. onion, diced
- 1 sm. green pepper, diced
- 1 sm. can mushrooms
- Pepper and salt to taste
- 2 c. water
- 1 10 ½-oz. can mushroom soup
- 1 c. sour cream
- 1 8-oz. pkg. wide noodles, cooked
- ½ lb. buttered bread crumbs

Brown meat; add onion, pepper, mushrooms with liquid and seasonings. Cover with water; cook slowly for 1 hour and 30 minutes. Add mushroom soup, sour cream and noodles; put in casserole. Top with buttered crumbs; bake in 350 degree oven for 30 minutes.

Mrs. Harry W. Vogt, St. Petersburg, Fla.

SUPPER DISH

- 1 ½ lb. pork steak, cut in cubes
- 1 ½ lb. veal, cut in cubes
- 1 pkg. fine noodles
- 1 can chicken-noodle soup
- 1 lge. green pepper, chopped
- Salt to taste
- ¼ lb. (about) mild cheese, grated
- 1 sm. can pimento, diced
- 1 No. 2 ½ can corn
- Cracker crumbs

(Continued on next page)

Boil meats in water to cover for 45 minutes. Add noodles, soup and chopped pepper. Cook for 20 minutes. Add grated cheese and pimento. Place in a buttered baking dish. Place corn on top; sprinkle with cracker crumbs. Bake 30 to 45 minutes at 350 degrees. Yield: 10 servings.

Mrs. Walter J. Peterson, Raleigh, N. C.

CHICKEN CRUNCH

½ c. chicken broth or milk
2 10 ½-oz. cans mushroom soup
1 7-oz. can tuna, drained and flaked
3 c. diced, cooked chicken
¼ c. minced onion
1 c. diced celery
1 5-oz. can water chestnuts, sliced thin
1 3-oz. can chow mein noodles
⅓ c. toasted almonds (opt.)

Blend broth into soup in 2-quart casserole. Mix in remaining ingredients except almonds. Bake at 325 degrees for 40 minutes. Just before serving, sprinkle with almonds which have been slightly toasted. Yield: 8 servings.

Mrs. Grace L. Kearns, Lexington, Ky.

CHICKEN CRUNCH

2 cans cream of mushroom soup
½ c. chicken broth
2 ¼ soup cans milk
3 c. diced chicken
1 can tuna
¼ c. minced onion
½ c. diced celery
1 can diced water chestnuts
1 lge. or 2 sm. cans chow mein noodles
⅓ c. slivered almonds

Dilute soup with chicken broth and 2 1/4 soup cans milk. Combine all other ingredients, reserving almonds for top. Bake 30 to 35 minutes at 350 degrees. Yield: 10-12 servings.

Mrs. Darley Caudill, Leander, Ky.

COMPANY'S CASSEROLE

¾ lb. ground beef
¼ lb. ground pork
4 med. onions, chopped
2 c. finely chopped celery
1 can cream of mushroom soup
1 can tomato soup
1 ¼ c. water
Salt and pepper to taste
1 tsp. chili powder
2 c. chow mein noodles

Brown meats. Add onions and celery; cook until vegetables are transparent. Mix in remaining ingredients except 1/4 cup noodles. Pour into greased casserole; top with crushed noodles. Bake at 350 degrees for 45 minutes. Yield: 6 servings.

Mrs. Walter Meek, Clarksville, Ark.

PENNY-WISE CASSEROLE

1 lb. hamburger
½ lb. ground pork
1 onion, chopped
1 green pepper, chopped
Water
1 c. cooked macaroni
1 can cream-style corn
1 can chicken soup
½ c. bread crumbs

Mix hamburger and pork; cook slowly in skillet until done. Drain off grease. Add onion and pepper; add a little water. Cook until almost done. Mix all ingredients except bread crumbs in large casserole. Sprinkle crumbs on top. Bake in 350-degree oven for 45 minutes. Yield: 12 servings.

Spug Garmon, Greenville, Ky.

CASSEROLE OF TURKEY WITH RICE

2 med. onions, chopped
Butter
½ lb. sliced mushrooms
2 c. diced cold turkey
½ c. diced ham
1 c. crumbled leftover stuffing
2 tbsp. chopped parsley
Pinch of thyme
Salt and freshly ground black pepper to taste
1 tbsp. curry powder
1 c. rice
2 c. hot turkey or chicken broth

Saute onions in butter until just tender. Add mushrooms; saute for 2 minutes. Combine in casserole with turkey, ham, stuffing, parsley, thyme, salt and pepper. Add an additional tablespoon of butter and the curry powder to skillet used for sauteing the onions and lightly saute rice. Add to mixture in a preheated 375-degree oven. Cook until the rice is tender and liquid is absorbed. Add more heated broth, if necessary. Yield: 4-6 servings.

Mrs. Bruce Wallace, Asheville, N. C.

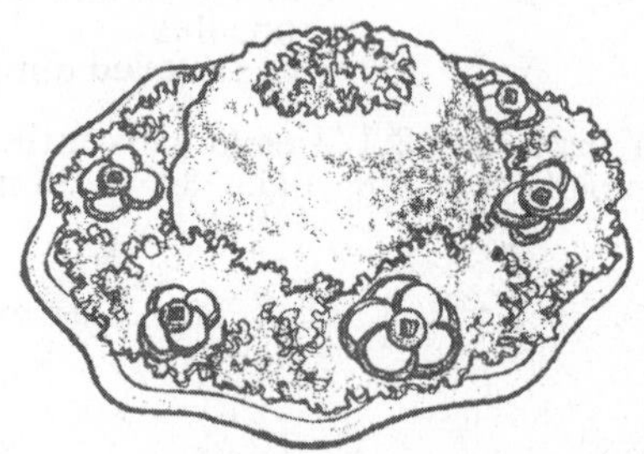

CHICKEN-RICE CASSEROLE

1 4-oz. pkg. dried beef
6 slices bacon
6 halves chicken breast, boned
Black pepper (opt.)
1 can cream of mushroom soup
1 c. sour cream
1 c. cooked rice

Place dried beef in shallow greased casserole. Wrap a slice of bacon around each half of chicken breast; place on top of beef. Sprinkle with black pepper. Blend undiluted soup with sour cream and rice. Pour over chicken. Bake at 275 degrees for 3 hours.

Mrs. Robert A. Sell, Winston-Salem, N. C.

Atop Lookout Mountain, Chattanooga, Tennessee.

CHICKEN AND RICE CASSEROLE

1 3 to 4-lb. chicken
Celery
Whole onion
Salt
1 pkg. white and wild rice, mixed
2 med. onions, chopped
Sausage drippings
½ lb. hot sausage, browned and crumbled
2 cans undiluted mushroom soup
1 c. or more of buttered bread crumbs

Cook chicken with celery, whole onion and salt until tender; cool. Cook rice according to box directions, using chicken stock instead of water; do not add butter. Saute chopped onions in sausage drippings. Combine onions, sausage and soup. Place in bottom of greased casserole; top with chunks of chicken. Put rice on top; cover heavily with bread crumbs. Bake at 350 degrees, uncovered, for 30 minutes. Casserole may be made ahead of time and frozen. Yield: 6 servings.

Mrs. J. D. Johnston, Brundidge, Ala.

CHICKEN-SAUSAGE CASSEROLE

1 ½ lb. mild sausage
2 sm. packages yellow rice, cooked
2 cans cream of mushroom soup
½ c. milk
1 lge. can mushrooms, undrained
1 3-lb. chicken, cooked and boned
Buttered bread crumbs

Fry sausage, breaking into pieces. Combine with remaining ingredients except chicken and bread crumbs. Place 1/2 of mixture in greased casserole; cover the chicken. Top with remaining sausage mixture. Sprinkle with bread crumbs. Bake at 350 degrees for 30 to 35 minutes.

Louise W. Peck, Fayetteville, Tenn.

SHRIMP JAMBALAYA

1 c. sliced celery
2 c. diced green peppers
2 med. onions, thinly sliced
4 tbsp. butter or margarine
1 or 2 cloves of garlic
1 lb. boiled ham, minced
2 lb. shrimp, cleaned
1 ½ tsp. salt
¼ tsp. pepper sauce
½ tsp. chili powder
1 tsp. sugar
2 1-lb. cans tomatoes
3 c. cooked rice

Cook celery, green peppers and onions in 2 tablespoonfuls butter until tender. Add garlic and ham. Cook for 5 minutes. Add remaining ingredients except tomatoes and rice. Cook, stirring frequently, until shrimp are pink. Add tomatoes; heat. Stir in rice.

Maude B. Fordham, Cochran, Ga.

SAVORY MEATBALL CASSEROLE

1 lb. ground beef
¼ lb. pork sausage
½ c. dry bread crumbs
1 ⅔ c. evaporated milk
2 tbsp. chopped onion
1 ½ tsp. chili powder
⅛ tsp. pepper
1 can cream of mushroom soup
1 can cream of celery soup
½ c. water
1 ½ c. flour
3 tsp. baking powder
¼ tsp. salt
⅓ c. shortening
1 egg
1 ½ c. shredded American cheese

Combine meats, crumbs, 1/3 cup milk, onion, 1 teaspoonful chili powder and pepper. Shape into balls and brown. Cook, covered, for 10 minutes. Place in 2 1/2-quart casserole. Combine soups, 1 cup milk and water. Heat until steaming. Pour over meatballs. Sift flour with baking powder, 1/2 teaspoonful chili powder and salt. Cut in shortening until particles are fine. Combine egg with 1/3 cup milk. Add dry ingredients. Roll 12-inch square. Sprinkle with shredded cheese. Roll up and cut into slices. Place on top of casserole. Bake at 400 degrees for 20 to 25 minutes.

Mrs. R. E. Pauschert, Hickory Ridge, Ark.

SCALLOPED CHICKEN AND OYSTERS

1 sm. hen, cooked
Saltine crackers, coarsely crushed
Butter
Salt and pepper to taste
2 lb. fresh mushrooms
4 ½ doz. lge. oysters
Milk

Remove chicken from bones; cut in bite-sized pieces. Remove fat from top of broth. Put layer of crackers in casserole. Dot generously with butter; sprinkle with salt and pepper. Add chicken; cover with sliced mushrooms. Sprinkle with salt and pepper. Add layer of crumbs; dot with butter. Add oysters, sprinkled with salt and pepper. Top with crumbs and butter. Mix equal parts of chicken

(Continued on next page)

broth and milk. Pour in enough liquid to almost cover casserole. Bake, uncovered, at 400 degrees for 45 minutes. Turn heat to 500 degrees for 5 minutes for final browning. Yield: 8 servings.

Mrs. John P. Norman, West Point, Ga.

CHICKEN AND SEAFOOD TETRAZZINI

1 4-lb. hen, cooked and boned
1 pkg. spaghetti
Broth
1 sm. onion, chopped
1 clove garlic
Bacon drippings
1 can oysters, drained
1 to 2 lb. boiled cleaned shrimp
1 can crab meat
1 can mushroom soup
1 can tomato soup
1 tbsp. Worcestershire sauce
Sharp cheese, grated

Cut chicken in small pieces. Cook spaghetti in broth. Saute onion and garlic in bacon drippings; add oysters, cooking until oysters curl. Combine chicken and oyster mixture with remaining ingredients except cheese. Top with cheese; bake for 45 minutes or until hot. Serve with spaghetti. Yield: 12 servings.

Mrs. Malcolm Sevier, Tallulah, La.

MEAT-SPAGHETTI CASSEROLE

1 lb. ground beef
½ lb. ground lean pork
1 c. diced onions
2 c. diced celery
½ lb. thin spaghetti, broken
1 c. sharp cheese, cubed
1 4-oz. can mushrooms
1 can tomato soup
Salt and pepper to taste

Cook ground meats in frying pan, stirring and breaking apart. Add onions and celery; continue to cook until onions and celery are soft. Cook spaghetti in salted boiling water until almost done; drain. Add meat mixture, cheese, mushrooms, soup and seasonings; mix thoroughly. Turn into large casserole. Bake at 350 degrees for 30 to 40 minutes. Yield: 6-8 servings.

Mrs. Roland P. Matchett, Covington, Ky.

MORE

1 med. onion, chopped
Fat
2 lb. ground beef
¾ lb. ground pork
Salt and pepper
¾ lb. spaghetti, cooked
1 No. 2 ½ can tomatoes
1 No. 2 can English peas
1 No. 2 can whole kernel corn
1 tall can ripe olives
1 sm. can pimento, finely cut
½ lb. grated American cheese

Brown onion in hot fat; add meat and seasonings. Cook until done. Combine meat and remaining ingredients except cheese; season to taste. Place in large flat pan; top with cheese. Bake at 350 degrees for 30 minutes. Yield: 16 servings.

Eunice Grisham, Dermott, Ark.

MORE CASSEROLE

2 lb. ground beef
½ lb. sausage
1 lge. onion, chopped
1 lb. cooked spaghetti
1 No. 2 can whole kernel corn, drained
1 No. 2 can peas, drained
1 can sliced ripe olives
1 can diced pimentos
1 can cream of mushroom soup
1 soup can water
2 cans tomato soup
Grated cheese

Brown meats; add onion and continue to cook until onion is tender. Mix all ingredients together except cheese. Pour into large casserole. Cover with grated cheese. Bake at 275 degrees 1 hour. Yield: 8 servings.

Mrs. Charles W. Bryant, North Little Rock, Ark.

MY FAVORITE CASSEROLE

1 lb. ground chuck
¼ lb. ground pork
1 tbsp. butter
1 med. onion, minced
1 ½ c. uncooked spaghetti
1 No. 2 can tomato juice
1 buffet can peas
1 can pimento, chopped
1 can pitted ripe olives
1 c. grated cheddar cheese

Have meats ground together. Melt butter in heavy pan; lightly brown minced onion. Add meat and cook until pink color disappears, stirring constantly. Cook spaghetti in boiling salted water until tender; drain. Combine spaghetti, meat, tomato juice, peas, pimentos, olives and 1/2 of shredded cheese. Blend lightly; turn into a 2-quart casserole. Sprinkle remaining cheese over top. Bake in 400-degree oven about 20 minutes or until cheese is melted. Yield: 6-8 servings.

Mrs. Naomi H. Doosing, Cuero, Tex.

UPSIDE-DOWN HAM LOAF

½ c. brown sugar
2 tbsp. pineapple syrup
1 No. 2 can sliced pineapple, drained
Maraschino cherries
Whole cloves
1 ½ lb. ground smoked ham
1 lb. ground veal
¾ c. cracker crumbs
⅓ c. chopped onion
1 tsp. dry mustard
2 eggs, beaten
1 c. milk

Mix brown sugar and pineapple syrup; pour into a greased 6 x 9 x 1/2-inch loaf pan. Place pineapple slices in syrup. Stick a clove in each cherry; place cherries in center of each pineapple slice. Combine remaining ingredients; press carefully but firmly over pineapple. Bake at 350 degrees for 1 hour and 15 minutes. Unmold on platter; garnish with remaining pineapple and cherries. Yield: 8 servings.

Mrs. Harold D. Combs, Mount Dora, Fla.

VEAL ROLL-UPS

Seasoning to taste
6 veal cutlets
6 thin slices turkey, chicken or ham sandwich meat
6 thin slices American cheese
1 can cream of mushroom soup, diluted

(Continued on next page)

Season veal cutlets; top each with slice of turkey and cheese. Roll up; fasten with toothpicks. Brown rolls slightly in margarine; place in baking dish. Pour in diluted soup. Bake at 325 degrees for 30 minutes. Garnish with mushrooms. Yield: 6 servings.

Mrs. Jack E. Browder, Cleburn, Tex.

ACAPULCO TAMALE PIE

¼ lb. bulk pork sausage
1 lb. ground lean beef
1 c. onions, diced fine
½ c. chopped celery
½ c. green pepper, diced fine
2 ½ c. sieved tomatoes
1 ½ c. whole kernel corn, drained
2 tsp. chili powder
1 tsp. salt
¼ tsp. black pepper
½ c. yellow cornmeal
1 c. sliced ripe olives

Place sausage in large skillet; add 2 tablespoons cold water. Cover and cook slowly for 10 minutes. Pour off fat. Add ground meat and brown over medium heat. When meat begins to brown, add onions, celery and green pepper. Cook slowly until vegetables are soft. Mix in tomatoes, corn, chili powder, salt and black pepper. Cover skillet; simmer for 15 minutes. Mix in separate bowl, 1 cup cold water and cornmeal; blend gradually into meat mixture. Cook until thickens. Mix in olives. Turn into 2-quart greased baking dish. Bake at 350 degrees until done.

Mrs. R. J. Reynolds, La Marque, Tex.

BAKED SAUERKRAUT

1 lb. hamburger
¼ lb. sausage
2 tbsp. flour
¼ c. chopped onion
1 egg
Salt and pepper to taste
3 tbsp. fat
2 c. sauerkraut
¼ c. catsup

Combine meats, flour, onion, egg and seasonings; brown in fat. Alternate layers of sauerkraut with meat mixture. Dot with catsup. Bake at 350 degrees for 1 hour. Yield: 6 servings.

Lourrine Lance, Mena, Ark.

FRIENDLY CLASS CASSEROLE

½ lb. veal
½ lb. beef
1 can tomato soup
1 c. milk
Onions, sliced
Green pepper, chopped
Potatoes, sliced
Potato chips or corn flakes

Combine veal and beef; add enough soup and milk mixture to soften meat. Place in baking dish. Layer onions, green pepper and sliced potatoes over meat. Cover with remaining soup mixture. Top with crumbled potato chips. Bake 2 hours at 350 degrees. Yield: 6 servings.

Mrs. C. A. J. Richards, Lakeland, Fla.

CLAM BAKE CASSEROLE

18 ears sweet corn
4 3-lb. chickens, quartered
12 med. sweet potatoes
Salt to taste
2 bunches celery
½ lb. butter, cut into sm. pieces
3 qt. hot water
4 doz. clams, well scrubbed

Husk corn, reserving husks. Place chickens on rack in bottom of electric roaster. Place potatoes on top of chicken; place corn on top of potatoes. Sprinkle each layer with salt. Split outer stalks of celery and lay on top. Dot with butter. Cover with inner husks; add water. Bake at 350 degrees for 1 hour and 15 minutes. Open roaster and add clams. Bake at 325 degrees for 1 hour and 15 minutes longer, keeping vent closed at all times. Yield: 8-10 servings.

Mrs. Dempsey Carnes, Osteen, Fla.

GROUND MEAT AND EGGPLANT CASSEROLE

2 lge. eggplants
1 lb. ground beef
Fat
1 lge. onion, chopped
2 cloves of garlic, chopped
⅓ c. chopped green pepper
4 oz. chicken liver, chopped
1 tbsp. parsley
½ c. bread crumbs or 1 c. cooked rice
Salt and pepper to taste
Butter

Peel eggplants; cut into 1-inch cubes. Brown ground meat in small amount of fat. Add onion, garlic and green pepper; saute. Add eggplants; cook over low heat until eggplants are tender. Add liver; cook for 5 minutes. Add parsley, bread crumbs, salt and pepper. Place in baking dish; cover with bread crumbs and dot with butter. Bake at 375 degrees for about 20 minutes. Yield: 4 servings.

Mrs. W. J. Griffin, Thibodaux, La.

KENTUCKY BURGOO

1 chicken breast, boned and cut into 6 pieces
3 tbsp. flour
2 tsp. salt
½ tsp. pepper
¼ c. cooking oil or shortening
2 lb. round steak, cubed
2 med. onions, chopped
2 c. water
2 1-lb. cans tomatoes
1 bay leaf
1 tbsp. chopped garlic
3 oz. bourbon whiskey (opt.)
6 med. carrots
12 sm. onions
4 c. shredded cabbage
2 c. fresh or frozen corn kernels

Coat chicken in mixture of flour, salt and pepper; brown in oil or shortening in heavy Dutch oven. Remove chicken. Coat meat with remaining flour mixture; cook in fat remaining in oven until well browned on all sides. Add chopped onions; cook until onions are browned, stirring occasionally. Add water, tomatoes, bay leaf, garlic and whiskey; bring to a boil. Cover; reduce heat to low and simmer for 1 hour. Add chicken, carrots and small onions; simmer for 30 minutes. Add cabbage and corn; simmer for 15 minutes longer. Correct seasoning to taste. Serve with bread and butter sandwiches. Yield: 6 servings.

Photograph for this recipe on frontispiece.

MARINA CAY CASSEROLE

1 lb. ground beef
½ lb. ground pork
4 med. onions, chopped
1 clove of garlic, crushed
Cooking oil
1 1-lb. 12-oz. can tomatoes
1 6-oz. can tomato paste
1 can French-style green beans, undrained
1 c. red wine
½ c. raisins
½ c. sliced stuffed olives
2 tbsp. capers
1 ½ tsp. salt
⅛ tsp. pepper
4 ripe plantains or bananas, sliced lengthwise
4 eggs

Fry meats until brown. Cook onions and garlic in 3 tablespoons cooking oil until golden. Add meat and next 9 ingredients. Fry plantains in 1/2 cup cooking oil until tender and golden. Drain on paper towel. Arrange alternate layers of meat mixture and plantains in 3-quart casserole, ending with meat sauce. Beat eggs; pour over meat sauce. Bake at 350 degrees for 30 minutes. May be served with rice. Yield: 10 servings.
PERSONAL COMMENT: This recipe is popular in the Bahamas.

Kathryn L. Carlin, Miami Beach, Florida

MEATBALLS AND VEGETABLE CASSEROLE

½ lb. ground beef
½ lb. ground veal
½ lb. ground fresh pork
1 ½ tsp. salt
⅛ tsp. pepper
½ sm. onion, minced
½ c. applesauce
½ c. bread crumbs
2 egg yolks
2 c. canned tomatoes
Flour
2 tbsp. fat
4 med. potatoes, diced
1 sm. carrot, diced
½ sm. onion, minced
1 stalk celery, minced
1 green pepper, minced

Mix first 9 ingredients thoroughly and shape into balls. Roll in flour and brown in fat. Place in casserole. To drippings in frying pan, add remaining ingredients. Bring to a boil; pour over meatballs. Bake at 350 degrees for 45 minutes.

Jane S. Scates, Florence, Ala.

MEAT-VEGETABLE COMBINATION DISH

1 lb. ground beef
½ lb. pork sausage
1 med. onion, chopped
3 tsp. salt
1 ½ tsp. black pepper
1 c. catsup
½ c. barbecue sauce
2 qt. cooked vegetables
8 med. potatoes
1 tsp. paprika

(Continued on next page)

Combine meats, onion, 1 teaspoon salt and 1/2 teaspoon pepper in large skillet. Cook until slightly brown. Add catsup and barbecue sauce; mix well and cook until meat is tender. Combine meats and vegetables in large baking pan; top with mashed potatoes that have been seasoned with remaining salt and pepper. Sprinkle paprika on top. Bake at 425 degrees for 15 minutes or until potatoes are slightly brown. Biscuits may be used in place of mashed potatoes. Yield: 10-12 servings.

Sallie M. Bradbury, Moseley, Va.

PORK AND CHICKEN CASSEROLE

4 center-cut pork chops
4 chicken thighs
Salt and pepper
Parsley flakes
4 med. potatoes, peeled and quartered
2 med. onions, sliced
3 lge. stalks celery, chopped
2 cans tomato soup
½ c. water

Place meats in greased casserole. Sprinkle with salt, pepper and parsley flakes. Layer over meats potatoes, onions and celery. Cover with soup and water. Cover with foil. Bake at 350 degrees for 1 hour and 30 minutes. Uncover last 30 minutes of cooking. Yield: 4 servings.

Eva Wiggins, Martinsville, Va.

SHANGHAI CASSEROLE

¾ c. thinly sliced onions
2 tbsp. oil
½ lb. boneless pork, cut in thin strips
½ lb. boneless veal, cut in thin strips
3 tbsp. soy sauce
½ tsp. onion salt
¼ tsp. monosodium glutamate
1 c. hot water
1 ½ c. diced celery
1 4-oz. can mushrooms, undrained
1 No. 2 can mixed chow mein vegetables
2 tbsp. cornstarch
3 tbsp. cold water

Saute onions in oil till golden; remove to small bowl and reserve. Brown pork and add soy sauce, onion salt and monosodium glutamate. Pour hot water over meat. Cover and simmer 30 to 45 minutes. Add celery; simmer 15 minutes. Add mushrooms, mixed vegetables and juice and browned onions, reserving 1 tablespoon for topping. Combine cornstarch and water. Add to meat mixture, stirring constantly. Pour in 2-quart casserole. Keep warm in 300-degree oven.

BISCUIT TOPPING:

1 c. flour
1 ½ tsp. baking powder
½ tsp. salt
1 tsp. celery seed
¼ c. shortening
1 egg, slightly beaten
½ c. milk

Sift together flour, baking powder and salt; add celery seed. Cut in shortening. Blend in reserved onions. Add slightly beaten egg and milk. Mix and drop by teaspoonfuls onto hot mixture. Bake at 400 degrees 20 to 25 minutes. Serve hot. Yield: 4-6 servings.

Mrs. Fred L. Myers, Waco, Tex.

Ground Beef Casseroles

RECIPE FOR CHEESE POLENTA ON PAGE 126

CHEESE POLENTA

1 c. farina or cornmeal
1 qt. hot milk
2 tsp. butter
1 tsp. salt
1 egg, beaten
1 c. shredded sharp American cheese

Slowly add farina to hot milk, stirring constantly. Add butter and salt and cook in double boiler, stirring occasionally for 15 to 20 minutes or until mixture is thickened. Add beaten egg and cheese, stirring to blend and pour into a buttered 8-inch square baking dish. Chill until firm.

SAUCE:

½ c. finely chopped onion
1 clove garlic, minced
1 tbsp. butter
½ lb. ground beef
1 c. sliced fresh mushrooms
½ tsp. salt
1 No. 303 can tomatoes
1 6-oz. can tomato paste
1 tsp. sugar
½ tsp. oregano
1 c. shredded sharp American cheese

Cook onion and garlic in butter until transparent. Add meat and cook and stir until meat has lost its color. Add mushrooms and cook until softened; add salt, tomatoes, tomato paste and sugar. Simmer, covered for 2 hours, adding a little water if necessary. Add more salt and sugar to taste and oregano and continue to cook until flavors are blended. Cut farina mixture into small squares and arrange in shallow baking dish. Cover with sauce; sprinkle with cheese. Bake in a 325-degree oven about 15 to 20 minutes or until cheese is melted and mixture is heated thoroughly. Yield: 5-6 servings.

Photograph for this recipe on page 125.

CHILI MEATBALLS

1 lb. ground beef
⅓ c. dried bread crumbs
2 tbsp. minced onion
1 tsp. salt
1 egg
1 can tomato soup
2 tbsp. shortening
1 tsp. chili powder
¼ c. water

Combine beef with dry bread crumbs, minced onion, salt, egg and 1/4 cup tomato soup; shape into 1-inch balls. Brown in shortening. Mix remaining soup, chili powder and water; pour over meatballs. Cover; bake at 350 degrees for 30 minutes. Yield: 4-5 servings.

Julia Rowland, Gretna, Va.

CHUCKIE'S GRITS PILAF

1 onion
2 tbsp. butter
1 c. uncooked grits
1 c. ground round steak
2 c. boiling water
2 c. canned tomatoes
Salt and pepper to taste
Grated cheese

Fry sliced onion in butter until soft and yellow. Add to other ingredients. Cook mixture in covered baking dish until grits are soft, about 1 hour. Uncover; sprinkle top with grated cheese. Bake at 350 degrees until cheese is melted, brown and bubbly.

Mrs. C. R. Fernandez, New Orleans, La.

GROUND BEEF CHOW MEIN

1 sm. onion
1 c. celery, chopped
Butter
1 can tomato soup
1 can mushroom soup
Salt and pepper to taste
½ tsp. soy sauce
1 lge. can chow mein noodles
1 ½ lb. ground beef

Saute onion and celery in butter until tender. Combine with remaining ingredients, half of noodles and meat; put into greased casserole. Top with remaining noodles. Bake 1 hour in 350-degree oven. Yield: 12 servings.

Mrs. Keith D. Blayney, Birmingham, Ala.

HAMBURGER-SOUP CASSEROLE

Oleo or shortening
Onion slices
Cracker crumbs
1 lb. finely ground hamburger
1 can mushroom or cream of celery soup

Grease loaf pan well with oleo. Cover bottom with onion slices and crumbs. Place hamburger in middle of pan; pour soup over all. Top with finely crushed cracker crumbs. Bake 45 minutes in 375-degree oven.

Mrs. Webster L. Simmons, Culpeper, Va.

BEEF AND MACARONI

1 lb. ground beef
1 lge. onion, chopped
1 box elbow macaroni, cooked
1 c. catsup
2 tsp. salt
1 tsp. pepper
1 can mushroom soup
¼ lb. cheese, grated

Brown beef and onion. Pour cooked macaroni over meat. Add catsup, salt and pepper; stir. Add soup; mix thoroughly. Top with cheese. Put in 450-degree oven until cheese melts. Yield: 6 servings.

Mrs. R. L. Dunagan, White Plains, Ga.

BEEF AND MACARONI DINNER

2 med. onions, chopped
1 c. chopped green peppers
2 tbsp. fat
1 lb. ground beef
1 tsp. salt
1 tsp. garlic powder
1 tsp. chili powder
2 c. cooked macaroni
2 c. grated cheese
2 8-oz. cans tomato sauce

Cook onions and green peppers in fat. Add meat, salt, garlic powder and chili powder; brown lightly. Arrange layers of meat mixture, macaroni and grated cheese in casserole. Pour 1 can tomato sauce over casserole. Repeat layers; pour remaining tomato sauce over layers. Bake at 400 degrees for 15 to 20 minutes or until cheese melts.

Mrs. Chloe Couch, Loganville, Ga.

CATTLE CLATTER HASH

1 lb. lean ground meat
¼ c. finely cut onion (opt.)
2 tbsp. chili blend
1 tsp. salt
1 8-oz. can tomato sauce
1 sm. pkg. macaroni, cooked and drained
½ lb. grated cheddar cheese
1 can cream of mushroom or cream of chicken soup

Brown meat; push to side of skillet. Cook onion until limp, but not brown. Add chili blend, salt and tomato sauce; mix well. Cover skillet and steam for 20 minutes. Add macaroni to meat mixture. Top with grated cheese; spread soup over macaroni. Bake at 375 degrees for 30 to 40 minutes. Yield: 6 servings.

Mrs. William S. Bevers, Post, Tex.

HEARTY CASSEROLE

1 c. elbow macaroni
2 med. onions, quartered
2 qt. boiling water
1 ¼ tsp. salt
2 tbsp. butter or margarine
1 lb. ground chuck
1 sm. onion, chopped
Dash of pepper
1 c. catsup
1 ½ tsp. prepared mustard
1 tsp. oregano
½ c. grated cheddar cheese

Cook macaroni and quartered onions in boiling water with 1 teaspoon salt; drain. Heat oven to 375 degrees. In butter in skillet, saute chuck and chopped onion until meat turns gray; stir in remaining salt, pepper, catsup, mustard and oregano. Add macaroni and onion mixture. Turn into 1 1/2-quart buttered casserole; top with cheese. Bake 15 to 20 minutes until cheese is melted. Yield: 6 servings.

Mrs. Herbert W. Morgan, Memphis, Tenn.

HOT CASSEROLE

1 tbsp. shortening
1 lb. ground beef
1 c. chopped onions
1 clove garlic, minced
⅛ tsp. oregano
1 can condensed cream of vegetable soup
1 c. cooked tomatoes
¼ c. water
1 8-oz. box cooked macaroni
¼ c. shredded mild process cheese

In a skillet with shortening, brown ground beef with chopped onions, garlic and oregano; mix in vegetable soup, tomatoes, water and macaroni. Pour into 2 1/2-quart casserole; top with shredded cheese. Bake in oven at 375 degrees for 30 minutes. Yield: 4 servings.

Mrs. Walter L. Gant, Virginia Beach, Va.

JOHNNY MARZETTI CASSEROLE

1 lb. ground round
2 c. cooked lge. macaroni, drained
1 can cream of tomato soup
1 can cream of mushroom soup
1 lge. chopped onion
¾ c. grated American cheese
Dash of paprika

Cook meat in skillet until done. Place in large mixing bowl; add macaroni, soups, onion and cheese. Mix together well; place in buttered casserole. Top with additional cheese and paprika. Bake at 375 degrees for 1 hour or until onion is done. Yield: 8 servings.

Mrs. Henry D. Ward, El Paso, Tex.

MACARONI MEAL CASSEROLE

½ lb. hamburger
Salt and pepper to taste
2 stalks celery
2 med. onions
1 green pepper
2 or 3 tbsp. shortening
½ lb. shell macaroni
3 pt. water
½ lb. Velveeta cheese
1 can condensed mushroom soup

Season hamburger with salt and pepper. Slice or chop vegetables; fry in shortening until translucent. Add crumbled hamburger; fry. Cook macaroni in boiling salted water until tender. Put in greased baking dish layers of macaroni, meat, cheese and soup, topping with cheese. Bake in 350-degree oven until cheese and soup melt through mixture. Stir once or twice; serve hot. Yield: 3-4 servings.

Mrs. J. W. Rankin, Clifton Forge, Va.

MACARONI AND MEATBALL CASSEROLE

1 box packaged macaroni and cheese
Salt and pepper
1 lb. ground beef
1 can mushroom soup
1 soup can cream or evaporated milk
1 c. grated cheese

Cook macaroni according to package directions, but do not add cheese. Salt and pepper ground beef; form into small balls. Fry in small amount of oil. Place macaroni and meatballs in an oiled 2-quart casserole. Drain fat from frying pan. Heat mushroom soup, cream and cheese from macaroni in frying pan. Stir until smooth; pour over macaroni and meatballs. Mix slightly; top with grated cheese. Heat 10 minutes in 350-degree oven or about 30 minutes if mixture has been refrigerated.

Mrs. Weldon Johnson, Cookville, Tex.

PASTITSIO

1 lge. onion, chopped fine
½ lb. butter
2 lb. ground meat
½ can tomato paste
½ c. water
½ tsp. ground cinnamon
½ tsp. ground nutmeg
Salt and pepper to taste
½ c. white wine
1 lb. elbow macaroni
1 lb. grated Kefalotyri or Parmesan cheese
2 eggs, well beaten
1 c. milk

Saute onion in small amount of butter. Add ground meat; stir until brown. Add tomato paste thinned with water. Add seasoning and wine; simmer slowly until thick. Cook macaroni in boiling salted water; drain. Melt remaining butter; pour over drained macaroni, mixing carefully. Spread half of macaroni in bottom of a 9 x 13-inch pan; sprinkle generously with cheese. Spread meat sauce over bottom layer of macaroni; cover with remaining macaroni. Top with another layer of grated cheese. Over all, pour a sauce made of eggs and milk mixed well. Bake at 350 degrees for 45 minutes. Allow to cool slightly; cut in squares to serve. Yield: 12 servings.

Mrs. George Dowqwillo, Montgomery, Ala.

AMERICAN LASAGNA

1 lb. ground beef
⅓ c. chopped onion
⅓ c. chopped peppers
1 can tomato paste
1 can water
1 can tomato juice
1 tsp. oregano
½ tsp. chili powder
1 tbsp. brown sugar
1 1-lb. pkg. wide noodles
½ lb. sharp cheese, grated
1 lb. cottage cheese
Salt and pepper to taste

Brown beef; add all other ingredients except noodles and cheeses. Cook slowly 1 hour. Cook noodles until tender; drain. Alternate layers of noodles and meat sauce; sprinkle each with cheeses. Salt and pepper to taste. Sprinkle Parmesan cheese over top of casserole. Bake 30 minutes at 350 degrees. Yield: 10-12 servings.

Mrs. C. E. Frazier, Grottoes, Va.

BEEF CASSEROLE

2 lb. ground beef
2 tbsp. fat
1 tsp. salt
2 c. chopped celery
¼ c. chopped green pepper
¼ c. chopped onion
¼ c. chopped pimentos
1 can mushrooms
1 can mushroom soup
¼ c. soy sauce
1 5-oz. pkg. noodles, cooked
1 c. sour cream
½ c. water chestnuts
½ c. sliced almonds

Saute meat in fat. Add salt, celery, green pepper, onion, pimentos, mushrooms, soup and soy sauce; cover and simmer for 30 minutes. Add noodles and sour cream. Place in casserole; top with water chestnuts and almonds. Bake at 325 degrees for 30 minutes. Yield: 10 servings.

Mrs. J. W. Fox, Nunnelly, Tenn.

BEEF IN CASSEROLE

1 lb. ground beef, round or chuck
2 tsp. salt
2 tsp. sugar
1 16-oz. can tomatoes
1 8-oz. can tomato sauce
2 cloves of crushed garlic or ½ tsp. garlic puree
Pepper to taste
1 5-oz. pkg. egg noodles, cooked and drained
1 c. sour cream
1 3-oz. pkg. cream cheese
6 green onions, chopped with tops
1 c. American cheese, grated

Combine beef, salt, sugar, tomatoes, tomato sauce, garlic and pepper in skillet; cook over low heat for 5 to 10 minutes. Combine egg noodles with sour cream, softened cream cheese and green onions. In a greased 3-quart casserole, arrange meat mixture and noodle mixture in alternate layers. Top with grated American cheese. Bake in oven at 350 degrees for 35 minutes. Yield: 6-8 servings.

Mrs. Harry J. Garrett, Jr., Dallas, Tex.

BEEF-NOODLE CASSEROLE

1 lb. ground beef
2 tbsp. butter
Garlic to taste
1 tsp. salt
1 tsp. sugar
Dash of pepper

(Continued on next page)

2 8-oz. cans tomato sauce
1 7-oz. pkg. flat noodles
6 green onions
1 lge. pkg. cream cheese
1 c. sour cream
½ c. grated sharp cheese

Cook beef until crumbly in butter; add garlic, salt, sugar, pepper and tomato sauce. Cook over low heat for 15 to 20 minutes. Cook noodles according to directions on package; drain. Chop onions, including tops; mix with cream cheese and sour cream. After meat sauce and noodles have cooled, grease a 2-quart casserole; alternate layers of noodles, then layer of cheese mixture and layer of meat sauce. Repeat. Sprinkle top with cheese. Bake in 350-degree oven for 15 to 30 minutes or until cheese is bubbly.

Mrs. Lurleen B. Wallace, Governor of Alabama, Montgomery, Ala.

CHEF'S CASSEROLE

1 pkg. egg noodles
1 lb. ground beef
1 sm. chopped onion
2 tbsp. butter
1 can cream of mushroom soup
1 c. sliced ripe olives
1 tsp. garlic salt
Pepper to taste
½ lb. diced cheese
⅓ c. tomato sauce

Cook noodles in boiling water. Brown beef and onion in butter. Mix browned mixture and cooked noodles with other ingredients; place in a 2-quart casserole dish. Cover; bake 45 minutes to 1 hour at 350 degrees. To serve, top each serving with grated Parmesan cheese, if desired. Yield: 4 servings.

Mrs. Kenneth H. Arnold, Atlanta, Ga.

FOSSILANE

1 lge. onion, cut fine
1 green pepper, cut fine
1 ½ lb. ground beef
1 med. pkg. noodles
1 can tomato soup
1 lb. sharp cheese, grated
1 sm. can ripe olives, pitted
1 med. can cream-style corn

Brown onion, green pepper and meat. Cook noodles separately. Combine all ingredients; place in greased casserole. Bake at 350 degrees for 1 hour. Yield: 6 servings.

Mrs. J. Ward McPherson, Houston, Tex.

GROUND BEEF AND NOODLES CASSEROLE

1 lb. ground beef
2 tbsp. salad oil
2 med. onions, chopped
1 med. bell pepper, chopped
1 8-oz. pkg. sm. noodles
1 12-oz. can whole kernel corn
1 10-oz. can condensed tomato soup
¼ tsp. cumin
¼ tsp. oregano
¼ tsp. pepper
1 tsp. salt
6 slices bacon (opt.)
¼ lb. cheddar cheese (opt.)

(Continued on next page)

Ground Beef with Noodles

Brown ground beef in oil; add onions and bell pepper. Cook noodles according to directions on package. Add noodles, corn, tomato soup and seasoning to beef mixture. Simmer on surface unit of range at medium heat or bake at 350 degrees for 30 minutes. Bacon or grated cheese may be put on top if baked. Yield: 8-10 servings.

Mrs. Joe Henery Nuckols, Dumas, Ark.

GROUND BEEF-SOUR CREAM CASSEROLE

1 lb. ground beef
Salt and garlic salt to taste
1 tsp. sugar
2 cans tomato sauce
½ pt. sour cream
1 3-oz. pkg. cream cheese
1 5-oz. pkg. egg noodles, cooked and drained
Parmesan cheese

Brown beef. Add salt, sugar and garlic salt while browning. Add tomato sauce and simmer for 15 minutes. Mix sour cream and cream cheese; set aside. Alternate layers of noodles and ground beef mixture in a casserole. Cover with sour cream mixture. Sprinkle Parmesan cheese on top. Bake at 350 degrees for 15 minutes. Yield: 6 servings.

Mrs. John A. Henig, Montgomery, Ala.

HACIENDA HAMBURGER

¾ c. ripe olives, chopped
¾ c. diced onion
1 c. diced celery
1 c. diced American cheese
2 tbsp. vegetable oil
½ lb. ground chuck
1 clove pressed garlic
1 ½ tsp. salt
¼ tsp. pepper
1 No. 303 can tomatoes
2 c. wide noodles, uncooked

Chop olives, onion, celery and cheese; put aside. Heat oil in fryer; add meat and cook 5 minutes. Add onion and celery; cook 5 minutes more. Add garlic, salt, pepper, tomatoes and chopped ripe olives. Mix well; place in greased casserole dish over uncooked noodles. Put cheese on top; toss all together. Cover casserole; bake in 350-degree oven for 20 to 30 minutes until noodles are done and cheese melted. Yield: 6-8 servings.

Mrs. Hugh W. Sheffield, Dallas, Tex.

HAMBURGER-CHEESE BAKE

1 lb. ground beef
1 med. onion, chopped
2 8-oz. cans or 1 15-oz. can tomato sauce
1 tsp. sugar
¾ tsp. salt
¼ tsp. garlic salt
¼ tsp. pepper
4 c. uncooked med. noodles
1 c. cream-style cottage cheese
1 8-oz. pkg. cream cheese, softened
¼ c. sour cream
⅓ c. sliced green onion
¼ c. chopped green pepper
¼ c. shredded Parmesan cheese

In skillet, brown ground beef with chopped onion. Stir in tomato sauce, sugar, salt, garlic salt and pepper; remove from heat. Cook noodles according to package directions; drain. Combine cottage cheese, cream cheese, sour cream, green

(Continued on next page)

onion and green pepper. Spread half the noodles in 11 x 7 x 1/2-inch baking dish; top with a little of the meat sauce. Cover with cheese mixture. Add remaining noodles and remaining meat sauce; sprinkle with Parmesan. Bake in 350-degree oven for 30 minutes. Yield: 8-10 servings.

Mrs. C. W. Robertson, Jr., Jamestown, Tenn.

HAMBURGER-CHEESE CASSEROLE

1 lb. ground beef
2 tbsp. fat
1 green pepper
1 lge. onion
1 No. 2 can tomatoes with juice
1 can mushroom soup
1 8-oz. pkg. noodles
½ lb. cheddar cheese

Cook ground beef in fat. Add chopped green pepper, chopped onion, tomatoes and mushroom soup. Simmer about 10 minutes. Cook noodles in boiling salted water; drain. Add beef mixture; place in greased baking dish. Add cubed cheddar cheese. Bake about 10 minutes in 350-degree oven. Yield: 8 servings.

Mrs. T. A. Parrish, Morganfield, Ky.

HAMBURGER DELIGHT

1 ½ lb. ground beef
½ c. onion, chopped
½ c. green pepper
2 c. cooked tomatoes
1 c. canned whole kernel corn
3 tbsp. chili powder
Salt and pepper to taste
2 c. cooked noodles
1 ½ c. sharp cheese, grated

Brown beef, onion and green pepper; add tomatoes and corn. Simmer until thick; add chili powder and season to taste. Add noodles; put in greased casserole. Top with cheese. Bake at 350 degrees for 20 minutes. Yield: 6-8 servings.

Mrs. Frank G. Tucker, Temple, Tex.

JACKPOT CASSEROLE

1 lb. ground beef
2 tbsp. salad oil
¼ c. chopped onion
1 can tomato soup
1 ½ c. water
½ 8-oz. pkg. noodles
Salt and pepper to taste
1 No. 2 can creamed corn
¼ c. chopped ripe olives
1 c. grated American cheese

Brown meat in oil; add onion. Cook until golden. Add soup, water and noodles; cook until noodles are tender, stirring frequently. Season; add corn, olives and 1/2 cup cheese. Pour into a 2-quart casserole; sprinkle with remaining cheese. Bake in 350-degree oven for 45 minutes. Yield: 6 servings.

Ruth Carson, Clinton, Tenn.

JOHNNY MARZETTI

1 stalk celery, chopped
2 green peppers, chopped
Butter
3 lb. hamburger
½ bottle stuffed olives, sliced
1 onion, chopped
1 can tomato soup
1 can mushroom soup
1 can tomato paste
2 cans tomato sauce
1 lge. pkg. noodles, cooked

Saute celery and green peppers in butter for 15 minutes. Combine all ingredients and place in large casserole. Bake, uncovered, at 350 degrees for 1 hour. Slices of cheese can be placed on top of casserole as a topping. Yield: 16 servings.

Mrs. Frank Field, Jr., Johnson City, Tenn.

LASAGNA

1 lb. ground beef
Oil
1 clove garlic
1 med. onion, chopped
⅓ c. chopped celery
1 can tomatoes
1 can tomato paste
1 paste can water
1 pkg. sliced mozzarella cheese, cut in 1-in. sq.
1 pkg. Romano cheese, grated
Parmesan cheese
1 pkg. wide noodles, cooked

Brown beef in small amount oil; add remaining ingredients except cheeses and noodles. Place part of noodles in baking dish; layer part of mozarella, Romano and meat mixture. Repeat layers until all is used; top with Parmesan cheese. Bake at 375 degrees until casserole bubbles. Yield: 10 servings.

Mrs. Fred Spears, Smackover, Ark.

LUNCHEON CASSEROLE

1 8-oz. pkg. med. noodles
2 tbsp. butter
1 ½ lb. ground beef
1 tsp. salt
¼ tsp. pepper
¼ tsp. garlic salt
1 c. tomato sauce
1 c. creamed cottage cheese
1 c. sour cream
6 green onions, chopped
¾ c. grated sharp cheddar cheese

Cook noodles until tender in boiling salted water; drain. Melt butter in skillet; add ground beef. Cook and stir until meat loses red color. Add salt, pepper, garlic salt and tomato sauce; simmer gently 5 minutes. Remove from heat. Combine cottage cheese, sour cream, onions and noodles. Alternate layers of noodles and meat mixture in 2-quart casserole; top with grated cheese. Bake at 350 degrees for 30 minutes or until browned on top. Yield: 6-8 servings.

Mrs. R. H. Winslow, Lexington, Tenn.

NEW ORLEANS CASSEROLE

1 ½ lb. ground beef
2 med. onions, chopped fine
2 cans tomato soup
1 sm. pkg. cream cheese
2 tbsp. sugar
1 ½ tsp. salt
¼ tsp. pepper
1 tbsp. Worcestershire sauce
2 5-oz. pkg. noodles, cooked
Cornflakes or cracker crumbs

(Continued on next page)

Brown meat and onions. Add soup and cream cheese. Add seasonings. Put cooked noodles in uncovered casserole; pour meat mixture on top. Sprinkle cornflakes on top. Bake in 350-degree oven for 20 minutes. If desired, add slivered almonds on top 5 minutes before removing from oven. Yield: 12 servings.

Mrs. Avery C. Stott, Chattanooga, Tenn.

NOODLE CASSEROLE

½ lb. ground beef
1 med. bell pepper
1 sm. onion
Salt to taste
1 pkg. egg noodles
1 can mushroom soup
1 can whole kernel corn

Brown ground beef, chopped pepper and onion; add salt to taste. Cook noodles; drain well. Mix all ingredients. Bake at 300 degrees for 20 minutes.

Judy A. Fasion, Headland, Ala.

NOODLES AND CORN

1 med. onion, chopped
2 cloves garlic, chopped
1 green pepper, chopped
1 lb. ground beef
3 tbsp. oil
1 sm. can tomato sauce
1 sm. can tomato paste
1 sm. can whole kernel corn
1 sm. can mushrooms
½ lb. egg noodles, cooked
Salt and pepper to taste
1 sm. jar chopped olives
½ lb. cheese, grated

Cook onion, garlic, pepper and meat in oil until gray and moist; add remaining ingredients except olives and cheese. Pour in baking dish; top with olives and cheese. Bake at 350 degrees until cheese melts and dish is hot and bubbly. Yield: 8-10 servings.

Mrs. T. W. Burson, Fulton, Ark.

ONE-DISH DINNER

1 lb. ground round steak
3 tbsp. vegetable oil
1 ½ tsp. salt
½ tsp. pepper
¼ tsp. monosodium glutamate
1 c. chopped onion
1 c. chopped mushrooms
½ c. chopped sweet pepper
1 No. 2 can whole kernel corn
1 8-oz. pkg. med. noodles
1 c. grated American cheese
3 c. canned tomatoes

In a large skillet, cook meat in oil until meat is not pink. Add salt, pepper, monosodium glutamate, onion, mushrooms, sweet pepper and corn. Put in large serving casserole or pan. Sprinkle noodles over top; sprinkle cheese over noodles. Pour tomatoes over all. Cover; simmer 1 hour. One can chili tomatoes may be added, if desired. Yield: 8 servings.

Mrs. Travis Gordon, Chicota, Tex.

PLANTATION SUPPER

1 lb. ground steak
½ c. chopped onions
1 8-oz. pkg. flat noodles
¾ c. milk
1 can mushroom soup
1 8-oz. pkg. cream cheese
¼ c. chopped pimento
1 can whole kernel corn, drained
½ tsp. salt

Brown meat in a greased skillet; add onions. Cook meat and onions until tender. Cook noodles until done. Into noodles, stir in milk, soup, cream cheese and pimento. Combine meat and noodle mixtures; add corn and salt. Pour into a casserole. Cook 30 minutes at 350 degrees. Yield: 6 servings.

Eleanor Vickers, Jackson, Miss.

SPANISH NOODLES

1 onion, chopped
5 or 6 pieces celery, chopped
1 green pepper, chopped
2 lb. ground meat
3 tbsp. (heaping) chili powder
Salt and pepper to taste
2 cans tomatoes
1 lb. Velveeta cheese
2 pkg. egg noodles

Brown onion, celery and green pepper; add ground meat. Cook until meat is gray. Add chili powder, salt and pepper. Pour in tomatoes; add cheese and noodles. Bake at 350 degrees for 30 minutes. This casserole freezes well.

Gene Johnson, Brownfield, Tex.

TAGLIARINI

½ med. green pepper, chopped
1 med. onion, chopped
2 cloves of garlic, chopped
1 lb. ground beef
¼ lb. butter
1 qt. tomato juice
3 c. tomato sauce
1 12-oz. pkg. egg noodles
1 No. 303 can cream-style corn
Salt and pepper to taste
Mushrooms
Ripe olives
Grated sharp cheese

Saute green pepper, onion, garlic and meat in butter in large Dutch oven. Add tomato juice and sauce; bring to a boil. Add noodles; cook until tender. Add corn, seasonings, mushrooms and ripe olives. Pour into casserole; top with grated cheese. Bake at 350 degrees for 45 minutes. Yield: 10 servings.

Mrs. W. F. Delancey, Yazoo City, Miss.

TAGLIARINI CASSEROLE

1 onion, chopped
1 clove garlic, minced
1 tbsp. fat
1 ½ lb. ground beef
Salt to taste
1 c. water
1 can cream-style corn
2 c. raw noodles
1 can tomato soup

Saute onion and garlic in hot fat; add ground beef. Partially cook, stirring as meat cooks. Add salt to taste. Add remaining ingredients; mix well. Put in casserole dish. Bake at 375 degrees for 45 minutes.

Mrs. Hallie M. Dudley, Altavista, Va.

TAGLIARNI

1 med. onion, minced
1 lb. ground beef
2 tbsp. butter
1 No. 2 can tomatoes
2 c. noodles
Salt and pepper to taste
1 c. whole kernel corn
1 sm. can ripe olives (opt.)
1 c. grated cheddar or longhorn cheese

Fry onion and beef in butter, stirring, until brown. Add tomatoes, noodles, salt and pepper. Stir and cook until noodles are tender. Add corn and olives. Place in greased casserole dish; sprinkle with cheese. Bake 45 minutes in 325-degree oven. Turn off oven. Let casserole remain in oven 15 minutes. Yield: 4-6 servings.

Mrs. John Whitt, Alice, Tex.

TRUDY'S MARZETTI CASSEROLE

1 lb. ground meat
1 or 2 onions, diced
½ green pepper, diced
1 can tomato soup
½ lb. American cheese
1 can mushrooms
½ c. ripe olives, diced
½ pkg. noodles

Put meat in skillet with onions and green pepper. Cook 20 minutes; add soup and 1/2 of cheese. Cook 10 minutes; add mushrooms, olives and cooked noodles. Put in casserole; top with remaining cheese. Bake 20 minutes at 350 degrees.

Trudy Dickerson, Midland, Tex.

BABKA

PASTRY:

½ c. shortening
1 ¼ c. sifted self-rising flour
3 tbsp. milk
1 egg, beaten

Cut shortening into flour; add milk and egg. Shape into ball; wrap and chill.

FILLING:

½ lb. ground beef
⅓ c. finely chopped onion
2 tbsp. butter
1 can cream of mushroom soup
½ c. finely chopped celery
½ tsp. salt

Brown meat and onion in butter; add 3/4 can soup, celery and salt. Divide pastry in half; knead and roll out. Fill with half of meat mixture. Roll up as jelly roll. Repeat with other half of dough. Place rolls in greased pan; bake at 375 degrees for 25 minutes. Combine remaining soup with water; heat and serve over rolls.

Mrs. Bessie A. Bass, Cumberland City, Tenn.

BEEF AND CHEESE PIE

1 to 2 tbsp. fat
¾ lb. ground beef
1 8-oz. can tomato sauce
½ tsp. Worcestershire sauce
¼ tsp. salt
2 drops Tabasco sauce

Heat fat in skillet; add beef. Cook over medium heat until lightly browned, breaking into small pieces. Remove from heat; slowly blend in remaining ingredients. Simmer for 5 minutes; set aside.

(Continued on next page)

CHEESE LAYER:

1 3-oz. pkg. cream cheese, softened
1 8-in. pie shell
½ c. cottage cheese
¼ c. thick sour cream
2 tbsp. minced onion
1 tbsp. chopped green pepper
1 tbsp. chopped pimento
½ tsp. monosodium glutamate
¼ tsp. salt

Spread one-half the cream cheese in pie shell; blend remaining cheese with remaining ingredients. Spread over cream cheese in pie shell; cover with meat mixture. Bake at 425 degrees for 10 minutes. Reduce heat to 325 degrees and bake for 30 minutes longer. Yield: 6 servings.

Mrs. E. B. Goza, Kosciusko, Miss.

BURGER UPSIDE-DOWN CORN BREAD

2 tbsp. butter or margarine
1 c. minced onion
1 ½ lb. ground chuck
1 tsp. chili powder
1 tsp. salt
⅛ tsp. pepper
¼ c. sliced ripe olives
1 8-oz. can tomato puree
1 tbsp. flour
1 12-oz. pkg. corn muffin mix
1 tbsp. minced parsley

In large skillet melt butter; saute onion, about 5 minutes, until golden brown. Add beef; cook, stirring frequently, over medium heat until browned, about 5 minutes. Add chili powder, salt, pepper, olives and puree; simmer 5 minutes longer. Combine flour and 1 tablespoon water, stirring until smooth; add to meat mixture. Cook, stirring constantly, 3 minutes or until slightly thickened. Spread evenly over bottom of 9 x 9 1/2 x 1-inch pan. Prepare corn muffin mix as package directs; turn batter onto hot meat, spreading evenly. Bake in 400-degree oven 20 minutes. Invert on serving platter; garnish with parsley.

Mrs. Nell White, Miami, Fla.

CHEESE CRUSTED HAMBURGER PIE

PASTRY:

1 ½ c. sifted flour
½ tsp. salt
½ c. shortening
¾ c. shredded cheese
3 to 4 tbsp. cold water

Thoroughly blend flour, salt, shortening and cheese. Add cold water; mix until dough sticks together.

FILLING:

½ sm. onion, chopped
3 tbsp. cooking oil
1 lb. ground beef
2 tbsp. chopped green pepper
¼ c. flour
1 tsp. salt
1 No. 2 can tomato juice
½ c. chopped celery
2 tsp. Worcestershire sauce

Saute onion in oil for 5 minutes. Add meat and green pepper; brown well. Stir in flour and salt; add tomato juice. Cook until thickened, stirring constantly. Add celery and Worcestershire sauce. Pour into an 8-inch square baking dish. Roll pastry 1/4 inch thick; cut out an 8-inch square. Cover filling with pastry. Cut remaining pastry into 1/2-inch strips; place in lattice design over crust. Bake at 400 degrees for 40 minutes. Yield: 4 servings.

Mrs. Odell Talley, Bell Buckle, Tenn.

CORN BREAD TAMALE PIE

1 lb. ground beef
1 lge. onion, chopped
1 can tomato soup
2 c. water
1 tsp. salt
¼ tsp. pepper
1 tbsp. chili powder
1 c. whole kernel corn, drained
½ c. chopped green pepper
¾ c. cornmeal
1 tbsp. flour
1 tbsp. sugar
½ tsp. salt
1 beaten egg
⅓ c. milk
1 tbsp. cooking oil
1 ½ tsp. baking powder

Brown ground beef and onion in skillet; add tomato soup, water, seasonings, corn and green pepper; simmer for 15 minutes. For topping, sift together dry ingredients. Add beaten egg and milk stirring lightly until combined. Fold in melted fat. Place meat mixture in greased baking dish; cover with corn bread topping. Bake at 425 degrees for 20 to 25 minutes until corn bread is brown.

Mrs. Marion Montgomery, McKinney, Ky.

CORN-CHILI CASSEROLE

1 lb. ground beef
1 med. onion, cubed
1 tbsp. butter
1 can tomato soup
1 ½ tsp. salt
½ tsp. pepper
1 tsp. chili powder
1 can cream-style corn
¾ c. cornmeal
½ c. flour
1 tsp. sugar
1 ½ tsp. baking powder
1 tbsp. shortening
1 egg
½ c. milk

Brown beef and onion in butter; add tomato soup, 1 teaspoon salt, pepper, chili powder and corn. Simmer for 15 minutes; turn into casserole. Combine cornmeal, flour, sugar, baking powder, remaining salt, shortening, egg and milk; put on top of meat mixture. Bake at 350 degrees for 30 minutes.

Mrs. Ray Frazier, Boynton Beach, Fla.

CORN AND HAMBURGER CASSEROLE

1 ½ lb. hamburger
2 tbsp. oil
1 c. cornmeal
½ tsp. soda
1 tsp. salt
⅓ c. liquid shortening
¾ c. milk
1 egg
1 No. 2 can cream-style corn
1 4-oz. can chopped green chilies
1 ½ c. grated cheese

Brown meat lightly in oil; set aside. Combine remaining ingredients, except cheese; pour half the cornmeal mixture into 9 x 9-inch pan. Cover with meat mixture; sprinkle with half the cheese. Put remaining cornmeal mixture over cheese; top with remaining cheese. Bake at 400 degrees for 45 minutes.

Mrs. C. F. Pirtle, McAllen, Tex.

CORNMEAL-MEAT PIE

4 tbsp. flour
½ c. cornmeal
2 tsp. baking powder
2 ½ tsp. salt
1 tsp. sugar
1 egg
½ c. milk
3 tbsp. melted margarine
¾ lb. hamburger
2 tbsp. bacon drippings
2 tbsp. chopped celery
2 tbsp. chopped green pepper
1 med. onion, chopped
2 tsp. chili powder
½ c. tomato juice
½ c. cooked rice
4 green pepper rings
4 sm. cubes cheese
Grated cheese

Sift together flour, cornmeal, baking powder, 1/2 teaspoon salt and sugar. Beat egg slightly; add milk. Add egg mixture and margarine quickly to dry ingredients. Reserve 4 tablespoons batter; pour remaining batter into greased 9-inch pie plate. Lightly cook meat in bacon drippings with celery, chopped green pepper and onion. Add remaining salt, chili powder, tomato juice and rice; spoon meat mixture carefully over batter. Place green pepper rings over meat mixture; fill each ring with 1 tablespoon reserved batter. Place 1 cube cheese in each green pepper ring. Sprinkle grated cheese over top. Bake at 425 degrees for 35 minutes.

Mrs. Mary K. Schulman, St. Petersburg, Fla.

CORN PONE PIE

1 lb. ground beef
1 lge. onion, chopped
1 can tomato soup
2 c. water
1 ½ tsp. salt
½ tsp. pepper
1 tbsp. chili powder
1 c. whole kernel corn
½ c. chopped green pepper
¾ c. cornmeal
1 tbsp. flour
1 tbsp. sugar
1 ½ tsp. baking powder
1 egg, beaten
⅓ c. milk
1 tbsp. melted fat

Brown beef and onion in skillet; add soup, water, 1 teaspoon salt, pepper, chili powder, corn and green pepper. Simmer for 15 minutes. Sift together cornmeal, flour, sugar, remaining salt and baking powder; add egg and milk. Mix lightly; fold in fat. Add meat mixture; turn into baking dish. Bake at 375 degrees for 20 to 25 minutes.

Mrs. Geraldine L. Philpott, Roanoke, Va.

FILLED GRITS PIE

½ c. chopped onion
2 tbsp. butter
½ lb. ground beef
1 tsp. chili powder
½ tsp. salt
⅛ tsp. pepper
3 c. grits, cooked
2 slices green pepper
1 sliced tomato
¼ c. bread crumbs

Saute onion in melted butter until glossy, but not brown. Combine meat, chili powder and seasonings; add to onion. Cook until meat is well browned. Place cooked grits in a 9-inch pie plate; shape as pie pastry. Pour meat mixture over grits. Top with green pepper rings; place tomato slices over rings. Sprinkle crumbs in center. Bake at 325 degrees for 20 minutes or until done.

Mrs. John R. Taylor, Jr., Jonesboro, Tenn.

HAMBURGER CORN PONE

1 lb. ground beef
⅓ c. chopped onion
1 tbsp. shortening
2 tsp. chili powder
¾ tsp. salt
1 tsp. Worcestershire sauce
1 c. canned tomatoes
1 c. drained canned pinto beans
¾ c. milk
1 sm. egg
1 c. self-rising cornmeal
1 tbsp. hot fat

Brown meat and onion in shortening. Add seasonings and tomatoes. Cover; simmer 15 minutes. Add beans. Pour into greased casserole. Add milk and egg to meal; stir until blended. Add hot fat to batter. Pour over mixture in casserole. Bake at 425 degrees for 20 minutes or until bread is done.

Mrs. William F. Hall, Seymour, Tenn.

HOT TAMALE PIE

1 ½ c. cornmeal
1 c. cold water
1 lb. ground beef
1 med. onion, chopped
1 clove garlic, minced (opt.)
1 tsp. salt
¼ tsp. black pepper
1 tsp. chili powder
1 pt. canned tomatoes
Grated cheddar cheese

Soak cornmeal in water for 10 to 15 minutes. Brown ground beef in skillet with onion and garlic; season with salt, pepper and chili powder. Stir in tomatoes and cornmeal; pour into greased 1 1/2-quart casserole. Bake at 350 degrees for 45 minutes. Sprinkle with cheese; return to oven until cheese is melted. Yield: 6 servings.

Mrs. H. L. Spillyards, Pine Bluff, Ark.

HOT TAMALE PIE

3 tbsp. shortening
1 med. onion, chopped
1 lb. ground beef
4 c. water
½ can tomatoes
2 tbsp. plus 1 tsp. chili powder
2 tsp. salt
1 c. meal

(Continued on next page)

Place shortening in skillet; add onion. Simmer; add beef. Cook for a few minutes, stirring. Add 1 cup water, tomatoes, 2 tablespoons chili powder and 1 teaspoon salt. Simmer for 1 hour. Combine remaining water, chili powder and salt in a kettle; bring to boil. Add meal, stirring to prevent lumping. Cook for a few minutes; add more water if necessary. Place a layer of mush in bottom of baking dish; add a layer of meat. Continue until all is used. Bake at 350 degrees for 30 minutes. Yield: 4-5 servings.

Mrs. T. E. Boyett, Jr., Mobile, Ala.

LIDA'S HOT TAMALE PIE

- 1 onion, finely chopped
- ½ green pepper, finely chopped
- 1 tbsp. cooking oil
- 1 lb. hamburger
- 2 tsp. chili powder
- 1 tsp. salt
- ½ tsp. pepper
- 1 c. tomato sauce
- 2 tsp. catsup
- 1 c. whole kernel corn
- 1 c. self-rising cornmeal
- 1 c. milk
- 1 egg

Brown onion and green pepper in oil. Add hamburger; crumble with fork and brown. Add chili powder, salt, pepper, tomato sauce, catsup and corn; pour into baking dish. Mix remaining ingredients; pour on top of meat mixture. Bake at 425 degrees for 30 minutes or until brown. Yield: 4 servings.

Mrs. Donald E. Hendrix, Oak Ridge, Tenn.

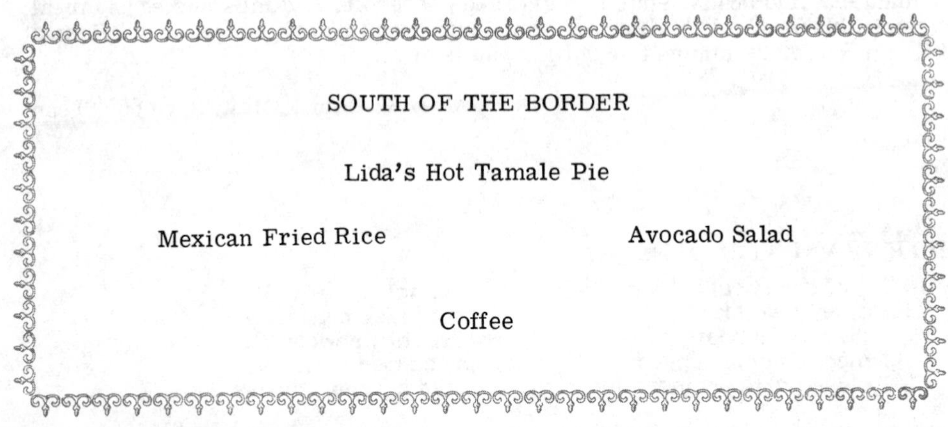

SOUTH OF THE BORDER
Lida's Hot Tamale Pie
Mexican Fried Rice
Avocado Salad
Coffee

MEAT-ZA PIE

- 1 lb. ground beef
- ⅔ c. evaporated milk
- ½ c. fine dry bread crumbs
- 1 tsp. garlic salt
- ⅓ c. tomato paste or catsup
- 1 2-oz. can sliced mushrooms
- 1 c. shredded sharp cheddar cheese
- 2 tbsp. grated Parmesan cheese
- ¼ tsp. oregano, crumbled finely

Place meat, milk, bread crumbs and garlic salt in a pie plate. Mix thoroughly. Pat this mixture evenly on the bottom and sides of pie plate. Pull up over rim and press firmly into place. Spread tomato paste over meat. Sprinkle mushrooms over. Top with cheeses and sprinkle with oregano. Bake at 375 degrees for 25 minutes. Yield: 4-5 servings.

Mary F. Ragsdale, Dumas, Tex.

MILLIE'S HAMBURGER PIE

1 lb. hamburger meat
Cooking oil
1 med. onion, chopped
1 stalk celery, chopped
½ green pepper, chopped
⅛ tsp. garlic salt
1 No. 1 can tomato juice
1 tbsp. Worcestershire sauce
1 tsp. sugar
1 ½ tsp. chili powder
1 c. grated cheese
1 recipe pie pastry

Brown meat in small amount of cooking oil. Add onion, celery and green pepper; cook, stirring. Add remaining ingredients except cheese and pastry; simmer for 30 minutes. Add cheese to pie pastry when preparing crust. Place cheese crust over pie. Bake at 400 degrees for 10 minutes or until crust is brown. Turn off heat and leave pie in oven for 10 minutes longer. Yield: 6 servings.

Mrs. Dale Moore, Taylorsville, Miss.

TAMALE PIE

½ c. oil
1 lge. green pepper, chopped fine
1 lge. onion, chopped fine
1 lb. ground beef
3 tsp. chili powder
1 can whole kernel corn
1 No. 303 can tomatoes
1 ½ c. cornmeal
1 tsp. salt
¼ tsp. pepper

Put 1/4 cup oil in frying pan. When hot, add green pepper and onion. Cook until tender; remove from pan. Brown meat, adding chili powder to meat as it cooks. Heat remaining oil in large saucepan; add corn and tomatoes. When hot, stir in cornmeal slowly. Add salt and pepper. Cook for about 15 minutes, stirring constantly. Combine meat and meal mixtures; bake in 350-degree oven until browned slightly on top.

Mrs. M. C. Pitts, Middletown, Ky.

TRUDY'S CHURCH PIE

1 sm. onion, diced
1 lb. ground beef
½ green pepper, diced
Dash of garlic salt
1 can tomato soup
1 No. 2 can mixed vegetables
Pastry

Saute onion; add meat, green pepper and garlic salt. Cook until brown; remove from heat. Add soup and vegetables; turn into pastry-lined casserole. Top with remaining pastry cut in strips. Bake at 350 degrees for 30 minutes. Yield: 8 servings.

Trudy Dickerson, Midland, Tex.

BEEF CASSEROLE

1 ½ lb. ground beef
1 med. onion
3 tbsp. oil
½ c. catsup
1 can tomato soup
Salt to taste
1 ½ c. rice
3 beef bouillon cubes
Buttered bread crumbs

(Continued on next page)

Brown beef and onion in oil; add catsup, soup and salt. Cook rice with bouillon cubes; do not drain. Place rice in buttered dish; spread with beef mixture. Cover with bread crumbs. Bake at 350 degrees until golden brown.

Mrs. Charles Hyatt, Roebuck, S. C.

BEEF CHOW MEIN

1 lb. ground beef
1 med. onion, chopped
2 stalks celery, diced
1 c. cooked rice
1 can cream of chicken soup
1 can cream of mushroom soup
½ c. water
3 tbsp. soy sauce
Chow mein noodles

Cook beef in large skillet until brown; pour off fat. Add remaining ingredients except noodles; mix well. Pour into a greased baking dish; top generously with chow mein noodles. Bake at 350 degrees for 30 minutes. Yield: 8 servings.

Mrs. J. R. Brinkhoff, Tuscaloosa, Ala.

BEEF-RICE CASSEROLE

1 lb. ground beef
1 tbsp. fat
½ c. rice
1 can condensed chicken soup
1 ¼ c. water
1 tsp. salt
½ c. chopped celery
¼ c. chopped green pepper

Brown beef in hot fat. Add rice, soup, water, salt, celery and green pepper; mix thoroughly. Place in greased 2-quart casserole. Cover and bake 1 hour and 15 minutes at 350 degrees. Yield: 6-8 servings.

Mrs. Fred Gobbell, Lawrenceburg, Tenn.

BEEF-RICE CASSEROLE

1 lb. ground beef
Chopped onion
Chopped green pepper
½ c. rice
1 potato, diced
1 can tomato soup

Fry beef with onion and green pepper; place in casserole. Add rice and potato. Pour tomato soup over all. Bake for 30 to 45 minutes in 350-degree oven.

Mrs. Amy Cordes, Sarasota, Fla.

BEEF-RICE CASSEROLE

1 lb. ground beef
1 c. uncooked rice
1 sm. onion, chopped
2 tbsp. cooking oil
1 tsp. salt
1 tsp. paprika
1 sm. bottle stuffed olives, sliced
2 c. tomato juice
1 ½ c. boiling water
½ c. cheddar cheese, grated

(Continued on next page)

Cook beef, rice and onion in cooking oil until lightly browned. Add salt, paprika, sliced olives, tomato juice and boiling water; turn into 1 1/2-quart casserole. Bake at 300 degrees, covered, for 1 hour. Uncover; sprinkle with cheese. Bake 10 minutes or until cheese is melted.

Mrs. E. L. Burns, Conehatta, Miss.

BEEF AND RICE CASSEROLE

1 lb. ground beef
1 c. rice
1 sm. onion, chopped
1 tsp. salt
¼ tsp. pepper
1 tsp. paprika
1 sm. bottle stuffed olives, sliced
2 c. tomato juice
1 ½ c. boiling water
½ c. grated cheese

Cook beef, rice and onion in skillet till lightly brown, breaking meat into small bits. Pour off excess grease. Add seasonings, olives, tomato juice and water; mix well. Place in 1 1/2-quart casserole or 9 x 12-inch dish. Cover. Bake 1 hour at 350 degrees. Uncover; sprinkle with cheese. Bake for 10 minutes.

Mrs. Jewel Cromer, Carrollton, Tex.

BUSY-DAY CASSEROLE

Thinly sliced potatoes
Thinly sliced carrots
Uncooked rice
1 lb. ground beef, browned
Thinly sliced onions
1 qt. canned tomatoes
1 tbsp. sugar
Salt and pepper

Layer all ingredients in casserole in order given; sprinkle with sugar, salt and pepper. Bake in oven at 325 degrees for about 2 hours.

Margery Brookhart, Miami, Fla.

BEEF AND TOMATO CASSEROLE

⅓ c. uncooked rice
Salt to taste
1 lb. ground beef
Chopped green peppers
Sliced onions
1 can tomatoes, undrained
Bread crumbs

Place rice evenly in bottom of buttered casserole; sprinkle with salt. Place meat over rice; sprinkle with salt. Place green peppers over meat; place onions over green peppers. Pour tomatoes over onions; sprinkle with bread crumbs. Bake at 350 degrees for 1 hour.

Mrs. Ruth Morris, Durham, N. C.

CHINESE HAMBURGER CASSEROLE

1 ½ lb. ground beef
2 med. chopped onions
¾ c. quick-cooking rice
2 c. chopped celery
1 can mushroom soup
2 c. hot water
1 sm. can chopped mushrooms
Soy sauce

Brown meat and onions together. Place rice in greased casserole; add celery. Add meat and onions. Combine soup, water and mushrooms; pour over meat. Sprinkle liberally with soy sauce. Bake at 350 degrees for about 45 minutes or until celery is tender. Yield: 6 servings.

Mrs. Barbara Davis, Knoxville, Tenn.

CHOP SUEY CASSEROLE

1 lb. hamburger or ground chuck
1 med. onion
3 tbsp. soy sauce
½ c. instant rice
2 c. celery, cut fine
1 c. water
1 can cream of mushroom soup
¼ tsp. salt

Brown meat in skillet; brown chopped onion. Add remaining ingredients; mix well. Bake in greased casserole dish until thick, 35 to 45 minutes at 350 degrees.

Mrs. H. L. Deans, Durham, N. C.

EASY MEATBALLS

1 lb. ground beef
1 c. instant rice, uncooked
Dash of salt
2 med. onions, thinly sliced
1 can tomato soup

Combine beef, rice and salt; mix thoroughly. Make into tiny balls; place in casserole. Put sliced onions on top; pour tomato soup over all. Bake in covered casserole in 350-degree oven for about 35 minutes. Remove cover; brown about 10 minutes longer.

Mrs. John Schoel, Russellville, Ala.

GROUND BEEF CASSEROLE

¾ c. raw rice
1 ½ tsp. salt
1 can tomato sauce
1 c. hot water
1 c. diced green pepper
1 c. diced onion
1 lb. ground beef
Dash of pepper
Dash of chili powder
1 can whole kernel corn
4 slices bacon

Place rice and salt in bottom of a 1 1/2-quart casserole dish. Pour 1/2 can tomato sauce over rice. Pour in hot water; add green pepper and onion. Place seasoned ground beef over top; add remaining tomato sauce. Add pinch of salt, pepper and chili powder. Place corn on top; add bacon. Bake at 350 degrees for 1 hour, covered. Uncover; bake 15 minutes more until bacon is browned.

Mrs. John D. Abshire, Sulphur, La.

HAMBURGER DELIGHT

1 lb. ground beef
1 c. chopped onion
1 c. chopped celery
1 pkg. frozen peas, thawed
1 can mushroom soup
1 can chicken soup
1 soup can water
½ c. uncooked rice
¼ c. soy sauce
¼ tsp. pepper
1 3-oz. can chow mein noodles

Brown meat until crumbly; add onion, celery, peas, soups, water, rice, soy sauce and pepper. Bring to boil. Put into greased 1 1/2-quart baking dish. Cover; bake at 350 degrees for 30 minutes. Remove cover; cook an additional 30 minutes. Top with noodles; bake 15 minutes longer. Yield: 8 servings.

Mrs. E. A. Mixon, Heidelberg, Miss.

MEAT CASSEROLE

1 c. cooked rice
1 lb. ground meat
Salt and pepper to taste
1 can drained green beans
Garlic powder
1 can cream of mushroom soup
1 c. chopped onion
1 can tomatoes

Place rice in bottom of deep ovenproof dish. Cook meat until red disappears; place over rice. Sprinkle with salt and pepper. Add beans; sprinkle with garlic powder. Cover with soup; top with onion and tomatoes. Bake at 325 degrees for 45 minutes.

Mrs. Hoyt Moore, Corsicana, Tex.

PEAS AND RICE CASSEROLE

2 c. cooked rice
2 c. garden peas, undrained
1 tsp. salt
2 tbsp. butter
1 med. onion, finely chopped
½ tsp. pepper
½ c. sweet milk
1 ½ lb. ground beef

Place all ingredients, except beef, in casserole. Shape beef into patties; place in casserole over vegetables. Bake at 350 degrees for 40 minutes. Serve hot.

Mrs. N. A. Barber, Clearwater, Fla.

QUICK CASSEROLE

1 lb. ground beef round
1 lge. onion
½ c. diced celery
2 tbsp. cooking oil
1 c. precooked rice
1 c. boiling water
1 1-lb. can tomatoes
1 1-lb. 4-oz. can kidney beans
1 ¼ tsp. salt
⅛ tsp. pepper
½ tsp. Worcestershire sauce
1 tsp. chili powder

Brown meat, onion and celery in oil. Add rice; cook until golden. Stir in remaining ingredients. Simmer 20 to 30 minutes in casserole at 350 degrees. Yield: 6 servings.

Trudy Dickerson, Midland, Tex.

RICE CASSEROLE

1 lb. ground beef
Salt and pepper
1 c. diced celery
1 c. diced onion
1 green pepper, chopped
1 can mushroom soup
1 can cream of chicken soup
1 c. uncooked rice

Cook beef, salt, pepper, celery and onion until tender and brown. Add remaining ingredients; simmer 15 minutes. Place in casserole dish; bake at 350 degrees for 20 minutes.

Mrs. Hallie Dudley, Altavista, Va.

RICE CASSEROLE SUPREME

½ lge. onion, chopped
½ lge. green pepper, chopped
2 tbsp. fat
1 lb. ground meat
½ c. raw rice
1 can cream of mushroom soup
1 can chicken-noodle soup
½ c. grated Parmesan cheese
½ tsp. salt
⅛ tsp. pepper
Rice cereal

Saute onion and green pepper in fat. Add meat; brown. Add remaining ingredients except cereal. Mix well. Put into greased casserole; top with rice cereal. Bake 1 hour in 350-degree oven.

Mrs. Lee O. Boudoin, Lake Charles, La.

RICE JAMBOREE

1 c. chopped onions
2 tbsp. shortening
1 lb. ground beef
1 tsp. salt
¼ tsp. pepper
1 c. canned peas
¼ c. liquid drained from peas
2 ½ c. tomatoes
½ c. uncooked rice
2 c. oven-toasted rice cereal
1 ½ tsp. melted butter or margarine

Cook onions in heated shortening until lightly browned. Add beef and seasonings; continue cooking until beef is browned. Add peas, liquid, tomatoes and rice to meat mixture, stirring lightly. Place in greased 2-quart casserole. Cover; bake in 325-degree oven about 45 minutes. Remove cover; sprinkle top with finely crushed cereal mixed with butter. Return to oven, uncovered; bake 15 minutes. Yield: 8 servings.

Della Worford, Irvine, Ky.

RICE AND MEAT CASSEROLE

1 lb. raw ground meat, beef or beef and pork mixed
1 c. raw rice
1 can plain onion soup, undiluted
1 can cream of mushroom or cream of chicken soup, undiluted
Salt and pepper to taste
Chopped bell pepper
Chopped parsley to taste

(Continued on next page)

Mix all ingredients together in deep dish. Bake 1 hour at 350 degrees. Stir at 15 minute intervals until done. May be frozen.

Mrs. R. L. Manuel, Crowley, La.

SEVEN-LAYER CASSEROLE

1 c. rice, washed and drained
1 can whole corn, drained
2 cans tomato sauce
Dash of salt and pepper
½ c. chopped onion
½ c. bell pepper, diced
¾ lb. ground beef
Dash of Worcestershire sauce
4 slices bacon, cut in half

Place rice in greased 2-quart casserole. Add corn and 1 can tomato sauce with 1/2 sauce can water; sprinkle with salt and pepper. Add onion, bell pepper and ground beef in layers. Add Worcestershire sauce, remaining tomato sauce and 1/4 sauce can water. Place bacon halves over top. Bake, covered, for 1 hour. Remove cover; continue baking for 30 minutes or until bacon is brown. Yield: 8-10 servings.

Mrs. Kennon Mixon, St. Joseph, La.

STEAK FLORIDIAN CASSEROLE

2 med. onions, diced
2 celery stalks, diced
1 lb. round steak, ground
2 tbsp. uncooked rice
1 can tomato soup
1 soup can water
Dash of salt and pepper

Brown onions, celery and ground round steak in skillet; place in casserole. Add rice, soup, water and seasonings. Bake at 350 degrees for 1 hour and 30 minutes to 2 hours. Serve on buns. Yield: 4 servings.

Mrs. James C. Slavik, St. Petersburg, Fla.

TEXAS HASH

3 lge. onions, sliced
1 lge. green pepper, minced
3 tbsp. fat
1 lb. ground beef
2 c. cooked tomatoes or
1 No. 303 can stewed tomatoes
½ c. uncooked rice
1 tsp. chili powder
2 tsp. salt
⅛ tsp. pepper

Heat oven to 350 degrees. In skillet, brown onions and green pepper in fat until onions are yellow. Add meat; fry until mixture falls apart. Stir in remaining ingredients. Pour into greased 2-quart baking dish. Cover; bake 1 hour, removing cover the last 15 minutes.

Mrs. Ernest C. Latham, Longview, Tex.

WEST TEXAS CASSEROLE

3 tbsp. cooking oil
2 med. onions, chopped
2 green peppers, chopped
1 lb. hamburger meat
2 c. canned tomatoes
1 c. cooked rice
1 tsp. chili powder
1 tsp. salt
¼ tsp. pepper

Heat oil in skillet; saute onions and green peppers until tender. Add hamburger; heat until red has disappeared from meat. Add tomatoes, rice and seasonings; arrange in greased baking dish. Bake at 350 degrees for 25 minutes.

Mrs. William H. Wade, Monahans, Tex.

WILD RICE CASSEROLE

2 c. boiling water
1 c. uncooked wild rice
1 can chicken gumbo soup
1 can sliced mushrooms, undrained
½ c. water
1 tsp. salt
1 bay leaf
¼ tsp. celery salt
¼ tsp. garlic salt
Pepper
Onion salt
Paprika
3 tbsp. chopped onion
3 tbsp. salad oil
1 lb. lean ground beef

Pour boiling water over rice; cover and let stand 15 minutes. Drain; place in 2-quart casserole. Add soup, mushrooms, water and seasonings. Mix gently; let stand a few minutes. Saute onion in oil until glossy; add to casserole. Add meat to oil remaining in pan; fry until brown and crumbly. Add to rice. Cover and bake at 350 degrees for 1 hour and 15 minutes. Mixture may be refrigerated and baked for 2 hours when needed.

Mrs. James Woods, Bedford, Ky.

BAKED SPAGHETTI

1 minced onion
1 tbsp. butter or margarine
1 lb. ground round steak
1 med. green pepper
3 stalks celery, chopped
1 can tomato soup
1 sm. bottle olives
2 sm. cans mushrooms
Salt and pepper
1 8-oz. pkg. thin spaghetti, cooked
½ lb. sharp cheese, grated
1 can cream of mushroom soup

Brown onion in butter; add meat, bell pepper and celery. Add tomato soup, juice of olives and mushroom juice; coat with salt and pepper. Alternate layers of spaghetti, sauce and grated cheese; top with mushroom soup. Cook at 325 degrees 45 minutes. Slice olives; put on top before serving. Yield: 8-10 servings.

Mrs. Bose Ethridge, Anderson, S. C.

CHILI-MEAT CASSEROLE

1 ½ lb. ground beef
1 c. chopped onion
1 No. 2 can tomatoes
½ c. green pepper, chopped
1 ½ tsp. salt
2 tsp. chili powder
1 tsp. paprika
4 c. cooked spaghetti
¼ lb. cheddar cheese, grated

(Continued on next page)

Cook beef slowly until crumbly, but not hard. Add onion, tomatoes, green pepper and seasonings. Cover; simmer 45 minutes. Alternate layers of cooked spaghetti and meat mixture in casserole; sprinkle with grated cheese. Bake 20 to 30 minutes in 375-degree oven until cheese is melted and brown.

Mrs. J. L. Temple, Gulfport, Miss.

CHEESE-SPAGHETTI CASSEROLE

1 lb. ground meat
2 c. tomato sauce
3 c. water
2 1 ½-oz. pkg. spaghetti sauce mix
1 ½ tsp. salt
1 1-lb. pkg. spaghetti
¼ c. butter
5 tbsp. flour
2 c. milk
1 ½ c. shredded process American cheese
¼ c. grated Parmesan cheese

Brown meat in large saucepan; pour off liquid. Add tomato sauce, water, spaghetti sauce mix and 1/2 teaspoon salt. Simmer, uncovered, stirring often, for 30 minutes. Break spaghetti into thirds; cook according to package directions. Rinse and drain well. Melt butter in saucepan; stir in flour and remaining salt. Add milk slowly, stirring constantly, over medium heat until thickened. Add 1 cup American cheese and Parmesan cheese; stir until melted. For two 12 x 7 1/2 x 2-inch casseroles, divide spaghetti, tomato sauce and cheese sauce in half, using half of each in 1 casserole. To prepare casserole, layer half of spaghetti, tomato sauce, cheese sauce, remaining spaghetti and tomato sauce. Top with 1/4 cup American cheese. Prepare second casserole in same order using remaining half of ingredients and remaining cheese. Bake in 350-degree oven for 15 to 20 minutes or until bubbly; serve at once. Casseroles may be prepared in advance and refrigerated. Add shredded American cheese before baking. Bake as directed for 20 to 30 minutes or until bubbly.

Mrs. Cecil R. Randolph, Dallas, Tex.

ITALIAN DELIGHT

Salt and pepper
1 lb. ground beef
1 green pepper, chopped
1 med. to lge. onion, chopped
½ 7-oz. pkg. spaghetti
1 lge. can mushrooms
1 can corn niblets
1 can tomato soup
1 tbsp. Worcestershire sauce
8 to 10 ripe olives, finely chopped
Sharp grated cheese

Lightly brown seasoned meat, green pepper and onion. Cook spaghetti; drain. Add all ingredients to meat except cheese; put into 2-quart casserole. Bake in 350-degree oven for 30 minutes. Sprinkle grated cheese over the top; let melt. Yield: 6-8 servings.

Mrs. Ronald Sharp, Columbia, Tenn.

MEAT-SPAGHETTI CASSEROLE

3 onions, chopped
½ green pepper, chopped
2 tbsp. oleo
¾ lb. ground beef
1 tbsp. salt
1 tsp. pepper
¼ c. sugar
1 can tomatoes, mashed well
4 c. cooked spaghetti
¼ c. sharp cheese, grated

(Continued on next page)

Ground Beef with Spaghetti

Brown onions and green peppers in oleo; add ground meat, salt and pepper. Cook until well done. Add sugar to tomatoes; pour over cooked meat. Spread layer of spaghetti over bottom of casserole dish; add a layer of meat mixture. Add another layer of spaghetti and meat mixture. Cover with grated cheese. Bake 1 hour at 350 degrees 5 inches above oven bottom.

Mrs. W. W. Nance, Alexandria, Va.

MEXICAN SPAGHETTI

1 green pepper, chopped fine
1 lge. onion, chopped fine
1 tbsp. shortening
1 lb. hamburger meat
1 sm. can chopped pimento
1 sm. jar or ½ c. stuffed olives
2 8-oz. or 1 15-oz. can tomato sauce
½ pkg. spaghetti, broken into 2-inch pieces
1 tsp. chili pepper
½ tsp. salt
¼ tsp. black pepper
½ lb. sharp cheese, cut in cubes

Cook green pepper and onion in shortening over low heat until soft and golden brown in skillet. Remove to bowl. Cook meat until brown and done. Add green pepper, onion, pimento, olives and tomato sauce; mix with cooked spaghetti. Season. Put in casserole; cover with cheese. Bake in oven for 15 to 20 minutes until cheese melts.

Mrs. J. J. Jackson, Montevallo, Ala.

SPAGHETTI AMORE

1 lb. ground beef
½ c. chopped onions
¼ c. green pepper
2 tbsp. shortening
1 can cream of mushroom soup
1 can cream of tomato soup
1 soup can water
1 c. sharp cheese, shredded
1 7-oz. pkg. spaghetti

Brown together ground beef, onions and green pepper in shortening, stirring occasionally. Add soups and water; simmer until onions and pepper are tender, about 10 minutes. Blend in 1/2 cup cheese. Cook spaghetti according to directions on package; drain. Place half of spaghetti in buttered 3-quart casserole; top with half of meat mixture. Repeat spaghetti and meat layers; top with remaining cheese. Bake at 350 degrees about 30 minutes or until cheese is melted. Yield: 6-8 servings.

Dorothy C. Brewer, Clinton, Tenn.

SPAGHETTI-BEEF CASSEROLE

1 med. onion
1 green pepper
1 garlic clove
½ sm. bottle olive oil
¾ lb. ground beef
½ tsp. salt
¼ tsp. pepper
1 can tomato soup
1 sm. can mushroom pieces
1 can whole kernel corn
1 tbsp. Worcestershire sauce
2 cans spaghetti in tomato-cheese sauce
1 c. grated American cheese

(Continued on next page)

Chop onion, green pepper and garlic; fry in olive oil until light brown. Remove from fire; remove onion mix from oil. In remaining oil, fry meat until light brown; add salt and pepper. Add soup, mushrooms, corn, Worcestershire sauce, spaghetti and onion mix. Stir to mix well. Put in greased casserole; sprinkle grated cheese on top. Bake 45 minutes in 375-degree oven.

Mrs. Howard Snavely, Pine Bluff, Ark.

SPAGHETTI CASSEROLE

6 slices bacon
1 ¼ lb. lean ground chuck
1 can tomato soup or tomato sauce
1 1-lb. can tomatoes
⅓ c. water
1 med. onion, sliced
1 med. green pepper, sliced
2 lge. stalks celery
½ tsp. salt
25 dashes soy sauce
½ lb. cooked spaghetti, rinsed with cold water
6 slices American cheese

Fry bacon in a 10-inch skillet. When crisp, remove to plate; break in pieces. Pour off all grease. Brown beef; break into pieces with a spoon while frying. Spoon out any excess grease. Add soup, juice from tomatoes and water. Continue cooking on low heat. Slice onion, green pepper and celery into meat; add salt and soy sauce. Cover; reduce heat to simmer. Cook 30 minutes. Add tomatoes and bacon; blend together. In casserole or baking pan, put half the spaghetti and half the sauce; repeat. Bake at 325 degrees for 1 hour. Add cheese the last 10 minutes. Yield: 6 servings.

Mrs. W. J. Kiefer, Greenville, S. C.

SPAGHETTI CASSEROLE

1 med. onion
2 cloves garlic
1 lb. ground beef
1 8-oz. can tomato sauce
1 6-oz. can tomato paste
1 12-oz. can niblet corn
1 ½-lb. box spaghetti
½ lb. sharp cheese
1 6-oz. jar sliced stuffed olives

Cook onion, garlic and beef until beef is done; add tomato sauce and paste. Cook slowly for 1 hour and 30 minutes; add corn. Cook another 30 minutes; set aside. Cook spaghetti in boiling salted water until done; drain. In 1 1/2-quart casserole, layer spaghetti and meat sauce; sprinkle with cheese and sliced olives. Continue layers until all ingredients are used, ending with cheese and sliced olives. Cook at 350 degrees until cheese melts and casserole is hot, about 45 minutes. Yield: 4 servings.

Mrs. Ben B. Harbin, Norfolk, Va.

ZUTONI CASSEROLE

2 lb. ground chuck
2 onions, chopped
2 green peppers, chopped
½ c. vegetable oil
Salt, pepper and paprika
2 cloves garlic
2 cans tomato soup, undiluted
2 cans tomato sauce
2 sm. cans mushrooms
1 No. 303 can cream-style corn
1 med. pkg. broken spaghetti, cooked according to directions
2 c. grated sharp cheese
Sliced ripe olives

(Continued on next page)

Brown ground beef, onions and green peppers in oil. Add salt, pepper, garlic, tomato soup and tomato sauce. Stir in mushrooms and canned corn; mix well. Add cooked spaghetti and half of cheese, reserving enough for topping. Place in large baking dish; cover with remaining cheese. Garnish with sliced ripe olives and paprika. Bake for 25 to 30 minutes at 350 degrees. Yield: 8-10 servings.

Mrs. Homer Olsen, Austin, Tex.

MEXICAN CASSEROLE

1 lb. ground beef
1 onion, chopped
½ tsp. salt
¼ tsp. pepper
1 can enchilada sauce
1 can cream of mushroom soup
½ soup can water
1 can chopped green chilies
2 c. grated cheddar cheese
6 to 8 tortillas

Fry together ground beef and onion until all pink disappears and onion is clear. Add enchilada sauce. Mix together mushroom soup, water and chopped green chilies. Break tortillas into several pieces. In a 2-quart casserole dish, put in a layer of tortillas, meat mixture, soup mixture, then cheese. Repeat layers, ending with cheese. Refrigerate overnight or all day. Bake at 350 degrees for 1 hour. Yield: 6 servings.

Mrs. F. T. Black, El Paso, Tex.

LOCAS DE CREMA

1 lb. ground chuck
1 med. onion, chopped
Dash each of garlic salt, pepper and oregano
1 can tomato sauce
1 can water
1 can tortillas
American cheese slices
1 can green chili peppers
1 carton sour cream

Brown meat and onion; add garlic salt, pepper and oregano. Add tomato sauce and water; simmer for 15 minutes. Separate tortillas; place a slice of cheese on each. Cut peppers in strips; place a strip on top of cheese. Roll up tortillas; place close together in a casserole. Add sour cream to meat mixture; heat through. Pour sauce over tortillas. Cover; bake 45 minutes in 350-degree oven.

Mrs. Joseph W. Lunn, Valparaiso, Fla.

BAKED BEANS WITH MEAT

1 lb. hamburger meat
2 onions
½ stick oleo
2 cans pork and beans
3 cans Ranch Style beans
¼ c. prepared mustard
1 c. brown sugar
¼ c. maple syrup
1 c. catsup

Brown meat and chopped onions in oleo. Mix all together and bake in slow oven at 300 degrees for 2 hours. Yield: 20 servings.

Nellie S. Moore, Perrin, Tex.

President Franklin Roosevelt's Little White House near Warm Springs, Georgia

BEEF-BEAN CASSEROLE

1 ½ lb. ground beef
½ c. catsup
½ tsp. dry mustard
2 tbsp. vinegar
3 tbsp. dark brown sugar
1 sm. onion, minced
1 No. 303 can green lima beans
1 No. 303 can red kidney beans
1 No. 303 can pork and beans
1 tsp. salt

Brown meat in skillet. Combine with remaining ingredients. Divide into two parts. Place each portion in 1 1/2-quart casserole. Bake at 350 degrees for 30 minutes. Yield: 12 servings.

Mrs. Eddie Powers, Marston, N. C.

BEEF AND BEAN CASSEROLE

1 clove garlic, minced
1 onion, minced
1 green pepper, chopped
3 tbsp. butter or margarine
1 lb. ground beef
¾ tsp. chili powder
2 tbsp. bottled steak sauce
1 tsp. salt
1 10 ¼-oz. can spaghetti sauce with mushrooms
1 1-lb. can lima beans, undrained

Saute garlic, onion and green pepper until tender in butter. Add ground beef; brown, breaking up with a fork. Combine chili powder, steak sauce, salt, spaghetti sauce and lima beans; stir into beef mixture. Turn into 2-quart casserole. Bake at 375 degrees 40 minutes. Yield: 4-6 servings.

Mrs. Charles W. Bryant, North Little Rock, Ark.

GROUND BEEF CASSEROLE

1 ½ lb. hamburger meat
1 lge. onion
1 tsp. salt
½ tsp. pepper
1 sm. bell pepper, cut up
1 No. 303 can tomato sauce
1 can pork and beans
Grated cheese

(Continued on next page)

Brown ground beef and onion in frying pan; remove with spatula to boiler. Add salt, pepper, bell pepper and tomato sauce. Cook slowly, about 1 hour. When mixture has cooked down, alternate with pork and beans in a casserole dish. Sprinkle grated cheese on top. Heat in 300-degree oven until cheese is melted.

Mrs. Charles M. Campbell, Homca Path, S. C.

CHALUPES

- 1 lb. lean ground beef
- 4 tbsp. chili powder
- 1 tbsp. oregano
- 2 tbsp. garlic salt
- 2 No. 303 cans of refried or barbecued beans
- 1 pkg. frozen tortillas
- Salt
- 2 tomatoes, sliced
- 1 head lettuce, sliced
- 2 c. grated cheddar cheese

Sear meat in a 3 or 4-quart saucepan; add chili powder, oregano and garlic salt. Stir until well blended. Drain off grease into 10-inch skillet. Add beans to meat; continue to cook over low heat for 20 minutes. Fry tortillas until crisp in skillet with grease; drain. Salt each tortilla well. Serve meat and bean mixture while hot; top each serving with sliced tomatoes, lettuce and grated cheese. Serve with tortillas. Yield: 6-8 servings.

Mildred Hill, Hillsboro, Tex.

DEEP-SOUTH CHILI

- 1 c. grits
- 1 tsp. salt
- 4 c. boiling water
- 1 tbsp. butter
- 2 lb. ground round steak
- 2 tbsp. fat
- 2 c. sliced onions
- 1 tsp. sugar
- ½ c. tomato juice
- 1 ½ c. tomato puree
- Salt and pepper to taste
- 3 tbsp. chili powder
- 1 No. 2 can chili or kidney beans

Prepare grits by cooking in salted water according to directions on package; add butter. Keep hot over very low heat while preparing chili. Brown ground meat in hot fat. Add sliced onions; cook lightly. Add remaining ingredients; mix well. Alternate layers of cooked grits and chili mixture in greased baking dish or in individual casseroles, beginning with grits and ending with chili. Bake about 30 minutes in 350-degree oven.

Mrs. Charlotte Corley, South Miami, Fla.

HEARTY MAIN-DISH CASSEROLE

- 1 lb. ground beef
- 1 tsp. salt
- 1 can tomatoes with green chilies
- 1 med. onion, chopped
- 1 tbsp. green pepper, chopped
- 1 4-oz. can mushrooms
- 1 can Ranch Style beans
- ¼ lb. grated cheddar cheese

Saute ground beef in small amount of fat until red color disappears. Add salt and tomatoes; simmer about 10 to 15 minutes or until almost dry. Add onion, green

(Continued on next page)

pepper, mushrooms and beans; mix well. Pour into casserole; top with cheese. Bake in 375-degree oven for 35 minutes. Yield: 6-8 servings.

Mrs. John T. Brown, Pine Bluff, Ark.

MOUSAKA KREAS

1 clove garlic
2 tbsp. oil
1 lb. hamburger
1 bay leaf, crumbled
1 tsp. ground sage
Salt and pepper
6 c. thinly sliced potatoes
1 c. sliced onions
1 No. 2 can tomatoes
Paprika

Brown half a clove of garlic in oil in large skillet. Discard garlic; brown meat slowly with bay leaf and sage. Add 1 teaspoon salt and dash of pepper. Remove meat. Brown remaining sliced garlic in drippings; remove. Add potatoes; brown, stirring often. Add onions and 2 teaspoons salt. Arrange layers of potato mixture, hamburger and tomatoes in 2 1/2-quart casserole; top with layer of potato mixture and tomatoes. Cover; bake in 375-degree oven about 1 hour or until tender. Sprinkle with paprika before serving. Yield: 4 servings.

Mrs. H. F. Jeanguenat, Fort Myers, Fla.

ONE-DISH MEAL

4 tbsp. oleo
1 lb. ground beef
¼ c. chopped onion
1 c. uncooked rice
2 tsp. salt
2 tsp. chili powder
¼ tsp. garlic powder
2 1-lb. cans kidney beans
1 tsp. black pepper
2 c. canned tomatoes

Melt oleo in skillet; saute beef and onion. Remove from skillet; set aside. Add rice to skillet; cook until brown. Add remaining ingredients; add beef mixture. Cook until steaming; turn into greased baking dish. Bake at 350 degrees for 30 minutes. Yield: 6-8 servings.

Mrs. J. B. Frances, Marion, Va.

RANCH-STYLE BAKED BEANS

2 tbsp. butter
1 lb. ground chuck
1 envelope onion soup mix
2 1-lb. cans pork and beans in tomato sauce
1 1-lb. can kidney beans, drained
1 c. catsup
½ c. cold water
2 tbsp. mustard
2 tsp. cider vinegar

Preheat oven to 400 degrees. In large skillet, melt butter; brown meat. Stir in soup mix, beans, catsup, water, mustard and vinegar. Pour into a 2 1/2-quart casserole or bean pot. Bake 30 to 45 minutes until hot and bubbly.

Mrs. W. J. Burton, Pell City, Ala.

WESTERN BEEF CASSEROLE

2 to 4 tbsp. butter or margarine
2 c. chopped onions
1 lb. ground beef
1 tsp. salt
1 c. catsup
2 tbsp. prepared mustard
2 tsp. vinegar
2 1-lb. 12-oz. cans pork and beans
4 bacon slices (opt.)

Heat butter in skillet; add onion and cook over medium heat until soft. Add ground beef; cook, stirring until meat loses red color. Add remaining ingredients except bacon; turn into 2-quart casserole. Top with bacon slices. Bake at 375 to 400 degrees for 30 to 40 minutes or until bacon is browned. Yield: 8 servings.

Mrs. Frank Meyer, Covington, Ky.

WESTERN LIMA CASSEROLE

1 lb. dried lima beans
3 tsp. salt
½ lb. ground beef
1 med. onion, finely chopped
3 tbsp. fat
2 8-oz. cans tomato sauce
1 tbsp. brown sugar
Dash of poultry seasoning

Wash beans; soak overnight in 2 quarts water. Bring to boil; simmer for 30 minutes. Add 2 1/2 teaspoons salt; continue simmering for 30 minutes to 1 hour or until tender. Drain all but 1/2 cup liquid from beans. Brown meat and onion in fat; add to beans. Add remaining salt, tomato sauce, sugar and poultry seasoning; turn into baking dish. Bake at 325 degrees for 1 hour.

Mrs. Ray Frazier, Boynton Beach, Fla.

BEEF AND CORN CASSEROLE

1 lb. lean ground beef
¼ c. diced onion
¼ c. diced green pepper
¾ tsp. salt
⅛ tsp. pepper
1 10 ½-oz. can condensed cream of mushroom soup
1 c. shredded cheddar cheese
2 12-oz. cans golden whole kernel corn, drained

Brown beef, onion and green pepper in small amount of shortening in large heavy frying pan; mix in remaining ingredients. Spoon into greased 1 3/4-quart casserole. Bake at 350 degrees for about 40 minutes. Yield: 4-6 servings.

Mrs. Charles L. McCarty, New Orleans, La.

CORN CREOLE

1 sm. green pepper
1 lge. onion
3 tbsp. vegetable oil
1 lb. ground beef
1 No. 2 can corn
1 egg
2 c. milk
½ c. cornmeal
2 tsp. salt
Pepper
½ c. bread crumbs
2 tbsp. butter or oleo

Chop green pepper and onion; saute in oil until wilted. Add meat; cook until brown. Add corn; cook 1 minute. Beat egg; add milk. Mix milk with meat mixture. Add cornmeal and seasonings; stir well. Pour in greased baking dish; top with bread crumbs. Dot with butter. Bake in 350-degree oven for 45 minutes.

Mrs. W. L. Blalock, Bunkie, La.

BEEF-VEGETABLE CASSEROLE

½ c. chopped onion
1 green pepper, sliced
2 tbsp. shortening or drippings
1 lb. ground beef
1 ½ tsp. salt
¼ tsp. pepper
1 No. 1 can whole kernel corn, drained
4 tomatoes, sliced
¼ c. dry bread crumbs
1 tsp. butter or margarine

Saute onion and green pepper for 3 minutes in shortening. Add meat; brown. Pour off drippings; season. Remove from heat. Place 1/2 of corn in bottom of a 2-quart casserole. Add half of meat mixture, then a layer of tomatoes. Repeat layers. Add bread crumbs to melted butter; sprinkle over casserole. Bake in 300-degree oven for 40 minutes. Yield: 6 servings.

Mrs. R. C. Bouse, Jr., Port Bolivar, Tex.

HEARTY CASSEROLE

4 tbsp. butter
1 med. onion, chopped
2 green peppers, sliced
1 lb. lean ground beef
1 ½ tsp. salt
¼ tsp. pepper
Monosodium glutamate to taste
Paprika to taste
2 eggs
2 c. fresh-cut or canned whole kernel corn
4 med. tomatoes, sliced
Sugar to taste
½ c. dry bread crumbs
Chicken bouillon (opt.)

Melt butter in skillet; add onion and green peppers and cook for 3 minutes. Add meat; mix well. Add salt, pepper, monosodium glutamate and paprika; remove from heat. Add eggs; mix well. Place 1 cup corn in casserole; cover with half the meat mixture. Sprinkle tomatoes with sugar; place half the tomatoes over meat mixture. Place remaining corn over tomatoes; cover with remaining meat mixture. Place remaining tomatoes on top; sprinkle with bread crumbs. Dot generously with additional butter. Bake at 375 degrees for 35 minutes, basting with bouillon occasionally.

Mrs. H. H. Allen, Clearwater, Fla.

EGGPLANT CASSEROLE

1 med. onion, chopped
Chopped green pepper to taste
2 tsp. sugar
1 c. ground meat
Corn oil
1 c. cooked eggplant, drained
2 c. cream-style corn
¼ c. milk
2 eggs
Salt and pepper to taste
1 ½ slices dry toast
4 crackers, crushed
Grated cheese

Cook onion, green pepper, 1 teaspoon sugar and meat in small amount of oil until done. Combine eggplant, corn, milk, eggs, remaining sugar, salt and pepper; crumble 1 slice toast and add. Add crackers and 1 tablespoon corn oil; add meat mixture. Turn into baking dish; sprinkle cheese and remaining toast over top. Set baking dish in pan of hot water. Bake at 350 degrees for about 30 minutes.

Mrs. A. J. Frazier, Llano, Tex.

EGGPLANT CASSEROLE

1 med. eggplant
1 med. onion, minced
1 lb. hamburger
Salt and pepper to taste
1 c. soft bread crumbs
1 egg, beaten

Pare and boil eggplant until tender; drain and mash. Saute or fry minced onion in small amount of shortening until golden brown. Drop hamburger into minced onion and shortening; cook until meat is done or redness has disappeared. Salt and pepper to taste. Combine eggplant, bread crumbs softened in a little water or milk, egg and meat; mix well. Pour in oiled casserole. Bake in 400-degree oven until done or browned.

Mrs. Sam H. Fields, San Antonio, Tex.

EGGPLANT CASSEROLE

1 lge. eggplant, peeled
1 ½ lb. hamburger
1 lge. onion, chopped
1 c. bread crumbs
½ c. corn bread crumbs
½ stick margarine
¾ c. grated cheddar cheese
2 eggs
¼ tsp. garlic powder
3 lge. tomatoes or 1 can tomatoes
3 stalks celery, chopped
½ green pepper, chopped
Salt and pepper to taste

Cook eggplant in salted water until tender. Saute hamburger and onion until onion is tender but not brown. Mix bread crumbs with margarine and cheese; divide in half. Reserve half the mixture for top. Mix remaining ingredients; pour into oiled baking dish. Top with remaining crumb mixture. Bake, covered, at 350 to 375 degrees for 30 minutes. Uncover and brown. Yield: 10 servings.

Mrs. Fay L. Price, Dover, Ark.

EGGPLANT-CHEESE CASSEROLE

1 lge. eggplant, peeled and sliced
1 egg
2 tbsp. water
1 lb. hamburger
2 onions, chopped
2 cans tomato sauce
1 tsp. salt
1 tsp. pepper
¼ tsp. sweet basil
1 clove garlic, crushed
½ lb. shredded cheddar cheese

Beat egg with water; dip eggplant in egg. Fry in oil until light brown; drain on paper towel. Brown hamburger with onion; add tomato sauce, salt, pepper, basil and garlic. Arrange alternate layers of eggplant, meat sauce and cheese in oiled 2-quart casserole, ending with cheese. Bake at 350 degrees for 35 to 40 minutes.

Mrs. Clay Pope, Lebanon, Tenn.

GROUND MEAT CASSEROLE

1 lb. ground meat
½ c. onion, cut fine
1 c. potatoes, diced
1 c. cracker crumbs
1 tsp. salt
½ tsp. pepper
1 tsp. hot sauce
1 egg
4 slices bacon

(Continued on next page)

Mix all ingredients together except bacon; place in casserole. Place slices of bacon on top. Bake at 350 degrees until done, about 30 minutes.

Mrs. Fonnie Rodgers, Ferris, Tex.

HAMBURGER-POTATO PIE

- 1 lb. ground beef
- 1 egg, beaten
- 1 c. bread crumbs
- 3 tbsp. catsup
- 2 tsp. salt
- 2 tsp. pepper
- 8 med. potatoes
- 3 tbsp. margarine or butter
- Paprika

Combine meat, egg crumbs, catsup, 1 teaspoon salt and 1 teaspoon pepper; mix well, adding more crumbs, if needed, to make mixture firm. Put into ungreased glass pie plate. Bake at 350 degrees for 20 minutes or until brown. Cook potatoes until done; mash. Add remaining salt and pepper and margarine. Spread over meat mixture and on sides of pie plate; sprinkle with paprika. Return to oven for 15 minutes or until light brown. Slice as for pie. Garnish with parsley, if desired.

Mrs. Joel Weiner, Raleigh, N. C.

HOMINY PIE

- 1 to 1 ½ lb. hamburger
- 1 med. onion, chopped
- 1 tsp. salt
- ½ tsp. pepper
- 1 tsp. chili powder
- 1 tbsp. (heaping) flour
- 2 c. canned tomatoes
- 2 ½ c. hominy
- ¼ lb. grated American cheese

Sear meat until brown. Add onion; brown lightly. Add salt, pepper and chili powder; blend well. Add flour and tomatoes. Cook for a few minutes, stirring constantly. Add hominy. Place mixture in a shallow baking dish; sprinkle cheese on top. Bake at 325 degrees until bubbling hot. Yield: 6-8 servings.

M. S. Malphrus, Savannah, Ga.

SQUASH CASSEROLE

- 1 lb. ground lean beef
- 1 c. raw rice, washed
- 1 sm. green pepper, chopped
- 1 onion, chopped
- ¼ c. salad oil
- 1 No. 2 ½ can tomatoes
- 1 tsp. salt
- ½ tsp. basil
- 4 green or yellow summer squash, about 7 in. long, sliced
- Grated cheese (opt.)
- Dash of sweet paprika

Brown beef, rice, green pepper and onion in oil in a heavy skillet. Add tomatoes and seasonings. Place sliced squash in a casserole; top with meat mixture. Cover; bake at 350 degrees for about 30 minutes. Stir once. Top with grated cheese and sweet paprika. Return to oven for another 15 to 20 minutes or until done. Yield: 4-6 servings.

Mrs. Cephas Brainerd, Hot Springs, Ark.

AU GRATIN VEGETABLE CASSEROLE

2 tbsp. melted butter
1 sm. onion, chopped
1 lb. hamburger
1 lb. mixed vegetables, cooked
1 can cream of vegetable soup
2 slices toasted bread, crumbled
½ c. grated sharp cheese

Melt butter in skillet; saute onion until tender. Add meat; cook until meat changes color. Add vegetables and soup; pour into buttered casserole. Top with bread crumbs and cheese. Bake at 350 degrees about 30 minutes. Yield: 6 servings.

Mrs. C. L. Dellinger, Raleigh, N. C.

DUTCH DINNER

1 ½ lb. ground beef
4 lge. potatoes, diced
4 lge. carrots, sliced
1 med. onion, diced
Salt and pepper to taste

Spread ground beef evenly on bottom of heavy shallow pan. Spread potatoes, carrots and onion evenly over meat. Season to taste. Cover tightly with foil. Bake at 350 degrees for 1 hour. Yield: 4-6 servings.

Mrs. Buddy Bocksnick, Dover, Ark.

EIGHT-IN-ONE CASSEROLE

2 c. thinly sliced potatoes
2 c. thinly sliced onions
1 c. thinly sliced carrots
1 c. thinly sliced celery
1 c. diced yellow turnips
1 box frozen fordhook lima beans
Dash of garlic salt
Pepper to taste
1 ½ tsp. salt
½ lb. ground beef

In 3-quart casserole mix together vegetables with garlic salt, pepper, 1 teaspoon salt and 1 cup water. Add remaining salt to beef; shape into 4 patties. Arrange patties on vegetables in casserole. Cover; bake in 400-degree oven for 1 hour. Uncover; bake another 15 minutes or until vegetables are tender.

Mrs. J. W. Hopkins, Abilene, Tex.

GARDEN CASSEROLE

1 c. sliced onions
1 lb. ground beef
3 tbsp. fat
1 green pepper, chopped
1 c. chopped celery
1 c. diced carrots
4 lge. firm tomatoes, quartered
¾ tsp. salt
⅛ tsp. pepper
1 tbsp. brown sugar
3 c. seasoned mashed potatoes
2 tbsp. melted butter or margarine
Parsley sprigs

(Continued on next page)

Lightly brown onions and beef in fat, stirring constantly. Add green pepper, celery, carrots, tomatoes, seasonings and sugar; simmer for 20 minutes. Pour into 2-quart casserole; top with potatoes. Brush lightly with butter or margarine. Bake at 350 degrees until golden brown. Garnish with parsley.

Twila Champlin, Loranger, La.

HAMBURGER CASSEROLE

1 lb. hamburger
1 tbsp. salad oil
Dash of thyme
Salt and pepper to taste
3 med. potatoes
2 med. onions
2 15-oz. cans red kidney beans, drained
1 c. chili sauce

Brown hamburger in salad oil; season with thyme, salt and pepper. Slice potatoes and onions thin. Arrange in greased casserole, beginning with hamburger, a layer of potatoes, onions and beans. Pour chili sauce over each layer, ending with hamburger on top. Cover; bake at 350 degrees for 1 hour. Yield: 6 servings.

Robbye Miller, Robertsdale, Ala.

QUICK SUPPER CASSEROLE

2 lb. ground beef
1 med. onion
2 cans green beans, drained
2 cans tomatoes
Mashed potatoes
Paprika

Brown beef and onion in hot oil in large skillet. Add beans and tomatoes; mix well. Cook slowly until excess moisture is absorbed, about 45 minutes. Put in baking dish. Bake at 350 degrees for about 15 minutes. Before serving, cover with mashed potatoes; sprinkle with paprika.

Mrs. Paul Rawson, Hope, Ark.

RUTABAGA CASSEROLE

Salt and pepper to taste
1 lb. ground beef
1 tbsp. flour
2 c. milk
1 No. 303 can diced rutabagas, drained
1 can English peas
3 to 4 c. whipped potatoes

(Continued on next page)

Salt and pepper ground beef; form into small balls. Brown in small amount of oil; remove meatballs and place in 2-quart casserole. Add flour to oil in pan; add milk, salt and pepper to make gravy. Add rutabagas and peas; add gravy and mix lightly. Top with whipped potatoes. Bake at 450 degrees about 30 minutes.

Mrs. Weldon Johnson, Cookville, Tex.

SHIPWRECK CASSEROLE

1 lb. ground beef
¼ tsp. onion salt
¼ tsp. garlic salt
1 tsp. cumin powder
½ tsp. chili powder
¼ tsp. pepper
2 med. potatoes, sliced
2 med. onions, sliced
1 c. celery, chopped
¼ tsp. salt
¼ c. uncooked rice
1 well-beaten egg
1 can kidney beans
1 can undiluted tomato soup

Mix ground beef, onion salt, garlic salt, cumin powder, chili powder and pepper. In large greased casserole, place sliced potatoes, sliced onions, then chopped celery in layers; sprinkle salt over top. Add rice over celery. Place ground beef over top; pat down smooth. Spread egg over beef. Pour kidney beans over all; add tomato soup. Bake, covered, for 1 hour at 325 degrees. Uncover; bake 30 minutes longer. Yield: 8-10 servings.

Mrs. Ida M. Burris, Russellville, Ark.

SHIPWRECK CASSEROLE

1 med. onion, sliced
2 to 3 med. potatoes, sliced paper thin
½ lb. chopped beef
¼ c. uncooked rice
½ c. sliced celery
1 med. can kidney beans
1 sm. can tomato sauce
Salt and pepper
Dash of paprika (opt.)

Arrange onion in buttered 1 1/2 or 2-quart casserole; add a layer of sliced potatoes. Layer beef, rice, celery and beans. Combine tomato sauce, salt, pepper and paprika; pour over casserole. Bake 1 hour at 350 degrees. Yield: 6 servings.

Mrs. Don Bolden, Burlington, N. C.

SIX-LAYER DINNER

Sliced potatoes
¼ c. rice
1 lb. lean ground hamburger
1 lge. onion, sliced
Sliced carrots
Green pepper
1 No. 303 can or 2 c. tomatoes
Salt and pepper

Place potatoes in 2-quart casserole. Sprinkle rice over potatoes; add ground hamburger. Add a layer of onion, carrots and green pepper. Pour tomatoes over all; sprinkle with salt and pepper. Cover; bake 2 hours at 300 degrees.

Mrs. R. E. Elkins, Boys Ranch, Tex.

RECIPE FOR ORIENTAL CHICKEN CASSEROLE ON PAGE 196

BAKED CHICKEN CASSEROLE

1 6-oz. can boned chicken, diced
1 10 ½-oz. can cream of chicken soup
1 c. diced celery
2 tsp. minced onion
½ c. almonds or pecans
½ tsp. salt
¼ tsp. pepper
1 tbsp. lemon juice
¾ c. mayonnaise
3 hard-cooked eggs, thinly sliced
2 c. crushed potato chips

Combine chicken and broth with soup. Mix remaining ingredients except potato chips; combine with chicken mixture. Place in casserole. Sprinkle with potato chips. Bake at 350 degrees for 30 minutes. Leftover chicken or turkey may be substituted for canned chicken. Yield: 6-8 servings.

Mrs. Fred J. Frieling, Austin, Tex.

CHICKEN BREASTS WITH MUSHROOM SAUCE

¾ stick butter or margarine
6 large chicken breasts, halved
1 med. onion, chopped fine
1 c. half and half cream
1 can cream of mushroom soup, undiluted
⅓ c. dry sherry
Salt and pepper to taste
Paprika

Melt butter in skillet. Flour chicken and cook in butter until light brown, not completely cooked. Remove from skillet and place in casserole. Saute chopped onion in grease remaining in skillet. Add half and half, mushroom soup and sherry. Cook until it bubbles and is well mixed. Season to taste. Pour over breasts and sprinkle generously with paprika. Bake about 1 hour and 30 minutes at 350 degrees, covered.

Mrs. Grady P. Gregory, Roanoke, Va.

CHICKEN CASSEROLE

1 c. boned cooked chicken, diced
1 c. chopped celery
4 tsp. chopped onion
3 boiled eggs
Salt and pepper
1 can cream of chicken soup
2 tsp. mayonnaise
1 tsp. lemon juice
2 c. crushed potato chips

Place chicken in casserole dish. On top of chicken, spread celery, onion and boiled eggs. Sprinkle with salt and pepper. Mix soup, mayonnaise and lemon juice. Pour over mixture in casserole. Put crushed potato chips over top. Bake for 20 to 25 minutes in a 350-degree oven.

Mrs. Barnett Ragan, Pine Bluff, Ark.

CHICKEN CASSEROLE

2 c. cubed chicken
2 c. chopped celery
½ c. slivered almonds, blanched and toasted
½ tsp. salt
2 tsp. grated onion
2 tbsp. lemon juice
1 c. mayonnaise
½ c. shredded cheese

(Continued on next page)

Combine first 7 ingredients and pile lightly in 8 1/2-inch round baking pan. Sprinkle cheese over; bake in a 425-degree oven for 15 minutes.

Mrs. A. Smith, Ormond Beach, Fla.

CHICKEN CASSEROLE

1 c. diced chicken breast
½ c. mayonnaise
1 can cream of chicken soup
2 hard-cooked eggs, sliced
1 c. finely chopped celery
1 tsp. grated onion
½ c. soda cracker crumbs
2 tbsp. Worcestershire sauce
½ c. slivered almonds
Potato chips

Cook chicken in salt water until tender. Remove meat from bone and dice. Mix with next 8 ingredients and pour into buttered shallow 9 x 5-inch baking dish. Sprinkle potato chips on top. Bake in a 350-degree oven for about 20 minutes.

Mrs. John Schoel, Russellville, Ala.

CHICKEN CASSEROLE

1 can cream of chicken soup
2 chopped boiled eggs
1 c. boned chicken
½ c. mayonnaise
1 c. chopped celery
2 tbsp. minced onion
2 c. Ritz cracker crumbs
⅓ c. slivered almonds

Mix first 6 ingredients well. Pour in baking dish and cover with cracker crumbs and almonds. Bake at 350 degrees for 30 minutes. Yield: 4-6 servings.

Mrs. John Crook, Evergreen, Ala.

CHICKEN-CHEESE CASSEROLE

Salt
1 frying chicken
1 can cream of mushroom soup
¼ lb. cheese, grated

Salt chicken lightly. Place in baking dish; pour over mushroom soup. Rinse can with 2 or 3 tablespoons water and with a fork work mushrooms to a good consistency for spreading over entire chicken. Sprinkle grated cheese over top. Bake uncovered at 350 degrees for 1 hour to 1 hour and 30 minutes, depending on size of chicken.

Mrs. J. M. Barnett, Ozark, Ark.

CHICKEN-EGG CASSEROLE

1 sm. fryer
2 c. corn flakes
6 slices toast, cubed
1 sm. onion, chopped
2 c. chicken broth
Chopped giblets
3 hard-cooked eggs, chopped
1 can cream of chicken soup

(Continued on next page)

Cook chicken until tender; reserve broth. Combine cornflakes, toast, onion, chicken broth and chopped giblets in casserole dish. Alternate layers of chicken and eggs. Cover with chicken soup. Bake at 300 degrees for 30 minutes. Yield: 6-8 servings.

Mrs. Ralph Ballington, Lexington, S. C.

CHICKEN HUNNINGTON

1 c. macaroni
Chicken stock
3 lb. cooked chicken, diced
1 sm. jar pimento
1 can green peas
1 can mushroom soup
1 c. bread crumbs
½ c. Parmesan cheese

Cook macaroni in stock. Mix well with next 4 ingredients. Pour in 2-quart casserole. Sprinkle bread crumbs and cheese on top. Bake at 325 degrees for 1 hour. Yield: 6 servings.

Elizabeth M. Clark, Chattanooga, Tenn.

CHICKEN POTPIE AND BAKED DUMPLINGS

1 fowl, cut in joints
2 ¼ c. flour
1 tsp. salt
Black pepper
3 level tsp. baking powder
¼ c. shortening
Milk or cream

Cover fowl with boiling water; let simmer till tender. Remôve to baking dish. Mix 1/4 cup flour, 1/2 teaspoon salt and pepper with cold water to make a smooth paste; use to thicken broth. Pour gravy over fowl until it is nearly covered and reserve rest to serve separately. Sift together remaining flour, baking powder and salt 3 times. Work shortening into dry ingredients. Use to make a dough less stiff than biscuits. Drop by spoonfuls into baking dish completely covering fowl. Bake about 25 minutes at 350 degrees.

Mrs. Harvey L. Curlee, Yorktown, Va.

CHICKEN STRATA

6 slices bread
2 c. diced chicken
½ c. mayonnaise
1 c. chopped celery
1 chopped pepper
1 med. onion
Seasoning
4 eggs
3 c. milk
1 can mushroom soup
Grated cheddar cheese
Paprika

Dice 4 slices of bread and arrange over bottom of a greased 13 x 9 x 2-inch baking dish. Combine next 5 ingredients. Season to taste; spread over diced bread. Cut crust from 6 slices of bread and place over chicken. Beat eggs with milk and pour over chicken mixture; refrigerate overnight. Bake at 350 degrees for 15 minutes. Remove from oven and spread undiluted mushroom soup over top. Sprinkle with cheddar cheese and paprika; bake 1 hour longer. Yield: 6-8 servings.

Mrs. Jack Brown, Birmingham, Ala.

CHICKEN SPOON BREAD

3 c. chicken broth
1 c. cornmeal
3 eggs
2 c. chopped chicken
1 ½ tsp. salt
¼ lb. sharp cheese

Heat chicken broth to boiling point. Add cornmeal. Cook until thick. Separate eggs; beat yolks. Add chicken, egg yolks and salt to cooked meal. Fold in beaten egg whites. Bake in greased pan at 325 degrees for 1 hour. Cut in squares. Melt cheese; add enough milk for desired consistency. Serve over squares. Yield: 8 servings.

Mrs. E. H. Gentry, Talladega, Ala.

CHICKEN CASSEROLE

1 5 lb. stewing hen or 2 fryers
2 qts. water
5 tsp. salt
1 carrot
½ c. chopped celery
1 med. onion, chopped
6 sprigs chopped parsley
½ c. plus 4 tbsp. butter
1 ½ loaves 2-day old bread
⅛ tsp. pepper
1 tsp. poultry seasoning
4 c. plus 6 tbsp. broth
1 c. milk
1 c. sifted flour
1 c. melted chicken fat
4 eggs, slightly beaten

Cook hen, water, 2 teaspoons salt and carrot until tender. Remove bread crusts; crumble and reserve for top of casserole. Saute celery, onion and parsley in 1/2 cup butter 5 minutes. Break bread and add to sauteed ingredients with giblets and 1 teaspoon salt, pepper and poultry seasoning. Add 6 tablespoons broth. Heat remaining chicken broth and milk. Do not boil. Make a paste of flour and melted chicken fat; stir into heated broth mixture. Add salt and eggs. Grease casserole. Cover bottom with dressing; add cut-up chicken and top with sauce. Mix crumbled crusts with remaining butter; sprinkle on top of casserole. Bake for 20 minutes at 375 degrees. Yield: 20 servings.

Mrs. F. C. Abraham, Tracy City, Tenn.

CHICKEN CASSEROLE

1 med. onion
6 c. corn bread, crumbled
½ tsp. poultry seasoning
½ tsp. celery seed (opt.)
⅛ tsp. pepper
¾ tsp. salt
2 tbsp. parsley
½ c. butter, melted
5 c. stewed chicken, cut up

Saute onion; combine with next 7 ingredients and pour in large greased casserole. Arrange chicken over corn bread mixture. Pour sauce over chicken and bread mixture. Bake about 1 hour at 350 degrees. Cut in squares to serve.

SAUCE:

¼ c. melted butter
¼ c. flour
1 ½ tsp. salt
2 c. chicken broth
2 eggs, beaten
1 qt. milk

Mix first 4 ingredients together and heat. Cool. Add eggs and milk. Cook over medium heat until slightly thickened.

Mrs. Donald M. Pinckley, Old Hickory, Tenn.

CHICKEN CASSEROLE

- 3 to 4 c. leftover chicken
- 1 ½ qt. bread
- ½ tsp. sage or poultry seasoning
- ⅛ tsp. pepper
- ½ tsp. salt
- ¼ c. chopped onion
- 2 c. chicken broth or gravy

Grease big baking dish. Cube leftover meat and place in bottom of dish. In a separate dish, break up 1 1/2 quarts bread; add seasonings and sauteed onion. Spread bread mixture over chicken. Add broth thickened with flour or leftover chicken gravy. Pour on slowly making wells and bake at 350 degrees for 30 to 35 minutes.

Mrs. Paul S. Grahu, Largo, Fla.

CHICKEN CASSEROLE

- 2 chickens, with broth
- 2 sticks margarine
- 1 c. flour
- 2 c. milk
- 8 eggs
- 3 c. corn bread crumbs
- 1 c. light bread crumbs
- 1 c. finely chopped celery
- ⅓ c. finely chopped onions

Cook chickens in water until done. Remove from broth; cool and remove meat from bones. Cut into large bite-size pieces. Blend margarine and flour for sauce. Season with salt and black pepper. Slowly add four cups broth and milk; cook until thick, stirring constantly. Hard cook 6 eggs; cool. Peel and slice. Combine corn bread crumbs and light bread crumbs with celery, chopped onions and remaining eggs, well beaten. Mix thoroughly; add salt and black pepper to taste. Arrange chicken, slices of egg and dressing in alternate layers in 2-quart casserole. Cover with sauce. Bake 1 hour at 350 degrees. Yield: 16 servings.

Eva S. Ray, Lake View, S. C.

CHICKEN 'N' DRESSING BAKE

- 1 7-oz. pkg. herb-seasoned stuffing
- 1 can cream of mushroom soup
- 2 c. chicken broth
- 2 well-beaten eggs
- 2 ½ c. diced cooked chicken
- ½ c. milk
- 2 tbsp. chopped pimento

Toss stuffing with half the can of soup, broth and eggs. Spread in 11 1/2 x 7 1/2 x 1 1/2-inch baking dish. Top with chicken. Combine remaining soup with milk and pimento. Pour over all. Cover with foil. Bake at 350 degrees for 45 minutes or until set. Yield: 6-8 servings.

Mrs. Emmett Chewning, Rhoadesville, Va.

CHICKEN LAYERED CASSEROLE

- 1 c. chicken fat
- 3 eggs, well beaten
- ½ c. flour
- 3 c. milk
- Salt and pepper
- ¼ c. onion, chopped
- ½ c. celery, chopped
- ½ c. margarine
- 4 c. bread crumbs
- 1 tsp. sage
- Chicken broth
- 1 large cooked hen, diced
- Buttered crumbs

(Continued on next page)

Combine chicken fat, eggs and flour; mix well. Add milk and season to taste. Cook over low heat, stirring constantly. Saute onion and celery in margarine; add bread crumbs, sage, 1 teaspoon salt and 1/4 teaspoon pepper. Moisten with chicken broth. Place layer of dressing in buttered casserole; alternate layers of sauce, chicken and dressing, ending with sauce. Top with buttered crumbs. Bake at 350 degrees until top is browned and dressing is done. Yield: 12-15 servings.

Mrs. Helen Roberts, Alvin, Tex.

CHICKEN-MUSHROOM CASSEROLE

1 can cream of chicken soup
1 4-oz. can sliced mushrooms
¼ tsp. Worcestershire sauce
1 c. boned chicken or turkey, diced
1 c. packaged bread stuffing

Combine soup, mushrooms, Worcestershire sauce and chicken in 1-quart casserole. Sprinkle bread stuffing on top. Bake 25 minutes at 375 degrees. Yield: 8 servings.

Mrs. Elizabeth Simmons, Holland, Va.

CHICKEN 'N' STUFFING CASSEROLE

1 8-oz. pkg. herb stuffing mix
3 c. cubed chicken
2 sticks butter
4 c. chicken broth
½ c. flour
¼ tsp. salt
Dash of pepper
6 eggs
1 c. golden mushroom soup
¼ c. milk
1 sm. can chopped pimentos

Prepare dressing mix using 1 stick butter. Spread in 13 x 9 x 2-inch casserole and top with chicken. Set aside. Slowly blend chicken broth with remaining butter, flour, salt and pepper. Add beaten eggs. Pour over chicken and dressing and bake 40 to 45 minutes in a 325-degree oven. Let stand 5 minutes and cut in squares; set aside. Blend mushroom soup, milk and pimentos. Heat until well blended and pour over chicken and stuffing squares. Yield: 12 servings.

Mrs. Duane W. Hoisington, Florence, Ala.

FRANKLY FANCY BUFFET CHICKEN

1 sm. fat hen
1 med. onion
Chicken fat
1 loaf stale bread, crumbled
4 hard-cooked eggs, chopped
Salt and pepper
Sage
Broth
3 tbsp. flour
4 eggs, beaten
Milk

Cook hen until tender. Remove from bone; cut in small pieces. Cool broth; skim fat from top. Cook onion in chicken fat; add bread, chopped eggs and seasonings. Moisten with broth. Spread dressing in 9 x 15-inch baking pan; cover with chicken. Add flour to remaining fat; heat, stirring constantly. Add eggs to broth and enough milk to make 1 quart liquid; pour into fat and flour. Boil for 3 minutes; pour over chicken and dressing. Bake at 350 degrees for 5 minutes.

Alberta R. Fox, Maplewood, La.

SCALLOPED CHICKEN

1 6-lb. hen cooked tender and cut up
1 c. chicken fat
1 c. flour
1 tsp. salt
Pepper to taste
4 c. chicken broth
2 c. milk
4 c. bread crumbs
⅓ c. melted butter
1 c. chopped celery
⅓ c. finely chopped onion

Melt chicken fat; blend with flour. Season. Slowly add broth and milk, stirring constantly. Cook over medium heat until sauce thickens. Combine bread crumbs with butter, celery, onion, salt and black pepper. Arrange chicken and dressing mixture in alternate layers in large casserole. Cover with sauce and bake 1 hour at 350 degrees. Yield: 16 servings.

Mrs. J. C. Huckaby, Eatonton, Ga.

EASY CHICKEN WITH ONIONS

1 lge. fryer, cut up
½ tsp. salt
½ tsp. pepper
12 to 16 tiny onions or 1 8-oz. can onions
1 can mushroom soup
2 tbsp. cooking sherry
½ c. sharp cheese, shredded

Place chicken in shallow baking dish. Sprinkle with salt and pepper; add onions. Mix soup and sherry; pour over chicken. Sprinkle with cheese. Bake covered for 45 minutes at 350 degrees. Uncover and bake 45 minutes longer.

Mrs. H. A. Maison, Winter Park, Fla.

HERBED CHICKEN EN CASSEROLE

3 whole chicken breasts, cut in half
Salt and pepper
¼ c. butter or margarine
1 can condensed cream of chicken soup
¾ c. sherry
1 5-oz. can water chestnuts, drained and sliced
1 3-oz. can broiled sliced mushrooms, drained
2 tbsp. chopped green peppers
¼ tsp. crushed thyme

Lightly season chicken with salt and pepper; brown slowly in butter in skillet. Arrange browned chicken, skin side up, in a 11 1/2 x 7 1/2 x 1 1/2-inch baking dish. For the sauce, add soup to drippings in skillet; slowly add sherry, stirring smooth. Add remaining ingredients; heat to boiling. Pour sauce over chicken; cover with foil and bake at 350 degrees for 25 minutes. Uncover and continue baking 25 to 35 minutes longer or until chicken is tender. Yield: 6 servings.

L. F. Dickson, Dallas, Tex.

CHICKEN CASSEROLE

1 ½ c. fine noodles, cooked
2 cans boned chicken
1 can cream of chicken soup
1 c. diced celery
2 tbsp. diced onion
½ c. mayonnaise
½ c. slivered almonds
3 tbsp. cream or milk
2 c. rolled potato chips

(Continued on next page)

Cool noodles and mix all ingredients. Bake for 20 minutes at 425 degrees. Yield: 8 servings.

Mrs. Joe J. Wild, Jr., Signal Mountain, Tenn.

CHICKEN-ALMOND CASSEROLE

3 ½ c. noodles
1 c. condensed cream of chicken soup
1 6-oz. can evaporated milk or ⅔ c. light cream
1 tsp. salt
¼ tsp. pepper
½ tsp. dry mustard
1 ½ c. shredded sharp process cheese
2 c. diced cooked chicken or turkey
¾ c. sliced celery
⅓ c. chopped green pepper
⅓ c. chopped pimento
1 c. slivered blanched almonds, toasted lightly

Cook noodles in boiling salted water until tender; drain. Put in greased 2-quart casserole making well in center. Combine soup, evaporated milk, salt, pepper and dry mustard. Heat and stir till hot through. Add cheese, stirring till cheese is melted. Add chicken, celery, green pepper, pimento and half the nuts; pour over noodles. Sprinkle with remaining half of almonds and bake in 400-degree oven 20 minutes or till hot through. Makes 6 servings.

Mrs. K. R. Wood, Miami, Fla.

CHICKEN CASSEROLE

2 c. cooked medium-wide noodles
1 pkg. frozen broccoli
2 tbsp. butter or margarine
2 tbsp. flour
1 tsp. salt
¼ tsp. prepared mustard
¼ tsp. black pepper
2 c. milk
1 c. grated sharp cheddar cheese
2 c. chopped cooked chicken
¼ c. slivered almonds, buttered
Paprika

(Continued on next page)

Cook noodles and broccoli as directed on packages in separate saucepans. Cook until barely tender; drain. Melt butter in saucepan over low heat. Blend in flour, salt, mustard, pepper and milk. Cook stirring constantly, until thickened. Remove from heat and stir in cheese, stirring until melted. Dice broccoli stems and leave the flowerets whole. Arrange noodles, broccoli stems and chicken in buttered 1 1/2-quart casserole. Pour cheese over all. Arrange flowerets to make a border around the dish. Sprinkle buttered almonds on top and sprinkle with paprika. Bake at 350 degrees about 25 minutes or until bubbling hot. Yield: 6 servings.

Mrs. Albert F. Roddy, Chattanooga, Tenn.

CHICKEN CASSEROLE

- 1 4-lb. hen
- 1 qt. water
- Salt
- 1 c. chopped green peppers
- 1 c. chopped onions
- 1 c. chopped celery
- 1 stick butter
- ½ lb. Velveeta cheese
- 1 sm. jar stuffed olives, drained and sliced
- 1 lge. can sliced mushrooms
- 1 can cream of mushroom soup
- 1 4 ½-oz. pkg. artichoke-spinach noodles
- Buttered crushed cheese crackers

Boil hen in salted water. Reserve broth; cut chicken into bite-sized pieces. Saute green peppers, onions and celery in butter. Add cheese; stir gently until melted. Add olives, mushrooms and soup. Add broth if necessary. Boil noodles in reserved broth until tender. Mix with sauce and pour into greased casserole. Top with cheese cracker crumbs. Bake at 300 degrees for 45 minutes.

Mrs. Frank McCollum, Birmingham, Ala.

CHICKEN CASSEROLE

- 2 fryers
- 1 12-oz. pkg. noodles
- 4 c. onions, chopped fine
- 4 c. celery, chopped fine
- 1 stick oleo
- 2 cans mushrooms
- 2 cans mushroom soup
- 2 sm. cans chopped pimento and juice
- 2 cans cream of chicken soup

Stew fryers; drain and reserve broth. Cut chicken from bones into small chunks. Cook noodles in broth. Saute onions and celery in butter. Add mushrooms, mushroom soup, pimento and juice, chicken soup and chicken. Blend all together carefully with noodles. Bake in casserole at 375 degrees for 20 minutes.

Mrs. W. B. McNulty, Baytown, Tex.

CHICKEN CASSEROLE SUPREME

- ½ c. water
- 2 cans mushroom soup
- 2 c. diced cooked chicken
- 1 c. diced celery
- ½ c. grated onion
- 1 sm. can water chestnuts, drained and sliced
- 6 oz. cashews
- 1 4-oz. can sliced and drained mushrooms
- 2 sm. cans fried noodles

(Continued on next page)

Mix water and soup; pour over other ingredients, except 1 can noodles. Mix together lightly and pour into baking dish. Bake at 325 degrees for 40 minutes. Top with reserved can of noodles.

Mrs. Dan T. Williams, Macon, Ga.

CHICKEN-NOODLE CASSEROLE

1 5-oz. pkg. medium noodles, cooked
2 c. diced chicken
1 c. chopped celery
1 can condensed chicken soup
⅔ c. evaporated milk
1 ½ c. shredded cheese
¼ c. chopped pimento
1 tsp. salt
Buttered bread crumbs

Place well drained, cooked noodles in 2-quart casserole. Top with chicken and celery. Mix and heat while stirring soup, milk, cheese, pimento and salt. Pour over chicken and noodles; top with bread crumbs. Bake, uncovered, in 400-degree oven for about 20 minutes or until bubbly hot and brown.

Mrs. J. P. Smith, Snow Hill, N. C.

CHICKEN AND NOODLES BRINSFIELD

1 lge. pkg. thin noodles
2 cans mushroom soup
3 c. cooked chicken
Pepper to taste
Paprika to taste
3 tbsp. curry powder
1 8-oz. pkg. sliced American cheese
1 8-oz. pkg. sliced mozzarella cheese

Cook noodles until tender; drain. Add soup, chicken, pepper, paprika and curry powder; mix well. Alternate layers of noodle mixture and cheeses in a casserole. Bake at 350 degrees until bubbly. Yield: 8 servings.

Mrs. S. E. Brinsfield, Montgomery, Ala.

CHICKEN ROYAL

1 c. sliced mushrooms
2 tbsp. butter
1 lge. onion, chopped
1 clove garlic, minced
½ green pepper, chopped
2 c. diced cooked chicken
⅓ lb. wide cooked noodles
1 c. chopped walnuts
1 can ripe olives, chopped
2 cans mushroom soup
1 ½ c. water or chicken broth
Salt, pepper and garlic salt to taste
½ c. grated Parmesan cheese

Saute mushrooms in butter; add onion, garlic and green pepper. Cook until tender. Combine chicken and noodles with the mushroom and green pepper mixture. Add walnuts and olives. Place mixture in a greased 2-quart casserole. Combine soup and water and pour over the mixture. Add seasonings. Bake at 350 degrees for 45 minutes to 1 hour. Remove from oven and sprinkle cheese on top.

Mrs. Darrell Royall, Austin, Tex.

CHICKEN STAR BAKE

1 8-oz. pkg. lasagna noodles
1 can cream of mushroom soup
½ tsp. salt
½ tsp. poultry seasoning
⅔ c. milk
2 3-oz. pkg. cream cheese, softened
1 c. cream-style cottage cheese
⅓ c. sliced stuffed green olives
⅓ c. chopped onions (opt.)
⅓ c. chopped green pepper
¼ c. minced parsley
3 c. diced cooked chicken
1 ½ c. buttered soft bread crumbs
2 slices pimento, shaped into stars

Cook noodles in boiling salted water until tender. Drain; rinse in cold water. Mix soup, salt, seasoning and milk; heat. Beat cheeses together; stir in olives, onions, green pepper and parsley. Place half noodles in 11 1/2 x 7 1/2 x 1 1/2-inch baking dish; spread with half the cheese mixture, half the chicken and half the soup. Repeat layers. Top with crumbs. Bake in 375-degree oven for 30 minutes or until heated through. Trim with pimento stars. Let stand 10 minutes before serving. Yield: 8 servings.

Mrs. F. S. Fagan, Hendersonville, N. C.

CHICKEN SUPREME

2 2¼-lb. fryers
1 c. chopped green peppers
1 c. chopped onions
1 c. chopped celery
1 stick butter
½ lb. Velveeta cheese
1 bottle stuffed olives, sliced
1 can whole mushrooms
2 cans cream of mushroom soup
1 pkg. spinach noodles

Boil chickens until done; reserve stock. Cool chicken; cut into pieces. Saute green peppers, onions and celery in butter until tender. Add cheese, olives, mushrooms and mushroom soup; mix well. Cook noodles in chicken stock. Combine all ingredients with chicken pieces. Place in casserole. Heat in 350-degree oven. Serve hot with sliced almonds on top.

Mrs. Charles Mitchell, Memphis, Tenn.

CHICKEN-ALMOND BAKE

1 can cream of celery soup
¼ c. plus 2 tbsp. milk
1 6-oz. can boned chicken, diced or 1 c. cooked, diced chicken
½ c. minced celery
1 sm. minced onion
½ c. slivered almonds
¼ tsp. Worcestershire sauce
1 can Chinese noodles

Blend celery soup and milk. Add the diced chicken, celery, onion, almonds and Worcestershire sauce. Cover bottom of long baking dish with half the noodles. Pour in the chicken mixture. Top with remaining noodles. Bake in a 350-degree oven for 30 to 35 minutes. Yield: 4-5 servings.

Mrs. W. H. Yeary, Lexington, Ky.

CHICKEN-NOODLE CASSEROLE

Chow mein noodles
1 can mushroom soup
1 can chicken fricassee soup
1 c. evaporated milk

(Continued on next page)

Line baking dish with noodles. After mixing first 3 ingredients, spoon over noodles. Alternate layers of noodles and mixture, finishing with noodles. Put in oven for approximately 25 minutes at 300 degrees. Yield: 4 servings.

Mrs. B. H. Fallow, Sr., Charleston Heights, S. C.

CHICKEN CRUNCH

3 c. diced chicken
2 10 ½-oz. cans mushroom soup
½ c. chicken broth or sweet milk
¼ diced onion
1 c. diced celery
1 5-oz. can drained, sliced water chestnuts
1 3-oz. can Chinese noodles
½ c. toasted almonds

Mix first 7 ingredients in order listed; pour into greased casserole and bake 40 minutes at 325 degrees. Sprinkle with toasted almonds. Yield: 10-12 servings.

Mrs. W. I. Kinsey, Franklin, Tenn.

FIVE-CAN CASSEROLE

1 can whole chicken, boned and diced
1 can mushroom soup
1 can chicken and rice soup
1 sm. can chow mein noodles
1 sm. can evaporated milk
1 c. crushed potato chips

Mix first 5 ingredients and pour into 9 x 9-inch baking dish. Top with potato chips. Bake in a 400-degree oven for about 15 minutes or until bubbly. Yield: 6 servings.

Mrs. Woodrow W. Patterson, Austin, Tex.

SOUPER CHICKEN-NOODLE CASSEROLE

1 can cream of chicken soup
⅓ c. milk
1 c. cubed chicken or 1 sm. can boned chicken
1 c. cooked noodles
1 c. cooked green beans
1 tbsp. minced onion
Buttered bread crumbs

Blend soup with milk in a 1 1/2-quart casserole. Add chicken, noodles, green beans and onion. Top with bread crumbs. Bake in 400-degree oven for 25 minutes. Garnish casserole with tomato slices.

Mrs. Wilder Patterson, Meridianville, Ala.

ARROZ A LA FILIPINA

1 sm. chicken
3 ripe tomatoes
1 sm. onion
Achuete, red coloring
3 cloves garlic
3 tbsp. lard
Salt and pepper
3 med. green peppers
½ c. boiled rice
½ c. boiled malagkit, mocha rice
1 sm. pkg. raisins
1 hard-boiled egg

(Continued on next page)

Cut chicken into small pieces. Slice tomatoes and onion. Soak achuete in a small amount of water; set aside. Saute garlic, onion, tomatoes and chicken in fat; add salt and pepper to taste. Cover; when chicken is brown, add water. Cook until tender. Add sliced green pepper; cook for a few minutes. Add achuete water for coloring, then boiled rice, malagkit and raisins. Stir mixture occasionally to prevent burning. Continue cooking on low heat. Garnish with hard-boiled eggs and green pepper.

Mrs. Leonor L. Lapid, Elizabeth City, N. J.

ARROZ CON POLLO

- Salt and pepper
- 1 chicken, cut into serving pieces
- 3 tbsp. olive oil
- 1 clove garlic
- 1 c. rice
- 2 c. chicken broth
- ¼ tsp. saffron
- 1 pkg. frozen peas
- 1 sm. can white asparagus (opt.)
- 1 sm. jar pimento, cut into strips (opt.)

In a deep heavy pot, brown seasoned chicken in olive oil; add garlic clove. Cook for a few minutes; discard garlic. Add rice; brown slightly. Add chicken broth, saffron, 1 teaspoon salt and peas; bring to a boil. Cover tightly; reduce heat to low. Simmer until all the liquid has been absorbed and chicken is tender. Just before serving, heat asparagus. Heap rice in center of platter; put chicken around rice. Garnish with asparagus and pimento.

Doran R. Them, Charleston, S. C.

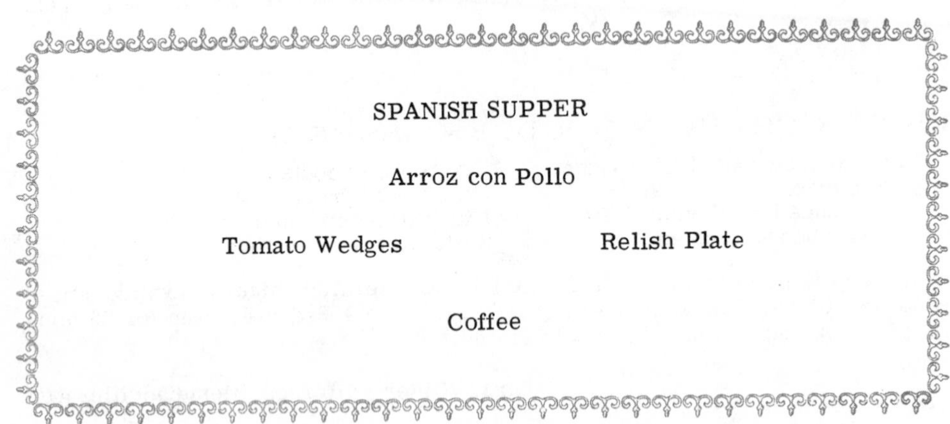

SPANISH SUPPER

Arroz con Pollo

Tomato Wedges

Relish Plate

Coffee

BAYOU TURKEY DINNER

- 3 c. cooked rice
- 2 green peppers, coarsely chopped
- 2 c. cooked turkey, diced
- 1 No. 2 can tomatoes
- 1 tsp. salt
- ⅛ tbsp. pepper
- 2 c. turkey gravy
- Dash of Tabasco sauce
- 2 tbsp. butter or margarine, melted

(Continued on next page)

Arrange alternate layers of rice, green peppers, turkey and tomatoes in a greased 2 1/2-quart baking dish. Season each layer with salt and pepper. Mix gravy, Tabasco sauce and butter; pour over casserole. Bake, uncovered, in preheated 350-degree oven for 30 minutes or until bubbling. Yield: 6 servings.

Mary Russell Cunningham, Evergreen, Ala.

CHICKEN AND BROWN RICE CASSEROLE

½ stick butter or margarine
6 med. onions, chopped medium fine
1 c. chopped celery, chopped medium fine
Salt and pepper to taste
1 c. brown rice
Chicken stock
3 c. diced cooked chicken
1 sm. can ripe olives (chopped)
¼ c. coffee cream

Combine butter, onions, celery, salt and pepper in skillet; saute slowly until tender and golden. Cook rice in chicken stock; add to onion mixture. Add chicken; toss mixture lightly. Add chopped olives; turn into large greased casserole. Dribble cream over top. Bake at 425 degrees for 15 to 20 minutes or until hot. Yield: 8 servings.

Mrs. I. E. Jackson, Winder, Ga.

CHICKEN CASSEROLE

1 ½ c. mayonnaise
1 c. chopped celery
1 can cream of chicken soup
1 can cream of mushroom soup
3 c. cooked chicken
6 hard-boiled eggs, chopped
1 c. chicken broth
1 c. milk
3 c. cooked rice
2 c. Chinese noodles
½ lb. cheese
Crushed potato chips

Mix all ingredients except potato chips. Put in baking dish. Bake 1 hour at 325 degrees. The last 15 minutes of baking, put crushed potato chips on top. Return to oven. This casserole may be frozen.

Mrs. Paul E. Root, Vidor, Tex.

CHICKEN CASSEROLE

1 c. uncooked rice
8 pieces uncooked chicken
1 pkg. onion soup mix
1 can cream of mushroom soup
1 soup can water

Place rice on bottom of greased round casserole; place chicken pieces on top of rice. Sprinkle onion soup mix over chicken; add mushroom soup mixed with water. Cover casserole; bake in 325-degree oven for 2 hours.

Mrs. Leonard Rice, Shreveport, La.

CHICKEN CASSEROLE

1 c. celery, diced
1 onion, chopped
2 ½ c. cooked chicken meat
1 ½ tsp. salt
1 bay leaf
1 c. uncooked rice
¼ c. peas and carrots
1 green pepper, cut in pieces
2 c. chicken broth
Sliced olives

Mix all ingredients except olives; place in baking dish. Bake at 350 degrees, covered, 35 minutes. Uncover; bake 40 minutes longer. Pour into chafing dish; serve hot. Garnish with olives. Yield: 6 servings.

Mrs. John R. Taylor, Jr., Jonesboro, Tenn.

CHICKEN CASSEROLE

3 c. cooked rice
3 c. cooked chicken, cubed
1 lb. Velveeta cheese
1 can cream of chicken soup
1 med. onion
½ c. celery
½ stick oleo
½ c. milk
1 can water chestnuts, sliced
Salt and pepper

Combine rice and chicken. Melt cheese in soup. Saute onion and celery in butter; add to soup mixture. Add milk; combine with chicken and rice. Add water chestnuts; season with salt and pepper. Pour into 9 x 13-inch dish. Bake in 350-degree oven for 45 minutes. Yield: 8-10 servings.

Mrs. Core S. Rosenbaune, Little Rock, Ark.

CHICKEN CASSEROLE

½ c. raw wild rice
Salt
1 c. raw white rice
Chicken stock
Cream
Seasoning to taste
Chopped parsley
Chopped onion
Chopped celery leaves
Mushrooms (opt.)
1 chicken, cooked and cut in pieces

Cook wild rice in salted water until done. Cook white rice according to package directions. Place in well-buttered casserole. Cook stock down; add enough cream to make consistency of thin gravy. Add seasonings, parsley, onion, celery and mushrooms. Pour over chicken and rice in casserole. Bake until slightly firm, but not dry, in 350-degree oven.

Mrs. Richard Steeves, Blytheville, Ark.

CHICKEN CASSEROLE DELIGHT

1 2 ½-lb. fryer
1 cup rice
1 can cream of chicken soup
1 can cream of celery soup
1 can cream of chicken soup
1 soup can water
½ stick margarine

Place cut-up chicken in casserole dish; add rice. Heat remaining ingredients in pan; pour over chicken. Cover; bake at 325 degrees 1 hour or until tender.

Mrs. Polly Click, Sardis, Ga.

CHICKEN CASSEROLE WITH MUSHROOM SAUCE

3 c. diced cooked chicken or turkey
1 c. cooked rice
2 c. soft bread crumbs
⅓ c. diced celery
¼ c. chopped pimento
2 tsp. salt
¼ tsp. poultry seasoning
2 c. chicken broth
4 beaten eggs

Combine chicken, rice, bread crumbs, celery and pimento. Add salt, poultry seasoning and broth to eggs; mix thoroughly. Stir into chicken mixture. Bake in greased 9 x 9 x 2-inch baking dish in 350-degree oven 55 minutes. Cut in squares; serve with Mushroom Sauce.

MUSHROOM SAUCE:

1 can cream of mushroom soup
⅔ soup can milk
1 3-oz. can drained mushrooms

Put all ingredients in saucepan; heat, stirring often. Yield: 8 servings.

Mrs. James L. Wright, Perryton, Tex.

CHICKEN CASSEROLE

1 ½ c. mayonnaise
1 c. chopped celery
1 can cream of chicken soup
1 can cream of mushroom soup
3 c. cooked chicken, chopped
6 hard-boiled eggs, chopped
1 c. chicken broth
½ c. milk
2 c. Chinese noodles
3 c. cooked rice
½ lb. Velveeta cheese, cubed

Mix all ingredients except crumbs. Put in greased baking dish. Bake 1 hour at 350 degrees. About the last 15 or 20 minutes of baking time, cover top with crushed potato chips. This casserole freezes well. Yield: 14-16 servings.

Mrs. John E. Ainsworth, Monticello, Ark.

CHICKEN-CORN PIE

1 chicken, cooked and boned
1 c. chicken broth
1 c. rice, cooked
2 tbsp. butter
4 ears corn, scraped from cob
½ tsp. salt
Dash of pepper
2 well-beaten eggs

Add butter to rice while hot. Place half of rice in buttered baking dish. Add chicken, corn, salt and pepper. Pour in chicken broth; add remaining rice. Pour eggs over all. Bake at 350 degrees about 20 minutes or until brown.

Mrs. E. W. Alexander, Galveston, Tex.

CHICKEN CURRY WITH RICE

1 c. uncooked rice
2 cans condensed mushroom soup
½ tsp. curry powder
8 ripe olives, chopped
1 sm. onion, chopped
2 c. cooked chicken, cut up
Parsley
1 sm. can sliced mushrooms

Cook rice according to package directions. Combine 1 can mushroom soup, 1/4 teaspoon curry powder, olives and onion; add to rice. Add chicken; mix together. Transfer to greased 2-quart baking dish; cover with foil. Bake in 375-degree oven for 25 minutes. Top with parsley. Heat remaining mushroom soup, remaining curry powder and sliced mushrooms. Serve sauce over each serving of chicken.

Mrs. William G. Stoner, Harrisonburg, Va.

CHICKEN AND DIRTY RICE

1 can onion soup
1 c. rice
1 chicken, cut up
Flour
Oil

Mix soup with enough water to make 2 cups liquid. Add rice; pour into casserole. Season to taste. Roll chicken in flour; fry in oil until golden brown. Add 1/3 cup drippings to rice mixture; top with chicken. Cover; bake at 400 degrees for 1 hour. Yield: 6 servings.

Mrs. J. W. Odom, Picayune, Miss.

CHICKEN A LA KING CASSEROLE

¾ c. chicken broth
¾ c. milk
1 sm. onion, stuck with 2 cloves
½ c. (about) butter
3 tbsp. flour
1 c. sliced mushrooms
¼ c. minced green pepper
¼ c. pimento, cut into ¼-in. pieces
2 c. diced cooked chicken
1 tsp. salt or to taste
¼ tsp. pepper or to taste
1 ⅓ c. long grain rice
½ c. grated Parmesan or Swiss cheese
2 egg yolks, beaten

Combine chicken broth, milk and onion; simmer 5 minutes. Remove onion; keep liquid hot. Melt 3 tablespoons butter; stir in flour. Cook, stirring constantly, for 2 minutes. Do not brown. Add hot liquid all at once; cook over low heat, stirring constantly, until sauce is smooth and thickened. Remove from heat. Add 4 tablespoons butter in another saucepan; cook mushrooms and green pepper 5 to 7 minutes, stirring frequently. Stir into sauce; add pimento, chicken, salt and pepper. Remove from heat. Cook rice in boiling water until barely tender; drain. Melt 3 tablespoons butter; combine with rice, 1/4 cup grated cheese and beaten egg yolks. Mix well. Put 2/3 of rice mixture into a 2-quart casserole. Press rice against bottom and sides, leaving a well in the middle. Put chicken filling into the well; spoon remaining rice over the filling, completely covering filling. Spread remaining cheese on top. Bake in preheated oven at 350 degrees for 1 hour.

Mrs. George R. Cowan, Milton, Fla.

CHICKEN AND RICE

5 oz. instant rice
½ pkg. dry onion soup mix
1 can cream of mushroom soup
1 ¼ c. boiling water
¼ c. dry sherry
2 tbsp. chopped pimento
Salt and pepper to taste
Paprika
½ stick butter, melted
Chicken breasts or whole chicken

Combine all ingredients except seasonings, butter and chicken; place in greased baking dish. Brush chicken with melted butter; place over soup mixture. Add salt, pepper and paprika. Bake, covered, at 375 degrees for 1 hour and 15 minutes; remove cover. Bake for 15 minutes. Yield: 4-6 servings.

Mrs. Carol Taylor, Maitland, Fla.

CHICKEN AND RICE

1 2 to 2 ½-lb. fryer
1 c. uncooked rice
Salt and pepper
Garlic powder
1 10 ½-oz. can cream of chicken soup
1 soup can water

Cut fryer into small pieces. Spread rice over bottom of a heavy roaster or large casserole dish. Arrange chicken evenly on top. Season with salt, pepper and garlic. Mix cream of chicken soup with water; pour over chicken and rice. Add more water if needed to barely cover chicken. Cover; bake in a 325-degree oven for 2 hours. Add additional water, if necessary during baking. Yield: 4 servings.

Mrs. Dan Schovajsa, Rosharon, Tex.

CHICKEN AND RICE

½ stick oleo, melted
1 c. raw rice
1 c. water
1 can cream of mushroom soup
1 can consomme
1 onion, chopped
Salt and pepper
1 fryer, cut in serving pieces

Melt oleo in 10 x 6 x 1 1/2-inch baking dish. Mix in rice , water, soup, consomme and onion. Salt and pepper chicken; place on top of rice mixture. Bake in a 350-degree oven for 1 hour and 15 minutes or until rice and chicken are done. Turn chicken 1 time during baking. Two cups stewed boned chicken may be substituted for chicken pieces and mixed in with rice mixture.

Mrs. Elbert Hays, Beaumont, Tex.

CHICKEN AND RICE

Salt and pepper
1 med. chicken, cut up
1 c. uncooked long grain rice
1 can cream of chicken soup
1 soup can water
Paprika (opt.)

(Continued on next page)

Salt and pepper chicken; place in long baking dish. Add remaining ingredients. Cover; bake in 350-degree oven for 1 hour to 1 hour and 30 minutes. Serve hot.

Mrs. Wanda J. Otts, Winnsboro, Tex.

CHICKEN-RICE CASSEROLE

1 ½ c. uncooked rice
½ c. water
1 can onion soup
1 chicken, cut up
Salt and pepper
1 can cream of chicken soup

Spread rice in buttered 4-quart casserole; pour water and onion soup over rice. Season chicken with salt and pepper. Place chicken, skin side up, on rice and soup mixture. Spoon chicken soup over chicken. Cover; bake at 350 degrees for 1 hour. Yield: 6 servings.

Mrs. Shirley Exley, Clyo, Ga.

CHICKEN-RICE CASSEROLE

3 whole chicken breasts, cut in half
Salt
1 c. converted rice
2 bouillon cubes
2 c. hot water
1 can mushroom soup
½ tsp. Worcestershire sauce
2 c. hot water
2 dashes of Tabasco
1 can pimentos, cut in strips
Butter

Cut chicken; wash and soak in salt water. Put rice in bottom of deep pan; sprinkle with small amount of salt. Dissolve chicken bouillon cubes in hot water; add mushroom soup, Worcestershire sauce and Tabasco. Mix well; pour over rice. Place pimentos over rice. Place chicken on top. Dot with butter. Bake in 350-degree oven for 1 hour and 30 minutes until chicken browns. Yield: 6 servings.

Mrs. Estelle B. Hill, Amherst, Va.

CHICKEN AND RICE CASSEROLE

1 c. chopped celery
1 can cream of chicken soup
½ c. chopped almonds
2 tbsp. chopped onion
¾ c. mayonnaise
3 hard-cooked eggs, chopped
1 c. raw rice, cooked
1 can boned chicken
2 c. crushed potato chips

Boil celery until tender; combine with soup, almonds, onion, mayonnaise and eggs. Alternate layers of rice, chicken and soup mixture in buttered casserole until all are used. Top with potato chips. Bake at 400 degrees for 20 minutes. Yield: 6-8 servings.

Bonnie Nettles, Vidalia, La.

CHICKEN-RICE CASSEROLE

1 c. uncooked rice
1 can cream of celery soup
1 can cream of chicken soup
1 c. water
6 chicken breasts
½ stick melted butter

Put rice in bottom of 2-quart casserole. Mix soups with water; pour over rice. Dip chicken breasts in melted butter; place on top of rice. Bake at 325 degrees for about 45 minutes.

Mrs. T. Marvin Vick, Raleigh, N. C.

CHICKEN AND RICE CASSEROLE

1 c. raw rice
1 envelope dry onion soup
1 can cream of mushroom soup
2 soup cans water
1 3-lb. fryer, cut up

Mix raw rice, dry onion soup, cream of mushroom soup and water in medium roasting pan or 4-quart casserole. Place cut-up chicken on top of rice mixture; cover with foil. Bake 30 minutes at 425 degrees. Remove foil; bake 30 minutes longer to lightly brown. Yield: 6 servings.

Mrs. F. W. Allain, Hammond, La.

CHICKEN AND RICE CASSEROLE

1 ¼ tbsp. salt
1 frying chicken, cut in pieces
4 tbsp. margarine or any shortening
5 c. water
1 ½ c. long grain rice

Sprinkle 1 tablespoon salt over chicken; brown in shortening. Place in large casserole or small roaster. Pour water in pan in which chicken was fried; add remaining salt. Bring to a boil, scraping side and bottom of pan. Pour over chicken; add rice. Cover; bake 1 hour. Turn off oven. Leave dish in oven another 15 minutes or longer. Add boiling water if necessary. Yield: 6-8 servings.

Mrs. Walter Jacob, Walburg, Tex.

CHICKEN AND RICE CASSEROLE

1 c. rice
1 pkg. prepared onion soup mix
1 2 ½-lb. chicken, cut up
1 1 ½-oz. pkg. prepared mushroom soup mix
3 c. water

Place rice in bottom of an ungreased casserole dish; sprinkle onion soup mix on top of rice. Arrange chicken on top; cover with mushroom soup mix and water. Bake at 350 degrees 1 hour and 30 minutes or until chicken is tender.

Mrs. John Doolittle, Mountain Home, Ark.

CHICKEN AND RICE CASSEROLE

1 fat hen
2 c. rice
2 cans cream of mushroom soup
1 tbsp. minced onion
Salt and pepper
1 c. slivered almonds
1 sm. can pimento
2 c. bread crumbs

Cover hen with salted water; cook until tender. Let cool in broth. Skim off fat; reserve. Remove chicken from bones; cut in small pieces. Wash rice; cook in 4 cups chicken broth, boiling rapidly for 20 minutes. Add mushroom soup, onion, salt and pepper to taste. Combine with chicken, almonds and pimento; pour into greased casserole. Heat reserved chicken fat in a skillet; saute bread crumbs. Mix thoroughly; spread over chicken-rice mixture. Bake in 350-degree oven 1 hour and 30 minutes to 2 hours. Casserole may also be baked in flat pan and served in squares. A sauce may be made with broth and thick cream and served with chicken, if desired. Garnish with small strips of pimento.

Mrs. Otto Murphy, Springfield, Tenn.

CHICKEN-RICE CREOLE

⅓ c. flour
1 ½ tsp. paprika
½ tsp. poultry seasoning
1 ½ tsp. salt
½ tsp. pepper
1 frying chicken, cut in pieces
Cooking oil
1 c. uncooked rice
½ c. chopped onion
½ c. chopped green pepper
3 c. chicken broth

Combine dry ingredients in paper sack. Add meaty pieces of chicken; shake until well floured. Brown in skillet in small amount of cooking oil. Place rice, onion, green pepper and additional seasoning in baking dish; top with cooked chicken. Pour broth over all. Bake 45 minutes at 400 degrees.

Mrs. Ray Dorsey, Edna, Tex.

CHICKEN SCALLOP

⅓ c. uncooked rice
2 c. chicken broth
2 ½ c. diced chicken
⅓ c. chopped celery
¼ c. pimento
2 eggs, beaten
¾ tsp. salt
⅛ tsp. poultry seasoning
¼ c. chopped onion
3 tbsp. butter
3 tbsp. flour
½ c. sour cream
1 c. mushrooms, drained

Cook rice in 2 cups broth for 10 minutes. Add chicken, celery, pimento, eggs, salt and poultry seasoning. Cook onion in butter until tender. Blend in flour. Stir in remaining broth, sour cream and mushrooms. Add rice; pour into large greased baking dish. Bake at 325 degrees for 40 minutes. Yield: 4-6 servings.

Mrs. Carolyn Weisheit, Montgomery, Ala.

CHICKEN-RICE VEGETABLE LOAF

1 4 to 5-lb. chicken
3 c. cooked rice
1 ½ c. chicken broth
1 c. milk
½ c. condensed milk or cream
1 tsp. salt
1 tsp. pepper
½ tsp. paprika
1 tsp. sage
2 tbsp. chopped pimento
½ c. chopped green pepper
1 c. chopped celery
1 tbsp. minced onion
½ c. canned green peas
4 beaten eggs

Steam chicken until tender; remove meat from bones and dice. Combine all ingredients in order given; mix well. If chicken stock is used, less salt may be added. Pack in buttered ring mold or loaf pan. Bake in oven at 325 degrees for 45 to 60 minutes. Allow to stand 10 minutes or longer in warm place. Turn out on platter; serve with chicken giblet gravy or Mushroom Sauce. Garnish with parsley.

MUSHROOM SAUCE:

3 tbsp. melted butter
3 tbsp. flour
¾ tsp. salt
1 can mushroom soup plus milk to equal 3 c. liquid
¼ tsp. white pepper
½ tsp. paprika
½ c. green peas

Melt butter in saucepan; blend in flour and salt. Add liquid gradually while stirring; add pepper and paprika. Bring to boiling. Boil 3 minutes. Add peas. Yield: 12 servings.

Mrs. J. F. Dorsey, Arkadelphia, Ark.

CHICKEN AND WILD RICE

1 pkg. long grain and wild rice, mixed
2 ¾ c. boiling water
2 lb. chicken
Salt and pepper
Garlic salt
Butter or margarine
1 can drained mushrooms (opt.)

Place rice in 2-quart casserole; stir in boiling water. Sprinkle chicken with salt, pepper and garlic salt; brush with butter. Arrange over rice in casserole. Add mushrooms. Bake in 375-degree oven for 1 hour and 30 minutes. Uncover; place under broiler to brown chicken on both sides. One-half cup sherry may be substituted for 1/2 cup of the boiling water.

Mrs. Jack L. Pink, Dallas, Tex.

EASY CHICKEN AND RICE CASSEROLE

1 c. (scant) cooked rice
1 c. chicken stock
4 hard-cooked eggs
2 c. cooked chicken, chopped
1 can cream of mushroom soup
Grated cheese

(Continued on next page)

Place rice in casserole; add stock. Cover with layers of egg slices and chicken. Pour soup over chicken. Top with cheese. Bake at 350 degrees for 20 minutes or until hot and bubbly. Yield: 6-8 servings.

Mrs. R. A. Clayton, Jr., Birmingham, Ala.

CHICKEN-WILD RICE CASSEROLE

2 3-lb. whole broiler-fryer chickens
1 c. water
1 c. dry sherry
1 ½ tsp. salt
½ tsp. curry powder
1 med. onion, sliced
½ c. sliced celery
1 lb. fresh mushrooms
¼ c. butter or margarine
2 6-oz. pkg. long grain and wild rice with seasonings
1 c. sour cream
1 10 ½-oz. can condensed cream of mushroom soup

Place chicken in a deep kettle. Add water, sherry, salt, curry powder, onion and celery. Bring to boil; cover tightly. Reduce heat; simmer 1 hour. Remove from heat; strain broth. Refrigerate chicken and broth at once. When chicken is cool, remove meat from bones; discard skin. Cut into bite-sized pieces. Wash mushrooms; pat dry. Saute in butter until golden brown, reserving enough to circle top of casserole. Measure chicken broth; use as part of liquid for cooking rice, following package directions for firm rice. Combine chicken, rice and mushrooms in 3 1/2 or 4-quart casserole. Blend sour cream and undiluted mushroom soup. Toss together with chicken mixture. Arrange reserved mushrooms in circle on top of casserole. Cover; refrigerate, if desired, for use the next day. Bake in 350-degree oven for 1 hour. Yield: 8-10 servings.

Mrs. C. Edward Gardner, Pennington Gap, Va.

CURRIED RICE CASSEROLE

1 tbsp. oleo or butter
1 c. rice
1 c. celery, chopped fine
¼ c. onion, chopped fine
1 can water chestnuts, sliced
1 can bamboo shoots
1 tsp. salt
2 tsp. curry powder
1 can cream of chicken soup
2 c. water
6 to 8 chicken breasts or meaty parts of 1 fryer, salted to taste

Grease casserole with butter. Combine rice, celery, onion, water chestnuts, bamboo shoots, salt, curry powder, chicken soup and 1 1/2 cups water. Mix well; pour into casserole. Place chicken breasts on top. Cover casserole; bake 1 hour and 30 minutes at 350 degrees. Add remaining water after mixture has cooked for 1 hour.
PERSONAL COMMENT: I won first place in the county "Miss Fluffy Rice" contest with this recipe.

Mary Lee Moyers, Hamburg, Ark.

The Governor's Palace at Colonial Williamsburg, Virginia.

CLUB CHICKEN CASSEROLE

- ¼ c. butter, margarine or chicken fat
- ¼ c. flour
- 1 c. chicken broth
- 1 14 ½-oz. can evaporated milk
- ½ c. water
- 1 ½ tsp. salt
- 3 c. cooked rice
- 2 ½ c. diced cooked chicken
- 1 3-oz. can broiled sliced mushrooms, drained
- ⅓ c. chopped green pepper
- ¼ c. chopped pimento
- ½ c. slivered blanched almonds, toasted (opt.)

Melt butter; blend in flour. Add broth, milk and water; cook and stir over low heat until thickened. Add salt, rice, chicken and vegetables. Pour into greased 11 1/2 x 7 1/2 x 1 1/2-inch baking dish. Bake at 350 degrees for 30 minutes. Top with almonds. Yield: 8-10 servings.

Mrs. Royce Crossnoe, Selmer, Tenn.

ORLEANS CHICK-N-RICE BAKE

- 1 stewing hen, cut into bite-sized pieces
- 1 can mushroom soup
- 1 sm. onion, chopped
- 1 c. quick-cooking rice
- 1 egg, beaten
- ¼ tsp. poultry seasoning
- 1 tsp. salt
- ½ tsp. pepper
- 2 ¼ c. chicken broth
- 2 slices toast or dry bread, pulled into small pieces
- 1 small can chopped or sliced mushrooms (opt.)

Cook stewing hen until tender; separate meat from bone. Reserve broth. Mix all ingredients in bowl; pour into buttered 10 x 10-inch pan. Cover with foil; bake 30 minutes at 350 degrees. Remove foil; dot with butter. Bake 15 minutes longer, uncovered. Serve hot. Yield: 6 servings.

Mrs. Betty Harwood, Ponchatoula, La.

RICE CASSEROLE

3 c. cooked rice
1 3-oz. can broiled mushrooms
½ c. chopped green pepper
½ c. chopped pimento
3 c. diced chicken
¼ c. butter
¼ c. flour
1 c. chicken broth
1 lge. can evaporated milk
1 ½ tsp. salt
½ c. slivered almonds

Mix rice, mushrooms, green pepper, pimento and chicken. Cook remaining ingredients, except almonds, over low heat until slightly thickened. Add to rice mixture; pour into greased 9 x 13-inch baking dish. Sprinkle almonds on top. Bake at 350 degrees for 25 to 30 minutes until lightly browned. This casserole may be made before serving time and refrigerated. Bake just before serving.

Iris Garrett, Johnson City, Tenn.

TASTY CHICKEN CASSEROLE

1 ½ c. dry rice
1 2 ½-lb. fryer, cut up
1 envelope onion soup
1 can cream of mushroom soup

Put dry rice in bottom of a heavy roast pan. Place fryer on top of rice. Add onion soup and cream of mushroom soup over the top of rice and chicken; barely cover with water. Cover; bake in a 325-degree oven for 1 hour and 30 minutes to 2 hours until chicken is tender.

Mrs. James B. Hopkins, Aransas Pass, Tex.

YELLOW RICE AND CHICKEN

1 3 to 3 ½-lb. chicken, cut in serving pieces
½ c. olive oil
1 med. onion, diced
2 buttons garlic, pressed
¾ c. tomatoes
1 ½ qt. chicken broth or water
1 bay leaf
2 tbsp. salt
2 c. raw white rice
½ tsp. saffron or 3 or 4 drops yellow food coloring
1 green pepper, diced
1 2-oz. can tiny peas
2 pimentos

Do not flour chicken. Fry in oil with onion and garlic for 35 minutes. Add tomatoes and broth. Boil for 5 minutes in deep skillet or pot. Add bay leaf, salt, rice, saffron or food coloring and green pepper. Blend. Place in baking dish. Bake in 375-degree oven for 20 minutes or until rice is tender and has absorbed moisture. Garnish with peas and pimento. Yield: 6 servings.

Mrs. Louise W. Henson, Bessemer, Ala.

RUBY'S CHICKEN CASSEROLE

2 c. cooked chicken, diced
2 c. celery, diced
1 c. slivered almonds
1 c. mayonnaise
4 tsp. onion, diced
2 tsp. lemon juice
2 cans cream of chicken soup
1 can pimentos, diced
6 hard-cooked eggs, diced
Salt and pepper to taste
1 c. potato chips, crushed

(Continued on next page)

Combine all ingredients except potato chips in a deep casserole. Sprinkle potato chips over top. Bake 60 minutes at 400 degrees. Yield: 8 servings.

Mrs. Robert F. Allen, Columbia, Tenn.

SOUTHERN CHICKEN UPSIDE DOWN DINNER

3 c. chicken broth
¼ c. chicken fat
½ c. flour
1 tsp. salt
Pinch of pepper and paprika
½ c. rich milk
3 c. cooked chicken, cut in 1 to 2-inch pieces
½ c. sliced stuffed olives
1 tbsp. lemon juice
Corn Bread Batter

Blend first 6 ingredients together and cook until thickened, adding chicken, olives and lemon juice to thickened mixture. Put 2/3 of mixture in bottom of 10-inch iron skillet and pour Corn Bread Batter over it. Spread with spoon to cover entire surface. Bake about 25 minutes or until corn bread is delicately browned at 400 degrees. Cut in wedges and serve upside down with remaining mixture over it.

CORN BREAD BATTER:

1 c. sifted plain flour
1 c. cornmeal
2 tbsp. sugar
2 tsp. double-action baking powder
½ tsp. soda
¾ tsp. salt
3 tbsp. shortening
1 c. buttermilk or sour milk

Sift dry ingredients into bowl. Cut shortening in with pastry blender till mixture looks like meal. Add buttermilk, stirring just enough to blend ingredients. Pour over hot mixture in skillet. Yield: 6-8 servings.

Mrs. R. L. Haskins, Huntsville, Ala.

AVOCADO-CHICKEN-SPAGHETTI CASSEROLE

8 oz. broken thin spaghetti
1 10½-oz. can cream of celery soup
¼ c. finely cut pimento
1½ c. diced cooked chicken
2 tbsp. butter or margarine
1 c. avocado cubes
½ c. grated cheese
⅓ c. buttered bread crumbs
Salt and pepper

Cook spaghetti till just tender in salted water; drain. Add soup, pimento, chicken and butter and put in buttered 1 1/2-quart casserole dish. Fold avocado cubes into first mixture; do not cook. Sprinkle with grated cheese and bread crumbs. Place under broiler to brown bread crumbs and meet cheese, about 3 to 4 minutes. Salt and pepper to taste. Yield: 4-6 servings.

Mrs. Lionel S. Carpenter, Ft. Myers, Fla.

BAKED CHICKEN SPAGHETTI

1 7-oz. pkg. spaghetti
1 No. 2 can tomatoes
3 bay leaves
1 tbsp. Worcestershire sauce
1 pt. chicken stock
1 can mushrooms, chopped or mushroom soup
1 hen, cooked and cubed
¾ lb. cheese, grated

(Continued on next page)

Cook spaghetti until done in salted water; drain. Make a sauce of tomatoes, bay leaves, Worcestershire sauce and chicken stock. Add sauce to spaghetti in baking dish. Add mushrooms and chicken. Bake for 1 hour in 350-degree oven. Mix in grated cheese; return to oven for 5 minutes. Serve immediately. Yield: 12 servings.

Mrs. Jack Doler, Winona, Miss.

CHICKEN-CURRIED SPAGHETTI

3 cans condensed cream of chicken soup, undiluted
2 cans condensed cream of mushroom soup, undiluted
1 c. milk
1 lb. thin spaghetti
6 qt. boiling water
2 tbsp. salt
¼ c. warm water
2 to 4 tsp. curry powder
1 6-oz. can mushroom buttons, undrained
1 tbsp. bottled onion juice
½ tsp. dried thyme
¼ tsp. basil
¼ tsp. oregano
1 ½ c. chicken chunks, cut
½ c. Parmesan cheese, grated

Simmer soups, milk and 1/2 cup water over low heat for 10 minutes. Stir while simmering. Cook spaghetti until barely tender in boiling water with salt. Drain. Combine warm water and curry powder; add to hot soup mixture. Add mushrooms and liquid, onion juice, dried thyme, basil and oregano. Simmer 10 minutes, stirring. Place spaghetti in 3 1/2-quart casserole. Pour soup mixture over it. Toss lightly with a fork. Add chicken and cheese. Bake 1 hour in a 300-degree oven. Yield: 12-15 servings.

Mary F. Brown, DeKalb, Miss.

CHICKEN MONTEGO

3 to 4 tbsp. flour
1 tsp. salt
⅛ tsp. pepper
3 chicken breasts, split
¼ c. shortening
1 4-oz. can button mushrooms, drained
1 can cream of celery soup
1 tsp. ground marjoram
2 c. sour cream
1 4-oz. pkg. spaghetti twists or elbow macaroni, cooked
1 16-oz. can small peas, drained

Mix flour, salt and pepper; dip chicken breasts in mixture. Cook chicken in shortening over moderate heat until lightly browned on both sides. Remove chicken. Add mushrooms to skillet and cook until lightly browned. Add soup and marjoram; mix well. Gradually add sour cream, stirring until blended. Pour spaghetti into a 3-quart shallow baking dish. Stir in peas and half the soup mixture. Arrange chicken over top of spaghetti mixture. Pour remaining soup mixture over chicken. Cover and bake at 350 degrees for 45 minutes. Remove cover and bake for 15 to 20 minutes or until chicken is fork tender. Sprinkle with paprika before serving. Yield: 6 servings.

Margery G. Middlebrooks, Jonesboro, Ga.

CHICKEN SPAGHETTI

1 sm. green pepper, chopped
2 stalks celery, chopped
2 med. onions, chopped
1 pt. chicken broth
2 pimentos
1 sm. can mushrooms, chopped
½ lb. sharp cheese, grated
1 4 to 5-lb. hen, cooked
1 8-oz. pkg. elbow spaghetti, cooked

Cook green pepper, celery and onions in chicken broth; add pimentos, mushrooms and cheese. Chop chicken into medium-sized pieces; add with spaghetti to mixture. Mix in casserole. Heat in 350-degree oven until hot. Yield: 8 servings.

Mrs. Max R. Leach, Scottsboro, Ala.

CHICKEN-SPAGHETTI CASSEROLE

3 tbsp. salad oil
1 med. onion, chopped
1 sm. green pepper, chopped
1 c. sliced mushrooms
2 8-oz. cans tomato sauce
1 tsp. salt
⅛ tsp. pepper
½ tsp. dried or 1 ½ tsp. fresh oregano, chopped
1 lb. spaghetti, cooked and drained
3 c. finely diced chicken
½ lb. mozzarella cheese, coarsely grated

Heat oil in skillet; saute onion and green pepper until onion begins to color. Stir in the mushrooms, tomato sauce, salt, pepper and oregano. Cover and simmer over very low heat for 25 to 30 minutes, stirring frequently. Check seasoning. Arrange layers of spaghetti sauce, chicken and cheese in large casserole; repeat layers, ending with cheese. Bake at 375 degrees for 30 minutes. Yield: 8 servings.

Mrs. Ommy Strauch, Victoria, Tex.

CHICKEN TETRAZZINI

1 chopped green pepper
1 chopped medium onion
1 c. chopped celery
Chicken fat or margarine
3 c. chopped chicken, cooked
1 can mushroom soup
½ c. grated sharp cheese
2 tbsp. pimentos
1 8-oz. pkg. thin spaghetti
3 c. chicken stock
½ c. Parmesan cheese

Saute green pepper, onion and celery in chicken fat. Mix with chicken, mushroom soup, cheese and pimentos. Cook broken spaghetti in chicken stock. Mix half the cooked spaghetti with chicken mixture; place in 13 x 9-inch baking pan. Top with remaining spaghetti and sprinkle with Parmesan cheese. Bake at 375 degrees for 30 minutes, covered.

Mrs. J. Thomas Gould, Raleigh, N. C.

CHICKEN TETRAZZINI

2 fryers
1 tsp. salt
½ tsp. pepper
1 onion
2 sprigs celery leaves
Pinch of garlic powder
1 8-oz. pkg. spaghetti or macaroni
2 cans mushroom soup
2 c. chicken stock
2 tbsp. sherry
Fine bread crumbs
3 tbsp. Parmesan cheese

(Continued on next page)

Cook chicken in water with salt, pepper, onion, celery and garlic powder until meat is tender. Cool; remove meat from bones and cut into bite-sized pieces. Cook spaghetti as directed on package. Thin mushroom soup with chicken stock. Add sherry. Spread alternating layers of spaghetti, chicken and mushroom soup. Top with fine bread crumbs. Bake for 30 minutes at 350 degrees. Serve with Parmesan cheese.

Mrs. Leota Reid Bryson, Sapphire, N. C.

CHICKEN VERMICELLI

1 3-lb. chicken
2 pkg. vermicelli
3 onions, chopped
1 stalk celery, chopped
1 can mushroom stems and pieces
2 tsp. margarine
¼ c. grated cheddar cheese
1 can pimento, chopped
3 cans cream of mushroom soup
1 can tomato soup

Cook and bone chicken. Cook vermicelli in broth. Saute onions, celery and mushrooms in margarine. Combine chicken, cheese, onion, celery, mushrooms, pimento and mushroom soup. Place in baking dish; add tomato soup. Place in oven until cheese melts; remove and add cooked vermicelli. Return to oven to heat thoroughly. Yield: 10 servings.

Mrs. James J. Antoon, Jr., Eldorado, Ark.

CASSEROLE MEXICANA

1 tbsp. flour
1 tbsp. salad oil
3 or 4 cloves garlic, minced
1 tbsp. chili powder
1 tbsp. comino seed
1 No. 2 can tomato juice
7 lge. chicken breasts
¾ c. onions, chopped
1 jalapeno pepper, chopped
1 pkg. tortillas
2 ¼ c. cheddar cheese, grated
1 can cream of chicken soup
1 6-oz. can evaporated milk
2 c. chicken broth

Combine flour, salad oil, garlic, chili powder, comino seed in saucepan; gradually add tomato juice and cook over low heat until mixture is slightly thick. Set aside. Cook chicken and bone meat. Fry onion; add chopped jalapeno. Line casserole with about 5 tortillas; add a layer of chicken and cheese. Add a layer of jalapeno and onions. Repeat layers, topping with cheese. Combine the sauce with remaining ingredients; mix thoroughly and pour over casserole. Refrigerate overnight. Heat for 1 hour at 350 degrees. Yield: 10 servings.

Mrs. Phyllis Watson, Corpus Christi, Tex.

CHICKEN ENCHILADA CASSEROLE

1 lge. fryer or stewing hen
1 can mushroom soup
7 or 8 commercial tortillas
1 lge. onion, chopped
2 tsp. chopped jalapeno chilies
1 c. grated cheddar cheese

(Continued on next page)

Boil chicken in salted water until tender. Let cool in chicken broth. Remove the meat from the bones and cube. Mix 1 1/2 cups broth with mushroom soup. Break enough tortillas to cover the bottom of a large casserole. Add a layer of chicken, onion, half the chili, half the broth and soup mixture and half the grated cheese. Repeat and end with cheese on top. Cover with foil and cook 50 minutes in 350-degree oven. Uncover and cook for 10 more minutes. Cream of chicken, cheese or celery soups may be substituted for mushroom soup. Use jalapeno chilies sparingly as they are hot.

Mrs. Billy J. Bunch, Ft. Worth, Tex.

CHICKEN SOPA

1 frying chicken
1 10 to 12-oz. pkg. tortillas
1 can cream of chicken soup
5 oz. Old English cheese
5 oz. cheddar cheese
1 4-oz. can green chili peppers
6 to 8 fresh green onions, chopped

Boil chicken until tender; bone and cut into large pieces. Reserve broth. Lightly fry tortillas. Mix chicken soup, broth, cheeses, chilies and onions; heat until cheeses melt. Arrange layers of tortillas, chicken and sauce in a 2-quart casserole until all ingredients are used. Bake at 325 degrees for 20 minutes. Yield: 12 servings.

Mrs. J. L. Knoz, Eden, Tex.

KING RANCH TRAIL DRIVE DISH

1 hen or lge. fryer
1 sm. onion
Celery
1 can cream of mushroom soup
1 can cream of chicken soup
½ can chili tomatoes
1 chopped onion
1 1-doz. can tortillas
¼ pkg. chili mix
1 c. grated cheddar cheese

Boil hen with small onion and celery; reserve 2 cups broth. Chop meat into chunks. Combine soups, tomatoes and chopped onion. Place a layer each of broken tortillas, chicken and soup mixture in casserole. Sprinkle with chili mix. Moisten with reserved broth. Sprinkle top with cheese. Bake at 350 degrees for 45 minutes to 1 hour. This dish freezes well.

Mrs. J. J. Stephen, Robston, Tex.

CHICKEN SPECIAL CASSEROLE

6 chicken breasts
Pinch of salt
2 ribs celery
3 cans broken asparagus
1 sm. can pimentos, chopped
¾ c. slivered almonds
3 cans mushroom soup
2 cans French-fried onion rings

(Continued on next page)

Cook chicken breasts in salted water with chopped celery until tender. Remove from bone and cut into bite-sized pieces. Place chicken, asparagus, pimentos, slivered almonds and soup in alternate layers in casserole. Cover with foil and bake 30 minutes at 350 degrees. During last 5 minutes, uncover casserole; top with onion rings. Yield: 6-8 servings.

Mrs. Hugh Colville, Jr., Bessemer, Ala.

ORIENTAL CHICKEN CASSEROLE

- 1 4-oz. can sliced mushrooms
- ¼ c. butter
- ¼ c. chopped onion
- ¼ c. flour
- 1 tsp. salt
- Dash of pepper
- ½ tsp. curry powder
- 1 tall can evaporated milk
- 1 c. cooked cut-up chicken
- 1 lb. fresh or 1 10-oz. pkg. frozen asparagus, cooked
- 1 3-oz. can chow mein noodles
- 1 c. shredded cheese

Drain mushrooms, reserving liquid. Melt butter in a large frypan. Add mushrooms and onion and cook over medium heat until onion is transparent. Remove from heat. Sprinkle evenly with flour, salt, pepper and curry powder, stirring to blend in smoothly. Add enough water to mushroom liquid to measure 1/2 cup total liquid. Slowly add to mushrooms and onion, stirring constantly to keep mixture smooth. Blend in evaporated milk. Cook and stir over medium heat until thickened. Add chicken, cooked asparagus and noodles, tossing lightly to mix. Turn into buttered 1 1/2-quart casserole. Top with shredded cheese. Bake in preheated 350-degree oven for 20 to 30 minutes or until mixture is heated through and cheese is melted. Yield: 5-6 servings.

Photograph for this recipe on page 165.

CHICKEN CASSEROLE

- 1 pkg. frozen broccoli
- 1 c. diced cooked chicken
- 1 can cream of chicken soup
- 2 tbsp. cooking sherry
- Buttered bread crumbs
- Grated cheese

Cook broccoli according to directions on package and drain well. Arrange broccoli in bottom of buttered casserole. Spread chicken on top of broccoli. Mix chicken soup with wine and pour over broccoli and chicken. Sprinkle with buttered bread crumbs and top with grated cheese. Bake at 400 degrees for 15 minutes or until bubbly. Yield: 4 servings.

Mrs. F. T. Black, El Paso, Tex.

CHICKEN CASSEROLE

- 4 lb. chicken breasts
- 2 c. water
- 1 pkg. prepared dressing
- 1 box frozen chopped broccoli
- 2 cans mushroom soup, diluted with liquid from chicken to make 4 cups
- Buttered bread crumbs

(Continued on next page)

Simmer chicken in water until tender; when cool, strip meat from bones. Prepare dressing according to directions for dry method. Break up frozen broccoli; place alternate layers of chicken, dressing, broccoli and soup in buttered casserole. Cover with bread crumbs dotted with butter or potato chips crumbled. Bake, uncovered, for 1 hour in a 350-degree oven. Yield: 8 servings.

Lucile K. Delano, Rock Hill, S. C.

CHICKEN DIVAN

- 2 10-oz. pkg. frozen broccoli spears
- 2 10 ½-oz. frozen creamed chicken
- ½ c. grated Parmesan cheese
- 2 tbsp. sherry
- 1 tsp. Worcestershire sauce
- ⅛ tsp. grated nutmeg

Cook frozen broccoli and creamed chicken according to package directions. Drain broccoli; arrange in single layer in a shallow baking dish, placing tops of spears at outer edge. Add grated cheese, reserving 2 tablespoons, sherry, Worcestershire sauce and nutmeg to chicken mixture; stir well. Spoon over broccoli spears. Sprinkle with reserved grated cheese. Bake in preheated 350-degree oven about 20 minutes or until heated. If desired, sprinkle with additional nutmeg before serving. For a more elaborate Chicken Divan, combine 1/4 cup heavy cream, whipped and 1/4 cup prepared Hollandaise sauce. Spread mixture over casserole before adding reserved grated cheese. Bake as directed. Yield: 6 servings.

Photograph for this recipe on cover.

CHICKEN DIVINE

- 1 lb. broccoli, cooked and drained
- Cooked chicken or turkey, sliced
- 1 can cream of chicken or mushroom soup
- ⅓ c. milk
- ½ c. grated cheddar cheese
- ¼ c. crushed potato chips

Arrange broccoli in a shallow baking dish; top with slices of chicken. Blend soup and milk; pour over all. Sprinkle with mixture of cheese and potato chips. Bake at 425 degrees until lightly browned on top and sauce is bubbly. Asparagus spears may be substituted for broccoli. Yield: 4 servings.

Mrs. Peggy G. Bracken, Brewton, Ala.

CHICKEN SUPREME

- 2 10-oz. pkg. frozen broccoli
- 6 single chicken breasts
- 2 cans cream of chicken soup
- 1 c. mayonnaise
- 1 tsp. lemon juice
- ½ tsp. curry powder
- ½ c. sharp shredded cheese
- ½ c. soft bread crumbs
- 1 tbsp. butter

Cook broccoli and drain. Boil chicken until done; remove from bone. Slice in thick slices. Arrange broccoli in greased baking dish; add sliced chicken. Combine soup, mayonnaise, lemon juice and curry powder. Pour over top of chicken and broccoli. Sprinkle with cheese, bread crumbs and butter. Bake at 350 degrees for 25 to 30 minutes. Yield: 6 servings.

Mrs. Carlisle Gunn, Alexander City, Ala.

CHICKEN-RICE DIVAN

2 10-oz. pkg. frozen broccoli spears
½ c. shredded Parmesan cheese
6 lge. slices cooked chicken
Salt and pepper
1 c. cooked rice
2 tbsp. butter or margarine
2 tbsp. all-purpose flour
1 c. milk
1 tbsp. lemon juice
1 c. sour cream

Cook broccoli according to package directions; drain. Arrange in 11 1/2 x 7 1/2 x 1 1/2-inch baking dish. Sprinkle with half the cheese; top with chicken. Season with salt and pepper; spoon on cooked rice. Melt butter in saucepan over low heat. Blend in flour; add milk all at once. Cook, stirring constantly, till mixture thickens and bubbles. Remove from heat; stir in lemon juice. Gently fold in sour cream; pour over chicken in casserole. Sprinkle with remaining Parmesan cheese. Bake in oven at 400 degrees for 15 to 20 minutes or till lightly browned. Yield: 6 servings.

Mrs. E. J. Courreges, Houston, Tex.

CLASSIC CHICKEN DIVAN

2 bunches fresh broccoli or 2 10-oz. pkg. frozen broccoli
¼ c. butter or margarine
¼ c. flour
2 c. chicken broth
½ c. light cream
3 tbsp. sherry wine
½ tsp. salt
Dash of pepper
3 chicken breasts, cooked and thinly sliced
¼ c. grated Parmesan cheese

Cook broccoli in boiling salted water; drain. Melt butter; blend in flour. Add chicken broth until thick. Stir in cream, sherry, salt and pepper. Place broccoli crosswise in 13 x 9 x 2-inch baking dish. Pour one-half the sauce over broccoli; top with chicken slices. Add Parmesan cheese to remaining sauce; pour over chicken. Sprinkle with additional Parmesan cheese. Bake at 350 degrees for 20 minutes or until heated through. Broil until sauce is golden. Yield: 8 servings.

Mrs. Carl Freund, Eustis, Fla.

CHICKEN BREASTS WITH ARTICHOKES

4 chicken breasts, halved
1 lge. onion, thinly sliced
½ c. chopped bell pepper
½ c. salad oil
Juice of 1 lemon
1 c. rice
1 can chicken broth
1 can artichokes, drained
Salt and pepper to taste
1 4-oz. can button mushrooms
12 stuffed olives

Saute chicken breasts, onion and bell pepper in salad oil. Drizzle lemon juice over breasts. Cook rice in chicken broth until tender; add remaining ingredients, being careful to keep artichokes whole. Place in a greased 8 x 3-inch casserole; place chicken breasts and sauteed vegetables on top. Cover and bake at 325 degrees for 1 hour. Toasted almonds may be sprinkled over top before serving. Yield: 6-8 servings.

Mrs. Bennie Ward, Lambert, Miss.

EASY CHICKEN CASSEROLE

1 c. bread crumbs
1 tbsp. melted butter
2 10-oz. pkg. frozen broccoli
2 c. cooked chicken
1 can cream of celery soup
1 can cream of mushroom soup
⅔ c. salad dressing
1 tsp. lemon juice
½ tsp. curry powder (opt.)
½ c. grated cheese

Combine bread crumbs and melted butter. Set aside. Cook broccoli in salted boiling water until tender and drain. Arrange broccoli in greased 11 x 7 1/2 x 1 1/2-inch baking dish. Place chicken on top. Combine soups, salad dressing, lemon juice and curry powder; pour over chicken. Sprinkle with cheese and buttered crumbs. Bake 30 minutes in a 350-degree oven. Pimentos may be added. Yield: 4-6 servings.

Mrs. Ira John Cox, Dallas, Tex.

CHICKEN CASSEROLE

1 5½-lb. stewing chicken, cut up
1 med. onion, chopped
Few celery tops
3 tsp. salt
½ tsp. peppercorns
1 c. water
1 10-oz. pkg. frozen green peas
2 hard-cooked eggs, shelled and chopped
2 pimentos, diced
¼ c. flour
1 c. cream
½ c. milk
Corn Bread Topping

Combine chicken with onion, celery tops, salt, peppercorns and water in a kettle; cover. Simmer 2 hours or until tender. Remove chicken from broth; let cool until easy to handle. Strain broth in 2-cup measure; let stand until fat rises to top. Skim off and save. Add water to broth to make 2 cups. Remove skin from chicken and take meat from bones; cut meat into bite-sized pieces. Cook peas according to label directions; drain. Add to chicken with eggs and pimentos. Place in a 12-cup baking dish. Measure 1/4 cup chicken fat in saucepan; stir in flour. Cook, stirring constantly, until bubbly. Stir in 2 cups broth, cream and milk; continue cooking until mixture thickens and boils 1 minute. Stir into chicken mixture. Spread Corn Bread Topping over chicken mixture. Bake in 425-degree oven for 30 minutes or until corn bread is firm and golden. Yield: 8 servings.

(Continued on next page)

CORN BREAD TOPPING:

¾ c. yellow cornmeal
¼ c. sifted flour
1 ½ tsp. baking powder
1 tsp. sugar
½ tsp. salt
1 egg
½ c. milk
¼ c. vegetable oil

Mix meal, flour, baking powder, sugar and salt in a large bowl. Beat egg slightly; stir in milk and oil. Add egg mixture all at once to cornmeal mixture; stir just until evenly moist. Spread over casserole. This recipe is excellent for any meat casseroles that call for toppings.

Mrs. J. L. Mitchell, Richardson, Tex.

CHICKEN BREASTS IN CREAM

8 chicken breasts
Salt and pepper
2 eggs, beaten
Bread crumbs
¼ c. butter
½ c. salad oil
2 pkg. frozen peas
2 c. heavy cream
¼ tsp. salt
½ tsp. garlic powder
½ tsp. paprika

Have butcher bone chicken breasts. Season breasts with salt and pepper. Dip in beaten egg and roll in bread crumbs. Saute until a golden brown in butter and salad oil mixed. Place breasts in large baking dish. Add frozen peas. Over them pour cream mixed with salt and garlic powder. Dust with paprika. Bake in a 350-oven for 1 hour, basting occasionally, or until chicken and peas are tender.

Mrs. Fletcher Sims, Jr., Canyon, Tex.

CHICKEN CASSEROLE ANNA

Breasts and thighs of chicken
Flour
Salt and pepper to taste
Oil
1 carrot, diced
1 onion, diced
1 stalk of celery, diced
1 c. dry wine
1 can beef bouillon
½ c. sliced mushrooms
20 green olives, sliced

Remove skin from chicken; dredge in mixture of flour, salt and pepper. Brown in oil; transfer to casserole. Cook carrot, onion and celery in chicken drippings until onions become transparent. Pour over chicken; add wine and bouillon. Bake, covered, at 350 degrees for 1 hour and 30 minutes. Ten minutes before serving, add sauteed mushrooms and green olives. Serve with rice. Yield: 6-8 servings.

Mrs. Edmund J. Butler, Jr., Vienna, Va.

CHICKEN IN CRUMB BASKETS

CRUMB BASKETS:

6 c. soft bread crumbs
¼ c. minced onions
1 tsp. celery salt
⅛ tsp. pepper
½ c. butter, melted

(Continued on next page)

Combine bread crumbs, onion, celery salt, pepper and melted butter. Line either individual buttered casseroles or one large one and press into place. Bake at 375 degrees for 15 minutes or until golden brown.

CHICKEN FILLING:

⅓ c. butter
⅓ c. flour
½ c. milk
1 ½ c. chicken broth
½ tsp. salt
⅛ tsp. pepper
1 tsp. Worcestershire sauce
3 c. cooked chicken, chopped
1 c. cooked or canned peas

Melt butter and blend in flour. Add milk, chicken broth and seasonings. Cook until thick, stirring constantly. Add chicken and peas just before serving. Pour into crumb baskets. Yield: 8 servings.

Mrs. Geraldine L. Philpott, Roanoke, Va.

CHICKEN CLEMENCEAU

1 chicken, cut up
Seasoned flour
1 to 2 c. cooking oil
4 lge. potatoes, diced
8 pods garlic
1 stick butter or margarine, melted
1 4-oz. jar pimento
1 3 ½-oz. can mushrooms
1 to 2 tsp. salt
1 to 2 tsp. pepper
1 4-oz. can peas

Dredge chicken in flour. Brown in cooking oil; place on platter. Brown potatoes in same oil; drain. Place in baking pan. Add garlic to butter; pour over potatoes. Add pimento, mushrooms, salt and pepper. Bake, covered, at 325 degrees for 30 minutes. Add peas; toss lightly. Spoon potato mixture over chicken; heat at 325 degrees for 15 minutes. Yield: 4 servings.

Mrs. S. L. Russell, Jr., Metairie, La.

CHICKEN PIE

1 2 ½-lb. chicken
1 tsp. salt
½ tsp. pepper
¾ c. cooked English peas
¾ c. cooked carrots, diced
¼ c. diced pimento
½ stick margarine, melted
3 tbsp. flour
2 c. chicken broth
1 can biscuits

Cook chicken until tender; remove from broth. Bone and dice. Sprinkle with salt and pepper; add peas, carrots and pimento. Blend margarine and flour in saucepan; stir in broth. Cook, stirring constantly, until thickened. Alternate layers of chicken mixture and sauce in a 9 x 15-inch baking dish. Place biscuits on top. Bake at 450-475 degrees until biscuits are browned. Yield: 10 servings.

Mrs. W. P. King, Russellville, Ala.

CHICKEN-POTATO CASSEROLE

1 2 ½ to 3-lb. fryer, cut up
5 lge. potatoes
1 lge. onion, diced
Salt and pepper to taste
Garlic salt to taste
1 stick margarine, sliced
1 chicken bouillon cube
1 c. water

(Continued on next page)

Place alternate layers of chicken, potatoes and onion in casserole; sprinkle with salt, pepper and garlic salt. Dot with margarine. Repeat. Mix bouillon cube with water; pour over mixture. Bake at 350 degrees for 1 hour or until done. Yield: 8 servings.

Mrs. Wayne DuBose, Silshee, Tex.

CHICKEN SUPPER

¾ c. chopped onion
½ c. chopped celery
1 tbsp. chopped green onion tops
¼ c. chicken broth
1 box frozen mixed vegetables, cooked and drained
1 10 ½-oz. can cream of chicken soup
1 c. sour cream
3 c. cooked, cubed chicken
1 4-oz. can sliced mushrooms, drained
3 slices crisp crumbled bacon
1 tsp. salt
1 tsp. Worcestershire sauce
⅛ tsp. pepper
¼ c. shredded cheddar cheese

Combine onion, celery, onion tops and chicken broth in saucepan; simmer 20 minutes. Cook frozen vegetables according to directions. Drain. Combine in 3-quart casserole soup, sour cream, chicken, drained vegetables, mushrooms, bacon, salt, Worcestershire sauce, pepper, cheese, cooked onions, celery, onion tops and chicken broth; mix well.

CONFETTI BISCUITS:

1 c. flour
2 tsp. baking powder
½ tsp. salt
2 eggs, slightly beaten
½ c. milk
1 tbsp. dried or chopped fresh green pepper
1 tbsp. dried sweet red pepper flakes or chopped pimento
1 c. shredded cheddar cheese

Combine in order given; mix just until blended. Drop by tablespoonfuls onto casserole. Bake at 350 degrees for 40 to 45 minutes until golden brown. Sprinkle with cheese. Return to oven to melt cheese. Yield: 6-8 servings.

Mrs. A. O. Hellums, Premont, Tex.

CHICKEN-SWEET POTATO CASSEROLE

1 fryer, cut in serving pieces
Salt
2 med. sweet potatoes, cut in ¼-in. slices
6 to 8 slices canned pineapple
½ c. pineapple juice
Brown sugar
Butter
Dash of cinnamon

Season chicken with salt. Place layers of chicken, potatoes and pineapple slices in a large foil-lined casserole dish. Pour pineapple juice over layers. Put 1/2 teaspoon brown sugar and a pat of butter in center of each pineapple slice. Sprinkle with cinnamon. Seal foil well. Bake at 400 degrees for about 1 hour or until chicken is tender. Yield: 6 servings.

Imogene Huffman, Hattiesburg, Miss.

CHICKEN, TATER & ONION CASSEROLE

1 frying chicken, cut in serving pieces
Salt, pepper and monosodium glutamate
6 med. potatoes, sliced
2 lge. white onions, sliced
1 can cream-style chicken soup
Strips pimento
Paprika

In a glass or ovenproof casserole, put pieces of frying chicken to cover bottom of casserole. Salt; pepper and sprinkle monosodium glutamate on chicken. Add layer of potatoes, a layer of onions and seasoning. Pour chicken soup over top; add a small amount water. Put pimento strips over top; sprinkle with paprika. Bake, covered, at 350 degrees for 1 hour and 30 minutes.

Mrs. Loren W. Stafford, Arlington, Va.

CHICKEN-VEGETABLE CASSEROLE

1 stewing chicken, ready to cook
Salt and pepper
Flour
2 tbsp. fat or oil
2 c. hot water
½ tsp. salt
2 med. carrots, sliced
1 ½ c. chopped celery
1 sm. onion, chopped
1 sm. green pepper, chopped
2 tbsp. flour

Cut chicken in serving pieces. Season with salt and pepper. Sprinkle with flour. Heat fat in heavy pan and brown chicken. Remove chicken to a casserole. Add hot water and salt; cover. Cook in oven at 325 degrees until almost tender, about 2 hours and 30 minutes. Add water as needed during cooking to keep liquid at original level. Add vegetables and cook 30 minutes longer. Remove a little fat and mix with flour for gravy. Add several spoonfuls of hot liquid from casserole. Cook 10 to 15 minutes longer. Yield: 6-8 servings.

Mrs. R. C. Bouse, Jr., Port Bolivar, Tex.

CHICKEN AND CORN CASSEROLE

1 ½ c. cracker crumbs
2 c. corn
2 c. diced, cooked chicken
½ tsp. salt
Pepper to taste
2 eggs, slightly beaten
1 c. milk
¼ c. grated cheese
2 tbsp. butter

Line bottom and sides of a greased casserole with crumbs, reserving some crumbs for top. Alternate layers of corn and chicken; add salt and pepper. Combine eggs and milk; pour over casserole. Top with reserved crumbs and cheese; dot with butter. Bake at 350 degrees until browned. Yield: 6 servings.

Mrs. Fred Johnson, Dawson, Ga.

CHICKEN LOAF

1 c. yellow cornmeal
½ tsp. seasoned salt
1 ½ c. boiling chicken broth or 1 ½ c. boiling water with 2 chicken bouillon cubes added
1 c. or more cooked diced chicken or 2 cans boned chicken
½ c. chopped celery
½ c. catsup
1 tbsp. cooking oil
2 eggs, beaten
1 tbsp. parsley, fresh or dried
1 can cream-style corn
1 tbsp. butter
1 tsp. sugar

(Continued on next page)

Put cornmeal in a large bowl. Season with salt; add boiling broth. Mix well. Add next 7 ingredients. Pour in well-greased loaf pan or casserole. Bake in a pan of water for 35 minutes at 375 degrees. Remove from pan of water and bake for 15 to 20 minutes longer or until brown. Let loaf set in dish a few minutes before turning it onto a platter or large plate. Heat corn, butter and sugar; pour over loaf while hot.

Mrs. J. H. Perkins, Beaumont, Tex.

CORN TAMALE LOAF

1 med. onion
1 clove garlic, minced
½ c. cooking oil
1 ½ c. yellow cornmeal
1 ¾ c. hot chicken broth
1 ½ c. diced cooked chicken
1 8-oz. can tomato sauce
1 tbsp. chili powder
1 tsp. salt
1 tsp. pepper
3 eggs, beaten
1 17-oz. can cream-style corn
1 tbsp. butter

Saute onion and garlic in oil till tender. Mix with next 8 ingredients; blend well. Pour mixture into well-greased 9-inch loaf pan. Set in pan of hot water. Bake at 375 degrees for 1 hour or till firm and brown. Heat corn with butter; turn out loaf on platter. Top with corn. Garnish with green onion and olive slices if desired. Yield: 6 servings.

Mrs. Joel Weiner, Raleigh, N. C.

NOODLE SURPRISE

½ stick butter
1 med. onion, sliced
2 tbsp. flour
1 c. seasoned turkey or chicken stock
1 3-oz. can mushrooms, drained and sliced
Salt
2 tsp. paprika
3 c. turkey or chicken, cut in med. chunks
2 egg yolks
1 c. sour cream
8 oz. noodles
½ stick melted butter
2 tsp. poppy seeds
½ c. Parmesan cheese
1 c. bread crumbs

Melt butter in skillet. Add onion. Cook without browning 5 minutes or until tender. Blend in flour. Add stock and cook, stirring constantly, until mixture thickens. Reduce heat to very low. Stir in mushrooms, 1/2 teaspoon salt, and paprika. Add turkey. Simmer for 5 minutes. Stir in small amount of sauce into egg yolks, then add mixture to skillet. Cook 2 minutes longer. Stir in sour cream. Heat a few minutes until sauce is hot. Cook 8 ounces noodles in boiling water until tender, about 10 minutes. Drain. Stir in 3 tablespoons melted butter and poppy seeds. Season to taste. Lightly fold the noodles into sauce mixture. Place in buttered casserole. Sprinkle with cheese topping and bake in 350-degree oven until topping has browned.

Mrs. H. W. Tinson, Miami, Fla.

TURKEY-AVOCADO SUPREME

1 ⅓ c. instant rice, cooked
Butter
½ tsp. salt
Lemon juice
2 avocados, mashed
½ tsp. garlic salt
Baked turkey slices
2 c. smooth cheese sauce

(Continued on next page)

Season rice with butter and salt. Add lemon juice to avocados; season with garlic salt. Place half of rice in casserole; add layers of turkey and avocado spread. Repeat layers. Top with cheese sauce. Bake at 300 degrees until thoroughly heated. This dish may be prepared ahead of time and heated when needed. Yield: 6 servings.

Mrs. Robert L. Behrens, El Paso, Tex.

FIVE-CAN CASSEROLE

- 1 sm. can boned turkey or chicken
- 1 sm. can evaporated milk
- 1 can cream of chicken soup
- 1 can cream of mushroom soup
- 1 5-oz. can Chinese noodles

Mix all ingredients together. Bake in buttered 1-quart casserole for 25 minutes at 350 degrees or heat and serve from chafing dish. Do not dilute the soups.

Mrs. Tom B. Coleman, North Little Rock, Ark.

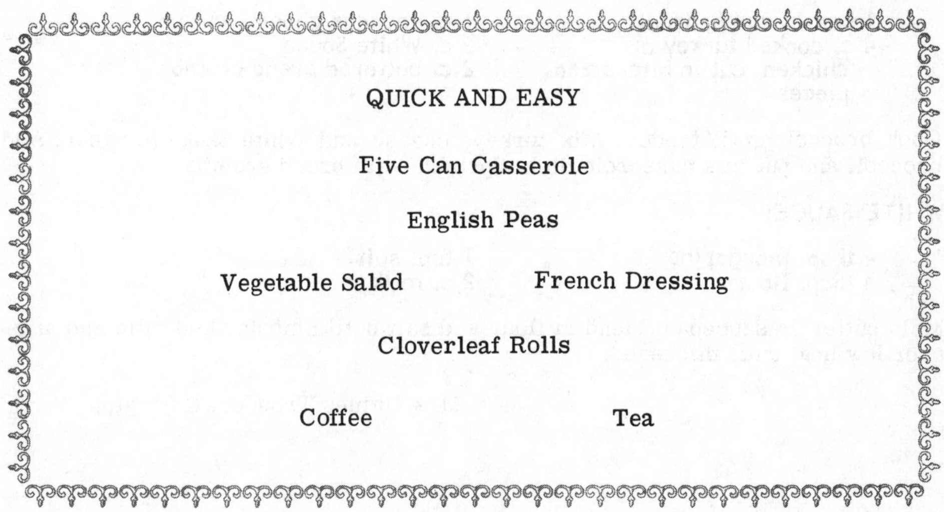

QUICK AND EASY

Five Can Casserole

English Peas

Vegetable Salad French Dressing

Cloverleaf Rolls

Coffee Tea

TURKETTI

- 2 ½ c. spaghetti, broken into 2-in. pieces
- 4 c. cooked diced turkey
- ½ c. diced pimento
- ½ c. chopped green pepper
- 1 sm. onion, chopped
- 2 cans cream of mushroom soup
- 1 c. turkey broth or water
- 1 tsp. salt
- ¼ tsp. pepper
- 3 ½ c. grated cheddar cheese

Cook spaghetti. Place turkey, pimento, green pepper and onion in large casserole. Pour in undiluted soup and turkey broth. Add salt, pepper, 2 1/2 cups cheese and spaghetti. Lightly toss until well mixed. Sprinkle remaining cheese over top. Bake at 350 degrees for 45 minutes or until bubbly throughout. Yield: 12 servings.

Mrs. L. Edward Williams, Jr., Demopolis, Ala.

TURKEY CASSEROLE

3 tbsp. chopped onion
⅓ c. chopped green pepper
3 tbsp. fat
1 tsp. salt
6 tbsp. flour
1 ½ c. milk
1 can cream of chicken soup
1 c. chopped turkey
1 tbsp. lemon juice
1 pkg. canned biscuits or
1 recipe biscuits
⅓ c. grated cheese

Brown onion and green pepper in melted fat; add salt and flour. Blend until moistened; add milk and soup. Cook until bubbly hot and thick, stirring occasionally. Add turkey and lemon juice. Pour into greased baking dish. Roll biscuits to form a rectangle 1/4 inch thick. Sprinkle grated cheese over dough and roll like jelly roll. Cut 1/2 inch thick; place on casserole. Bake in preheated 450-degree oven for 15 minutes. Reduce heat to 425 degrees; bake until swirls are browned. Yield: 6 servings.

Mrs. Mildred Tate, Lobelville, Tenn.

TURKEY CASSEROLE

1 box frozen broccoli
4 c. cooked turkey or chicken, cut in bite-sized pieces
1 c. cheddar cheese, cut up
2 c. White Sauce
2 c. buttered bread crumbs

Cook broccoli until tender. Mix turkey, cheese and White Sauce together. Add broccoli and put in a casserole dish. Sprinkle with bread crumbs.

WHITE SAUCE:

4 tbsp. margarine
4 tbsp. flour
1 tsp. salt
2 c. milk

Melt butter in saucepan; blend in flour and salt until smooth. Add milk and stir over low heat until thickened.

Mrs. James Trosper, Covington, Tenn.

TURKEY-CHEESE CASSEROLE

5 tbsp. flour
1 tsp. salt
¼ tsp. onion salt
¼ c. melted butter
2 ½ c. milk
1 ⅓ c. instant rice
1 ½ c. turkey broth
½ c. grated cheese
2 c. diced turkey
½ c. cooked peas
½ c. cooked carrots
6 unbaked biscuits

Stir flour, 1/2 teaspoon salt and onion salt into butter. Stir in milk. Cook over hot water, stirring occasionally, until thickened. Pour rice from box into a 2-quart baking dish. Combine broth and remaining salt and pour over rice. Sprinkle half of cheese over rice. Top with turkey, peas and carrots combined. Pour on sauce. Sprinkle with remaining cheese. Bake at 375 degrees for 20 minutes. During last 10 minutes, place biscuits on top to bake. Yield: 6 servings.

Mrs. Grady Astrop, Bristol, Va.

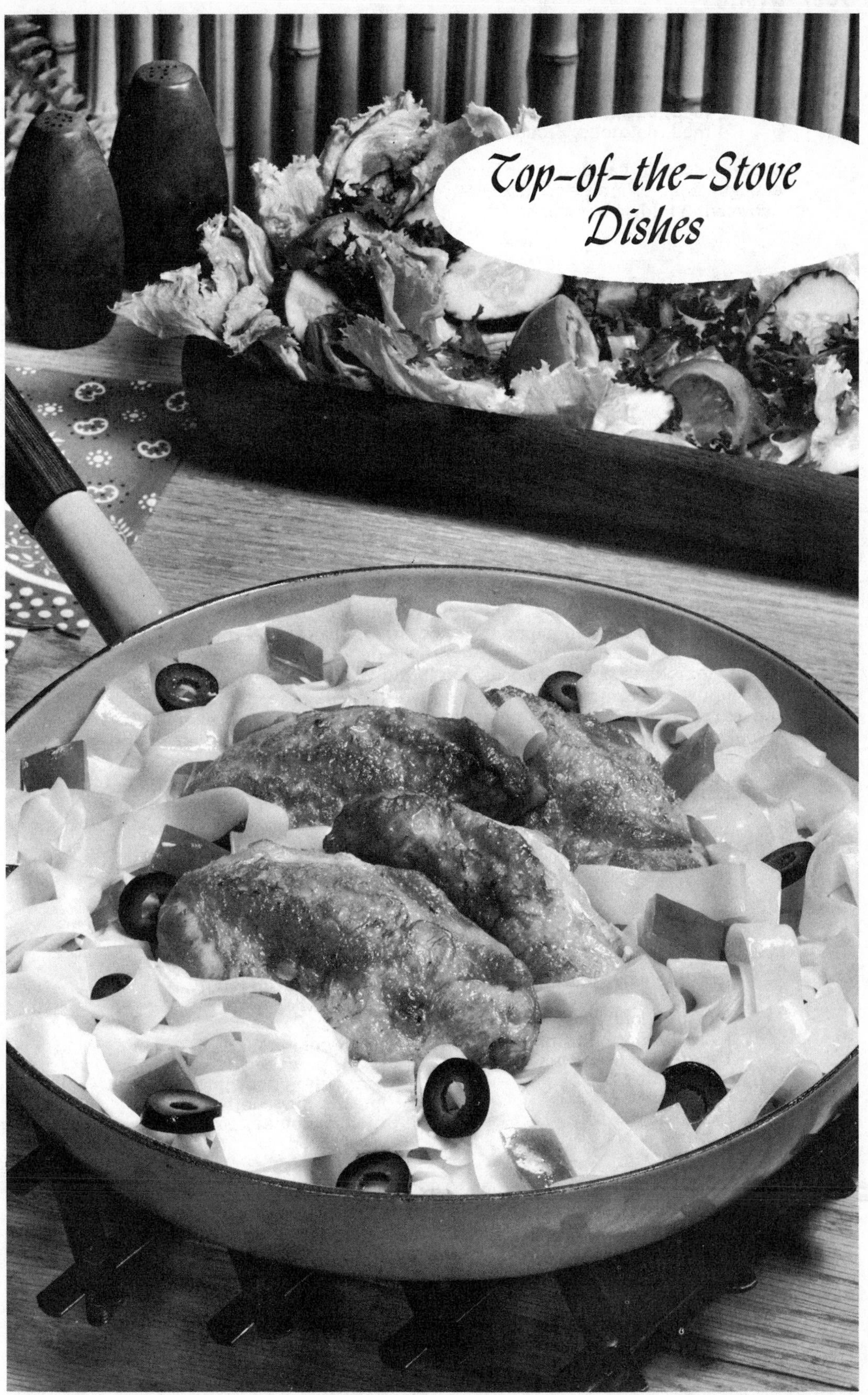

RECIPE FOR PATIO CHICKEN SKILLET ON PAGE 218

BEEF HASH

2 med. onions, sliced
2 tbsp. bacon drippings
4 med. potatoes, diced
2 c. cooked leftover beef, diced
Salt and pepper to taste
Milk

Saute onions in bacon drippings until soft. Add potatoes, beef, seasonings and enough milk to cover. Mix well; cover skillet and simmer until hash is well browned. Yield: 5 servings.

Mrs. Ollie Thompson, Troy, N. C.

BEEF STEW

1 ¾ lb. chuck or round beef, 1 ½-inch thick
⅓ c. flour
¼ tsp. pepper
Salt
3 tbsp. fat or drippings
¼ c. diced onion
1 clove of garlic, minced
2 ¾ c. boiling water
1 c. canned tomatoes
½ tsp. Worcestershire sauce
3 or 4 med. potatoes, pared and quartered
12 sm. white onions, peeled
12 carrots, peeled and cut into 2-in. pieces
1 c. frozen peas

Trim excess fat from meat; cut into 1 1/2-inch cubes. Combine flour, pepper and 1/4 teaspoonful salt in paper bag; add meat. Shake until pieces are coated. Melt fat in Dutch oven; add meat and brown on all sides. Add onion, garlic, boiling water, tomatoes, 1/2 teaspoonful salt and Worcestershire sauce. Cover; reduce heat to low and simmer for 2 hours or until meat is tender. Add potatoes, onions and carrots; cook for 20 minutes. Add peas; cook for 15 minutes longer. Drop dumplings may be added with peas. Stew may be served over cooked noodles, omitting potatoes. Yield: 4 servings.

Mrs. William T. Biltz, Palm Bay, Fla.

BEEF STEW BOURBONAIS

1 ½ lb. chuck, cut into 1-in. cubes
1 tbsp. shortening
1 clove of garlic, minced
1 med. onion, chopped
½ tsp. salt
⅛ tsp. pepper
1 can tomato soup
¾ c. red wine
¼ c. water
¼ tsp. powdered basil
¼ tsp. powdered thyme
½ c. catsup
3 med. carrots, cut into ½-in. pieces
1 ½ c. celery, cut into 1-in. pieces diagonally
4 med. potatoes, pared and quartered

Lightly brown beef in shortening. Add garlic and onion; saute until transparent. Sprinkle with salt and pepper. Stir in soup, wine and water. Cover and simmer for 30 minutes. Add herbs and catsup. Arrange vegetables on top of meat and in gravy. Cover and simmer for 1 hour and 30 minutes or until meat and vegetables are tender, adding more water if necessary. One-half cup lemon juice may be substituted for red wine. Increase water from 1/4 to 3/4 cup. Yield: 4-6 servings.

Michele M. Mixon, Eau Gallie, Fla.

BRAISED SHORT RIBS

3 lb. short ribs
Flour, salt, pepper
Cooking oil
1 ½ c. water
1 sm. can tomatoes
2 med. carrots, chopped
2 med. onions, chopped
2 stalks celery, chopped
½ head small cabbage, chopped

Roll ribs in flour; season with salt and pepper. Brown on both sides in cooking oil. Place ribs in baking dish and blend flour into drippings gradually by adding water. Add tomatoes and other chopped vegetables, covering ribs. Place cover on dish and simmer about 1 hour and 30 minutes until tender. Serve over noodles. Yield: 4-6 servings.

Mrs. R. G. Allison, Montgomery, Ala.

BROWN BEEF STEW

1 lb. beef chuck, cut in 1 ½-in. cubes
1 tbsp. fat
4 c. water
1 tbsp. Worcestershire sauce
1 clove garlic
1 med. onion, sliced
1 tbsp. salt
½ tsp. pepper
6 carrots, quartered
4 med. potatoes, quartered

Brown meat well in hot fat; add remaining ingredients except carrots and potatoes. Simmer 2 hours, stirring occasionally. Add carrots and potatoes and continue cooking 30 to 40 minutes longer or until vegetables are tender. Remove meat and vegetables; thicken liquid for gravy. Return meat and vegetables to thickened gravy and serve. Yield: 6-8 servings.

Mrs. Kenneth W. Rockett, Gloster, Miss.

CHINESE BEEF

6 tsp. sugar
3 tsp. cornstarch
5 tsp. soy sauce
2 tsp. Burgundy wine
¼ c. plus 2 tbsp. cooking oil
1 lb. sirloin tips, cut into thin strips
3 green peppers, cut into bite-sized pieces
3 tomatoes, cut into bite-sized pieces
3 stalks celery, chopped
1 onion, thinly sliced
1 tbsp. catsup
½ tsp. Worcestershire sauce
6 c. hot cooked rice

Combine 4 teaspoonfuls sugar, 2 teaspoonfuls cornstarch, 4 teaspoonfuls soy sauce, wine and 1/4 cup oil. Marinate meat in sauce for at least 30 minutes or overnight. Drain beef; cook in remaining oil for 2 minutes. Remove beef from pan; cook vegetables in same pan for 10 minutes or until tender. Add beef. Combine remaining sugar, cornstarch and soy sauce with catsup and Worcestershire sauce. Mix well and pour over meat. Cook for 5 minutes. Mix with rice. Yield: 6 servings.

Mrs. Sherwood Jones, Arlington, Va.

CHOP SUEY

1 lb. round steak, diced
2 tbsp. shortening
1 c. celery, diced
1 c. onion, diced
2 tbsp. soy sauce
2 tbsp. beaded molasses
2 c. water
1 can cream of mushroom soup
2 tbsp. flour
Salt and pepper to taste
Rice, cooked
Chinese noodles

Brown steak in shortening; add celery, onion, soy sauce, molasses and water. Cook 45 minutes. Stir in soup, flour, salt and pepper; simmer 10 minutes. Serve on rice; top with noodles. Yield: 10 servings.

Mrs. Jack Morris, Marion, N. C.

CURRIED BEEF

2 ½ lb. round steak
Salt and pepper to taste
Flour
Oil
2 c. chopped onion
2 c. chopped celery
2 lge. cans tomatoes
1 tbsp. curry powder
1 tbsp. catsup
1 tsp. sugar
1 tsp. Worcestershire sauce
2 lge. cans mushrooms

Cut steak into cubes. Salt, pepper and flour steak; brown in oil. Brown onion and celery in oil. Pour tomatoes into large pan. Mix curry powder in glass of water; add to tomatoes. Add steak, onion and celery and 1 cup water. Simmer 3 hours or until steak is tender. Thirty minutes before serving, add remaining ingredients. Serve over fluffy rice. Yield: 10-12 servings.

Mrs. John A. Freeman, Hot Springs, Ark.

EASY STEAK DINNER

1 1-lb. round steak, ½ in. thick
¼ c. flour
1 tsp. salt
4 sm. carrots, cut into strips
¼ c. shortening
4 sm. onions
4 sm. potatoes
1 can cream of mushroom soup

Cut steak into 3 x 5-inch pieces; dredge in flour seasoned with salt. Place three or four carrot strips on each piece of steak; wrap around carrots. Fasten with toothpicks. Brown rolls slowly in shortening; add onions and potatoes. Pour mushroom soup over all. Cover. Cook over low heat or simmer for 45 minutes. Yield: 4 servings.

Mrs. Ruth Wingo, Kaufman, Tex.

GRILLARDS AND GRAVY

2 lb. lean beef, cubed
2 tbsp. shortening
3 tbsp. flour
2 lge. onions, finely chopped
2 No. 1 cans tomatoes
1 can tomato paste
2 cloves garlic, finely chopped
2 c. finely chopped green pepper
2 c. chopped celery
½ c. minced parsley
Salt and pepper to taste

(Continued on next page)

Fry beef in shortening until brown; remove beef. Brown flour; add onions and saute lightly. Add tomatoes, tomato paste, garlic, green pepper, celery and parsley. Return meat to skillet. Add enough water to cover. Simmer for 1 hour and 30 minutes or until beef is tender. Stir occasionally. Add salt and pepper after cooking 30 minutes. Yield: 8-10 servings.

Mrs. W. R. Ferris, Vicksburg, Miss.

ONE-POT MEAL

- 2 lb. boneless stew meat
- 2 tbsp. shortening
- 6 to 8 carrots, peeled and cut into quarters
- 6 med. Irish potatoes, peeled and cubed
- 1 lge. onion
- 1 tsp. salt
- ½ tsp. pepper
- 1 c. water

Brown meat in skillet in shortening; place in bottom of pot. Place carrots over meat; cover with potatoes. Place onion in center. Sprinkle with seasonings; add water. Cook for 1 hour or until tender. Yield: 6-8 servings.

Mrs. B. K. Sanders, Goldonna, La.

ROAST HASH DELIGHT

- 1 stalk celery
- ½ green bell pepper
- 1 lge. carrot
- 1 lge. Idaho potato
- 1 med. onion
- Leftover roast, meat juice and gravy
- Hamburger seasoning to taste
- 1 tbsp. catsup
- 1 sprig parsley
- 1 tsp. flour

Chop all vegetables and add to chopped roast, juice and gravy. Add water as needed. Sprinkle in other ingredients, adding softened flour. Stir well and cook till vegetables are tender. Yield: 6-8 servings.

Mrs. W. A. Warren, Austin, Tex.

ROUND STEAK AND SPAGHETTI CASSEROLE

¼ c. flour
1 ½ tsp. salt
¾ tsp. pepper
2 lb. round steak
4 tbsp. shortening
1 med. onion, sliced
1 lge. green pepper, cut into rings
1 family-sized can tomato sauce
1 sauce can water
Dash of garlic salt
1 8-oz. pkg. spaghetti, cooked

Combine flour and 3/4 teaspoonful salt and 1/2 teaspoonful pepper; sprinkle over steak. Pound steak on both sides. Cook steak in shortening to desired tenderness. Place steak in baking dish. Cook onion and green pepper in pan drippings until lightly browned. Add tomato sauce and water, remaining salt, pepper and dash of garlic salt. Cook for 10 minutes. Place spaghetti around steak; pour sauce over spaghetti. Yield: 4 servings.

Mrs. Edward Parnell, Pensacola, Fla.

ROUND STEAK STEW

Flour
Salt and pepper
Round steak, cut into pieces
½ c. shortening
2 sm. cans stewed tomatoes
1 green pepper, cut into 6 to 8 pieces
3 or 4 potatoes, cut into pieces
1 or 2 onions, quartered
2 carrots, cut into pieces

Flour, salt and pepper steak; brown in shortening in Dutch oven. Remove steak. Add 2 tablespoonfuls of flour to drippings in Dutch oven. Cook until brown. Pour in 1 can stewed tomatoes; add meat. Pour remaining stewed tomatoes over meat. Cover; cook over low heat for 45 minutes, adding water as needed. Add green pepper, potatoes, onions and carrots. Simmer for 30 minutes or until tender. Yield: 6 servings.

Mrs. Charles Braddock, Ripley, Miss.

SAILORS' BEEF

1 lb. beef chuck or round steak, 1 in. thick
2 tbsp. butter or margarine
2 med. onions, sliced
1 ½ lb. potatoes, pared and thickly sliced
Salt and pepper
1 ¼ c. hot water

Wipe steak with damp cloth; cut into 1/2-inch slices. Pound meat with edge of saucer. Heat butter in heavy skillet until bubbly; saute meat until browned. Remove meat; saute onions until golden brown. Remove onions; layer potatoes, beef and onions in skillet, ending with potatoes. Sprinkle each layer with salt and pepper. Pour water over layers. Simmer, covered, for 1 hour to 1 hour and 30 minutes or until tender. Sprinkle with snipped parsley, if desired. Yield: 4 servings.

Mrs. Thomas G. Harrison, Fredericksburg, Tex.

SUNDAY NIGHT CASSEROLE

3 c. leftover macaroni and cheese
2 c. drained English peas, string beans or field peas
1 sm. cabbage, cut into quarters
Leftover steak, roast or fried chicken
1 can cream of mushroom soup

Arrange macaroni and cheese and English peas in electric frypan. Place cabbage in corners. Arrange meat on top; spoon soup over meat. Cover; simmer at 250 degrees for 15 minutes or until cabbage is tender.

Mrs. J. D. Hawkins, Fitzgerald, Ga.

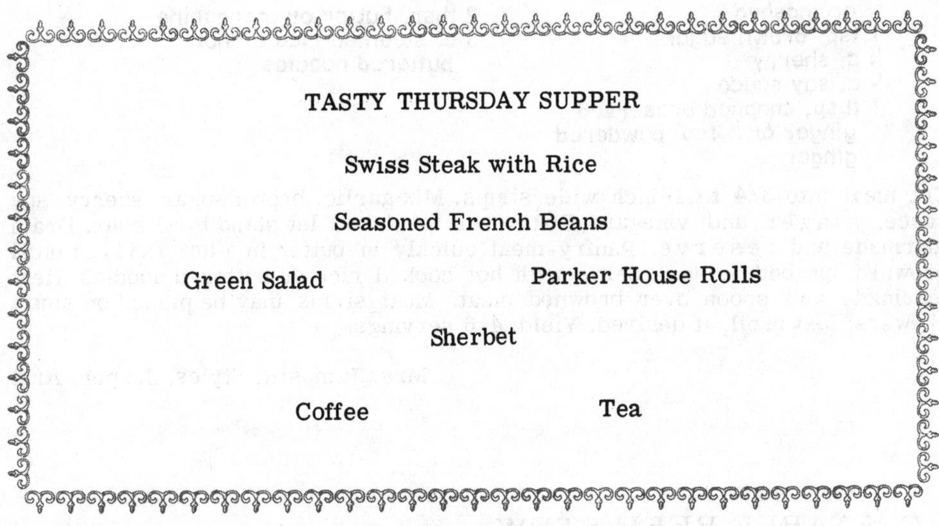

TASTY THURSDAY SUPPER

Swiss Steak with Rice

Seasoned French Beans

Green Salad — Parker House Rolls

Sherbet

Coffee — Tea

SWISS STEAK WITH RICE

2 lb. round steak, 1 in. thick
2 tsp. salt
Pepper to taste
3 tbsp. flour
Fat
6 onions, sliced
1 c. rice
1 bay leaf
1 can tomato soup
½ c. water or 1½ c. tomato juice

Cut meat in serving pieces. Season and dredge in flour. Brown meat well on both sides in hot fat. Add onions; brown slightly. Add rice and bay leaf. Combine soup and water; pour over meat and rice. Cook for 15 minutes at 15 pounds pressure in pressure cooker. Yield: 5-6 servings.

Mrs. Gladys Skinner, Longview, Tex.

SWISS STEAK AND SPAGHETTI

1 lb. round steak
Salt and pepper to taste
½ c. flour
⅓ c. fat
½ c. diced onion
½ c. diced green pepper
1 clove garlic (opt.)
1 8-oz. can tomato sauce
¾ c. water
4 c. cooked spaghetti

(Continued on next page)

Cut meat into four pieces; salt and pepper. Pound flour into meat; brown on one side quickly in fat. Turn meat; reduce heat. Add onion, green pepper and garlic. Cover and simmer for 10 minutes. Add tomato sauce, water and 1/4 teaspoon salt. Simmer for 30 to 40 minutes. Serve gravy over spaghetti. Yield: 4 servings.

Mrs. C. R. Glass, Hueytown, Ala.

TERIYAKI STEAK

- 4 to 6 minute steaks
- 1 clove of garlic, minced or mashed
- 1 tsp. brown sugar
- ¼ c. sherry
- ¼ c. soy sauce
- 1 tbsp. chopped preserved ginger or ½ tsp. powdered ginger
- 1 tbsp. vinegar or lemon juice
- 2 tbsp. butter or margarine
- 3 c. steamed rice or hot buttered noodles

Cut meat into 3/4 to 1-inch wide strips. Mix garlic, brown sugar, sherry, soy sauce, ginger and vinegar. Pour over meat and let stand for 1 hour. Drain marinade and reserve. Panfry meat quickly in butter in a hot skillet until browned on both sides. Serve with hot cooked rice or buttered noodles. Heat marinade and spoon over browned meat. Meat strips may be placed on small skewers; fast broil, if desired. Yield: 4-6 servings.

Mrs. James R. Styles, Jasper, Ark.

VEGETABLE-BEEF STEW

- 1 lb. stew beef
- Salt and pepper to taste
- 4 med. potatoes, chopped
- 2 lge. carrots, chopped
- 1 med. onion, chopped
- 2 sticks celery, chopped
- 1 lge. pkg. frozen mixed vegetables
- 1 lge. can tomatoes
- 1 lge. can tomato sauce
- Garlic salt (opt.)

Brown beef in small amount of fat with salt and pepper. Add enough water to cover meat; simmer, covered, for 1 hour. Add potatoes, carrots, onion, celery and vegetables. Simmer, covered, for 2 to 3 hours. Add tomatoes and tomato sauce. Simmer for 1 hour longer, adding water as needed. Add garlic salt. Yield: 8 servings.

Mrs. Jan Anderson, Crestview, Fla.

SOUTHERN HASH

- 2 lge. onions
- 3 tbsp. fat or salad oil
- 1 lb. ground veal, shoulder or rump
- 1 No. 2 can or 2 ½ c. cooked tomatoes
- ½ c. uncooked rice
- 1 tsp. chili powder
- 1 tsp. salt
- Few grains pepper

(Continued on next page)

Slice onions; brown in fat. Add veal; brown. Add tomatoes, rice, chili powder, salt and pepper. Cover; cook slowly 30 minutes or until rice is tender, stirring occasionally. Yield: 4 servings.

Mrs. Alberta E. Veith, Louisville, Ky.

TEXAS VEAL BALLS

1 lb. chopped veal
1 tsp. garlic salt
2 tbsp. parsley
Pepper to taste
1 tsp. Kitchen Bouquet
1 egg
2 tbsp. bacon grease
1 can cream of mushroom soup

Mix meat with seasonings and egg; shape into balls. Brown in Kitchen Bouquet and bacon grease. Add soup; simmer for 20 minutes. Serve on noodles. Yield: 6 servings.

Mrs. Cletabel Bidwell, Lewisville, Tex.

VEAL FRICASSEE DINNER

2 lb. boneless veal
2 tbsp. margarine
1 ½ tsp. salt
Water
4 carrots, diced
3 onions, sliced
2 tbsp. finely cut parsley
4 potatoes, sliced

Wipe meat with a damp cloth. Cut into 1 1/2-inch cubes; brown in hot margarine. Sprinkle salt on meat; add water to cover. Cover skillet and simmer until meat is tender, about 1 hour and 30 minutes. Add vegetables 30 minutes before end of cooking time. Just before serving, thicken gravy, if desired, with flour and water paste, stirring over direct heat until it boils. Yield: 5 servings.

Arlene Campbell, Roseland, Va.

CHICKEN BOGG GRITS

3 c. chicken broth
⅔ c. quick-cooking white grits
1 c. chopped chicken
5 slices crisp-cooked bacon
Pepper
1 tsp. salt
2 tbsp. butter

Pour broth and grits into a 2-quart boiling pot. Place on medium heat; stir constantly. After mixture begins cooking, turn on low heat. Stir in chopped cooked chicken, crisp-cooked bacon, pepper, salt and butter. Cook until desired consistency. Yield: 5-6 servings.

Mrs. John T. Askins, Hartsville, S. C.

CHICKEN CACCIATORE

1 2½ to 3-lb. chicken, cut up
¼ c. olive oil
1 med. onion, chopped
1 clove garlic, chopped
1 tsp. basil
1 tbsp. parsley
¼ c. sherry or marsala
Salt and pepper to taste
1 17-oz. can tomatoes, cut up

Lightly brown chicken in hot olive oil. Add onion, garlic, basil and parsley; cook until chicken is golden brown and vegetables are soft. Add wine and heat until evaporated. Season with salt and pepper. Add tomatoes with liquid. Cover and simmer for 20 to 30 minutes or until chicken is tender and sauce has thickened. Yield: 8 servings.

Ruth Wall, Gadsden, Ala.

CHICKEN A LA GRITS

1 can cream of mushroom soup
½ c. cooked chopped chicken
2 tbsp. chopped pimento
½ c. light cream
2 tbsp. butter
2 c. cooked grits
Parsley

Mix ingredients except grits and parsley; cook slowly 10 minutes over medium heat. Bake grits earlier in day in greased loaf pan at 325 degrees until firm. Keep in warm oven. Cut out squares and serve chicken mixture over them. Garnish with parsley.

Mrs. John R. Taylor, Jr., Jonesboro, Tenn.

CHICKEN-NOODLE DISH

2 tbsp. butter or margarine
1 c. chopped onions
1 c. chopped celery
1 clove garlic, crushed
1 1-lb. 12-oz. can tomatoes
1 c. water
1 2-oz. can mushroom stems and pieces
1 chicken bouillon cube
½ tsp. salt
½ tsp. oregano
¼ tsp. pepper
¼ tsp. basil
3 c. chopped cooked chicken or turkey
8 oz. noodles

Melt butter in large saucepan. Add onions, celery and garlic; cook until onions are transparent. Stir in tomatoes, water, mushrooms and liquid, bouillon cube, salt, oregano, pepper and basil. Bring to a boil; reduce heat. Cover; simmer for 45 minutes, stirring occasionally. Stir in chicken and noodles; cover and simmer for 10 to 15 minutes longer or until noodles are tender, stirring occasionally. Serve immediately. Yield: 4-6 servings.

Requa K. Spears, Pikeville, Ky.

CHICKEN TETRAZZINI

1 5 to 5½-lb. hen
1 tbsp. salt
1 ½ qt. water
1 1-lb. pkg. macaroni or spaghetti, cooked
1 10-oz. pkg. frozen peas
1 4-oz. can mushrooms, undrained
1 4-oz. can pimento, chopped

(Continued on next page)

4 tbsp. butter
4 tbsp. flour
¼ c. milk
½ lb. Velveeta cheese, sliced

Cook chicken in salted water; allow to cool in broth. Remove from broth; cut into bite-sized pieces. Bring broth to boil; add spaghetti. Cook, uncovered, until tender. Add more water if necessary, but most of liquid should be absorbed. Cook frozen peas in separate pan; add mushrooms and pimento. Combine butter, flour, milk and Velveeta; cook, stirring constantly, until cheese melts. Add chicken, peas, mushrooms and cheese sauce to macaroni. Stir until mixed. Cover; heat very slowly until serving temperature. Yield: 16 servings.

Mrs. Eunice Gordon, Shattuck, Okla.

CHICKEN IN WINE-CHERRY SAUCE

1 can sweet dark cherries
1 c. port or Burgundy wine
3 tbsp. lemon juice
2 cloves of garlic
¼ tsp. ginger
½ tsp. oregano
1 2½ to 3½-lb. chicken, cut into serving pieces
½ c. flour
2 tsp. salt
Dash of pepper
¼ c. shortening
1 chicken bouillon cube

Drain cherries, reserving 1 cup juice. Combine cherry juice, wine, lemon juice, garlic, ginger and oregano. Pour over chicken; let stand for several hours or overnight. Remove chicken; wipe dry. Combine flour, salt and pepper. Dip chicken into flour mixture. Brown in shortening. Remove garlic from marinade; pour over chicken. Add bouillon cube; bring to a boil. Reduce heat and simmer. Add cherries; cook for 15 minutes. Yield: 4-6 servings.

Mrs. S. V. Susina, Birmingham, Ala.

FRENCH CHICKEN

4 chicken breasts
½ c. butter
2 to 3 bouillon cubes
¼ c. elbow macaroni, cooked
½ c. mixed chopped celery and green pepper
4 tsp. cornstarch
1 tbsp. lemon juice
1 tsp. sugar
1 tbsp. water
½ c. olives, cut up
2 tomatoes, sliced

Place breasts in skillet with butter; brown. Dissolve bouillon cubes according to directions; add to chicken with macaroni and simmer. Place celery and pepper, cornstarch, lemon juice, sugar and water in separate pot. Simmer. Place olives and sliced tomatoes on chicken; pour on sauce. Simmer for a few minutes longer. Yield: 4 servings.

Mrs. Charlotte Roper, Chickasaw, Ala.

HOMINY CROQUETTES

2 c. cooked grits
2 c. finely chopped chicken
⅛ tsp. pepper
1 tsp. salt
Bread crumbs
1 egg

(Continued on next page)

Combine cooked grits and meat. Add seasoning; chill. Shape into croquettes; roll in crumbs. Dip in beaten egg. Roll in dry crumbs again; panfry in moderately hot deep fat until golden brown. Beef, ham or flaked fish may be substituted for chicken.

Mrs. J. A. Stansbury, Clinton, Miss.

INDIAN CHICKEN CURRY

1 onion, thinly sliced
1 tart apple, peeled and diced
1 tbsp. curry powder
3 tbsp. butter
¼ c. raisins
1 ½ c. chicken stock
3 ½ tbsp. flour
1 c. light cream or evaporated milk
Salt and pepper to taste
2 lb. chicken breasts, cooked and diced

Saute onion, apple and curry powder in butter, stirring to blend well. Add raisins and stock. Blend flour with small amount of cream until smooth; add with remaining cream to mixture. Cook over low heat, stirring, until thick and creamy; add seasonings and chicken. Heat thoroughly; serve over rice with grated coconut, chopped peanuts, minced onion, chow-chow, raisins, sweet pickle relish and chutney as condiments. Flavor improves if made a day ahead and reheated in double boiler. Yield: 4-6 servings.

Mrs. Mae Belle Alcock, Chelsea, Ala.

PATIO CHICKEN SKILLET

2 chicken breasts, halved
¼ c. butter or margarine
4 tsp. seasoned salt
¼ tsp. crushed thyme
Ground pepper
1 med. green pepper, diced
1 sm. onion, chopped
¼ tsp. Tabasco sauce
1 qt. water
8 oz. wide egg noodles
1 10 ½-oz. can cream of celery soup
½ c. ripe olives, sliced

Brown chicken on both sides in butter in large skillet; sprinkle with 2 teaspoons seasoned salt, thyme and a dash of pepper. Cover and cook over low heat 30 minutes or until tender. Remove chicken. Mix green pepper, onion, Tabasco sauce, water, remaining seasoned salt and 1/8 teaspoon pepper with drippings in skillet; bring to a boil. Gradually add noodles; cover and cook over low heat 20 minutes, stirring occasionally, until noodles are tender. Stir in soup, olives and water, if needed. Add chicken and heat.

Photograph for this recipe on page 207.

QUICK CHICKEN SOUP

1 3 to 4-lb. chicken
1 lge. onion, diced
1 carrot, diced
2 pieces celery
½ pkg. shell macaroni
1 12-oz. can chili sauce
Salt and pepper to taste

Cook chicken until tender; add onion, carrot and celery. Cook until tender. Remove chicken from broth; bone and dice. Add enough water to broth to make 8 cups;

(Continued on next page)

bring to a boil. Add macaroni, chili sauce, chicken, salt and pepper. Cook for 15 minutes over medium heat. Add more water if too thick. Yield: 6 servings.

Mrs. George Kinsel, Lafayette, La.

CHICKEN WITH RICE

1 fryer, cut up
Butter
Salt and pepper
3 onions, chopped
1 to 2 tomatoes, cut up
¼ lb. bacon ends or ham
1 c. rice
1 can chicken stock
3 to 4 pimentos
Cooking oil
1 can or pkg. asparagus tips, cooked
1 can or pkg. English peas, cooked
Parsley

Cook chicken in butter until golden brown; season with salt and pepper. Fry onions, tomatoes and bacon ends in separate skillet; add onions and tomatoes to chicken. Stir in rice, salt and pepper; moisten with stock. Cook until rice is tender, adding more stock if necessary; place on hot dish. Fry pimentos in oil. Garnish chicken mixture with pimento, asparagus and English peas; sprinkle with parsley. Yield: 6 servings.

Mrs. Carl E. Odem, Bastrop, La.

CHICKEN AND YELLOW RICE

2 tbsp. shortening
1 fryer, cut into serving pieces and skinned
4 c. water
Salt and pepper to taste
1 16-oz. pkg. yellow rice

Melt shortening in 4-quart pot. Brown chicken lightly on both sides. Add water, salt and pepper; bring to boil. Reduce heat; boil for 15 minutes. Add yellow rice; stir. Cover; cook for 20 minutes or until water is absorbed into rice. Stir occasionally. Yield: 5 servings.

Mrs. Donna M. West, Haines City, Fla.

SKILLET CHICKEN WITH RICE

½ c. flour
1 tsp. paprika
1 ½ tsp. salt
⅛ tsp. pepper
1 lge. fryer, cut up
½ c. fat
¾ c. rice
3 c. boiling water
1 onion or 1 clove garlic (opt.)
Parsley

Combine flour, paprika, salt and pepper in paper bag. Add chicken and shake until well dusted. Brown in fat. Add remaining ingredients; cover and simmer at 350 degrees for 1 to 2 hours or until chicken is tender and water evaporated. Remove onion or garlic before parsley. Yield: 6-8 servings.

Mrs. J. W. Harrison, Magnolia, Miss.

CHICKEN AND SPAGHETTI

- 2 onions, chopped
- 2 green peppers, chopped
- 6 stalks celery, chopped
- 1 tbsp. shortening
- 2 qt. chicken broth
- 1 qt. tomato juice
- ¼ c. Worcestershire sauce
- ¼ c. Indian Grill sauce
- 4 tbsp. sugar
- 2 tbsp. prepared mustard
- 1 tbsp. hot sauce
- Salt to taste
- 2 hens, cooked
- 3 pkg. spaghetti
- 1 sm. can pimento
- 1 lb. Velveeta cheese, grated

Fry onions, green peppers and celery in shortening; add all remaining ingredients except chicken, spaghetti, pimento and cheese. Cook slowly until celery and pepper are barely tender. Cook spaghetti in salted boiling water for 7 minutes. Combine spaghetti, chicken, pimento and sauce in large pan. Stir gently until mixed. Add cheese. Yield: 10 servings.

Dorris Jewett, Panhandle, Tex.

CHICKEN AND SPAGHETTI

- 1 lge. chicken
- 3 c. chopped onions
- Cooking oil
- 2 lge. cans tomatoes
- 2 cans tomato paste
- 1 lge. stalk celery, diced
- 2 or 3 green peppers, diced
- 18 to 20 oz. spaghetti
- 1 can mushrooms

Boil chicken; reserve broth. Remove from bone; cut into pieces. Fry onions in a small amount of cooking oil. Mix onions with tomatoes, tomato paste, celery and peppers. Simmer for 2 to 3 hours; add water, if needed. Cook spaghetti in chicken broth until tender. Add spaghetti, chicken and mushrooms to tomato mixture; mix thoroughly. Simmer for 30 minutes. Yield: 18-20 servings.

Mrs. James P. Cook, Grenada, Miss.

CREOLE CHICKEN AND SPAGHETTI

- Salt and pepper
- 1 lge. fryer, cut up
- 2 8-oz. cans tomato sauce
- 1 6-oz. can tomato paste
- 1 c. water
- 2 tbsp. creole seasoning
- 1 pkg. thin spaghetti, cooked

Salt and pepper chicken; sear on both sides in heavy pot or pan without grease. Add tomato sauce, tomato paste, water, creole seasoning and additional salt and pepper. Cook until tender. Remove chicken to serving dish; add cooked spaghetti to sauce. Serve hot. Yield: 6 servings.

Inez Walker, Pensacola, Fla.

EASY CHICKEN SPAGHETTI

- 1 hen or fryer
- 1 onion, chopped
- 1 green pepper, chopped
- 3 stalks celery, chopped
- 1 10-oz. box spaghetti
- 1 can cream of mushroom soup
- 1 jar chopped pimento
- ½ lb. cheese, cubed

(Continued on next page)

Cook chicken until tender. Remove from broth; cool. Remove bones and chop. Cook onion, green pepper and celery in chicken broth until tender. Add spaghetti; cook until tender. Add soup, pimento, cheese and chicken; cook until cheese is melted. Yield: 8 servings.

Jan Clark, Brownwood, Tex.

CHICKEN AND CORN

1 frying chicken
Salt
Pepper
1 pt. raw creamed corn
½ c. flour
Pork lard or cooking oil

Prepare chicken for frying. Salt and pepper to taste. Prepare corn while chicken absorbs salt. Flour chicken lightly; place in hot fat. Cook slowly browning evenly. Remove chicken and drain excess grease, adding corn to drippings and cooking quickly. Cover and stir frequently. Add water, salt and pat of butter, if needed.

Mrs. Oeland R. Parker, Tallahassee, Fla.

CHICKEN IN THE CORN

½ c. yellow cornmeal
1 tsp. salt
¼ tsp. poultry seasoning
½ tsp. black pepper
1 fryer, cut up
¼ c. butter or margarine
¼ c. shortening
1 16-oz. can cream-style corn
2 tbsp. chopped pimento

Mix cornmeal, salt, poultry seasoning and pepper together. Coat pieces of chicken well. Melt butter and shortening in skillet. Brown chicken well on all sides. Turn to low heat and continue frying until tender, about 25 minutes. When chicken is tender move to side of skillet. Add corn and pimento; heat. Yield: 4 servings.

Mrs. R. C. Bouse, Jr., Port Bolivar, Tex.

CHICKEN A LA JARDINIERE

1 med. chicken, cut in small pieces
3 tbsp. flour
Salt and pepper
3 tbsp. cooking oil
8 green onions, chopped
2 pt. boiling water
¼ can mushrooms
1 sm. cauliflower, chopped
½ c. green peas
4 sm. artichoke hearts, cooked
1 sprig thyme
1 sprig parsley
1 bay leaf
Cooked rice

Roll chicken slightly in flour, salt and pepper; fry in hot oil until lightly browned. Add onions; cook until onions are soft. Add 1 pint boiling water; simmer, covered, for 1 hour or until tender. Stir in mushrooms, cauliflower, green peas and artichoke hearts; place over high heat. Add remaining water, mixing well; stir in salt, pepper and remaining ingredients except rice. Cook for 20 minutes; serve over rice. Yield: 4 servings.

Mrs. Paul R. Dirmann, New Orleans, La.

CHICKEN FRICASSEE WITH CARROTS

½ c. sliced onion
1 tbsp. chicken fat
3 tbsp. flour
2 c. chicken broth
1 stewed chicken, cut up
2 c. cooked shredded carrots
Salt to taste

Cook onion in fat for a few minutes. Blend in flour. Add broth; cook until smooth and thickened, stirring constantly. Combine chicken, carrots, sauce and salt. Serve over fluffy rice. Yield: 6-8 servings.

Mrs. G. G. Bennett, Vaiden, Miss.

CHICKEN-IN-A-POT

1 4-lb. chicken
Salt and pepper
⅓ c. salad oil
2 c. water
1 c. sliced onion
½ c. mushrooms
2 c. diced potatoes or potato balls
1 ½ c. sliced carrots
¾ c. wine
Cayenne

Cut chicken into serving pieces; sprinkle with salt and pepper. Brown in hot oil; place in a casserole. Pour water over chicken; cover tightly. Bake at 300 degrees for 1 hour to 1 hour and 30 minutes or until done. Lightly brown onion in remaining oil in skillet; add with vegetables to chicken. Pour wine over all; add salt, pepper and cayenne to taste. Return to oven and continue cooking for 30 to 45 minutes or until vegetables are tender. Yield: 6 servings.

Mrs. Frances Melvin, Fayetteville, N. C.

CHICKEN-IN-THE-POT

Salt and pepper
2 3-lb. broilers
Butter
½ c. chicken consomme
¼ c. white wine
2 c. diced white potatoes
2 tbsp. minced parsley
6 thick slices bacon
1 5-oz. pkg. fresh mushrooms
2 tbsp. diced pimento

Season chickens; brown in 1/4 cup butter in casserole. Lay birds on sides; add consomme and wine. Bake, covered, at 350 degrees for 1 hour and 30 minutes. Cook potatoes in 1/3 cup butter until tender; sprinkle with parsley. Cut bacon into small strips; fry until crisp. Wash mushrooms; trim ends. Cook in potato butter for 5 minutes. Add potatoes, bacon strips, pimento and mushrooms to chicken. Yield: 4-6 servings.

Mrs. Earl Wiggins, Jr., Rome, Ga.

PINEAPPLE-CHICKEN CHOW MEIN

¼ c. salad oil
1 c. sliced onion
3 c. sliced celery
1 No. 2 can bean sprouts
1 14-oz. can pineapple tidbits, drained
2 chicken bouillon cubes
½ c. water

(Continued on next page)

¾ tsp. salt
¼ tsp. pepper
2 tbsp. brown sugar
2 tbsp. cornstarch
¼ c. soy sauce
2 c. chicken
1 6-oz. can chow mein noodles

Heat salad oil in large saucepan or Dutch oven; add onion, celery, bean sprouts with liquor, drained pineapple, bouillon cubes dissolved in water, salt, pepper and brown sugar. Cover and bring to boil. Mix cornstarch with soy sauce; stir into vegetable mixture. Add chicken and cook, stirring, for 3 to 6 minutes or until thickened. Serve over chow mein noodles or cooked rice. Yield: 4 servings.

Mrs. Tal Flowers, Tuskegee, Ala.

QUICK BRUNSWICK STEW

3 lb. cut-up chicken
2 1-lb. cans tomatoes
2 c. water
1 tbsp. salt
½ tsp. oregano
½ tsp. black pepper
1 10-oz. pkg. frozen baby lima beans

In Dutch oven or large saucepan, combine chicken, tomatoes, water, salt, oregano and pepper. Bring mixture to boil; reduce heat. Cover and simmer 30 minutes, or until chicken is tender. If necessary, remove excess fat. Stir in lima beans and bring to boil; reduce heat and simmer while preparing cornmeal dumplings.

CORNMEAL DUMPLINGS:

¾ c. self-rising cornmeal
¾ c. self-rising flour
2 tbsp. butter or margarine
½ c. chopped onions
1 egg, beaten
3 to 6 tbsp. milk

In mixing bowl, stir together cornmeal and flour. Cut in butter until mixture resembles coarse crumbs. Stir in onions; blend together egg and 3 tablespoons milk. Add liquid all at once to cornmeal mixture. Stirring to blend if necessary, add more milk to make a thick drop batter. Drop dumplings by rounded tablespoonfuls into boiling mixture. Cover and steam 10 minutes. Remove; cover and cook 10 minutes longer. Yield: 6 servings.

Mrs. Reba Mabe, Atlanta, Ga.

BEEF LA CACCIATORE

3 tbsp. lard
1 lb. hamburger
Onion, diced
Green pepper, diced
2 tsp. salt
¼ tsp. pepper
1 can tomato soup
⅔ c. uncooked rice

On medium-high heat melt lard and brown hamburger, diced onion and green pepper. Add salt, pepper, tomato soup, 1 can water and rice. Mix all together and turn to low for 25 to 30 minutes. Cover tightly. Stir once or twice. Yield: 8 servings.

Mary Simmons Rakes, Stanardsville, Va.

CHILI

1 lb. ground beef
2 tbsp. shortening
1 sm. green pepper, diced
1 sm. onion, diced
2 c. diced tomatoes
2 c. cooked chili beans
2 tsp. sugar
1 tbsp. chili seasoning
Salt and pepper to taste

Brown beef in shortening; add remaining ingredients. Simmer for 1 hour, stirring occasionally.

Mrs. Winnie Mae Pilcher, Dublin, Ga.

CIRCUS CITY SPECIAL

1 lb. ground beef
½ c. chopped onion
1 tbsp. fat
¼ c. uncooked rice, washed and drained
1 tsp. salt
1 can cream of mushroom soup
½ soup can water
1 pkg. frozen peas and carrots

Brown ground beef and onion lightly in fat in frying pan. Add rice, salt, soup and water. Cover; simmer for 30 minutes, stirring occasionally. Add vegetables; simmer for 10 to 15 minutes or until tender. Serve hot. Yield: 6 servings.

Mrs. Vannie Tate, Pulaski, Tenn.

HAMBURGER SKILLET MEAL

2 slices bacon, diced
½ lb. ground beef
1 onion, chopped
1 green pepper, chopped
½ tsp. salt
Dash of pepper
1 tbsp. parsley flakes
½ c. water
2 c. egg noodles
1 No. 2½ can tomatoes
½ c. chili sauce

Heat diced bacon, ground beef and onion in skillet over high heat. Reduce heat until meat is slightly browned. Add remaining ingredients; when steaming, cook over low heat for 35 minutes. Yield: 6 servings.

Mrs. Mildred J. Foxworth, Bishopville, S. C.

HAMBURGER STEW

1 ½ lb. ground beef
Garlic salt
Pepper and salt
1 egg
1 ½ cans tomato paste
3 tbsp. cooking oil
½ green pepper
4 cans water
4 med. potatoes, diced
1 med. onion
3 carrots
1 can sweet peas

Mix meat with seasonings, egg and 1/2 can tomato paste. Shape into meatballs. Brown in hot cooking oil and green pepper. Add remaining tomato paste, water, potatoes, onion, carrots and peas. Cover. Simmer about 1 hour.

Mrs. John D. Abshire, Sulphur, La.

Along the Skyline Drive in Shenandoah National Park.

HAMBURGER STROGANOFF

- ½ c. chopped onion
- ¼ c. butter or margarine
- 1 lb. ground beef
- 1 tsp. salt
- 1 tsp. pepper
- ¼ tsp. paprika
- ¼ tsp. monosodium glutamate
- 1 tbsp. cornstarch or 2 tbsp. flour
- 1 sm. can water chestnuts, drained and sliced
- 1 sm. can mushroom stems and pieces
- 1 can cream of chicken soup
- 1 c. buttermilk
- ¾ c. raw rice, cooked
- 1 can chow mein noodles

Brown onion in butter. Add ground beef, salt, pepper, paprika and monosodium glutamate; cook until meat is gray. Add flour; stir well. Add water chestnuts, mushrooms and soup; cook over low heat for 10 minutes. Remove from heat; add buttermilk and stir. Heat until bubbly hot. Serve on cooked rice; top with chow mein noodles. Yield: 6 servings.

Mrs. J. T. Alexander, Livingston, Ala.

ITALIAN SPAGHETTI

- 1 lb. ground beef
- 1 onion, diced
- 1 bunch celery, diced
- 1 green pepper, diced
- 1 can tomato paste
- 1 can tomato sauce
- 1 can tomatoes
- Salt and pepper
- 1 can mushroom soup
- 1 8-oz. pkg. spaghetti
- Parmesan cheese

Brown beef. Add next 7 ingredients. After mixture starts boiling, add mushroom soup. Cover; simmer 1 hour. Cook noodles. Serve with sauce topped with Parmesan cheese.

Mrs. Sheridan E. Davis, Appalachia, Va.

MACARONI-BEEF CASSEROLE

1 lb. ground beef
1 grated onion
Dash each of onion and garlic salt
1 box macaroni or long spaghetti
1 can cream of tomato soup
1 sm. bottle stuffed olives, chopped
1 lb. grated Velveeta cheese

Brown beef, onion, onion salt and garlic salt. Cook macaroni; drain well. Add to beef mixture. Add soup and olives; stir in cheese. Simmer until thick.

Billie Faye Bullard, Gurdon, Ark.

MAMA'S SPAGHETTI SAUCE

4 lge. bell peppers
4 lge. onions
2 c. diced celery
2 tbsp. (about) bacon grease
3 lb. ground beef
1 bottle catsup
2 tbsp. 57 sauce
2 tbsp. A-1 sauce
1 lge. can tomatoes
1 bottle chili sauce
Salt and pepper

Cut up peppers and onions. Simmer with celery in bacon grease for at least 30 minutes. Brown ground beef and mix with peppers, onions, and celery. Add remaining ingredients. Simmer for at least 45 minutes. Serve over hot cooked spaghetti. Yield: 8 servings.

Mrs. Wade W. Herring, Macon, Ga.

MEAT SAUCE WITH BEANS

1 lb. ground beef
1 med. onion, chopped
1 med. green pepper, chopped
1 tsp. salt
½ tsp. pepper
2 tbsp. (heaping) flour
2 tbsp. bacon fat
1 can tomato sauce
½ can tomatoes and chili pepper
1 lge. can pork and beans
1 c. water

Combine beef, onion, green pepper, salt, pepper and flour; cook beef mixture slowly in fat until meat begins to brown, stirring to separate meat. Add remaining ingredients; cook slowly for 1 hour, adding water as needed. Yield: 8 servings.

Mrs. Maude Strothart, Coushatta, La.

MOCK VEAL CUTLETS IN MUSHROOM SAUCE

2 lb. ground lean beef
1 c. milk
1 tbsp. Worcestershire sauce
Dash of garlic salt
1 tsp. salt
¼ tsp. pepper
¼ c. flour
¼ c. cooking oil
1 can cream of mushroom soup

Mix meat, 1/2 cup milk and seasonings in bowl; pat out into thin oblong patties. Dip patties into flour; brown in oil in skillet covered with a tight-fitting lid. When

(Continued on next page)

brown on both sides; drain off fat. Add soup, diluted with remaining milk. Cover; cook gently for 10 minutes. Yield: 10-12 servings.

Ruby Robertson Duncan, Sanderson, Tex.

MUSH-MEAT

- 1 lb. ground beef
- 2 tbsp. chili seasoning mix
- Dash of salt
- ½ c. water or tomato sauce
- 2 c. white hominy

Brown beef in heavy pot; sprinkle with chili seasoning after turning once. Mix well; add salt, water and hominy. Simmer, covered, until hominy is heated; fold over hominy. Yield: 4-6 servings.

Mrs. Earl C. Lewis, Chalmette, La.

SPAGHETTI AND MEAT SAUCE

- 1 med. onion, diced
- 1 clove garlic, minced
- ¼ c. chopped parsley
- ¼ c. salad oil
- 1 can whole tomatoes
- 1 6-oz. can tomato paste
- ¾ c. water
- 1 tsp. salt
- ¼ tsp. pepper
- 3 cloves
- ½ lb. ground beef
- 1 lb. cooked spaghetti

Brown onion, garlic and parsley in salad oil. Stir in tomatoes, tomato paste, water, salt, pepper and cloves. Cover; simmer for 25 to 30 minutes, stirring occasionally. Brown ground beef in skillet; add to sauce. Serve with spaghetti. Sprinkle with Parmesan cheese, if desired. Yield: 4 servings.

Mrs. W. F. McLeod, Moss Point, Miss.

SWEET-SOUR RED BEANS WITH BEEF

- ¼ lb. ground beef
- ½ c. vegetable oil
- 1 med. onion, chopped
- 1 green pepper, chopped
- 2 c. canned tomatoes
- 1 tbsp. chili sauce
- 1 tbsp. sweet pickle relish
- 1 tbsp. brown sugar
- 1 tbsp. parsley
- ½ tsp. salt
- ¼ tsp. black pepper
- ½ tsp. oregano
- 2 c. red kidney beans, drained
- 1 12-oz. can whole kernel corn, drained
- Juice of 1 lemon

Fry meat in oil until done. Add onion; cook slowly for 5 minutes. Add pepper, tomatoes and seasonings; simmer for 10 minutes. Add beans and corn; heat thoroughly. Do not boil. Season with lemon juice. Yield: 4 servings.

Myrtice Dobson, Resaca, Ga.

TEXAS JAMBALAYA

1 c. uncooked rice
2 tbsp. drippings
¾ c. sliced onions
½ c. diced green pepper
1 clove of garlic, minced
1 lb. lean ground beef
2 10 ½-oz. cans tomato soup
½ soup can water
2 tsp. salt
¼ tsp. pepper
Hot sauce (opt.)
Chili powder (opt.)
Comino (opt.)

Add uncooked rice to drippings in heavy pan; stir constantly over medium heat until rice is browned. Add onions, green pepper, garlic and ground beef. Cook, stirring frequently, until meat is browned. Add remaining ingredients. Cover tightly; cook over low heat for 40 minutes or until rice and meat are tender and liquid is absorbed. Add water as needed. Garnish with parsley just before serving, if desired. Yield: 4-5 servings.

Mrs. Turnmire Carroll, Walnut Ridge, Ark.

TOP O' STOVE CASSEROLE

1 med. onion, chopped
1 med. bell pepper, chopped
1 garlic clove, minced
2 tbsp. oil
1 lb. lean ground beef
2 cans tomato sauce
2 cans water
2 tsp. Worcestershire sauce
2 dashes Tabasco
Salt and pepper to taste
½ pkg. elbow macaroni

Saute onion, pepper and garlic in oil until tender. Add ground beef; brown, stirring frequently. Add tomato sauce, water and seasonings; simmer 30 minutes. Cook macaroni according to package directions; drain. Add to sauce; simmer slowly for 20 minutes, stirring occasionally. Yield: 6 servings.

Mrs. Audrey Hunt, Columbia, S. C.

FRIED RICE

½ lb. roasted or fried ham, bacon, lobster or shrimp
2 eggs
3 c. cooked rice
1 tbsp. chopped onion
Dash of pepper
½ tsp. salt
1 tbsp. soy sauce

Cut ham in small pieces and fry. It is not necessary to heat or fry cold roasted meat, canned lobster or shrimp. Fresh shrimp or lobster should be sauteed in butter 3 minutes. Fry eggs slightly on both sides in a hot well-greased skillet. Add rice, onion, pepper, salt and meat. Mix thoroughly while cooking, about 3 minutes. Remove from heat. Add soy sauce and stir.

Mrs. Leona L. Lapice, Elizabeth City, N. C.

MEAT-POTATO HASH

6 med. potatoes, peeled
1 med. onion, peeled
2 c. cubed cooked pork or beef
3 strips bacon, cut into pieces
1 tsp. salt
⅛ tsp. pepper
½ c. water
½ c. gravy

(Continued on next page)

Put potatoes, onion and pork through medium blade of food chopper. Brown in preheated 350-degree electric skillet. Fry bacon until lightly browned. Add meat mixture and seasonings. Cook until well browned on bottom. Turn. Add water and gravy. Reduce heat. Cover; simmer for 1 hour. A bouillon cube dissolved in 1/2 cup water may be substituted for gravy. Yield: 6-8 servings.

Maggie Yates, Martin, Ky.

PORK CHOP CASSEROLE

6 pork chops
1 c. uncooked rice
1 c. water
6 slices tomato
6 slices onion
6 bell pepper rings
Salt and pepper

Brown chops; remove from pan. Add rice to pan and brown slightly. Add water. Place chops on rice. On each chop, place slice of tomato, slice of onion and a bell pepper ring. Salt and pepper chops to taste. Cook until rice is done. More water may be added if rice becomes too dry.

Mrs. B. W. Glade, Lufkin, Tex.

PORK CHOPS SUPREME

6 center-cut pork chops
Salt and pepper
Dry mustard
Shortening
1 med. onion, chopped
6 sliced potatoes
1 sm. can tomato sauce
Water

Season pork chops with salt, pepper and dry mustard. Brown in small amount shortening in deep pan. Add chopped onion; when chops are nicely browned, add potatoes, tomato sauce and an equal amount of water. Cover pan and allow to simmer on top of range for 1 hour. Yield: 6 servings.

Mrs. M. Wokurka, Forest Park, Ga.

PORK SUB GUM

1 lb. lean pork, cubed
¼ c. butter
½ c. chopped green onions
1 green pepper, cut into thin strips
½ lb. sliced mushrooms or 2 c. chopped celery
2 c. chop suey vegetables, chopped carrots or sliced string beans
½ c. sliced almonds or water chestnuts
1 ½ c. chicken stock
2 tbsp. cornstarch
1 tbsp. soy sauce
Salt and pepper
Chow mein noodles or hot rice

Brown pork in butter in large skillet. Cover and cook for 15 minutes. Remove pork from skillet. Place onions, green pepper and mushrooms in skillet; cook for 3 minutes or until tender. Add vegetables, nuts, chicken stock and pork. Combine cornstarch and soy sauce; stir until smooth. Add meat; season to taste. Bring to a boil; reduce heat and simmer for 10 to 15 minutes, stirring occasionally. Serve over chow mein noodles. Yield: 6 servings.

Mrs. James Strosnider, Woodstock, Va.

PORK FRIED RICE

1 to 2 c. cooked cubed pork
1 lge. onion, diced
2 to 4 tbsp. oil, butter or margarine
2 to 3 eggs, well beaten
3 c. cooked rice
Salt and pepper to taste
2 tbsp. soy sauce
2 tbsp. bottled brown sauce (opt.)

Saute pork cubes and onion in oil in large skillet until onion is transparent; push to one side. Pour eggs into skillet; stir over low heat until soft cooked. Mix with pork and onion; add remaining ingredients. Cook until very hot. Yield: 6 servings.

Mrs. Ted Cook, Carlisle, Ark.

RIB CASSEROLE

2 lb. ribs
8 med. potatoes
2 lge. onions
1 c. catsup
2 c. hot water
½ c. brown sugar

Brown ribs in skillet; place in foil-lined small roasting pan. Peel potatoes and onions. Put potatoes around ribs whole; cut onions in chunks and lay on meat. Then mix catsup, water and brown sugar. Pour mixture over meat and vegetables. Cover with foil and a lid. Bake at 325 degrees for 1 hour and 30 minutes or until tender. Season to taste after adding the liquid mix. Carrots that have been precooked partially may be added.

Mrs. Garnet Vance, Black Rock, Ark.

SKILLET CASSEROLE

4 loin chops, ¾ in. thick
3 c. hot water
6 bouillon cubes
1 c. uncooked rice
½ c. diced celery
Dash of Tabasco cauce
½ tsp. salt
¼ tsp. pepper
4 thick slices onion
4 slices green pepper
4 slices tomato

Brown chops on both sides in electric skillet at 350 degrees; remove chops. Pour water into pan; bring to boil. Add bouillon cubes and stir until dissolved. Add rice, celery, Tabasco sauce, salt and pepper; stir. Turn heat to 225 degrees. Place chops on rice; top each with a slice of onion, green pepper and tomato. Cover and cook for 30 minutes, or until meat is tender. Add more water if necessary to prevent rice from sticking. Yield: 4 servings.

Edith Bryant, Andalusia, Ala.

SKILLET PORK CHOPS AND VEGETABLES

3 tbsp. vegetable shortening
6 med., thick pork chops
½ tsp. salt
½ tsp. pepper
½ c. self-rising flour
1 c. water
3 lge. potatoes, sliced
2 lge. onions, sliced
2 lge. carrots, sliced

(Continued on next page)

Heat shortening in heavy 12-inch frying pan. Season chops with salt and pepper; roll in flour, coating well. Fry chops in hot shortening until golden brown. Remove chops; add water to hot pan. Stir to form gravy. Replace pork chops in gravy. Place potatoes, onions and carrots on top of chops. Cover; reduce heat. Simmer for 45 minutes. Yield: 6 servings.

Mrs. T. H. Hern, Bonsal, N. C.

DUTCH OVEN MEAT DISH

1 pt. canned or fresh sausage
¾ c. rice, washed and drained
3 tbsp. minced onion
1 pt. canned tomatoes
1 ½ tsp. prepared mustard
1 tsp. chili powder
½ tsp. salt
1 ½ tsp. Worcestershire sauce
3 c. water (more if needed)

Place sausage and liquid from jar into Dutch oven. Add rice; brown slightly. Add all other ingredients except water. Cover and simmer for 20 minutes, stirring occasionally, and as needed, add the water to keep mixture from becoming dry.

Mrs. Virginia Stickley, Stephens City, Va.

FRIED RICE

Rice
½ lb. sausage
1 med. onion, diced
1 lge. green pepper, diced
3 med. carrots
1 egg
Salt
1 sm. can sliced mushrooms (opt.)
3 tbsp. soy sauce

Prepare rice to make 4 cups cooked rice. Fry sausage which has been cut in small pieces; remove from skillet and add onion and pepper. Saute on medium heat just until tender. Boil carrots until done; dice. Beat egg with 2 tablespoons water and salt. Fry in same skillet and slice into small strips. Add mushrooms. Place all ingredients back into skillet; heat thoroughly. Sprinkle soy sauce and 1 teaspoon salt over all; mix well. If there is not sufficient grease left from sausage, add a little bacon grease.

Mrs. William F. Hale, Fort Campbell, Ky.

MEXICAN LUNCHEON SKILLET DISH

2 lb. bulk pork sausage
1 c. diced onions
1 c. diced green peppers
1 can tomatoes
2 c. uncooked elbow macaroni
2 tbsp. sugar
1 tbsp. chili powder
1 tsp. salt
1 c. sour cream

Brown sausage, onions and green peppers in skillet. Pour off drippings; add tomatoes, macaroni, seasonings and sour cream. Cover. Cook slowly on low heat for 10 minutes. Uncover; simmer for 15 to 20 minutes. Serve immediately. Yield: 6 servings.

Lou Wigley, New Market, Ala.

SAUSAGE 'N' RICE

12 link sausages
Cooking oil
1 ⅓ c. instant rice
1 can onion soup
Water
Salt and pepper
2 doz. pimento-stuffed olives, sliced

Brown sausages in a small amount of cooking oil; mix rice with onion soup and enough water to make 2 cups liquid. Salt and pepper to taste. Pour rice and onion soup mixture over sausages; simmer until rice is done. Top with sliced olives. Other type meats may be substituted for sausages. Yield: 6 servings.

Romie Stewart, Grand Prairie, Tex.

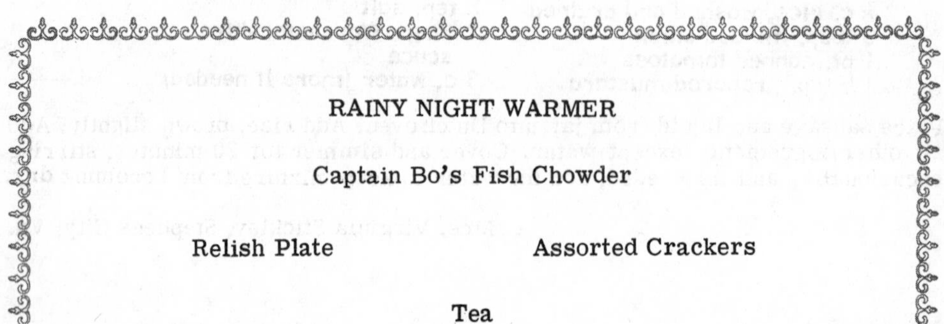

RAINY NIGHT WARMER

Captain Bo's Fish Chowder

Relish Plate Assorted Crackers

Tea

CAPTAIN "BO'S" FISH CHOWDER

2 c. diced potatoes
1 lge. green pepper, chopped fine
1 lge. onion, chopped fine
1 lge. clove garlic, minced
½ c. chopped celery
1 c. salad oil
1 No. 2 can tomatoes
1 sm. can tomato paste
2 c. water
2 bay leaves
2 tbsp. Worcestershire sauce
Salt and pepper to taste
3 lge. carrots, cleaned and sliced
3 lb. fillet of flounder
2 c. shrimp
1 sm. lemon, sliced
3 hard-cooked eggs, sliced
2 tbsp. chopped parsley

Brown potatoes, green pepper, onion, garlic and celery in salad oil. Add tomatoes, tomato paste, water, bay leaves, Worcestershire sauce, salt, pepper and carrots. Simmer for at least 30 minutes. Add fish, shrimp, lemon , eggs and parsley and cook an additional 15 minutes or until fish and shrimp are done. Yield: 8-10 servings.

Mrs. Russell O. Behrens, Apalachicola, Fla.

CREAMY FISH CHOWDER

6 lb. fish
1 stalk celery with tops
3 onions
1 bay leaf
Salt to taste
Fat from 2-in. sq. of salt pork
3 lge. Irish potatoes
2 c. cream
3 c. milk

(Continued on next page)

Clean and scale fish, leaving on heads, tails and fins. Wash thoroughly and place in cold water to cover. Chop celery and onions very fine. Add these, bay leaf and salt to fish. Bring to boil and simmer for 20 minutes. Remove from fire. When cool, bone and skin fish. Strain fish broth. To broth, add fat and potatoes. Boil until potatoes are done. Add fish, cream and milk. Simmer for 5 minutes and serve with crackers. Do not boil.

Ruby Scott, Shreveport, La.

CREAMED TUNA ON TOAST

3 tbsp. margarine or butter
3 tbsp. flour
1 tsp. salt
Dash of pepper
1 ½ c. milk
1 7-oz. can tuna, drained
2 hard-cooked eggs, sliced

Melt butter over medium heat; add flour, salt and pepper and blend well. Add milk; heat, stirring constantly, until thickened. Add tuna and eggs. Cook over low heat for 5 minutes. Serve on toast or hot biscuits. Yield: 6 servings.

Mrs. R. A. Johnson, Jr., Tuscaloosa, Ala.

HENDRY'S SKILLET SHRIMP AND SPAGHETTI

½ c. salad oil
½ c. chopped green onion
2 lb. cooked cleaned shrimp
2 tsp. grated lemon peel
Salt and pepper to taste
1 tbsp. lemon juice
½ c. sliced ripe olives
½ lb. thin spaghetti, cooked

Heat oil in skillet over medium heat; add onion. Cook for 3 minutes; add shrimp, lemon peel, salt and pepper. Cook until heated through. Stir in lemon juice; add olives and spaghetti. Mix well. Keep warm. Yield: 4-6 servings.

Mrs. D. A. Hendry, Baton Rouge, La.

SHRIMP CREOLE

½ c. butter
1 ⅓ c. diced green peppers
1 ⅓ c. chopped onions
2 ½ c. diced celery
½ c. flour
3 1-lb. 13-oz. cans tomatoes
1 ½ tbsp. salt
½ tsp. pepper
2 tbsp. (firmly packed) brown sugar
3 bay leaves
8 whole cloves
4 lb. fresh shrimp
2 tsp. Worcestershire sauce
⅛ tsp. Tabasco sauce
1 tbsp. lemon juice
⅔ c. white wine
7 c. raw instant rice, cooked

Melt butter in 8-quart heavy kettle. Add green peppers, onions and celery; saute for 10 minutes or until vegetables are tender. Remove from heat. Add flour; blend thoroughly. Add tomatoes gradually, stirring constantly. Add salt, pepper, sugar, bay leaves and cloves. Bring to a boil. Reduce heat; simmer, uncovered, over low heat for 45 minutes, stirring occasionally. Add shrimp to thickened tomato sauce; cook for 5 minutes. Stir in Worcestershire sauce, Tabasco sauce, lemon juice and wine. Serve over hot rice. Yield: 18 servings.

Mrs. Dean H. Lucas, Camden, S. C.

SHRIMP MARENGO

3 ½ lb. shrimp
7 slices bacon
1 clove garlic, crushed
1 lb. mushrooms, wiped and sliced or 1 8-oz. can mushroom pieces
1 med. onion, chopped
2 14-oz. cans Italian tomatoes
1 6-oz. can tomato paste
1 10 ½-oz. can consomme
1 tsp. monosodium glutamate
1 ½ tsp. oregano
1 tbsp. sugar
1 ½ tsp. sweet basil
1 tbsp. salt
⅛ tsp. black pepper
3 drops liquid hot pepper seasoning
6 to 7 tsp. prepared mustard
¼ c. flour
½ c. water

Cook shrimp 7 minutes in a large amount of boiling water. Shell and devein shrimp. Cut bacon into small pieces and cook until crisp; remove bacon. Saute shrimp in bacon drippings to which crushed garlic has been added. Add mushrooms and onion and continue to saute for a few minutes longer. Add tomatoes, tomato paste, shrimp, bacon and consomme. Season with monosodium glutamate, oregano, sugar, sweet basil, salt, pepper, hot pepper seasoning and mustard. Cook 10 minutes, stirring often; taste for seasoning and correct if needed. Mix flour with water until smooth; add to shrimp mixture, stirring briskly. Cook about 1 minute. This dish should be prepared in advance. Yield: 10 servings.

Mrs. Susan Sockwell, Decatur, Ga.

SHRIMP PILAU

4 slices bacon
1 c. uncooked rice
3 tbsp. butter
½ c. chopped celery
2 tbsp. chopped green pepper
Salt and pepper
2 c. shrimp, peeled
6 tbsp. Worcestershire sauce
1 tbsp. flour

Fry bacon crisp. Cook rice, adding bacon grease to water. Melt butter; add celery and green pepper, cooking slowly for 10 minutes. Salt and pepper shrimp; add Worcestershire sauce. Sprinkle flour over shrimp, mixing well; add shrimp to butter, celery and pepper. Cook slowly for 30 minutes or until shrimp is well done. Remove from heat; mix rice with shrimp mixture until well mixed. Sprinkle crumbled crisp bacon over top.

Sandra R. Carter, Clemson, S. C.

SWEET-SOUR TUNA CHOW MEIN

2 tbsp. salad oil
1 c. sliced onions
1 ½ c. diced celery
⅛ tsp. pepper
1 can sliced mushrooms
1 ½ c. vegetable or chicken stock
¼ c. molasses
2 tbsp. vinegar
1 1-lb. can bean sprouts
2 tbsp. cornstarch
3 tbsp. soy sauce
2 cans tuna in oil

Heat salad oil in large skillet. Add onions, celery and pepper. Cook for 2 minutes, stirring occasionally. Drain mushrooms; add mushroom liquid to vegetable stock. Stir in molasses and vinegar. Add to skillet with mushrooms and bean sprouts. Cover; simmer for 10 minutes. Blend cornstarch with soy sauce; quickly stir into hot mixture. Add tuna; mix well. Cook, stirring constantly, for 2 to 3 minutes or until mixture is thickened and heated through. Serve over hot cooked rice or canned fried noodles. Yield: 6 servings.

Mary Sue Bonner, Fairfield, Tex.

TUNA SPECIAL

1 7 ½-oz. can tuna, drained and flaked
1 15-oz. can mixed vegetables, drained
1 4-oz. can mushroom stems and pieces, drained
1 tbsp. dehydrated onion flakes
½ tsp. dehydrated parsley flakes
4 lge. eggs, slightly beaten
¼ tsp. seasoning salt
⅛ tsp. monosodium glutamate
Salt and pepper to taste
2 tbsp. butter or margarine

In a large bowl, combine all ingredients except butter. Stir until well blended. Melt butter in a heavy 8 or 9-inch skillet. Pour into fish mixture; cover. Cook over moderately low heat for 30 minutes or until firm. Cut into squares. Yield: 4 servings.

Mrs. V. T. Bowen, The Plains, Va.

AMERICAN CHOP SUEY

¼ lb. ground pork
¼ lb. ground veal
¼ c. chopped green pepper
¼ c. chopped onion
¼ c. chopped celery
Salt and pepper to taste
1 No. 2 ½ can tomatoes
¼ c. rice (uncooked)

Brown meat in skillet in 1 tablespoon fat. Spread evenly over bottom. Sprinkle over meat, pepper, onion and celery which have been mixed together. Add salt and pepper to taste. Pour in tomatoes. Last, sprinkle with rice which has been washed. Cover. Turn to high until steaming then to low for 30 minutes. Yield: 4 servings.

Catherine H. Wilder, Kinston, N. C.

BRUNSWICK STEW

3 squirrels
2 hens
3 lb. stew meat
Salt and red pepper to taste
Mustard to taste
2 No. 2 cans tomatoes
2 No. 2 cans corn
2 lb. frozen butter beans
2 cloves garlic, chopped (opt.)
1 bottle Worcestershire sauce
8 lge. Irish potatoes, chopped
2 sm. cans tomato paste
1 ½ sticks margarine
4 to 6 stalks celery, chopped
2 cans chili
5 med. onions, chopped
Juice of 3 lemons

Cook squirrels, hens and beef in pressure cooker for 45 minutes. Cool and pick out all bones. Return meats to broth; add seasonings. Combine all remaining ingredients; heat to boiling. Add to meats and cook slowly for 2 hours. Yield: 25 servings.

Mrs. A. W. Cook, Pass Christian, Miss.

CABBAGE ROLLS

2 lge. cabbages
1 lb. ground beef
½ lb. ham, ground
2 c. uncooked rice
2 lge. onions, chopped
2 tsp. salt
1 tsp. red pepper
1 lge. can whole tomatoes or tomato sauce
6 slices bacon

(Continued on next page)

Wilt cabbage leaves in hot water. Blend meats, rice, onions, salt and pepper. Place 3 heaping tablespoonfuls of mixture in each cabbage leaf; roll firmly and secure with toothpicks. Brown cabbage rolls on all sides; simmer in tomato sauce with bacon for 1 hour and 30 minutes. Yield: 4-6 servings.

Mrs. Virginia R. Smith, Bunkie, La.

CAMP STEW

- 3 lb. boneless stew meat
- 2 lb. lean pork, cut up
- 6 chicken thighs
- 6 chicken breasts
- 8 lge. potatoes, chopped
- 3 lge. onions, chopped
- Salt and pepper to taste
- 2 cans tomatoes
- 1 lge. bottle catsup
- 1 bottle chili sauce

Boil stew meat, pork and chicken until tender. Grind beef and pork; bone and chop chicken. Cook potatoes and onions in water to cover. Combine all ingredients in meat broth; simmer 30 to 40 minutes, stirring often.

Mrs. George Folmar, Luverne, Ala.

CHICKEN NEPTUNE

- 2 doz. fresh shrimp
- 2 doz. lge. oysters
- 1 sm. can crab meat
- 6 fresh mushrooms, sliced
- ½ green pepper, finely chopped
- 4 tbsp. butter or oil
- 2 tbsp. flour
- 1 pt. cream
- ¼ tsp. paprika
- 1 ½ tsp. salt
- ¼ tsp. pepper
- 2 c. diced cooked chicken
- ½ pimento, finely chopped

Wash shrimp; cook for 20 minutes in boiling water. Shell and devein. Wash oysters; cook slowly in their own liquid until edges curl. Carefully clean crab meat. Combine mushrooms and green pepper; saute for 3 minutes in 2 tablespoonfuls butter. Melt remaining butter in top of bouble boiler. Add flour gradually to melted butter, stirring constantly until smooth. Add cream and seasoning slowly, still stirring mixture. Cook until thoroughly blended. Combine with chicken, oysters, shrimp, crab meat, mushrooms, green pepper and pimento. Heat thoroughly. Serve on small slices of toast, if desired. Yield: 10 servings.

Mrs. J. B. Anderson, Jr., Eupora, Miss.

CHILI

- 2 lge. onions
- 3 tbsp. butter or oleo
- ½ lb. beef kidney suet
- 2 lb. lean beef
- 2 or 3 cloves garlic
- 1 tbsp. salt
- 3 tbsp. chili powder
- 1 tbsp. cumin seed, ground
- Tabasco sauce
- 3 No. 303 cans red kidney beans
- ⅓ (or more) c. flour

Chop onions and cook with butter; add finely chopped suet. Cook slowly until suet is rendered and onion cooked almost to nothing. Add beef cut in 3/4-inch cubes, chopped garlic and salt. Brown meat well; add chili powder, cumin seed and heavy dash tabasco sauce. Cover with 1 1/2 quarts boiling water and let simmer over

(Continued on next page)

low heat about 2 hours and 30 minutes or until meat is tender. Stir to prevent sticking. Drain and wash beans; add to sauce. Stir paste of flour and water into mixture to thicken as desired. Flavor improves after setting a day or more.

L. F. Dickson, Dallas, Tex.

CHOP SUEY

- 1 onion, chopped
- 1 pork chop, cut up
- ½ slice ham, chopped
- 12 pieces shrimp
- Salt and pepper to taste
- Water
- 2 tbsp. soy sauce
- 2 stalks celery
- 1 sm. cabbage
- 1 sm. cauliflower
- 1 tbsp. flour

Saute onion; add pork chop, ham, shrimp, salt and pepper. Saute until brown. Add 1/2 cup water; bring to a boil. Add soy sauce and vegetables; boil for 5 minutes. Mix flour and 1 tablespoon water; stir into chop suey. Yield: 6 servings.

Mrs. Lourdes M. Pascual, Tuskegee, Ala.

CHOW MEIN

- 2 cans bean sprouts
- 2 bunches celery, cut diagonally
- 6 onions, sliced
- 1 lb. ground beef
- 1 lb. ground pork
- Salt and pepper to taste
- ½ bottle (or more) soy sauce
- ½ c. sugar
- Cornstarch
- Chinese noodles
- Rice

Drain bean sprouts; cook celery in bean sprout liquid until tender. Add onions and bean sprouts. Simmer until onions are tender. Cook meats in frying pan in small amount of oil until done. Season with salt and pepper. Add to onion mixture with soy sauce and sugar; cook. Thicken with cornstarch. Serve on noodles with rice. Yield: 12 servings.

Mrs. Willie H. Rountree, Whaleyville, Va.

GOULASH WITH SAUERKRAUT

- ¼ c. flour
- 2 tsp. salt
- ½ tsp. pepper
- 2 lb. veal, cut in 2-in. cubes
- 2 lb. pork, cut in 2-in. cubes
- 3 tbsp. fat or oil
- 3 med. onions, sliced
- 1 tbsp. paprika
- 2 lb. sauerkraut
- 1 tbsp. caraway seeds
- ½ pt. sour cream

Mix together flour, salt and pepper. Toss veal and pork in mixture. Heat fat in heavy saucepan; brown meat and onions. Sprinkle with paprika. Cover and cook 30 minutes over low heat. Wash sauerkraut under running water and drain. Add to meat with caraway seeds; add water if pan is dry. Cover and cook 1 hour and 30 minutes. Stir in sour cream. Do not boil. Yield: 6-8 servings.

Hazel H. Snyder, Houston, Tex.

HOT CABBAGE ROLL

1 lge. head cabbage
1 lb. pork sausage
½ lb. hamburger meat
1 c. uncooked rice
1 tbsp. salt
½ tsp. each black pepper, red pepper, chili powder
1 can tomato paste
1 garlic button

Pull off 12 leaves cabbage, wilt them in boiling water. Mix sausage, hamburger meat, uncooked rice, salt, pepper, garlic and chili powder. Place about 1 tablespoon mixture crossways cabbage leaf and roll. Place crisscross in a boiler. Pour tomato paste, garlic and salt over rolls; cover rolls with water and cook about 2 hours.

Mrs. C. L. Roberson, Sr., Shreveport, La.

MARZETTI

1 lb. ground chuck
½ lb. ground pork
1 can tomato soup
3 to 4 lge. stalks celery, diced
1 c. chopped onion
1 med. can mushrooms
½ tsp. Italian seasoning
½ tsp. summer savory
½ tsp. salt
½ lb. grated longhorn cheese
1 8-oz. pkg. noodles, cooked
½ c. cooking wine

Cook meats with tomato soup, celery and onion until tender. Add mushrooms, seasonings and cheese; blend well. Alternate layers of meat sauce and noodles in casserole; add wine and top with additional grated cheese. Yield: 8-10 servings.

Mrs. Errol R. Lawshe, Vero Beach, Fla.

MOTHER'S BEEF AND KIDNEY DISH

1 sm. beef kidney, cubed
1 lge. round steak, cubed
1 onion, chopped
1 sm. green pepper, chopped
3 sm. cloves garlic, finely chopped
Salt and pepper to taste
2 tbsp. vegetable oil
½ tsp. chili powder
2 8-oz. cans tomato sauce
½ c. water

Combine meats, onion, green pepper, garlic, salt and pepper; brown in oil. Add chili powder; mix well. Stir in tomato sauce and water; simmer until meat is tender. May be served over shell or cut macaroni and sprinkled with Italian cheese. Yield: 4 servings.

Mrs. Adeline Roitsch, Galveston, Tex.

PAELLA

1 chicken, boiled and cut up
1 lb. veal, cut up (opt.)
½ onion, chopped
Chopped green pepper
Dash of garlic powder
1 tomato, chopped
Salt and pepper
1 lb. shrimp, boiled
Clams
Saffron
2 c. long grain rice
4 c. chicken and or shrimp broth

(Continued on next page)

Brown chicken; add veal, onion, green pepper, garlic powder, tomato, salt and pepper. Cook for 2 minutes. Add shrimp, clams, saffron and rice; cook, stirring constantly, for 5 minutes. Add broth; cover and simmer for 10 minutes. Uncover; cook for 10 minutes longer. Let set for 10 minutes before serving. Yield: 6-8 servings.

Mrs. Grover L. Hall, Beaufort MCAS, S. C.

PAELLA

2 c. uncooked rice
½ c. oil
1 broiler chicken, cut into serving pieces
2 cans or 1 ½ lb. fresh shrimp
1 lge. onion, chopped
2 cloves of garlic
1 can tomato sauce
1 can chicken consomme
1 can or 8 artichoke hearts
1 jar pimento strips
¼ c. minced parsley
½ tsp. powdered saffron
1 pkg. frozen peas

Brown rice in 3 tablespoonfuls oil in heavy skillet. Remove rice; brown chicken in remaining oil. Remove chicken; fry shrimp lightly in same oil. Add chicken, onion, garlic, tomato sauce and consomme. Cover; simmer until chicken is tender. Add rice, shrimp and remaining ingredients. Simmer until rice is done. Yield: 8 servings.

Mrs. L. W. Hoener, Brownsville, Tex.

PICADILLO II

2 med. onions, chopped
1 lge. green pepper, chopped
Olive oil
2 sm. cans tomatoes
2 tsp. salt
1 tsp. garlic powder
Pepper
1 lb. ground beef
1 lb. ground pork
2 tbsp. brown sugar
¼ c. vinegar
¼ c. olives, chopped
½ c. raisins
1 tbsp. capers
2 beef bouillon cubes

Brown onions and green pepper in olive oil. Add tomatoes, salt, garlic powder, pepper and meat, stirring to break into small pieces. Add remaining ingredients; cook slowly until meat is tender, about 1 hour. Serve over rice, spaghetti or toasted split hamburger buns. Yield: 10 servings.

Mrs. G. L. Pettit, Kosciusko, Miss.

SAUCE PIQUANT

1 tbsp. flour
2 tbsp. oil
1 lge. onion
1 med. green pepper
1 clove of garlic, minced
1 sm. can tomato sauce
1 can mushroom steak sauce
½ c. water
1 4-lb. hen, cooked and diced
½ lb. smoke sausage
1 tbsp. Worcestershire sauce
2 tsp. salt
¼ tsp. pepper
Parsley
Chopped onion tops
1 bay leaf
¼ c. dry wine

(Continued on next page)

Brown flour in oil in 4 or 5-quart pot; add onion, green pepper and garlic. Cook until tender. Add tomato sauce, steak sauce and water. Cook for 15 minutes. Add chicken, sausage, Worcestershire sauce, salt and pepper. Simmer for 45 minutes. Add a handful parsley, a handful onion tops, bay leaf and dry wine. Simmer for 20 minutes. Serve over rice, if desired. Yield: 6 servings.

Mrs. Bill Moore, Baton Rouge, La.

SOUTHERN CAMP STEW

6 lb. pork
2 lge. hens
2 lb. hamburger
6 lb. potatoes, cubed and cooked
2 lb. onions, cubed and cooked
3 qt. canned tomatoes
4 lge. cans tomato paste
4 cans sm. lima beans
3 cans English peas
4 cans creamed corn
Juice of 8 lemons
1 sm. bottle Worcestershire sauce
Salt and pepper to taste
Hot sauce to taste
6 lge. bottles catsup

Cook pork and hens until tender; cut into small pieces. Cook hamburger until done; drain off juice. Combine all ingredients with enough stock from pork and hens to make juicy. Simmer until thickened. Yield: 70 servings.

Mrs. Hayt Sheppard, Shorter, Ala.

VEAL SKILLET WITH SAUSAGES

4 link pork sausages
1 slice veal cutlet
3 tbsp. flour
2 tsp. salt
¼ plus ⅛ tsp. pepper
1 med. onion, sliced
¾ c. raw rice
½ c. thinly sliced celery
1 No.2 ½ can tomatoes
1 tbsp. Worcestershire sauce
Chopped parsley

Brown sausages in a large skillet; reserve the fat. Cut veal in 4 pieces; wrap each piece around a sausage and secure with a wooden pick. Coat the rolls with flour seasoned with 1 teaspoon salt and 1/4 teaspoon pepper. Brown rolls in sausage fat in skillet; remove rolls. Add onion and rice to fat in skillet and cook for 5 minutes, stirring. Add veal rolls, celery, tomatoes, 1 teaspoon salt, 1/8 teaspoon pepper and Worcestershire sauce. Cover and simmer, stirring occasionally, until veal rolls and rice are tender and liquid has been absorbed, about 40 minutes. Serve sprinkled with chopped parsley. Yield: 4 servings.

Effie Moore, Houston, Tex.

VIRGINIA BRUNSWICK STEW

1 veal shin bone
1 2-lb. chicken
1 piece of bacon, cut in strips
1 lge. onion
3 qt. cold water
1 qt. butter beans
12 med. ripe tomatoes, skinned
4 lge. Irish potatoes, diced
Juice of 1 lemon
6 lge. ears of corn, cut
1 tbsp. Worcestershire sauce
Salt and pepper to taste

(Continued on next page)

Boil veal, chicken, bacon and onion very slowly until meat falls off the bones. Shred meat, discarding bones. Add butter beans, tomatoes, potatoes and lemon juice to meat and stock. Simmer for 1 hour, stirring often. Add corn and cook for 30 minutes. Remove from heat and add seasonings. Yield: 6 servings.

Caroline W. Dozier, Toano, Va.

WILD DUCK AND OYSTER GUMBO

- 1 c. cooking oil
- 1 c. flour
- 1 lge. onion, chopped
- 2 wild ducks, cut up
- Salt to taste
- Cayenne pepper to taste
- 2 qt. warm water
- 2 tbsp. pepper sauce
- 1 qt. oysters
- 2 tbsp. minced parsley (opt.)
- 2 tbsp. minced onion tops (opt.)
- Gumbo file

Make roux of oil and flour in heavy skillet or Dutch oven; brown for 5 minutes. Add onion and cook. Season ducks with salt and pepper; fry in roux and onion until oil separates and runs to sides of pan. Add warm water. Cook, covered, for 2 hours. Add pepper sauce and seasonings to taste. Add oysters 20 minutes before serving. Place ducks in bowl. Sprinkle with parsley, onion tops and gumbo file. Serve over rice. Yield: 6-8 servings.

W. W. McKeithen, Jackson, Miss.

CORNED BEEF AND CABBAGE

- 1 4 to 5-lb. corned beef brisket
- 2 tsp. monosodium glutamate
- 1 sm. onion, sliced
- 1 bay leaf
- 1 stalk celery with leaves
- 2 whole cloves
- 4 peppercorns
- 6 med. potatoes, pared
- 1 cabbage, cut into wedges

Place brisket in deep kettle; cover with cold water. Add monosodium glutamate, onion, bay leaf, celery, cloves and peppercorns. Bring to boil; cover. Reduce heat; simmer for 4 to 5 hours or until fork tender. Skim off excess fat 30 minutes before end of cooking time. Add potatoes; cook for 20 minutes. Add cabbage; cook for 15 minutes. Yield: 6 servings.

Mrs. Fred Forehand, Green Cove Springs, Fla.

CREOLE LIVER

4 slices bacon, diced
1 lb. beef liver, sliced ¼ in. thick
3 tbsp. flour
⅓ c. diced green pepper
1 No. 2 can tomatoes
⅛ tsp. cayenne pepper
1 ½ tsp. salt
⅛ tsp. chili powder

Saute bacon in skillet until nearly crisp; remove bacon and set aside. Roll liver in flour; brown in bacon fat. Add bacon and remaining ingredients. Cover and simmer for 45 minutes. Yield: 4 servings.

Mrs. A. L. Simmons, Marion, N. C.

CURACAS

1 4-oz. pkg. dried beef
1 No. 2 can tomatoes
2 to 4 tbsp. chili powder
1 ½ c. grated Wisconsin cheese
2 to 3 eggs, beaten
2 tbsp. Worcestershire sauce
Salt to taste

Chop beef up fine; add slightly sweetened tomatoes and chili powder. Cook until thickened. Add cheese, eggs, Worcestershire sauce and salt. Cook for 5 minutes. Serve over dried toast or crackers. Yield: 4 servings.

Mrs. Alva Sanders, Cameron, Tex.

FRANKFURTER CASSEROLE

1 lb. frankfurters, sliced
¾ c. diced onions
2 tbsp. butter or margarine
2 ¼ c. uncooked noodles
1 can tomato soup, diluted
1 soup can milk

Brown frankfurters and onions in butter for 5 minutes, stirring frequently. Add noodles, soup and milk. Heat to boiling; cover and simmer for 30 minutes, stirring occasionally. Sprinkle with chopped parsley and grated cheese if desired. Yield: 4 servings.

Mrs. D. F. Mowbray, Charlottesville, Va.

INSTANT CORN CHOWDER

4 slices bacon
½ c. chopped onion
1 ⅔ c. or 1 13 ½-oz. can chicken broth
1 tsp. celery salt
1 pkg. instant mashed potatoes
2 c. cream-style corn
1 ⅔ c. undiluted evaporated milk
2 thinly sliced frankfurters

Cut bacon into small pieces; brown in 2-quart saucepan over medium heat. Add onion. Cook mixture over low heat until onion is tender. Add chicken broth and celery salt; bring mixture to boil. Remove from heat. Stir in remaining ingredients. Heat to serving temperature. Yield: 6 servings.

Mrs. Linnie Collier, Dallas, Tex.

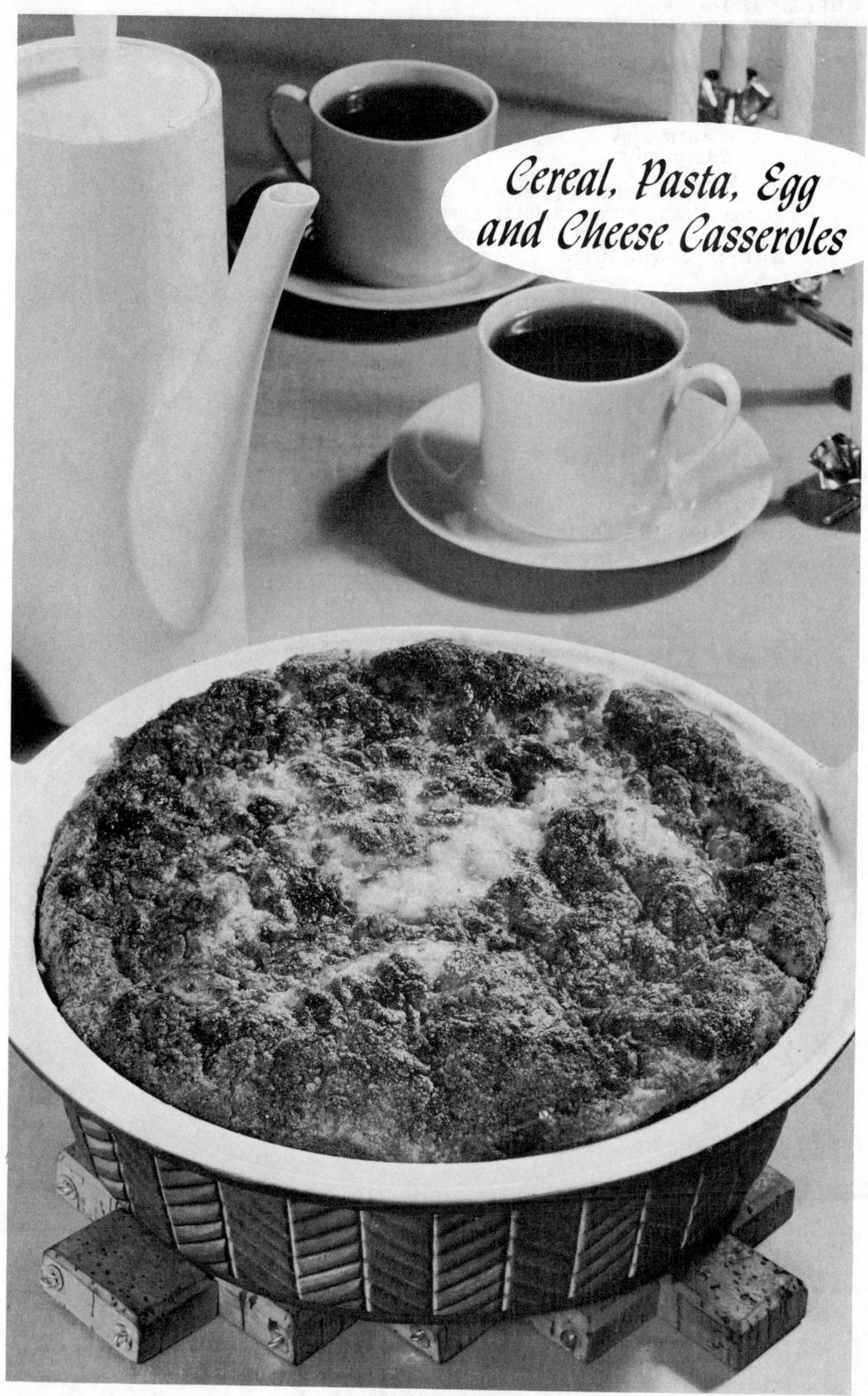
Cereal, Pasta, Egg
and Cheese Casseroles

RECIPE FOR CHEESE CHARLOTTE ON PAGE 261

BAKED GRITS

1 c. uncooked quick grits
½ stick oleo
2 whole eggs
2 tbsp. milk
1 c. grated cheese
½ can undiluted mushroom soup

Cook the grits using the method on the package. Add butter to the grits. Add eggs beaten slightly with milk; fold in grated cheese, reserving enough to sprinkle over top. Add soup. Sprinkle cheese over top. Sprinkle lightly with paprika. Bake in 350-degree oven until firm.

Mrs. Hugh Moreland, Starkville, Miss.

CHEESE GRITS

2 c. dry grits
¼ lb. butter
1 lb. sharp cheese
3 eggs
⅛ tsp. garlic salt
¼ tsp. Worcestershire sauce

Cook grits as directed. Mix remaining ingredients with grits while hot. Bake in 350-degree oven about 20 minutes or until thoroughly hot. Good with chicken or ham.

Mrs. M. L. Thompson, Dallas, Tex.

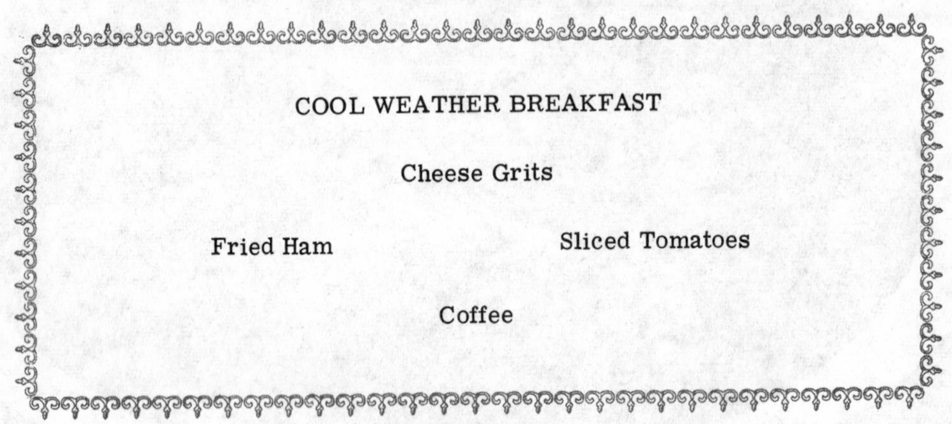

COOL WEATHER BREAKFAST

Cheese Grits

Fried Ham

Sliced Tomatoes

Coffee

CHEESE GRITS

1 c. grits
2 c. water
2 c. milk
1 stick margarine or butter
1 roll garlic cheese
1 roll nippy cheese
2 eggs, well beaten

(Continued on next page)

Put grits in pan; gradually stir in water and milk. Cook until very thick. Add butter; stir until butter is melted. Add cheeses and well-beaten eggs. Stir until all white has disappeared and mixture is smooth. Pour into well-greased 1 1/2-quart casserole. Bake at 350 degrees for 35 minutes or until mixture bubbles. Allow to set a few minutes before serving. Yield: 8 servings.

Mrs. E. J. Hauck, Owensboro, Ky.

FLUFFY, GOLDEN GRITS BREAD

2 c. milk
⅓ c. quick-cooking grits
1 (scant) tsp. salt
1 tsp. sugar
3 beaten egg yolks
3 stiffly beaten egg whites
2 tbsp. (heaping) butter, melted (no substitute)

Scald milk. Stir in the grits, along with salt and sugar. Cook 5 minutes, stirring often. Let cool. Stir in beaten egg yolks. Fold in stiffly beaten egg whites. Preheat oven to 375 degrees. Melt butter in a baking dish and put batter on butter. Bake about 30 minutes. If a deep souffle dish is used, bake about 40 minutes. Serve it hot with more butter.

Mrs. R. R. Ritter, Falls Church, Va.

GARLIC-CHEESE GRITS

1 c. grits
1 roll garlic cheese
1 stick oleo
2 beaten eggs
½ c. milk
Buttered cornflakes or corn chips

Cook grits according to directions on box. While still in pan, melt in cheese and oleo and mix thoroughly. Add eggs and milk. Mix. Bake in buttered casserole at 350 degrees about 45 minutes. Sprinkle crushed buttered cornflakes on top for last 20 minutes of baking time.

Mrs. Sara O'Kelley, North Little Rock, Ark.

GRITS AU GRATIN

1 c. quick grits, cooked
⅓ lb. sharp cheese, grated
½ c. milk
Buttered bread crumbs
Paprika

Alternate layers of cooked grits and grated sharp cheese in greased baking dish. Pour milk over grits and cheese. Sprinkle with buttered bread crumbs and paprika. Bake in 325-degree oven about 20 minutes. Yield: 6 servings.

Mrs. Frank Cress, Salisbury, N. C.

GRITS AU GRATIN

1 c. uncooked grits
½ stick oleo
½ lb. cheddar cheese
1 clove garlic, cut fine
Dash of red pepper
2 tbsp. Worcestershire sauce
2 egg whites

Cook grits according to directions on box. And oleo and grated cheese to grits. Add garlic, red pepper and Worcestershire sauce to grits and cheese mixture. Fold in stiffly beaten egg whites last. Bake in 350-degree oven about 30 minutes.

Bivian M. Richmond, Odessa, Tex.

GRITS AU GRATIN

1 c. quick hominy grits
1 tsp. salt
6 slices breakfast bacon, fried crisp and crumbled
Parmesan cheese or sharp cheese, grated fine

Stir grits into 4 cups boiling salted water. Cook for 3 to 5 minutes, stirring occasionally. Remove from heat; stir in breakfast bacon. Serve immediately with sprinkling of cheese over each serving.

Mrs. Charles B. Quade, Arlington, Va.

GRIT CASSEROLE

1 c. grits
3 ½ c. boiling water
1 c. grated cheese
¾ stick butter
3 eggs
Milk
1 tsp. salt
Cornflake crumbs

Add grits to boiling water and cook 5 minutes. Remove from heat; add cheese and butter. Return to stove and cook 2 minutes, stirring constantly. Remove from heat. Break eggs in cup; fill with milk. Beat slightly. Add to grits mixture; add salt. Pour in greased casserole; top with cornflake crumbs. Bake for 30 minutes at 350 degrees.

Mrs. W. B. Jolly, Taylorsville, Ga.

GRITS CASSEROLE

1 qt. milk
Oleo or butter
6 wedges Gruyere cheese
1 tsp. salt
⅛ tsp. pepper
1 c. grits
⅓ c. Parmesan cheese

Bring milk to a boil; add 1/2 cup oleo and Gruyere cheese. Stir until melted and add salt and pepper. Add grits and boil until thick, stirring constantly. Remove from heat and beat vigorously for 5 minutes. Pour into a 1-quart casserole. Melt 1/3 cup oleo and pour over grits. Sprinkle with Parmesan cheese. Bake for 30 minutes at 400 degrees. Yield: 8 servings.

Mrs. George H. Yenowine, Middletown, Ky.

GRITS CASSEROLE

1 qt. sweet milk
1 tsp. salt
1 stick margarine
1 c. quick grits
1 c. grated sharp cheddar cheese

Heat milk, salt and 1/2 stick margarine. When the margarine melts, add the grits slowly. Cook until slightly thick. Remove from heat and beat with electric beater for 5 minutes. Pour into an 8 x 13-inch pan to set; cut in oblong pieces about 1 x 2-inches. Stack in casserole; sprinkle with grated cheese and remaining melted margarine. Bake for 40 minutes at 350 degrees. Serve piping hot. Yield: 6 servings.

Mrs. W. E. Semands, Houston, Tex.

GRITS AND CHEESE CASSEROLE

1 c. quick-cooking grits
4 c. boiling water
¼ tsp. salt
1 6-oz. pkg. cream cheese
1 stick margarine
2 eggs
Milk
Grated cheese

Cook grits in water until soupy; add salt. Cut cheese in small pieces and stir into grits. Add margarine. While cheese and margarine melt, break eggs in cup; fill cup with milk. Beat together and add to grits. Pour into greased, 2-quart casserole. Bake 45 minutes at 300 degrees. Sprinkle top with grated cheese. Bake 10 minutes longer.

Mrs. William F. Hall, Seymour, Tenn.

GRITS, GRANNY-STYLE

1 c. coarse grits
1 sm. can tomatoes
½ c. chopped onions
5 or 6 slices crisp bacon

Cook grits until almost done. Add tomatoes and onions. Crumble bacon. Add with onions and tomatoes. Bake in casserole at 400 degrees until dry, about 1 hour and 30 minutes.

Mrs. Nell Dorsey, Opp, Alabama

GRIT SOUFFLE

1 c. grits
2 c. boiling water
1 tsp. salt
Dash of Tabasco sauce
⅛ tsp. garlic salt
½ stick butter
4 beaten egg yolks
1 c. milk
½ lb. sharp cheese
4 beaten egg whites

Cook grits until thick in boiling water to which salt, Tabasco and garlic salt has been added. Remove from heat. Cook butter, egg yolks, milk and cheese together until thick. Remove from heat and let this mixture stand for 15 minutes. Then combine with grits; fold in egg whites. Bake in greased casserole for 1 hour and 15 minutes. Yield: 12 servings.

Mrs. Dee S. Lenfesty, Ft. Lauderdale, Fla.

GRITS SOUFFLE

2 c. quick grits
8 c. boiling water
1 tsp. salt
1 roll garlic cheese
2 tbsp. sherry
2 sticks margarine or butter
1 tbsp. Tabasco sauce
2 tbsp. Worcestershire sauce
2 eggs, beaten
Grated cheese

Cook grits in boiling salted water for 2 to 3 minutes or follow directions as given on package. Add garlic cheese and sherry to hot grits. Add remaining ingredients except cheese. Sprinkle grated cheese on top. Place in lightly greased casserole. Bake for 1 hour at 300 degrees.

Mrs. George E. Hinds, Fort Worth, Tex.

GRITS SOUFFLE

6 c. water
1 ½ c. grits
Salt
½ stick butter
1 c. grated cheese
4 eggs, separated
Pepper to taste

Boil water; add grits and 3 teaspoons salt. Return to boil. Cover and cook over low heat 30 to 40 minutes. Remove from heat and stir in butter and cheese, stirring until well blended. Cool to lukewarm; add beaten egg yolks and stir. Fold in beaten egg whites; add salt and pepper to taste. Pour into buttered baking dish and bake for 45 minutes in a 350-degree oven. Yield: 8 servings.

Mrs. W. L. Martin, Shreveport, La.

HOMINY-TOMATO AND CHEESE CASSEROLE

1 8-oz. can tomato sauce
4 c. water
1 tsp. salt
¼ tsp. pepper
2 tsp. Worcestershire sauce
1 c. enriched hominy grits
1 c. grated cheddar cheese

In large saucepan, stir together tomato sauce, water, salt, pepper and Worcestershire sauce. Bring to a boil. Slowly stir in grits; cover and cook slowly, stirring often for 25 minutes or until grits thicken. In a greased, round, ovenproof 1 1/2-quart casserole, spread a layer of cooked grits; sprinkle with some grated cheese. Repeat for 2 more layers. Bake at 325 degrees for about 20 minutes. Yield: 6 servings.

Mrs. W. C. Young, Paducah, Ky.

JOHNSON CITY GARLIC GRITS

1 (rounded) tsp. salt
4 ½ c. boiling water
1 c. grits
1 stick margarine
1 ½ rolls garlic cheese, cut fine
2 eggs
⅔ c. (about) milk
2 c. crushed cornflakes
Dash of Tabasco sauce
Paprika

Add salt to water and bring to boil. Add grits slowly and cook 3 to 5 minutes, stirring occasionally to prevent lumping. Turn off heat and add butter and cheese;

(Continued on next page)

stir until melted. Beat eggs in cup; measure and finish filling cup with milk. Add to grits mixture. Pour into well-greased casserole and sprinkle with crushed cornflakes. Dot with butter and dash of paprika. Bake at 350 degrees for 1 hour.

La Venia Neal, Birmingham, Ala.

OLD-SOUTHERN CASSEROLE

1 c. quick grits
4 c. milk
1 stick butter or margarine
1 roll garlic cheese
2 eggs

Mix grits and milk. Cook over medium heat until thick. Remove from heat. Add butter and cheese and stir to melt. Beat the two eggs in measuring cup, then add enough milk to fill cup. Fold into the grits mixture. Put in greased casserole and bake in 250-degree oven for 30 to 40 minutes. Serve hot or warm. Yield: 10 servings.

Mrs. H. I. Miranda, Lexington, Ky.

SOUTHERN GRITS DELUXE

1 ½ c. yellow grits
6 c. boiling water
1 ½ sticks oleo
1 lb. grated American cheese
2 tsp. savory salt
2 tsp. salt
6 drops Tabasco sauce
4 eggs, well beaten

Slowly cook the grits 20 minutes in the boiling water. Add all the ingredients; pour into a buttered casserole. Bake for 1 hour at 250 degrees. This is delicious to serve for a large group.

Mrs. W. E. Frashuer, Robstown, Tex.

WEST TEXAS-STYLE GRITS

2 c. hot cooked grits
2 c. sharp cheese
1 stick butter or oleo
2 buds minced garlic
2 eggs, well beaten
1 sm. can finely minced green chilies

Mix all ingredients together till cheese and butter are well melted. Bake for 1 hour at 300 degrees. This hot, spicy dish is a favorite with men. Yield: 8-10 servings.

Mrs. Donald N. Jones, Tulia, Tex.

PEANUT CHEESE LOAF

⅔ c. cooked oatmeal, wheat cereal or rice
¼ c. chopped green pepper
3 tbsp. minced onion
1 tsp. salt
2 tsp. lemon juice
1 c. chopped salted peanuts
⅔ c. fine crumbs
¼ lb. cheese, grated
1 egg
⅓ c. milk

Combine all ingredients. Put mixture into a greased loaf pan. Bake at 350 degrees about 1 hour. Serve hot with mushroom or tomato sauce. Yield: 4 servings.

Mrs. Minnie Pennington, Northport, Ala.

BAKED EGGS IN RICE

2 c. milk
4 tbsp. butter
4 tbsp. flour
2 tsp. salt
1 c. grated cheese
2 c. cooked rice
8 eggs
2 tsp. salt
Pepper to taste
Paprika to taste

Make a sauce of first 5 ingredients; cook in double boiler until smooth and thick. Add half the cheese sauce to rice. Mix lightly with fork. Line well-oiled individual dishes with rice mixture. Break 1 egg in each dish; season. Place dishes in pan of warm water. Bake in a 375-degree oven until whites of eggs are firm. Serve with remaining cheese sauce. Yield: 8 servings.

Mrs. C. A. Davidson, Amarillo, Tex.

BAKED RICE AND CHEESE

1 c. uncooked rice
1 qt. boiling water
1 c. tomatoes
1 med. onion, diced
2 tsp. salt
5 tbsp. sugar
¾ lb. cheese, grated

Boil rice in water with tomatoes, onion, salt and sugar. When rice is soft, place a layer of mixture in a greased baking dish. Add a layer of cheese. Add remaining rice mixture and top with cheese. Bake at 350 degrees for 35 to 40 minutes. Yield: 6 servings.

Mrs. Lawrence Hunter, Millington, Tenn.

BAKED RICE AND CHEESE

3 c. cooked rice
2 c. shredded cheese
2 tbsp. finely chopped green pepper
2 eggs, beaten
1 ¼ c. milk
1 tsp. salt
Cayenne pepper to taste
½ c. coarse bread crumbs
1 tbsp. melted butter

Arrange alternate layers of cooked rice, cheese and green pepper in buttered baking dish. Combine beaten eggs, milk, salt and pepper. Pour over rice and cheese mixture. Toss bread crumbs in melted butter. Sprinkle over top of casserole. Bake at 350 degrees for 45 minutes or until set. Yield: 6 servings.

Joanne West, Richmond, Va.

BAKED RICE WITH CHEESE

2 c. cooked rice
4 tbsp. butter
4 tbsp. flour
1 ½ tsp. salt
¼ tsp. pepper
½ tsp. dry mustard
½ tsp. paprika
2 ½ c. milk
1 c. grated cheese
1 tsp. Worcestershire sauce

Cook rice as directed on package; rinse and drain. Melt butter; stir in flour, salt, pepper, mustard and paprika. When well blended, add milk, stirring continually over low heat till mixture thickens and boils. Add cheese and Worcestershire sauce; stir till cheese is melted. Add drained rice and pour mixture into greased 2-quart baking dish. Bake at 400 degrees about 20 minutes or till brown. Yield: 6 servings.

Evelyn B. Landreth, Greenville, S. C.

CHEESE-RICE CASSEROLE

½ c. canned mushrooms, stems and pieces
1 tbsp. chopped onion
¼ c. coarsely chopped almonds
1 tbsp. butter or margarine
½ c. uncooked rice
2 tbsp. chopped parsley
½ c. shredded cheese
1 ½ tsp. salt
1 ½ c. hot water and mushroom liquid

Drain mushrooms; reserving liquid. Lightly brown mushrooms, onion and almonds in fat. Add uncooked rice, parsley and cheese; mix thoroughly. Place mixture in a greased casserole. Add salt to water and mushroom liquid and pour over rice mixture. Bake at 375 degrees for 45 minutes to 1 hour, until rice is done. Yield: 4-6 servings.

Mrs. A. Flowers, Lexington, Miss.

EPICUREAN WILD RICE

⅓ c. butter or margarine
½ c. snipped parsley
½ c. chopped green onions
1 c. diagonally sliced celery
1 ¼ c. wild rice
1 10 ½-oz. can condensed consomme, undiluted
1 ½ c. boiling water
1 tsp. salt
½ tsp. dried marjoram
½ c. sherry

In Dutch oven or heavy skillet with tight-fitting cover, melt butter; add parsley, onions and celery. Saute until soft but not browned. Add rice, consomme, water, salt and marjoram. Cook, covered, over low heat, for about 45 minutes, stirring occasionally with a fork. Add a little hot water if mixture becomes dry and starts to stick. When rice is tender and all liquid has been absorbed, stir in sherry. Cook, uncovered, about 5 minutes or until sherry is absorbed, stirring occasionally. Yield: 6 servings.

Mrs. Dan P. Johnston, Dallas, Tex.

EXOTIC RICE CASSEROLE

2 c. rice
2 cans beef consomme
2 lge. onions, chopped
1 c. chopped celery
1 stick butter
1 5-oz. can water chestnuts, chopped
1 4 ½-oz. can mushrooms, chopped

Cook rice by directions on package, substituting consomme for water. Set aside. Saute onions and celery in butter until soft and slightly brown. Add chestnuts and mushrooms with juices and simmer for 10 to 15 minutes. Into a 10 x 14-inch casserole, put a layer of rice, a layer of mixture and repeat until both are used. Cover casserole with foil and bake in a 300-degree oven for 30 minutes. Yield: 10-12 servings.

Mrs. Mayme McLean, Liberty, Tex.

GREEN RICE

2 c. raw rice
2 c. top milk
⅔ c. cooking oil
2 c. grated cheese
2 green peppers, chopped
2 sm. onions, chopped
1 c. chopped parsley
2 beaten eggs

Cook rice as usual and add to other ingredients. Place ingredients in baking dish set in a pan of water. Bake at 325 degrees for 45 minutes. Yield: 12 servings.

Mrs. Flora B. Mims, Memphis, Tenn.

HAWAIIAN RICE

1 c. uncooked rice
1 can bouillon or consomme
1 stick oleo, melted
1 c. water
1 sm. can chopped green chilies

Mix together in casserole and bake at 350 degrees for 1 hour.

Mrs. Paul Wecker, Midland, Tex.

RICE CASSEROLE

1 stick margarine
1 can onion soup
1 can beef consomme soup
1 c. uncooked rice
1 sm. can mushrooms (opt.)

Grease casserole and cut up margarine. Combine other ingredients and bake at 350 degrees for 1 hour in covered casserole. Yield: 8 servings.

Inez Hendrix, Greensboro, N. C.

Stevedores unload cargo at Charleston, South Carolina.

RICE CASSEROLE

- 1 lge. onion
- 1 lge. sweet pepper
- ½ stick oleo
- 1 c. raw rice
- 2 cans beef consomme
- 1 chicken bouillon cube
- 1 can cream of mushroom soup
- 1 tsp. parsley flakes
- ½ tsp. Italian seasoning
- ¼ tsp. salt
- ¼ tsp. pepper

Chop onion and sweet pepper; add to oleo. Fry until almost tender. Mix all ingredients together and put into a 2-quart casserole. Bake for 1 hour at 350 degrees.

Mrs. Alys Hebard, Van Buren, Ark.

RICE AND CHEESE CASSEROLE

- ⅔ c. crisp crumbled bacon
- 3 tbsp. bacon drippings
- 1 c. minced onion
- 1 c. diced celery
- 3 c. cooked rice
- 1 c. sliced stuffed olives
- ½ tsp. salt
- 1 tsp. thyme
- ½ tsp. pepper
- 1 10 ½-oz. can cream of chicken soup or 1 can chicken broth
- 2 c. cheddar cheese

Fry bacon in large skillet until crisp. Remove from pan; drain well on absorbent paper. Crumble into small pieces. Drain all but 3 tablespoonfuls drippings from pan. Add onion and celery; cook until tender. Remove from heat and stir in rice, sliced olives and seasonings. In a saucepan, heat chicken soup and one cup cheese until cheese has melted. Add sauce and bacon to rice mixture. Turn into a greased casserole; top with remaining cheese. Bake at 375 degrees for about 15 minutes or until browned. Yield: 6-8 servings.

Mrs. Jane S. Howard, Stuttgart, Ark.

RICE CASSEROLE

1 c. uncooked rice
⅔ c. melted butter
1 can cream of chicken soup
1 ½ soup cans water

Mix all ingredients together. Pour in a buttered casserole and bake at 375 degrees for 1 hour..If mixture becomes dry, add more water.

Mrs. J. Clayton Hargrove, Eatonton, Ga.

RICE CASSEROLE

2 c. cooked rice
1 can mushroom soup, undiluted
1 sm. jar pimento, chopped
1 ½ c. evaporated milk, undiluted
½ 5-oz. can toasted almonds, chopped
¼ lb. sharp cheese, grated

Combine all ingredients. Bake in a greased casserole for 30 minutes at 350 degrees. Yield: 8 servings.

Mrs. William Ruffner, Homewood, Ala.

RICE CASSEROLE

1 c. rice
3 tbsp. corn oil
1 c. consomme, undiluted
1 can mushroom soup, undiluted

Brown uncooked rice in oil; add remaining ingredients. Bake in casserole at 325 degrees for 35 to 40 minutes or until done.

Mrs. Robert D. Dixon, New Bern, N. C.

RICE AND CHEESE DISH

½ c. crunchy peanut butter
3 c. cooked rice, salted
1 ½ c. milk
¼ lb. sharp cheese, grated
1 sm. onion, minced or 2 tsp. dry instant onion
Dash of Tabasco sauce
Paprika (opt.)

Mix all ingredients and place in large baking dish or casserole and bake in 350-degree oven for 30 minutes.

Mrs. Bertie R. Coley, Lithonia, Ga.

RICE-CHILIES AND SOUR CREAM CASSEROLE

1 c. rice
1 tbsp. butter or oleo
Salt to taste
1 c. sour cream
⅓ lb. grated cheese
1 6-oz. can chilies, chopped

(Continued on next page)

Cook rice according to package directions. Add butter and salt. Fold in sour cream. Alternate layers of rice mixture, cheese and chilies in a casserole, ending with cheese. Bake at 350 degrees for 20 minutes or until heated through. Yield: 6-8 servings.

Henrietta Cooper, Austin, Tex.

RICE PILAF

1 can beef consomme
1 consomme can water
1 stick margarine
2 c. long grain uncooked rice
⅔ c. chopped carrots
⅔ c. chopped celery
⅔ c. chopped green onion tips
⅔ c. chopped blanched almonds
1 tsp. monosodium glutamate
1 tsp. parsley leaves

While preheating oven to 325 degrees, place a 2-quart ovenproof dish in oven. Add consomme and 1 can water in saucepan. Bring to boil. Melt margarine in another pan; add rice. Stir constantly for 2 to 3 minutes or until rice is hot. Pour consomme and rice into hot ovenproof dish and cover. Cook for 45 minutes. Remove cooked rice from dish into another dish. Let stand until cool. Mix other ingredients; add to rice. Replace in oven, covered, for 10 minutes at 325 degrees.

Mrs. T. L. Graham, Eclectic, Ala.

SAVORY RICE

2 med. onions, finely chopped
1 clove garlic, chopped
3 tbsp. butter
1 c. uncooked converted rice
3 c. chicken broth
1 tsp. dried marjoram
½ tsp. dried thyme
1 tsp. dried chervil
2 tsp. minced parsley

Cook onions and garlic in butter until tender, but not brown. Add rice and brown slightly, stirring constantly. Add broth and herbs; bring to boil. Reduce heat; cover and cook until rice is tender and the liquid has been absorbed, about 20 minutes. Salt to taste. Yield: 4-6 servings.

Mrs. Vaughn Snow, Loudon, Tenn.

SPANISH RICE PRONTO

¼ c. bacon drippings or butter
1 med. onion, thinly sliced
½ med. green pepper, diced
1 ⅓ c. instant rice
2 8-oz. cans tomato sauce
1 ½ c. hot water
1 tsp. salt
Dash of pepper
½ tsp. prepared mustard

Melt fat in skillet. Add onion, green pepper and rice. Cook and stir over high heat until browned. Add remaining ingredients. Mix well. Bring quickly to a boil; reduce heat. Simmer, uncovered, 5 minutes. Yield: 4 servings.

Brenda Warren, Andalusia, Ala.

SCRAMBLED RICE BREAKFAST

3 c. leftover cooked rice
4 eggs
Salt
Pepper
Butter

Beat rice and eggs in bowl; add salt and pepper to taste. Melt butter in frying pan; add rice and egg mixture. Cook as for scrambled eggs or until dry, stirring constantly.

Mrs. M. L. Baggette, Daphne, Ala.

SPANISH RICE

¼ c. salad oil
1 clove garlic, peeled
1 med. onion, minced
¼ c. chopped green pepper
3 c. boiled rice
1 tsp. salt
2 ½ c. canned tomatoes

Heat salad oil in large frying pan. Add garlic, onion, green pepper and rice. Cook 3 minutes, stirring continuously. Add salt and tomatoes. Mix well; cover and cook over low heat till tomato juice is absorbed, about 15 minutes. Yield: 6 servings.

Evelyn B. Landreth, Greenville, S. C.

WILD RICE CASSEROLE

1 c. wild rice
2 ribs celery, chopped
1 sm. onion, chopped
½ green bell pepper, chopped
2 tbsp. butter
1 4-oz. can mushrooms, drained
½ lb. processed American cheese, diced
Salt and pepper to taste
½ c. table cream

Cook rice according to package directions until tender, fluffy and dry. While rice cooks, saute celery, onion and bell pepper in butter in skillet until limp. Combine sauteed vegetables with wild rice. Add, blending lightly, mushrooms, cheese, salt and pepper to taste. Turn mixture into greased casserole and pour cream over all. Bake at 350 degrees for 30 minutes or until sauce cooks down a bit. Yield: 6 servings.

Mrs. I. E. Jackson, Winder, Ga.

AUNT BRUNER'S SPAGHETTI CASSEROLE

1 8-oz. pkg. spaghetti
1 onion, chopped
2 tbsp. chopped green pepper
1 tbsp. oleo
1 No. 2 can of tomatoes
1 can mushroom soup
¼ c. chopped green olives
1 tsp. salt
1 tsp. sugar
1 c. grated cheese

Cook spaghetti until tender; drain well. Brown onion and green pepper in oleo. Mix spaghetti, browned onion and green pepper and remaining ingredients together.

(Continued on next page)

Place in a greased casserole dish. Bake at 325 degrees for 45 minutes. Yield: 6-8 servings.

Adelia A. Davis, Jackson, Miss.

CREAMY MACARONI-CHEESE BAKE

2 c. macaroni
⅓ c. mayonnaise
¼ c. chopped pimento
¼ chopped green pepper
¼ c. chopped onions
1 can of mushroom soup
½ c. milk
1 c. sharp cheese

Cook macaroni. Combine with next 4 ingredients. Blend soup, milk and 1/2 of the cheese; stir into macaroni. Put in casserole. Put remaining cheese on top. Bake at 400 degrees for 25 to 30 minutes.

Betty Keown, Starr, S. C.

GREEN NOODLES CASSEROLE

3 c. green noodles
¾ tsp. Tabasco sauce
¼ c. butter
¼ c. flour
1 tsp. salt
2 ½ c. milk
1 c. diced sharp cheddar cheese
¼ c. grated Parmesan cheese
1 4-oz. can pimento, diced
3 hard-cooked eggs, sliced

Cook noodles according to package directions adding 1/4 teaspoon of the Tabasco to cooking water. Drain and rinse. Melt butter. Stir in flour, salt, and remaining Tabasco. Add milk and stir over medium heat until mixture is smooth and slightly thickened. Add cheddar and Parmesan cheeses and stir until melted. Add diced pimento and cooked noodles and mix. Pour into 1 1/2-quart casserole. Bake at 350 degrees about 30 minutes. Top with egg slices last 5 minutes of cooking time. Yield: 6-8 servings.

Anna Kate Eatman, Tuscaloosa, Ala.

MACARONI CASSEROLE

1 c. macaroni
½ tbsp. butter
½ tbsp. flour
⅛ tsp. salt
⅛ tsp. paprika (opt.)
⅛ tsp. pepper
¾ c. milk
½ c. grated cheese, sharp or medium sharp
Bread crumbs

Cook macaroni for 10 minutes in salted water. Melt butter; blend in flour and seasonings. Add milk and cook, stirring constantly until thickened. Add part of cheese and stir until cheese melts. Combine sauce with macaroni. Top with bread crumbs and remaining cheese. Bake at 375 degrees for 25 minutes. Yield: 2 servings.

Mrs. Kenneth O. Long, Tavares, Fla.

MACARONI AND CHEESE

2 6-oz. pkg. macaroni
¼ c. green pepper, chopped
¼ c. onions, chopped
¼ c. pimento, chopped
¾ c. mayonnaise
¾ lb. cheese, grated
1 can mushroom soup
1 can mushrooms and liquid

Cook macaroni according to package directions; drain. Mix with other ingredients. Bake for 40 minutes at 375 degrees. Yield: 12 servings.

Mrs. Reuben O'Neal, Lanett, Ala.

MACARONI AND CHEESE

1 box elbow macaroni
1 can mushroom soup
1 c. mayonnaise
¼ c. pimentos, chopped
¼ c. onion, chopped
3 tbsp. butter
1 lb. sharp cheese, grated
1 can mushrooms
Cheese crackers, crushed

Cook macaroni according to package directions. Mix all ingredients except cracker crumbs. Pour into a buttered casserole. Cover with crumbs. Bake 25 minutes at 300 degrees. Yield: 8-10 servings.

Mrs. George F. Steward, Atlanta, Ga.

MACARONI AND CHEESE

1 ½ c. milk
2 eggs
2 c. cooked macaroni, drained
1 c. cheddar cheese, grated
Salt and pepper

Mix milk and eggs. Add to macaroni while stirring. Add cheese, reserving 1/4 cup for topping. Season to taste. Turn into a buttered baking dish. Sprinkle with reserved cheese. Bake in 350-degree oven about 45 minutes or until set and slightly brown. Yield: 6 servings.

Mrs. H. D. Alexander, Jackson, Miss.

MACARONI SAUTE

1 8-oz. pkg. elbow macaroni
½ c. onion, chopped
½ c. green pepper, chopped
1 clove garlic, minced
1 lb. ground beef (opt.)
½ c. cooking oil
1 8-oz. can tomato paste
2 ½ c. water
1 to 1 ½ tsp. salt
¼ tsp. pepper
2 tsp. Worcestershire sauce

Saute macaroni, onion, green pepper, garlic and beef if desired, in hot oil until macaroni turns slightly yellow. Add remaining ingredients and bring to a boil. Cover and simmer over low heat about 20 minutes, stirring occasionally. If beef is added, use larger amount of salt. Yield: 6 servings.

Mrs. Hollis Morgan, Smithville, Miss.

NOODLE CASSEROLE

1 4-oz. pkg. med. noodles
½ stick butter or margarine
1 c. chopped celery
½ c. chopped onion
2 c. creamed cottage cheese
½ c. sour cream
1 tsp. salt
1 tsp. Worcestershire sauce
¼ tsp. Tabasco sauce
¼ c. grated Parmesan cheese

Cook noodles according to package directions; drain. In small skillet melt the butter; add celery and onion. Saute 8 minutes. Combine noodles, sauteed vegetables, cottage cheese, sour cream and seasonings. Turn into buttered casserole; sprinkle Parmesan cheese over top. Bake at 350 degrees for 20 minutes. Yield: 8 servings.

Mrs. W. M. Crowe, Plant City, Fla.

SO EASY MACARONI AND CHEESE

1 8-oz. pkg. elbow macaroni
2 cans cream of chicken soup
⅓ c. chopped onions
2 tbsp. chopped pimento
4 hard-cooked eggs, diced
½ lb. Edam or cheddar cheese, diced
½ lb. fresh mushrooms
2 tbsp. butter

Cook macaroni according to package instructions but reduce salt to 1 teaspoon. Rinse and drain. Combine undiluted soup, onions, pimento, eggs and cheese with macaroni in 2-quart casserole. Saute mushrooms in butter to garnish top of casserole. Bake 25 to 30 minutes in preheated 350-degree oven.

Mrs. William B. Marks, Harrisonburg, Va.

SPAGHETTI CASSEROLE

Bunch of celery, finely chopped
1 16-oz. can mushrooms, finely chopped
4 tbsp. butter
2 1-lb. cans spaghetti
¼ lb. Velveeta cheese, finely cut

Cook celery and mushrooms in butter over medium heat until tender. Place spaghetti in a colander; rinse off most of the tomato sauce. Place spaghetti in casserole. Mix mushrooms, butter and celery through the spaghetti. Sprinkle cheese over top. Bake at 375 degrees for about 20 minutes or until thoroughly heated.

Mrs. Violet Ross, Ashland, Miss.

SPAGHETTI CASSEROLE

- 1 lge. box spaghetti
- ½ green pepper, diced
- 1 med. onion, diced
- 1 tbsp. margarine
- 2 cans condensed tomato soup
- 1 can mushrooms
- Salt
- Pepper
- Oregano
- Grated cheese

Cook spaghetti according to box directions in salted water. Fry green pepper and onion in margarine until slightly brown. Drain spaghetti; mix with soup, browned green pepper, onion and mushrooms. If dry add a little water. Season with salt and pepper; sprinkle with oregano and grated cheese. Bake at 350 degrees until bubbly. Yield: 8 servings.

Mrs. C. E. McSwain, Huntersville, N. C.

TEXAS-STYLE MACARONI AND CHEESE

- 2 c. uncooked elbow macaroni
- 1 tsp. onion, finely chopped
- ½ green pepper, finely chopped
- ¼ c. butter or margarine
- 1 ½ c. scalded milk
- 1 c. soft bread crumbs, packed
- 1 tbsp. minced parsley or ¼ tsp. dehydrated parsley flakes
- 1 pimento, diced
- 1 tsp. salt
- 1 c. grated sharp cheddar cheese
- 1 c. canned tomatoes
- 3 eggs, well beaten

Cook macaroni in boiling salted water for 12 to 15 minutes; drain. While macaroni is cooking, saute onion and green pepper in the butter on low heat, until partially tender. Pour milk over crumbs. Reserve 1/4 cup cheese for topping. Add remaining ingredients, ending with eggs last. Pour over macaroni and sprinkle cheese on top. Set buttered 2-quart baking dish, covered, in a pan of hot water. Remove cover the last 10 minutes of cooking. Bake at 350 degrees for 40 to 45 minutes. Yield: 8 servings.

Mrs. Robert J. Soto, Fort Worth, Tex.

YUMMY CHEESE CASSEROLE

- ½ lb. bacon
- 1 onion, chopped
- 3 tbsp. flour
- 1 1-lb. can tomatoes
- Salt, pepper, oregano and sweet basil
- ½ lb. mozzarella cheese
- 1 pkg. cooked twist noodles

Fry bacon; drain and crumble. In 3 tablespoons bacon grease, saute onion. Stir in flour until smooth. Add tomatoes; season. Stir in cheese until it melts and fold in noodles. Add bacon. Bake 20 minutes at 350 degrees. Yield: 4 servings.

Mrs. Wade W. Herring, Macon, Ga.

BREAKFAST CASSEROLE

- 6 slices bread, broken in pieces
- ½ lb. mellowed cheese, cut in small cubes
- 1 tsp. dry mustard
- 1 tsp. salt
- 3 tbsp. butter or margarine
- 4 eggs
- 2 ½ c. sweet milk

(Continued on next page)

Grease bottom and sides of casserole dish. Line bottom of dish with half of the bread. Cover with half of the cheese; sprinkle with half of the mustard and salt. Repeat layers; dot with the butter. Beat eggs and milk together; pour over casserole. Refrigerate overnight. Bake at 350 degrees for 30 minutes. Yield: 6-8 servings.

Mrs. Betty Hixon, Andalusia, Ala.

CHEESE CHARLOTTE

- 3 tbsp. butter
- 3 eggs, separated
- 1 ½ tbsp. flour
- 2 c. diced white bread
- 1 c. milk
- ½ lb. Swiss cheese, shredded
- ¼ tsp. salt
- ½ tsp. nutmeg
- ½ c. heavy cream
- 1 ½ tsp. Augostura bitters
- 6 whole slices bread, trimmed

Let butter soften at room temperature and beat together with egg yolks and flour. Soak diced bread in milk until moistened. Add to egg mixture. Add cheese, salt and nutmeg. Stir in cream and Augostura bitters and mix all together thoroughly. Butter a deep 1-quart baking dish. Dip whole bread slices in milk and line bottom and sides of baking dish with them. Beat egg whites until stiff and fold gently into cheese mixture; pour into baking dish and bake in 350-degree oven for 30 minutes. Serve immediately very hot. Yield: 6 servings.

Photograph for this recipe on page 243.

CHEESE FLUFF

- 4 eggs, separated
- 1 c. sweet milk
- 1 c. cracker crumbs
- 1 c. grated cheese
- Salt and pepper to taste

Beat egg yolks in baking dish; add milk and cracker crumbs. Beat egg whites until stiff. Fold egg whites and grated cheese into first mixture. Season to taste. Place baking dish in a shallow pan of water and place in a 375 to 400-degree oven. Bake until puffy and brown. When done, a knife inserted will come out clean.

Mrs. Bill Morrison, Alexander City, Ala.

CHEESE STRATA

- 4 slices bread
- 3 eggs, beaten slightly
- 1 ¼ c. milk
- ½ rounded tsp. brown sugar
- ⅛ tsp. paprika
- 1 sm. finely minced onion
- ¼ tsp. dry mustard
- ¼ tsp. monosodium glutamate
- ¼ tsp. salt
- ¼ tsp. black pepper
- ¼ tsp. Worcestershire sauce
- ¼ tsp. red pepper
- ¾ lb. grated cheddar cheese

Butter bread. Cut off crusts and cut each slice into small squares. Butter large casserole. Combine eggs and milk and next 9 ingredients. Arrange layer of buttered bread squares in casserole. Next arrange layer of grated cheese. Repeat until all bread and cheese are used. Pour egg and milk mixture over all. Cover with waxed paper and place in refrigerator. Take out 30 minutes before cooking. Set in pan of cold water. Put in cold oven. Bake at 300 degrees for 1 hour.

Mrs. James T. Sowell, Montgomery, Ala.

CHEESE FONDUE

4 eggs, beaten
2 c. hot milk
2 c. soft bread crumbs
½ lb. cheese, shredded
¼ tsp. salt

Combine all ingredients. Pour into greased baking dish. Bake at 350 degrees for 40 minutes. Serve at once. Yield: 6 servings.

Mrs. Jack Philbeck, Bostic, N. C.

CREOLE EGGS GRINALDS

1 med. onion, chopped fine
2 tbsp. bacon fat
1 lge. can tomatoes
Salt and pepper to taste
1 stick butter
3 tbsp. flour
Milk
8 hard-boiled eggs, sliced
1 c. toasted bread crumbs

Brown onion in hot bacon fat. Add tomatoes and simmer until onion is done. Add salt and pepper to taste. Make a white sauce of 1/2 stick butter, flour and enough milk to be very thick. Add tomato mixture to sauce; stir well. Layer tomato mixture in buttered casserole with sliced eggs and bread crumbs. Fill dish full. Dot the top with remaining butter. Bake in 400-degree oven for 25 minutes.

Mrs. G. C. Booker, Theodore, Ala.

CORNMEAL SOUFFLE

¾ c. cornmeal
2 c. milk
1 tsp. salt
1 tbsp. melted fat
4 eggs, separated

Cook cornmeal in milk until thick. Add salt and melted fat. Add beaten egg yolks; fold in stiffly beaten egg whites. Bake in greased casserole at 350 degrees for 1 hour.

Mrs. Lloyd H. Smith, Easley, S. C.

COTTAGE-CHEESE AND PEANUT LOAF

1 c. cottage cheese
1 c. cold, cooked rolled oats
1 c. milk
1 egg, slightly beaten
1 tbsp. fat
½ tsp. salt
Dash of pepper
1 tsp. poultry seasoning
Few drops Worcestershire sauce
1 tbsp. chopped onions
½ c. peanuts, chopped

Combine ingredients in order given adding peanuts last. When thoroughly combined, place in a well-oiled bread tin. Bake in 350-degree oven until brown.

TOMATO SAUCE:

1 lge. can tomatoes
1 sliced onion
8 cloves
3 tbsp. butter
3 tbsp. flour
Salt and pepper to taste

Cook tomatoes, onion and cloves for 20 minutes. Brown butter in a frying pan; add the flour and cook until smooth and brown, stirring constantly. Season to taste. Add the tomatoes. Serve hot tomato sauce over Cottage Cheese and Peanut Loaf.

Mrs. Grace Hutzler, Houston, Tex.

RECIPE FOR EGGPLANT CASSEROLE ON PAGE 282

ALMOND-ASPARAGUS CASSEROLE

1 can asparagus
2 hard-boiled eggs
1 c. sliced almonds
1 can mushroom soup
1 c. crushed potato chips
½ c. grated cheese

Place alternate layers of asparagus, eggs and almonds in baking dish. Pour soup over layers. Top with crushed potato chips and grated cheese. Bake at 350 degrees for 30 minutes. Yield: 4-6 servings.

Mrs. R. D. Bond, Pulaski, Va.

ASPARAGUS CASSEROLE

1 ½ c. bread crumbs
2 tbsp. butter, melted
1 10 ½-oz. can green asparagus, drained
Thick white sauce
1 ½ c. cheese, grated

Save 1/2 cup bread crumbs for top and mix with butter. Put drained asparagus in bottom of casserole dish; add white sauce, cheese and add remaining bread crumbs. Mix together and put buttered bread crumbs on top. Bake in a 350-degree oven and heat until bread crumbs on top are browned. Yield: 8 servings.

THICK WHITE SAUCE:

2 tbsp. butter
4 tbsp. flour
½ tsp. salt
Speck of black pepper
1 c. milk

Melt butter; stir in flour, salt and pepper. Blend well and add milk gradually. Cook until thick, stirring constantly.

Mrs. Charles V. Wright, Decatur, Miss.

ASPARAGUS CASSEROLE

2 cans asparagus
1 can cream of mushroom soup
½ c. chopped pimento
2 hard-boiled eggs
1 c. grated cheddar cheese
Cracker crumbs
Oleo

Drain liquid from asparagus. Add mushroom soup and pimento. Place layer of mixture in greased casserole; add sliced hard-boiled eggs and grated cheese. Repeat layers. Sprinkle top with cracker crumbs and dot with oleo. Place in a 325-degree oven and cook for 25 minutes. Yield: 6 servings.

Mrs. Louise W. Peck, Fayetteville, Tenn.

ASPARAGUS CASSEROLE

⅔ c. milk
1 10 ½-oz. mushroom soup
2 14 ½-oz. cans green tip asparagus spears
1 ½ c. potato chips, slightly crushed
Grated cheese
Paprika

(Continued on next page)

Butter a 10 x 6 x 2-inch baking dish. Add milk to soup and mix well. Line baking dish with asparagus; pour soup mixture over vegetable. Add potato chips sprinkled with grated cheese and paprika. Bake at 350 degrees for 25 minutes.

Mrs. James P. Thomas, Cape Charles, Va.

ASPARAGUS CASSEROLE

2 cans asparagus tips
3 sliced hard-boiled eggs
1 c. grated cheese
1 can mushroom soup

Arrange asparagus tips in buttered casserole dish. Add a layer of egg slices. Top with grated cheese. Cover with mushroom soup. Heat in 350-degree oven until cheese melts.

Mrs. B. W. Glade, Lufkin, Tex.

ASPARAGUS CASSEROLE

1 med. can asparagus, drained, reserving juice
1 can cream of mushroom soup
Butter or margarine
1 ½ c. grated cheese
¾ c. cracker crumbs, coarsely broken
½ c. slivered almonds
1 med. can chow mein noodles

After draining asparagus, stir 2/3 of the juice into mushroom soup. Using a 1 1/2-quart casserole or an 8 x 8-inch glass baking dish, spread soft butter on bottom and sides of dish. Layer asparagus, cheese, cracker crumbs, almonds and mushroom soup alternately; top with chow mein noodles. Bake at 350 degrees until bubbly and top is browned, approximately 30 minutes. Yield: 8-10 servings.

Mrs. Martha J. Sipes, Pleasure Ridge Park, Ky.

ASPARAGUS-MACARONI CASSEROLE

2 cans macaroni
1 lge. can asparagus, drained and cut in bite-sized pieces
1 c. sharp cheese, grated
½ c. buttered saltine cracker or bread crumbs

In a buttered casserole, layer macaroni, asparagus and grated cheese alternately. Top with cracker crumbs. Bake at 350 degrees until hot and bubbly, about 30 to 40 minutes. Yield: 6-8 servings.

Mrs. W. E. Robinson, Jr., Milledgeville, Ga.

ASPARAGUS CASSEROLE

1 stick butter or margarine, softened
2 c. cracker crumbs
1 can asparagus
4 tbsp. butter
3 tbsp. flour
1 ½ c. milk
½ tsp. salt
½ tsp. pepper
1 med. can Parmesan cheese

(Continued on next page)

Mix butter and cracker crumbs, reserving 3/4 cup. Spread remaining in bottom of baking dish; pour asparagus over crumb mixture. Make sauce of butter, flour and milk. Add salt, pepper and Parmesan cheese. Cook five minutes; cool. Pour sauce over asparagus and sprinkle reserved cracker crumbs on top. Bake for 15 minutes at 350 degrees. Yield: 8 servings.

Mrs. Lula Pottinger, New Haven, Ky.

ASPARAGUS CASSEROLE SUPREME

¼ c. butter
¼ c. flour
1 ¾ c. chicken broth
¼ c. light cream
Pinch of nutmeg
Salt and pepper to taste
3 hard-cooked eggs, sliced
24 asparagus spears, drained
Grated Parmesan cheese

Preheat oven to 400 degrees. In saucepan, melt butter; add flour and stir with wire whisk until blended. Bring chicken broth and cream to boil; add all at once to butter and flour mixture, stirring vigorously. Stir until sauce is thickened and smooth. Season with nutmeg, salt and pepper. Place alternate layers of sauce, egg and asparagus in a buttered casserole ending with layer of sauce. Sprinkle with Parmesan cheese and bake 5 to 10 minutes at 350 degrees.

Lucile Freese, Nashville, Tenn.

ASPARAGUS-NOODLE CASSEROLE

1 8-oz. pkg. med. noodles
1 c. shredded sharp cheese
½ c. mayonnaise
½ c. sweet milk
1 No. 2 or No. 300 can cut green asparagus
1 can cream of mushroom soup
¼ c. buttered bread crumbs.
Paprika
Tabasco sauce

Cook noodles as directed on package. Drain well; add cheese to hot noodles. Stir until melted. Add mixture of mayonnaise and milk, asparagus, including liquor and mushroom soup. Mix well. Put half of crumbs on bottom of 3-quart casserole. Add noodle-asparagus mixture. Top with remaining crumbs. Sprinkle paprika and 4 to 5 dashes Tabasco sauce over all. Bake at 325 degrees for 20 minutes or until bubbly. Yield: 10-12 servings.

Mrs. Ernest E. Hodges, Bogue Chitto, Miss.

ASPARAGUS EN CASSEROLE

2 c. asparagus
1 pimento, cut up
3 eggs, beaten
1 c. grated cheese
1 ¼ c. finely rolled cracker crumbs
1 tsp. salt
½ tsp. pepper
1 c. milk
¼ c. butter

(Continued on next page)

Mix together all ingredients except butter. Pour into oiled baking dish. Melt butter and pour over top. Bake, uncovered, in a 350-degree oven for 20 to 30 minutes.

Mrs. G. C. Ford, Columbus, Miss.

CHEESE-ASPARAGUS CASSEROLE

2 No. 2 cans green cut asparagus
1 10 ½-oz. can cheddar cheese soup
4 to 6 hard-cooked eggs
Cracker crumbs

Drain asparagus, saving liquid. Mix 1/4 cup liquid with undiluted soup and heat until bubbly. Place asparagus and sliced eggs in a buttered casserole. Add soup and mix lightly. Top with crumbs. Bake for 25 minutes in a 350-degree oven until brown on top and heated thoroughly.

Mrs. Lester McCaleb, Columbia, Tenn.

ASPARAGUS CASSEROLE

4 tbsp. butter
½ tsp. salt
¼ tsp. paprika
3 tbsp. flour
1 ½ c. milk
½ lb. sharp cheese
3 tbsp. pimento, chopped
2 tbsp. onion, chopped
3 tbsp. celery, chopped
2 boiled eggs, chopped
1 can asparagus
Buttered bread crumbs (opt.)

Melt butter in saucepan; add salt, paprika and flour. Stir until smooth. Gradually add milk. Cook until sauce thickens. Remove from heat; add cheese and stir until cheese melts. Add pimento, onion, celery and eggs; stir well. In a greased baking dish, layer sauce mixture and asparagus alternately. Sprinkle buttered bread crumbs on top. Bake in a 350-degree oven until brown. Yield: 8 servings.

Mrs. Ruby M. Polk, Winnsboro, La.

EGGS AND ASPARAGUS AU GRATIN

1 lb. or 1 No. 2 can asparagus, cooked
2 tbsp. butter or fortified margarine
2 tbsp. enriched all-purpose flour
½ tsp. salt
Dash of pepper
Liquid from asparagus and enough milk to make 1 ½ c.
1 c. grated cheese
4 hard-cooked eggs, sliced
½ c. soft bread crumbs

Drain asparagus, saving liquid. Melt butter; blend in flour, salt and pepper. Add liquid and bring to boil, stirring constantly until thickened. Remove from heat; add cheese. Place alternate layers of eggs, asparagus and cheese sauce in a greased baking dish. Cover with crumbs and bake in a preheated 350-degree oven for 25 minutes. Yield: 6 servings.

Mrs. Ruby B. Epting, Chapin, S. C.

EASY ASPARAGUS AU GRATIN

1 14 ½-oz. can asparagus
1 10-oz. can cream of celery soup
16 Ritz crackers, crushed
½ c. cheddar cheese, grated

Butter a flat oblong casserole. Drain asparagus and arrange in casserole. Pour undiluted cream of celery soup over asparagus; spread Ritz cracker crumbs over top. Bake at 400 degrees for 20 minutes. Top with grated cheese. Return to oven for 5 minutes longer.

Mrs. F. A. Duffy, Roanoke, Va.

EASY ASPARAGUS CASSEROLE

1 can asparagus and liquid
1 tsp. salt
Pimento
¼ lb. cheese
1 ¼ c. milk
1 ½ c. crackers, broken up

Mix all ingredients and bake in buttered casserole about 45 minutes in a 350-degree oven. Yield: 6 servings.

Mrs. George Wendel, Falls Church, Va.

ANNIVERSARY ELEGANCE

Baked Cornish Hens with Wild Rice

Old English Asparagus Casserole

Hot Rolls   Lemon Fluff

Coffee

OLD ENGLISH ASPARAGUS CASSEROLE

¼ lb. plus 4 tbsp. margarine
1 ½ c. cracker crumbs
1 No. 2 can green asparagus spears
½ c. toasted almonds (opt.)
3 tbsp. flour
1 ½ c. milk
1 jar Old English cheese

Melt 1/4 pound margarine and mix with crumbs. Pat in bottom of long casserole and up onto sides. Arrange asparagus on crumbs and sprinkle with almonds. Mix remaining margarine, flour and milk together for sauce. Add cheese to hot sauce and stir until melted and thick. Pour over asparagus. Top with additional crumbs. Bake in a 400-degree oven for 30 minutes.

Mrs. Harold B. Dalton, Bowling Green, Ky.

ELEGANT ASPARAGUS CASSEROLE

1 lge. can asparagus spears or tips, drained
1 can cream of mushroom soup
1 c. toast cubes, buttered
2 tsp. dried parsley flakes
Dash of black pepper
Dash of paprika
1 can cheese soup

Put asparagus in a 1 1/2-quart casserole. Some may be reserved to decorate top, if desired. Add mushroom soup that has been thinned with a little asparagus liquid. Cover with toast cubes. Mix seasonings with cheese soup which has also been thinned with asparagus liquid. Spread over top of casserole. Bake at 350 degrees until bubbly or about 30 minutes.

Mrs. Paul D. Spradlin, Russellville, Ala.

FAVORITE CASSEROLE

2 c. med. white sauce
1 c. cheese, grated
1 tsp. Worcestershire sauce
1 lge. can green asparagus
1 c. cashew nuts
3 hard-boiled eggs, chopped

Make white sauce; stir cheese and Worcestershire sauce into sauce. Arrange layer of asparagus; sprinkle with cashew nuts and chopped eggs in casserole. Cover with cream sauce. Repeat layers until all ingredients are used. Bake in a 400-degree oven until bubbly.

Mrs. W. B. Jolly, Taylorsville, Ga.

FRIED ONION-ASPARAGUS CASSEROLE

2 sm. cans asparagus tips
1 ½ c. grated American cheese
1 can mushroom soup
1 sm. can evaporated milk
1 3 ½-oz. fried onion rings

Drain asparagus tips and place in well-greased casserole. Cover with grated cheese. Mix soup and milk well; pour over asparagus and cheese. Cook 30 minutes at 350 degrees; sprinkle onion rings over top and brown 10 minutes longer. Yield: 8-10 servings.

Mrs. S. L. Norrell, Cleburne, Tex.

BAKED BEAN CASSEROLE

2 sm. onions
2 seeded green peppers
3 tbsp. butter
1 c. oven-baked beans
¾ c. grated cheese
½ c. fine fresh bread crumbs
6 slices of bacon

Chop and cook onions and green pepper in 2 tablespoons butter until tender and golden brown. Add beans in alternate layers with grated cheese, ending with a layer of beans. Top with bread crumbs mixed with remaining butter. Arrange slices of bacon over top. Bake for 35 minutes at 325 degrees. Yield: 4 servings.

Mrs. Margaret B. Davis, Holly Hill, Fla.

BAKED GREEN BEANS AND MUSHROOMS

14 slices fresh white bread, cubed without crusts
½ c. melted margarine
2 cans cut green beans, drained
2 cans sliced or chopped mushrooms, drained
Salt and pepper
1 sm. onion, diced
1 can cream of mushroom soup, undiluted
⅓ soup can milk
1 3 ¼-oz. pkg. toasted slivered almonds (opt.)

Preheat oven to 400 degrees. Toss bread cubes with oleo; spread half of mixture evenly into bottom of greased 2-quart casserole. Cover with beans; top with mushrooms. Sprinkle evenly with salt, pepper and onion. In medium bowl, combine soup and milk, mixing well; pour over beans. Top with remainder of bread cubes and almonds. Bake for 30 minutes. Yield: 8 servings.

Mrs. F. T. Murphy, Sarasota, Fla.

CHEESEY GREEN BEANS

1 No. 303 can cut green beans
2 tbsp. flour
2 tbsp. butter
1 c. milk
¼ tsp. salt
1 3-oz. jar Old English cheese spread
1 3-oz. jar chopped pimentos
1 can mushroom soup
1 c. crushed Ritz crackers

Heat green beans in a saucepan. Make a white sauce with flour, butter and milk. Add salt, cheese spread, pimentos and soup to white sauce. Pour beans into 1 1/2-quart casserole dish; pour soup mixture on top. Mix lightly; top with cracker crumbs. Brown in a 350-degree oven for 20 minutes. Yield: 6 servings.

Janis Callaway, Atlanta, Ga.

EASY GREEN BEAN CASSEROLE

2 cans whole green beans
1 can mushroom soup
New York sharp cheese
1 can French-fried onion rings

Cook green beans about 15 minutes; drain. Put half of beans in bottom of casserole; add half of mushroom soup. Cover with layer of sliced cheese; pour half of onions over cheese. Repeat layers. Bake at 350 degrees for 20 minutes.

Louise M. Byrd, Jackson, Miss.

FAVORITE GREEN BEAN CASSEROLE

3 9-oz. pkg. frozen French green beans
1 ½ c. water
1 ½ tsp. salt
1 5-oz. can sliced water chestnuts or slivered almonds
2 cans condensed cream of celery soup
½ tsp. pepper
½ c. milk
2 cans French-fried onion rings

(Continued on next page)

Combine beans, water and salt in a saucepan. Cover; bring to a boil over high heat. Reduce heat; cook gently until thawed, but still slightly crisp, about 4 minutes. Drain; put a layer of beans and a layer of chestnuts alternately in a 2-quart greased casserole. Mix celery soup and pepper with milk. Pour over beans in casserole. Bake in a 350-degree oven 25 minutes. Top with French-fried onions; bake until golden brown, about 10 minutes. Yield: 8-10 servings.

Mrs. Bette H. Campbell, Memphis, Tenn.

FRENCH BEAN CASSEROLE

1 can French-style green beans
1 can condensed mushroom soup
½ c. Cheez Whiz
1 can mushrooms
1 can drained water chestnuts, cut in quarters
1 can French-fried onion rings

Heat and drain beans. While still hot, add mushroom soup and Cheez Whiz; mix together. Add mushrooms and water chestnuts. Place in shallow oven dish; cover generously with onion rings. Heat at 300 degrees until beans are bubbly and onions are brown and crisp. Yield: 6-8 servings.

Mrs. John A. Fierro, Jr., Winter Haven, Fla.

FRENCH CLASSY BEANS

2 tbsp. butter
1 tbsp. flour
½ tsp. salt
1 tbsp. sugar
1 tbsp. grated onion or onion dry soup mix
1 c. sour cream
1 No. 2 can French-style green beans
¼ c. grated cheese
1 c. crushed potato chips

Melt butter; blend in flour, salt, sugar and onion. Stir in cream; heat, but do not boil. Combine sour cream mixture and drained beans; add grated cheese. Pour into buttered casserole; top with potato chips. Bake at 350 degrees for 25 minutes.

Mrs. E. P. Pruitt, Jr., Birmingham, Ala.

FRENCHED GREEN BEANS SUPREME

2 No. 2 cans French-style green beans, drained
2 cans cream of celery soup
Dash of salt, pepper and monosodium glutamate
1 can French-fried onions

Put green beans in an oblong baking dish; pour undiluted cream of celery soup over beans. Sprinkle seasonings over soup; top with French-fried onions. Cover with foil; bake for 20 minutes at 350 degrees. Uncover; bake for 10 minutes. Yield: 6-8 servings.

Mrs. F. Killingsworth, Denison, Tex.

FRENCH-STYLE GREEN BEAN CASSEROLE

2 10-oz. pkg. frozen French-style green beans
4 tbsp. butter, melted
½ c. minced onion
6 oz. slivered almonds or 1 small can water chestnuts, drained and chopped
4 tbsp. flour
2 tsp. salt
½ tsp. dry mustard
1 tsp. Worcestershire sauce
1 c. sour cream
1 c. grated sharp cheese

Cook beans in boiling water until just tender. Melt butter; add onion and almonds. Cook over medium heat until onion is transparent. Remove from heat; blend in flour, salt, mustard and Worcestershire sauce. Heat until mixture bubbles. Remove from heat; add sour cream. Return to low heat, stirring constantly for 2 to 3 minutes; do not boil. Drain beans; put in baking dish. Add sauce; toss gently until beans are well coated with sauce. Sprinkle with grated cheese. Bake, uncovered, 10 to 12 minutes at 350 degrees. Serve hot. Yield: 6-8 servings.

Mrs. Dan C. Stowe, Brandon, Fla.

GREEN BEAN CASSEROLE

1 can mushroom soup, diluted with ½ c. sweet milk
¼ c. sliced almonds
1 sm. can water chestnuts, cut up
1 No. 2 can green beans, drained
Salt and pepper to taste
1 can French-fried onions or potatoes

Mix mushroom soup, milk, almonds and water chestnuts. Add beans; mix well. Season with salt and pepper to taste. Bake in oven about 40 minutes at 350 degrees. Remove from oven; spread onions over top. Return to oven long enough to warm onions. Yield: 6 servings.

Mrs. O. G. Glausier, Montgomery, Ala.

GREEN BEAN CASSEROLE

1 lge. onion
½ c. oleo
½ c. flour
3 c. milk
1 tbsp. soy sauce
Salt and pepper to taste
¾ lb. sharp cheese, grated
1 can French-fried almonds, chopped
3 cans French-style beans
1 can mushrooms
1 can drained water chestnuts, sliced
Cracker crumbs

Chop onion fine; cook in oleo. Add flour, milk, soy sauce, salt and pepper. Add cheese and almonds. Drain beans, mushrooms and chestnuts; mix with sauce. Place mixture in greased casserole. Top with cracker crumbs. Bake in 350-degree oven for 30 minutes.

Mrs. H. C. Edgar, Edinburg, Tex.

GREEN BEAN CASSEROLE

2 1-lb. cans French-style green beans
1 can cream of mushroom soup
1 tbsp. milk
⅓ c. salad dressing
2 hard-boiled eggs, chopped

(Continued on next page)

Heat beans in juice from cans; drain. Pour beans into 1 1/2-quart casserole. Thin mushroom soup with milk; mix well with salad dressing and chopped eggs. Pour over beans. Heat in 400-degree oven. Yield: 6-8 servings.

Mrs. Vida C. Melton, Tyler, Tex.

GREEN BEAN CASSEROLE SUPREME

- 1 can consomme
- 2 pkg. frozen French-cut green beans
- 1 can cream of celery soup
- 1 tsp. Worcestershire sauce
- ¼ tsp. pepper
- ¼ c. Italian bread crumbs
- 3 tsp. butter
- 1 can French-fried onion rings

Heat consomme until boiling; add beans. Cook just until tender; do not overcook. Drain off consomme; add cream of celery soup, Worcestershire sauce and pepper. Mix thoroughly; put in greased casserole. Sprinkle with bread crumbs; dot with butter. Arrange onion rings on top. Bake at 350 degrees for 30 minutes or until bubbling hot. Yield: 8 servings.

Mrs. A. J. Doherty, Baton Rouge, La.

LIMA BEAN CASSEROLE

- 2 c. frozen lima beans, cooked according to package directions
- ½ c. chopped pimento
- 1 c. grated cheese
- 1 c. white sauce
- 2 tbsp. tomato catsup
- ½ c. bread crumbs
- 2 tbsp. butter (softened)

Combine beans, pimento cheese, white sauce and catsup in casserole. Cover with bread crumbs which have been buttered. Bake at 350 degrees for 30 minutes. Yield: 6-8 servings.

Mrs. Thomas Byrd, Nashville, Tenn.

SAUCY GREEN BEAN CASSEROLE

- 1 sm. stalk celery, thinly sliced diagonally
- 1 tbsp. melted butter
- 1 tbsp. flour
- 1 can cream of mushroom soup or golden mushroom soup
- 1 tbsp. Worcestershire sauce
- 1 lge. can green beans
- ½ c. grated Velveeta cheese

Simmer celery in a small amount of water until tender; drain. Mix melted butter and flour together; add mushroom soup, Worcestershire sauce, small amount of bean liquid, celery and grated cheese. Drain remaining liquid from green beans. Place beans in a greased 1-quart casserole; pour sauce on top. Bake 25 to 30 minutes in a 350-degree oven. Yield: 4 servings.

Mrs. Robert J. Soto, Fort Worth, Tex.

MIXED BEAN CASSEROLE

1 clove garlic, minced
1 med. onion, chopped
3 tbsp. bacon drippings
2 c. baked beans
2 ½ c. cooked kidney beans
2 ½ c. cooked green lima beans
½ c. catsup
3 tbsp. vinegar
1 tbsp. brown sugar
1 tsp. dry mustard
1 tsp. salt
½ tsp. pepper

Cook garlic and onion in bacon drippings in heavy frying pan until onion is tender. Combine with remaining ingredients; pour into a 2-quart casserole and bake 45 minutes in a 350-degree preheated oven. Yield: 4-6 servings.

Mrs. Simon L. Bean, Clifton, Tex.

ONION-RINGED VEGETABLE BAKE

1 10-oz. pkg. frozen green lima beans
1 can condensed cheese soup
½ c. milk
¾ c. sliced celery
¼ c. snipped parsley
1 3 ½-oz. can French-fried onion rings

Into bowl, empty package of limas. Pour boiling water over and break beans apart. Drain well. Blend together cheese soup and milk; add beans, celery, parsley and half the onion rings. Bake in a 350-degree oven for 35 minutes. Top casserole with remaining onion rings. Bake 10 minutes longer or till rings are crispy. Yield: 6 servings.

Mrs. R. E. Daniel, Knoxville, Tenn.

PASTA FAGOOLA

1 onion, chopped
1 green pepper, chopped
1 clove garlic, chopped
Olive oil
1 c. elbow macaroni
1 can kidney beans
Parmesan cheese

Saute first 3 ingredients in 1/4 cup olive oil. Cook macaroni as package directs and drain. Add kidney beans and top with plenty of cheese. Place in casserole; bake at 350 degrees until nicely browned. Yield: 6-8 servings.

Mrs. P. T. Dix Arnold, Gainesville, Fla.

SOUR CREAM-BEAN CASSEROLE

2 pkg. frozen French-style beans
2 tbsp. flour
1 tsp. salt
¼ tsp. pepper
2 tbsp. butter
1 carton sour cream
½ c. grated sharp cheese

Cook beans as directed on package; drain. Add flour, salt, pepper and butter; mix well. Mix cream with bean mixture; pour into shallow baking dish. Top with grated cheese. Bake in 350-degree oven for 15 minutes.

Mrs. Charles D. Cope, Atlanta, Ga.

STRING BEAN CASSEROLE

2 No. 2 cans string beans
1 can cream of mushroom soup
1 can French-fried onions

Drain beans; add soup. Top with onions. Place in 350-degree oven, uncovered. Bake until onions brown and beans heat.

Mrs. William Parker, Fayetteville, N. C.

TASTY GREEN BEAN CASSEROLE

1 can green beans, drained
1 can cream of mushroom soup, undiluted
Salt to taste
1 can French-fried onion rings

Mix beans, soup and salt; place in greased casserole. Bake at 350 degrees until thoroughly heated and bubbling. Remove from oven; top with French-fried onions. Return to oven till onions are crisp and brown, about 5 minutes. Yield: 4 servings.

Mrs. John Manley, Pompano Beach, Fla.

VEGETABLE CASSEROLE

1 10-oz. pkg. frozen green beans
1 10-oz. pkg. frozen lima beans
1 6-oz. can mushrooms, sliced
3 tbsp. flour
2 tsp. chicken fat
1 onion
1 c. chicken broth
1 c. sweet milk
1 c. sharp cheese, grated
1 c. bread crumbs

Cook beans and mushrooms; drain well. Make a white sauce of next 5 ingredients. Pour sauce over vegetables placed in a casserole. Top with cheese and bread crumbs; bake at 350 degrees for 20 minutes. Yield: 8 servings.

Mrs. H. C. Evans, Morristown, Tenn.

BROCCOLI CASSEROLE

½ c. onions, chopped
5 to 6 stalks celery, chopped
2 tbsp. butter
1 pkg. frozen chopped broccoli, steamed
2 c. cooked rice
1 can cream of mushroom soup
1 can cream of chicken soup
Sharp cheese

Saute onion and celery in butter. Add steamed broccoli, cooked rice, mushroom soup and chicken soup. Mix and put in casserole. Top with sharp cheese. Bake for 30 minutes at 300 degrees. Yield: 8 servings.

Mrs. R. D. Waters, San Antonion, Tex.

BROCCOLI-ONION CASSEROLE

2 pkg. frozen chopped broccoli
1 16-oz. can small onions, drained
½ c. grated sharp cheese
½ c. slivered almonds
1 can cream of chicken soup

Cook broccoli according to package directions until just tender; drain. Arrange alternate layers of broccoli, onions, cheese and almonds in buttered casserole; repeat layers. Pour soup over top. Bake at 375 degrees for about 30 minutes. Yield: 6-8 servings.

Mrs. William F. Cosby, Rockford, Tenn.

BROCCOLI SUPREME

1 box frozen chopped broccoli, thawed
1 c. bread crumbs
½ pt. sour cream
1 c. grated sharp cheese
Salt and pepper to taste

Mix all ingredients thoroughly; place in small casserole dish. Bake at 350 degrees for 1 hour. Yield: 4-6 servings.

Mrs. W. B. Harrell, Huntsville, Ala.

BROCCOLI-RICE CASSEROLE

1 ½ c. rice
1 c. chopped celery
1 med. onion, minced
½ stick oleo
1 pkg. chopped broccoli
1 can mushroom soup
1 8-oz. jar Cheez-Whiz

Cook rice. Wilt celery and onion in oleo. Place broccoli in collander over boiling water to thaw. Mix all ingredients together and bake 45 minutes at 350 degrees. Yield: 12-16 servings.

Mrs. Tom W. Barron, Metairie, La.

BROCCOLI CASSEROLE

2 pkg. frozen chopped broccoli
2 eggs, well beaten
1 can mushroom soup
1 c. grated sharp cheese
1 c. mayonnaise
Crushed Ritz cheese crackers
Butter

Cook broccoli for 5 minutes; drain. Combine eggs, soup, cheese and mayonnaise; fold in broccoli. Pour into casserole; cover with crackers. Dot with butter. Bake at 350 degrees for 30 minutes. Yield: 6-8 servings.

Mrs. Gaye Enkema, Kingsport, Tenn.

BROCCOLI SUPREME

½ c. chopped onion
2 stalks celery, chopped
1 stick butter or margarine
2 boxes frozen chopped broccoli
1 can condensed mushroom soup
1 sm. can mushrooms
1 roll garlic cheese
1 c. bread crumbs
Seasoning to taste

Saute onion and celery in butter; add broccoli. Simmer for 15 minutes; add soup, mushrooms, cheese, 1/2 cup bread crumbs and seasoning. Pour into greased 2-quart casserole; sprinkle with remaining crumbs. Bake at 350 degrees for 30 minutes. Yield: 10 servings.

Mrs. Kennon Mixon, St. Joseph, La.

SPAGHETTI-BROCCOLI AU GRATIN

6 green onions, chopped
4 tbsp. butter or oleo
1 bunch fresh or 2 pkg. frozen broccoli, cooked
½ tsp. salt
Dash of pepper
Dash of savory
1 8-oz. pkg. spaghetti, cooked
1 8-oz. pkg. processed American cheese slices
½ c. light cream

Cook onions in melted butter until limp. Cut broccoli in chunks; add to onions with salt, pepper and savory. Cook for 5 minutes over low heat. Put spaghetti in greased 2-quart casserole; cover with the cheese slices. Pour cream over cheese; add broccoli. Top with remaining cheese. Bake at 375 degrees for 30 minutes or until cheese is melted. Yield: 6 servings.

Kathryn S. Johnson, St. Petersburg, Fla.

DEVILED EGG CASSEROLE

6 hard-cooked eggs
3 tbsp. mayonnaise
⅛ tsp. dry mustard
Dash of pepper
2 10-oz. pkg. frozen chopped broccoli or spinach
¼ c. butter
2 tbsp. flour
2 c. milk
1 c. grated sharp cheese
½ tsp. Worcestershire sauce
½ tsp. salt
Dash of Tabasco sauce

(Continued on next page)

Cut eggs in half lengthwise. Remove yolks and mash well; add mayonnaise, mustard and pepper. Blend well; fill egg whites with yolk mixture. Cook broccoli as directed on package; drain well. Melt butter in saucepan; add flour and stir until blended. Add milk gradually; cook over medium heat until thickened, stirring constantly. Set aside 2 tablespoons grated cheese; add remaining cheese to sauce. Stir until cheese is melted; add Worcestershire sauce, salt and Tabasco sauce. Place broccoli in well-greased 1 1/2-quart baking dish; add half the cheese sauce, mixing broccoli and sauce with fork. Arrange eggs on top; pour remaining sauce over eggs. Sprinkle with reserved cheese. Bake at 375 degrees for 20 to 25 minutes or until bubbly and lightly browned. Yield: 6 servings.

Mrs. Doris Miles, Ferguson, N. C.

BRUSSELS SPROUTS CASSEROLE

3 boxes cooked Brussels sprouts
Lemon juice
Salt and pepper to taste
½ stick butter
2 tbsp. flour
1 c. evaporated milk
½ small pkg. Velveeta, grated
½ pkg. or roll sharp cheese, grated
Dash dry mustard
½ tsp. Worcestershire sauce
Dash of Tabasco

Cook sprouts; spread in casserole dish. Sprinkle with lemon juice, salt and pepper. Make white sauce with butter, flour and evaporated milk; add salt, pepper, cheeses and seasonings. Add white sauce to Brussels sprouts; cover with buttered crumbs and paprika. Bake at 350 degrees till bubbly. Yield: 8 servings.

Mrs. Frank Parrot, Salisbury, N. C.

CABBAGE-APPLE CASSEROLE

1 sm. head red cabbage
1 sm. head green cabbage
Salt and pepper to taste
½ c. butter
½ c. brown sugar
Juice of 1 lemon
Nutmeg to taste
3 c. diced apples
1 c. green pepper, minced
Buttered bread crumbs

Grind red and green cabbage separately. Season red cabbage with salt and pepper; place in greased casserole. Dot with butter. Add sugar, lemon juice and nutmeg to apples; place on top of red cabbage. Mix green cabbage, green pepper, salt and pepper; place over apples. Dot with butter; cover with bread crumbs. Bake in 375-degree oven for 25 minutes. Yield: 4-6 servings.

Mrs. Ray Gragg, Bell City, La.

CABBAGE WITH TOMATOES

2 tbsp. butter
½ c. chopped onions
1 c. chopped green peppers
1 c. sliced celery
2 c. diced fresh tomatoes
¼ med. head cabbage, shredded
1 tsp. sugar
1 ½ tsp. salt
¼ tsp. black pepper

(Continued on next page)

Melt butter in large heavy skillet. Toss remaining ingredients gently in bowl. Add to butter; cover and cook on low heat about 10 minutes or until vegetables are barely tender. Yield: 6 servings.

Mrs. Charles Brosius, Tampa, Fla.

CALIFORNIA CARROT CASSEROLE

18 to 20 med. carrots, peeled
Salt and pepper to taste
2 tbsp. evaporated milk
½ c. chopped walnuts
2 tsp. candied ginger, chopped fine
4 tbsp. butter or margarine

Simmer carrots, covered, in small amount of boiling salted water until tender. Drain; mash well. Season with salt, pepper and milk. Pile in buttered 1-quart casserole. Sprinkle with nuts and ginger; dot with remaining butter. Bake in oven at 350 degrees for 30 minutes. Yield: 6 servings.

Mrs. Barbara Hazel, Talladega, Ala.

CARROT CASSEROLE

2 c. diced carrots
1 c. cream of mushroom soup
½ med. onion, chopped fine
1 sm. bag potato chips, crushed

Alternate layers of carrots with soup and onion mixed in greased 1-quart casserole. Bake at 325 degrees for 20 to 25 minutes or until thoroughly heated. Just before removing from oven, sprinkle with crushed potato chips; brown slightly. Yield: 6 servings.

Mrs. A. R. Caldwell, Pocahontas, Ark.

CAULIFLOWER AND HAM CASSEROLE

1 lge. head cauliflower
1 c. ham, cut in small cubes
1 10-oz. can cream of mushroom soup
½ c. buttered bread crumbs
½ c. grated cheddar cheese

Cook the whole cauliflower in boiling water for about 20 minutes. Drain and break into pieces. Place cauliflower and ham in layers in casserole. Cover with soup. Sprinkle with bread crumbs and cheese. Bake in a 375-degree oven for 25 minutes or until slightly browned. Yield: 4-6 servings.

Mrs. William Segal, Jacksonville, Fla.

CELERY CASSEROLE

4 c. sliced celery
½ c. boiling water
1 10½-oz. can condensed cream of celery soup or cream of mushroom soup
½ c. sweet milk
½ c. chopped pecans
⅓ c. cracker crumbs
3 tbsp. butter

(Continued on next page)

Cook celery in boiling water until tender; drain. Combine with soup, milk and pecans; mix well. Turn into greased 1 1/2-quart casserole; sprinkle with cracker crumbs. Dot with butter. Bake at 350 degrees for 30 minutes. Yield: 6-7 servings.

Mrs. C. E. Barnette, Johnson City, Tenn.

CORN CASSEROLE

2 eggs
2 tbsp. sugar
2 tbsp. flour
Salt and pepper to taste
1 green pepper, diced or 1 sm. jar pimentos
¼ lb. cheese, grated
2 tbsp. melted butter
1 can whole kernel corn

Beat eggs; add sugar, flour, salt, pepper, green pepper, cheese and butter. Add corn with liquid. Bake in a 350-degree oven for 20 to 30 minutes. Yield: 6 servings.

Mrs. James L. Wright, Perryton, Tex.

CORN PIE

1 ¼ c. fine saltine cracker crumbs
½ c. plus 2 tbsp. melted butter or margarine
1 ¼ c. milk
2 c. fresh corn
½ tsp. salt
2 tbsp. flour
⅛ tsp. onion salt or seasoning salt
2 eggs, beaten

Combine crumbs and 1/2 cup melted butter. Take out 1/2 cup and reserve for topping. Press remaining crumbs in bottom and sides of a 9-inch pie pan. Combine remaining butter, 1 cup milk, corn and salt. Bring to boil. Reduce heat and cook 3 minutes. Blend flour with remaining milk to make smooth paste. Add slowly to hot corn-milk mixture, stirring. Cook 2 to 3 minutes or until slightly thickened. Cool slightly. Add onion salt. Stir in eggs slowly. Pour into crumb-lined pan. Sprinkle remaining crumbs over top. Bake in a 400-degree oven for about 20 minutes.

Mrs. Elbert Parrish, Greensboro, N. C.

DUTCH BAKED CORN

4 ears fresh or 1 No. 2 can corn
1 tbsp. butter
2 tbsp. flour
1 c. milk
2 tsp. sugar
1 tsp. salt and paprika
2 eggs, separated

Cut corn from cob. Melt butter; mix with flour and add milk gradually. Bring to a boil, stirring constantly. Add corn, seasonings and egg yolks, well beaten. Fold in stiffly beaten egg whites. Put in a buttered casserole. Bake 30 minutes at 350 degrees.

Mrs. Jack Bishop, Birmingham, Ala.

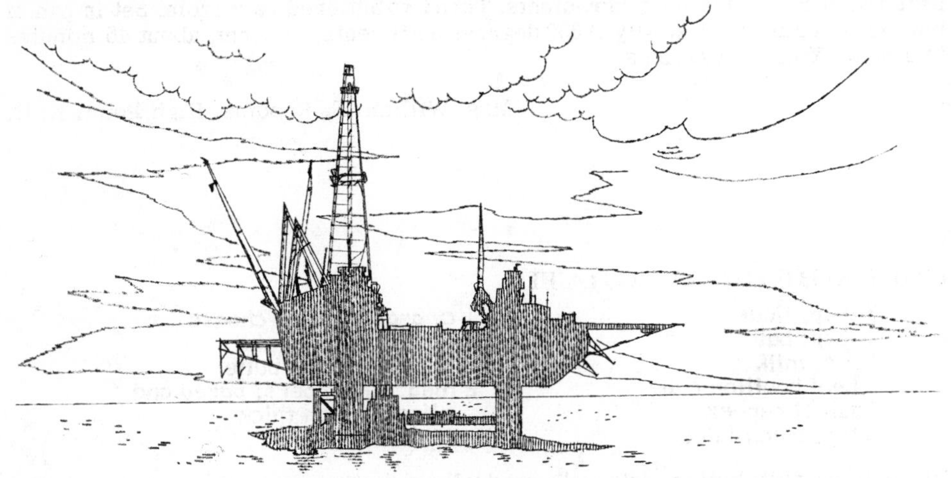

Drilling for oil offshore in Louisiana.

FRESH CORN CASSEROLE

- 2 c. fresh corn, cut from cob
- 1 ½ c. diced fresh tomatoes
- ¼ c. sliced celery
- ¼ c. chopped onions
- 1 ½ c. toasted bread cubes
- 2 tsp. salt
- ¼ tsp. pepper
- 1 tbsp. melted butter
- 3 eggs, well beaten
- Paprika

Combine all ingredients except paprika and turn into greased 1-quart casserole. Place in pan of hot water. Cover and bake at 325 degrees for 1 hour and 30 minutes or until a knife inserted in center comes out clean. Serve hot with garnish of paprika. Yield: 6 servings.

Mrs. L. L. Gallop, Hollins, Ala.

SOUTHERN CORN PUDDING

- 3 c. canned yellow corn
- 3 eggs, beaten well
- 3 tbsp. sifted flour
- 2 tsp. salt
- 1 tbsp. sugar
- 1 tbsp. melted butter
- 1 pt. milk, scalded

Grind corn using a medium-coarse grinder. Beat eggs and add flour, salt, sugar and melted butter; mix well. Add milk and ground corn to egg mixture, mixing well. Pour into well-buttered casserole and bake at 350 degrees until firm, approximately 40 minutes.

Mrs. George B. Weber, Louisville, Ky.

TASTY CORN PUDDING

- 3 tbsp. cornmeal
- ½ tsp. paprika
- 1 tbsp. salt
- ½ c. cold milk
- 2 c. hot milk
- 1 tbsp. butter
- 2 c. fresh corn pulp
- 2 eggs, slightly beaten

(Continued on next page)

Blend cornmeal with paprika, salt and cold milk. Add gradually to hot milk, stirring constantly. Cook over boiling water until mixture thickens. Remove from heat and stir in remaining ingredients. Turn into buttered casserole. Set in pan of boiling water and bake slowly at 350 degrees until center is firm, about 45 minutes to 1 hour. Yield: 6 servings.

Mrs. William E. Robbins, High Point, N. C.

CUCUMBERS AU GRATIN

3 tbsp. flour
3 tbsp. butter
1 ¼ c. milk
1 beef bouillon cube
Dash of pepper
¼ tsp. onion juice
1 c. grated sharp cheese
⅓ c. fine dry crumbs
1 ½ tbsp. melted butter
2 med. cucumbers, pared and sliced ⅛ inch thick

Blend flour with butter. Add milk gradually and stir constantly over direct heat until sauce thickens. Stir in bouillon cube, pepper, onion juice and remove from heat. Add cheese; stir until melted. Stir bread crumbs in the melted butter to coat well. Into a 6-cup buttered casserole, put alternate layers of cucumbers and hot sauce. Top with buttered crumbs; cover and bake at 325 degrees about 30 minutes. Remove cover and continue baking 10 minutes longer or until cucumbers are just tender and surface browned. Serve piping hot. Yield: 5 servings.

Mrs. M. J. Dutschke, Louisville, Ky.

EGGPLANT CASSEROLE

1 lge. eggplant
Salt
2 tbsp. margarine
2 lge onions, finely chopped
1 lb. ground beef
4 med. tomatoes, peeled and quartered
¼ tsp. pepper
¼ c. French dressing

Cut eggplant into 1/2-inch slices; pare. Sprinkle with salt and let stand several hours. Drain off water and dry slices with absorbent paper. Melt margarine in large skillet. Add onions, meat and tomatoes. Cook over medium heat until meat is browned and vegetables tender. Mix in 1/2 teaspoon salt and pepper. Line bottom and sides of 2-quart casserole with all the eggplant. Pour in meat mixture; pour French dressing on top. Cover. Bake in 375-degree oven until eggplant is tender, about 40 minutes. Serve hot. Yield: 6 servings.

Photograph for this recipe on page 263.

EGGPLANT CASSEROLE

1 eggplant, peeled, cubed, cooked and drained
1 c. milk
2 beaten eggs
1 c. grated sharp cheese
1 c. bread crumbs
1 tbsp. margarine or butter
½ tsp. salt
Pepper

(Continued on next page)

Combine all ingredients well. Pour into greased casserole and bake 40 minutes at 350 degrees. Yield: 4 servings.

Mrs. Ruby M. Polk, Winnsboro, La.

EXCELLENT EGGPLANT CASSEROLE

1 med. eggplant
1 egg, beaten
½ c. fine dry bread crumbs
⅓ c. oil
1 6-oz. pkg. sliced mozzarella cheese
1 envelope spaghetti sauce mix with tomato
1 ½ c. water

Peel eggplant and cut into 1/2-inch slices. Dip each slice into egg, then into crumbs and saute on both sides. Put half the slices in a 2-quart casserole. Top with half the cheese. Add remaining eggplant. Prepare spaghetti sauce using 1 1/2 cups water and pour over eggplant. Arrange remaining cheese slices over the top. Cover casserole and bake in a 350-degree oven for 20 minutes. Yield: 4-5 servings.

Mrs. A. Frank Arnold, Spruce Pine, N. C.

GREEN CHILI DISH

1 can cream of chicken soup
1 c. half and half cream
1 c. chopped green chili peppers
8 tortillas
½ lb. grated cheese
1 8-oz. pkg. cream cheese
½ c. chopped onion

Heat soup, cream and chili peppers; pour over 8 tortillas which have been fried and drained. Blend in 3/4 grated cheese, cream cheese and chopped onion. Top casserole with remaining cheese. Bake for 20 minutes at 350 degrees. Yield: 4 servings.

Mrs. Mack Gardner, Jackson, Miss.

GREEN ENCHILADAS

Cooking oil
1 pkg. tortillas
1 can cream of mushroom soup
1 can cream of chicken soup
1 can peeled green chilies, chopped, or to taste
½ c. diced onion
1 c. grated cheddar cheese

Pour cooking oil in frying pan to 1 inch; heat. Dip tortillas in hot fat; drain on paper towels. Combine soups, chopped chilies, onion and cheese. Dip tortillas in sauce. Stack in pan as hot cakes with sauce between each and over top. Bake at 350 degrees for 20 to 30 minutes. May be prepared by dipping hot tortilla in sauce and placing diced cheese and onion in center. Roll tight; secure with toothpick. Lay in 1 layer in large pan. Bake at 350 degrees for 20 to 30 minutes.

Darlene Coleman, Birmingham, Ala.

HOMINY AND CHEESE CASSEROLE

2 c. cooked hominy
5 tbsp. butter
3 tbsp. flour
Salt and paprika
1 ½ c. milk
1 to 2 c. grated cheese
½ c. fine cracker or pastry crumbs

In hot hominy, melt 3 tablespoons butter; add flour, salt and paprika. Stir and cook until puffy. Bring milk to boil while stirring; blend in cheese. Butter a baking dish and alternate layers of hominy and cheese mixture, ending with layer of cheese. Mix crumbs with remaining melted butter; season with sauce spread over top. Bake at 350 degrees till browned.

Anna Murphy, El Dorado, Ark.

TEXAS HOMINY

2 tbsp. butter
2 tbsp. flour
1 c. milk
1 No. 2 can hominy, drained
½ tsp. Worcestershire sauce
Salt and pepper
Chili powder
Ripe olives
Old English cheese

Combine butter, flour and milk for white sauce. Pour over hominy. Season with Worcestershire sauce, salt and pepper; add chili powder. Cut 10 ripe olives and add to mixture. Cook, uncovered, 30 to 45 minutes at 350 degrees. Top with cheese just before taking from oven.

Mrs. P. H. Hayes, Midland, Tex.

ONION CASSEROLE

1 c. spring onions
2 tbsp. butter
1 can cream of celery soup
2 tsp. prepared mustard
1 c. grated cheese
⅓ c. milk
1 ½ tbsp. flour
3 eggs
1 pie shell

Chop spring onions with tops. Cook in melted butter until tender, but not brown. Pour onions in bottom of pie shell. In frypan, pour cream of celery soup; add prepared mustard, grated cheese and milk mixed with flour. Mix well; add well-beaten eggs. Cook until thickened. Add mixture to onions. Preheat oven at 350 to 450 degrees; reset to 350 degrees when pie is put in oven. Bake for 25 minutes or until done.

Mrs. P. B. Sutton, Danville, Va.

GREEN PEA CASSEROLE

1 c. chopped onions
1 c. chopped celery
1 c. chopped green pepper
½ c. butter
1 1-lb. can green peas
1 can pimento
1 can sliced water chestnuts
1 can mushroom soup
Bread crumbs

(Continued on next page)

Preheat oven to 350 degrees. Cook onions, celery and pepper in butter until soft. Add next 4 ingredients; place mixture in casserole and sprinkle bread crumbs on top. Bake for 30 minutes.

Mrs. John C. Wright, Hollywood, Fla.

PEA CASSEROLE

- 1 stick butter
- 1 c. chopped onion
- ½ c. chopped celery
- ½ c. chopped green pepper
- 1 can sliced water chestnuts and liquid
- 1 can mushroom soup
- ½ c. chopped pimentos
- 2 No. 2 cans peas, drained

Melt butter; saute onion, celery and green pepper. Add water chestnuts and liquid, mushroom soup and pimento; add peas. Pour in greased casserole and bake for 30 minutes in a 350-degree oven. Yield: 6-8 servings.

Mrs. Irene Wood, London, Ky.

VENETIAN RICE AND PEAS

- 4 slices bacon
- 1 sm. onion, minced
- 3 tbsp. butter
- 1 10-oz. pkg. frozen peas
- ¾ c. uncooked rice
- 2 c. chicken broth
- 1 tsp. salt
- Dash of pepper
- ¼ c. Parmesan cheese

In heavy skillet, saute bacon. Remove bacon and grease. Saute onion in butter; add frozen peas. Cook 5 minutes; stir frequently. Add rice; cook until well coated with butter. Pour in chicken broth, salt and pepper. Cover and simmer. Stir occasionally for 20 minutes or until liquid is absorbed. Toss with crumbled bacon and Parmesan cheese. Yield: 6-8 servings.

Mrs. Tom W. Barron, Metairie, La.

DELUXE EGG CASSEROLE

- ½ lb. fresh mushrooms, sliced, or 1 4-oz. can mushrooms, drained
- ¼ c. butter or margarine
- ¼ c. flour
- 1 tsp. onion salt
- 1 tsp. celery salt
- ¾ tsp. salt
- ¼ tsp. ground pepper
- 3 c. milk
- 1 1-lb. pkg. frozen French fries
- ¼ lb. cheddar cheese, chopped or cubed
- 8 hard-cooked eggs, cut in chunks

Cook mushrooms in butter for 5 minutes or until tender but not brown; blend in flour and seasonings. Add milk all at once; cook, stirring constantly, until thickened. Stir in frozen French fries and cheese; pour half the mixture into greased 2-quart baking dish. Top with eggs; add remaining cheese mixture. Bake at 400 degrees for 20 minutes or until bubbly and golden brown on top. Yield: 6 servings.

Mrs. Louis Christensen, Cullman, Ala.

POTATO CASSEROLE

6 med. potatoes, peeled and cubed
1 sm. onion, cut in small pieces
1 c. grated cheese
¾ c. milk
1 can cream of mushroom soup
Butter
Pepper
Salt

Arrange alternate layers of raw potatoes, onion and cheese. Pour milk and soup over layers. Bake for 1 hour at 350 degrees.

Mrs. Evelyn Gunter, Milan, Tenn.

SCALLOPED POTATOES WITH HERBS

4 c. raw potatoes, thinly sliced
Salt and paprika
1 tbsp. mixed dried marjoram, savory, chives, thyme and parsley
3 tbsp. butter
1 c. milk
1 c. water
1 c. soft bread crumbs, buttered

Make a layer of potatoes in buttered baking dish; sprinkle with salt, paprika and part of herb mixture. Dot layer with butter. Repeat until all potatoes and herbs are used. Pour milk and water over potatoes. Cover; bake at 375 degrees for 40 minutes. Remove cover; sprinkle with bread crumbs and bake 15 minutes longer until brown. Yield: 6 servings.

Mrs. Frank Homiller, Ball Ground, Ga.

PINEAPPLE GREEN RICE

1 c. raw rice
2 tsp. salt
1 ½ c. water
1 9-oz. pkg. frozen spinach
1 13 ½-oz. can pineapple tidbits, well drained
2 eggs, beaten
1 c. evaporated milk
¼ c. melted butter
1 c. grated sharp cheddar cheese
1 tbsp. minced onion
⅓ c. finely chopped parsley
1 tsp. Worcestershire sauce

Combine rice, salt and water. Heat to boiling; cover and reduce heat to low. Steam for 15 minutes. Cook spinach as directed. Drain and press out as much liquid as possible. Combine all ingredients. Turn into buttered casserole; bake in a 350-degree oven for 40 to 45 minutes. Yield: 6 servings.

Mrs. P. G. Arnold, Chapel Hill, N. C.

SPINACH CASSEROLE

1 pkg. frozen chopped spinach
1 tsp. sugar
1 can mushroom soup
1 egg, slightly beaten
1 ½ c. grated sharp cheese
2 slices bread
3 tbsp. melted butter or oleo
Dash garlic salt

(Continued on next page)

Cook spinach according to directions in 1/2 cup water, using sugar and no salt. Drain thoroughly, mashing out all liquid with the back of a large spoon. Combine spinach with soup, egg and cheese; pour into a greased 1 1/2-quart casserole. Cube bread and toss lightly in butter to which garlic salt has been added. Top spinach mixture with bread cubes and bake 1 hour at 350 degrees. Yield: 6 servings.

Mrs. J. McLean Murphy, Lowell, N. C.

BAKED HUBBARD SQUASH

Hubbard squash
Butter
Brown sugar

Cut squash into pieces; remove seeds and strings. Place pieces in dripping pan in a 350-degree oven for 1 hour. Cover generously with butter and sprinkle with brown sugar. Cook for 1 hour longer, basting frequently. Add butter if necessary. Cooked squash may be scalloped with drained crushed pineapple, dotted with butter and covered with bread crumbs if desired. Bake until top is browned.

Mrs. Agnes Thomas, Townley, Ala.

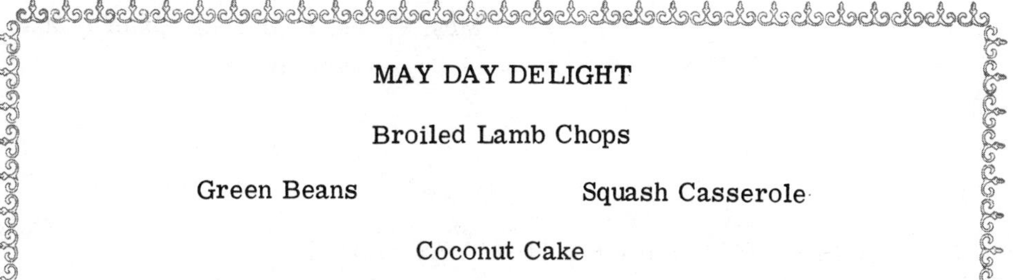

MAY DAY DELIGHT

Broiled Lamb Chops

Green Beans — Squash Casserole

Coconut Cake

Coffee — Tea

SQUASH CASSEROLE

6 med. yellow squash
1 egg, beaten
1 tbsp. finely chopped onion
½ stick butter
1 tsp. salt
Pepper

Boil squash until tender. Drain and mash. Add beaten egg, onion, butter, salt and pepper. For variety, chopped bacon or 1/4 cup grated cheese may be added. Place in a greased casserole dish and top with cracker crumbs. Bake at 350 degrees for about 25 minutes or until crumbs brown slightly.

Mrs. Charles R. Owen, Memphis, Tenn.

MUSHROOM-SQUASH CASSEROLE

3 lb. yellow squash
1 med. onion
2 tsp. salt
1 can mushroom soup
3 tbsp. butter
Milk (opt.)
Dash cayenne pepper
½ pkg. seasoned stuffing mix

Slice squash and onion thin; parboil in salted water until tender, but firm. Dilute soup with butter and a little milk if needed. Season squash with cayenne pepper. Layer squash and stuffing in a casserole, ending with stuffing on top. Pour soup mixture over all. Bake at 350 to 375 degrees until bubbly, about 25 to 35 minutes. Yield: 6-8 servings.

Mrs. W. G. Catron, Lebanon, Tenn.

SOUR CREAM-SQUASH CASSEROLE

½ c. grated sharp cheese
1 tbsp. butter
¼ c. sour cream
½ tsp. salt
½ tsp. paprika
1 egg yolk
1 tbsp. chives
3 strips bacon, fried
½ c. fried sausage
10 med. squash, simmered
Bread crumbs

Cream cheese and butter over low heat; combine first 10 ingredients, adding squash last. Top with bread crumbs and bake for 45 minutes at 350 degrees.

Mrs. Forest E. Barber, Oxford, Miss.

SQUASH-GREEN PEPPER CASSEROLE

3 tbsp. butter
1 c. hot milk
1 c. dry bread crumbs
2 c. cooked squash, mashed
1 tbsp. onion, grated
1 green pepper, finely chopped
2 eggs, beaten
Salt and pepper to taste

Melt butter in milk; stir into bread crumbs. Add remaining ingredients; pour into greased baking dish. Sprinkle with additional bread crumbs. Bake at 350 degrees for 20 to 30 minutes. Yield: 6 servings.

Mrs. Horace L. Weaver, Concord, N. C.

SQUASH SOUFFLE

2 lb. yellow squash, sliced thin
2 med. onions, cut fine
½ stick butter or margarine
2 eggs, separated
¼ c. fine cracker crumbs
½ c. cream
Salt and pepper to taste
Sugar
Buttered crumbs
Paprika

(Continued on next page)

Cook squash, onions and butter in small amount of water until done and water is cooked out. Cream thoroughly. Add well-beaten egg yolks, 1/4 cup crumbs, cream, salt, pepper and a small amount of sugar. Mix well. Fold in stiffly beaten egg whites. Pour into greased casserole and top with buttered crumbs. Sprinkle with paprika. Bake in 400-degree oven for 20 minutes.

Mrs. Eugen Hunt, Old Hickory, Tenn.

TEXAS ACORNS

1 acorn squash
2 tbsp. oleo
4 tbsp. brown sugar

Cut squash in half, lengthwise. Remove seeds and turn cut side down in 1/2 inch water in a shallow pan. Bake at 350 to 375 degrees until squash is tender when mashed with fingers; remove from oven. Drain any remaining water from pan. Turn squash cut side up. Melt oleo and brown sugar; spoon mixture over cut edges of squash and pour in cavity. Return to oven and cook until mixture is bubbly. Yield: 2 servings.

Mrs. L. L. Withrow, Ft. Worth, Tex.

YELLOW SQUASH CASSEROLE

2 lb. yellow squash
1 lge. onion
2 tbsp. butter
1 can frozen shrimp soup
1 can water chestnuts, sliced
Salt to taste
Bread crumbs

Chop squash and onions. Saute in butter over low heat until tender. Add frozen shrimp, soup and water chestnuts. Add salt to taste and pour into greased casserole. Cover with bread crumbs and dot with additional butter. Bake in a 350- degree oven for 30 minutes. Yield: 6-8 servings.

Mrs. John T. Brown, Pine Bluff, Ark.

ZUCCHINI CASSEROLE

3 med. zucchini squash
¼ c. sour cream
1 tbsp. butter
1 tbsp. grated cheddar cheese
½ tsp. salt
Dash paprika
1 egg yolk, beaten
1 tbsp. chopped onion
Cornflakes or cracker crumbs

Cut zucchini into small cubes; simmer in small amount of boiling water 6 to 8 minutes, or until tender. Drain well. Mix sour cream, butter, cheddar cheese and salt. Stir over low heat until cheese and butter are melted. Stir in paprika, egg yolk and onion. Place zucchini in well-greased baking dish and add cream mixture. Sprinkle top with cornflake crumbs and additional grated cheese. Bake in a 375-degree oven until top is golden brown. Yield: 6 servings.

Mrs. W. J. Helm, Paducah, Ky.

PEANUT CRUNCH SWEET POTATO CASSEROLE

2 tbsp. butter
½ to ¾ tsp. salt
½ c. (approx.) warm milk
3 c. fresh cooked or canned sweet potatoes
Marshmallows
½ to ¾ c. chopped salted peanuts

Add butter and salt to milk. When butter is melted, blend with mashed potatoes. Beat until light and fluffy. Add more milk, if needed. Pile lightly into greased casserole. Heat in a 375-degree oven about 20 minutes. Top with marshmallows; sprinkle with chopped nuts. Return to oven; heat until marshmallows brown lightly. Yield: 6-8 servings.

Mrs. A. B. Alexander, Winston-Salem, N. C.

SWEET POTATO CASSEROLE

10 to 12 sweet potatoes
¼ c. butter or margarine
2 tsp. grated orange rinds
1 c. orange juice
2 eggs, slightly beaten
Salt
Pepper
Cinnamon or 15 marshmallows

Scrub and boil potatoes; peel and press through ricer. Add butter, orange rinds and juice, eggs, salt and pepper to taste. Pile in greased 2-quart casserole; dot with additional butter and sprinkle lightly with cinnamon or top with marshmallows. Bake at 400 degrees for 10 minutes or until slightly browned. Yield: 12 servings.

Mrs. Edward T. Breathitt, Wife of Governor of Kentucky, Frankfort, Ky.

YUMMY YAMMY SOUFFLE

2 c. boiled and mashed sweet potatoes
¾ tsp. salt
2 c. sweet milk
½ c. honey
3 eggs, beaten
2 tbsp. cornstarch
1 ½ tsp. curacao
1 c. broken pecans
Marshmallows to cover

Blend potatoes, salt, milk, honey, eggs, cornstarch and curacao, having first dissolved the cornstarch in half cup of milk. Stir in broken pecan meats and put mixture in a well-buttered casserole. Preheat oven to 350 degrees. The casserole is done when a silver knife is inserted in souffle and comes out clean. Cover souffle with large marshmallows and return to oven until these are puffed and delicately browned.

Freda Avant Jay, West Palm Beach, Fla.

TOMATO PIE

½ pkg. pie crust mix
6 lge tomatoes, cut in ½ inch thick slices
Salt and pepper to taste
½ c. cornmeal
4 tbsp. butter or margarine
1 tsp. sugar
½ c. grated cheese
1 tbsp. melted butter

(Continued on next page)

Prepare pie dough as directed on package for 1 crust. Season tomatoes with salt and pepper. Coat with cornmeal; fry in butter. Turn with spatula to brown both sides. Sprinkle each slice with sugar. Line a pie pan with pastry dough. Place layer of tomatoes on bottom; sprinkle with grated cheese. Repeat. Top with cheese; sprinkle with melted butter. Bake at 425 degrees for 10 minutes. Lower heat; bake 15 minutes more.

Mrs. Richard Humphreys, Summerville, Ga.

ASPARAGUS-PEAS CASSEROLE

8 saltine crackers, crushed
1 can sweet peas
1 can asparagus
1 pkg. slivered almonds
1 can cheddar cheese soup
Paprika
Butter or oleo

Layer first 5 ingredients in order given in casserole. Repeat. Top with remaining cracker crumbs and paprika. Dot with butter. Bake at 350 degrees for 30 minutes. Yield: 6-8 servings.

Mrs. A. B. Grant, San Juan, Tex.

BAKED SQUASH WITH GREEN CHILIES

1 lb. squash
½ c. chopped onions
2 eggs
¼ c. milk
¼ tsp. salt
¼ tsp. pepper
2 tbsp. bacon drippings or oleo
1 can mild green chilies, chopped
1 c. grated cheese
1 c. crushed crackers

Cook squash and onions in water until tender enough to mash. Beat eggs; add milk, salt, pepper and bacon drippings. Add green chilies with half the cheese and cracker crumbs. Pour in greased casserole; sprinkle remaining cheese and crumbs on top. Cook 45 minutes at 350 degrees. Yield: 8 servings.

Henrietta Cooper, Austin, Tex.

BAKED TOMATOES AND ZUCCHINI CASSEROLE

3 fresh zucchini
5 sm. ripe tomatoes
6 sm. sweet onions
⅓ c. chopped fresh parsley
Salt
1 tsp. dried basil or 2 tsp. fresh basil
Ground pepper to taste
¼ c. imported olive oil

Scrub zucchini; cut off both ends. Parboil whole and unpeeled zucchini for 5 to 10 minutes, depending on size; drain. While zucchini cooks prepare and slice tomatoes and onions and slice zucchini in 1/2 inch thick rounds. Lay slices of zucchini in shallow casserole. Sprinkle with sliced onions and 1/2 the parsley. Season with salt and basil. Cover with sliced tomatoes; add parsley, pepper and olive oil to cover all contents of casserole. Bake in preheated oven at 350 degrees for 30 to 40 minutes or until vegetables are tender and just beginning to brown. Sprinkle with remaining parsley. Yield: 4 servings.

Mrs. Harvey C. Hamann, Aiken, S. C.

CARROT CASSEROLE

2 c. cooked carrots, mashed
1 c. cooked potatoes, mashed
1 tbsp. sugar
1 sm. onion, grated
1 sm. bell pepper, chopped
1 c. milk
2 tbsp. butter
Buttered bread crumbs
1 egg, separated

Mix all ingredients, folding in egg white last after whipping until stiff. Pour mixture into buttered casserole and top with buttered crumbs. Bake at 300 degrees for 45 minutes or until set. If top is not brown, run under broiler until golden. Yield: 6 servings.

Agnes Hunt, Birmingham, Ala.

CORN AND PEA CASSEROLE

1 10 ½-oz. can condensed cream of mushroom soup
¼ c. water
1 1 lb. 1 oz. can whole kernel corn, drained
1 1 lb. 1 oz. can peas, drained
1 tomato, sliced
2 tbsp. buttered bread crumbs

In a 1 1/2-quart casserole, combine soup, water, corn and peas. Top with tomato. Sprinkle with crumbs. Bake at 350 degrees for 30 minutes or until hot. Yield: 4-6 servings.

Susan Frugia, Venice, La.

EGGPLANT CASSEROLE

1 ½ lb. eggplant
6 tbsp. butter
1 med. onion, sliced thin
1 sm. can mushrooms, stems and pieces
1 c. canned tomatoes
1 c. grated cheese
1 tsp. salt
Pepper to taste
1 c. fine dry bread crumbs

Slice eggplant 1/2 inch thick. Pare off skin and dice to make 5 cups. Melt 3 tablespoons of butter in skillet and saute eggplant slowly for 5 minutes. Place in buttered casserole with alternate layers of sliced onion, mushrooms, tomatoes and 3/4 cup grated cheese. Season each layer with salt and pepper. Top with bread crumbs which have been mixed with remaining cheese. Dot with remaining butter. Bake at 375 degrees until vegetables are tender and top is nicely browned or about 35 minutes. Yield: 6 servings.

Eileen Aulenbach, Dallas, Tex.

GREEN BEAN CASSEROLE

1 bud garlic
1 1-lb. can French green beans, drained
1 can fancy mixed vegetables, drained
½ jar sliced pimentos, well drained
1 can mushroom soup
Dash of salt
1 c. grated cheddar cheese
1 can onion rings

(Continued on next page)

Butter casserole and rub garlic bud around dish. Add layers of French green beans, mixed vegetables, pimentos and mushroom soup in that order. Add salt and top with cheese. Cook in a 400-degree oven for 15 to 20 minutes or until cheese is bubbly. Put onion rings on top of casserole. Return to oven until top is browned, about 5 minutes. Yield: 4-6 servings.

Mrs. Louise W. Peck, Fayetteville, Tenn.

OKRA AND FRESH CORN CASSEROLE

3 c. cut okra
4 tbsp. butter or margarine
6 ears corn
Salt and pepper to taste
2 tbsp. flour
1 c. milk
¼ lb. sharp cheese
1 c. bread or cracker crumbs

Wash okra and drain well. Place in skillet with 2 tablespoons butter and cook slowly until the sticky substance has disappeared, stirring frequently. Cut corn from cob. Place okra and corn in alternate layers in greased casserole, sprinkling with salt and pepper. Then make a sauce with remaining butter, flour and milk. Stir well and do not brown. Add cheese; stir until melted. Pour over okra and corn; cover with crumbs. Bake at 350 degrees for 30 minutes or until slightly browned. Yield: 6 servings.

Mrs. J. Norris Hanning, New Orleans, La.

POTATO-ASPARAGUS CASSEROLE

3 med. potatoes
2 lge. onions
3 hard-boiled eggs
1 can asparagus tidbits
1 can cream of mushroom soup
Cracker crumbs
Paprika
Butter

Slice potatoes, onions and eggs. Arrange layers of potatoes, onions, asparagus, eggs and soup in casserole. Add second layer in same order. Top with cracker crumbs; sprinkle with paprika. Dot with butter. Grated cheese may be added. Bake at 350 degrees for 1 hour and 30 minutes. Yield: 6-8 servings.

Mrs. A. B. Grant, San Juan, Tex.

SPRING CASSEROLE

8 sm. new potatoes
8 baby carrots
1 sm. cauliflower
8 sm. onions
1 c. fresh or frozen peas
½ lb. American cheese
2 c. med. cream sauce
Parsley

Break cauliflower into flowerets. Cook vegetables until tender and drain well. Place in a casserole. Add sliced American cheese to hot cream sauce and stir until cheese is melted. Pour sauce over vegetables and place casserole in a 350-degree oven; bake for 20 minutes or until thoroughly heated. Garnish with parsley.

(Continued on next page)

MEDIUM CREAM SAUCE:

4 tbsp. butter
4 tbsp. flour
1 tsp. salt
2 c. milk

Melt butter in saucepan; add flour and salt. Blend until smooth. Gradually stir in cold milk and cook over direct heat stirring constantly until sauce boils and becomes thick and smooth. If lumps appear beat with rotary beater. Yield: 6 servings.

Evelyn J. Bailey, Louisville, Ky.

SPINACH CASSEROLE

1 3-oz. pkg. cream cheese
1 block butter or margarine
1 pkg. frozen chopped spinach
1 can water chestnuts
Salt and pepper to taste
1 sm. can artichoke hearts, packed in water
Bread crumbs

Cream cheese and butter; add prepared drained spinach. Slice water chestnuts very fine and add to spinach mixture. Salt and pepper mixture to taste. Line a 1 1/2-quart casserole dish with artichoke hearts and fill with spinach mixture. Top with bread crumbs and bake at 325 degrees until bubbly, about 25 to 30 minutes. Yield: 4 servings.

Mrs. Joseph P. Giustiniano, Gretna, La.

SQUASH CASSEROLE

3 c. cooked squash
½ c. chopped onion
½ c. chopped mushrooms
½ c. asparagus, chopped
½ tsp. salt
½ tsp. celery salt
¼ tsp. black pepper
2 eggs, well beaten
½ c. milk
1 c. cracker crumbs
1 can French-fried onions

Boil squash and onion till tender. Drain; combine with mushrooms, asparagus, salt, pepper and eggs. Pour into casserole. Add milk; cover with cracker crumbs. Bake at 350 degrees till firm. Remove from oven; arrange onion rings over top. Return to oven long enough to crisp onions.

Mrs. T. W. Nicholson, Eastmon, Ga.

VEGETABLE CASSEROLE

1 can cream-style corn
1 can drained English peas
1 can drained tomatoes, chopped
1 sm. onion, chopped
3 eggs, slightly beaten
1 stick melted oleo
½ c. bread crumbs

Combine first 4 ingredients; add eggs, oleo and bread crumbs. Cook 40 to 45 minutes at 325 to 350 degrees. Sprinkle grated cheese over top and return to oven until cheese melts.

Mrs. Frank Hester, Memphis, Tenn.

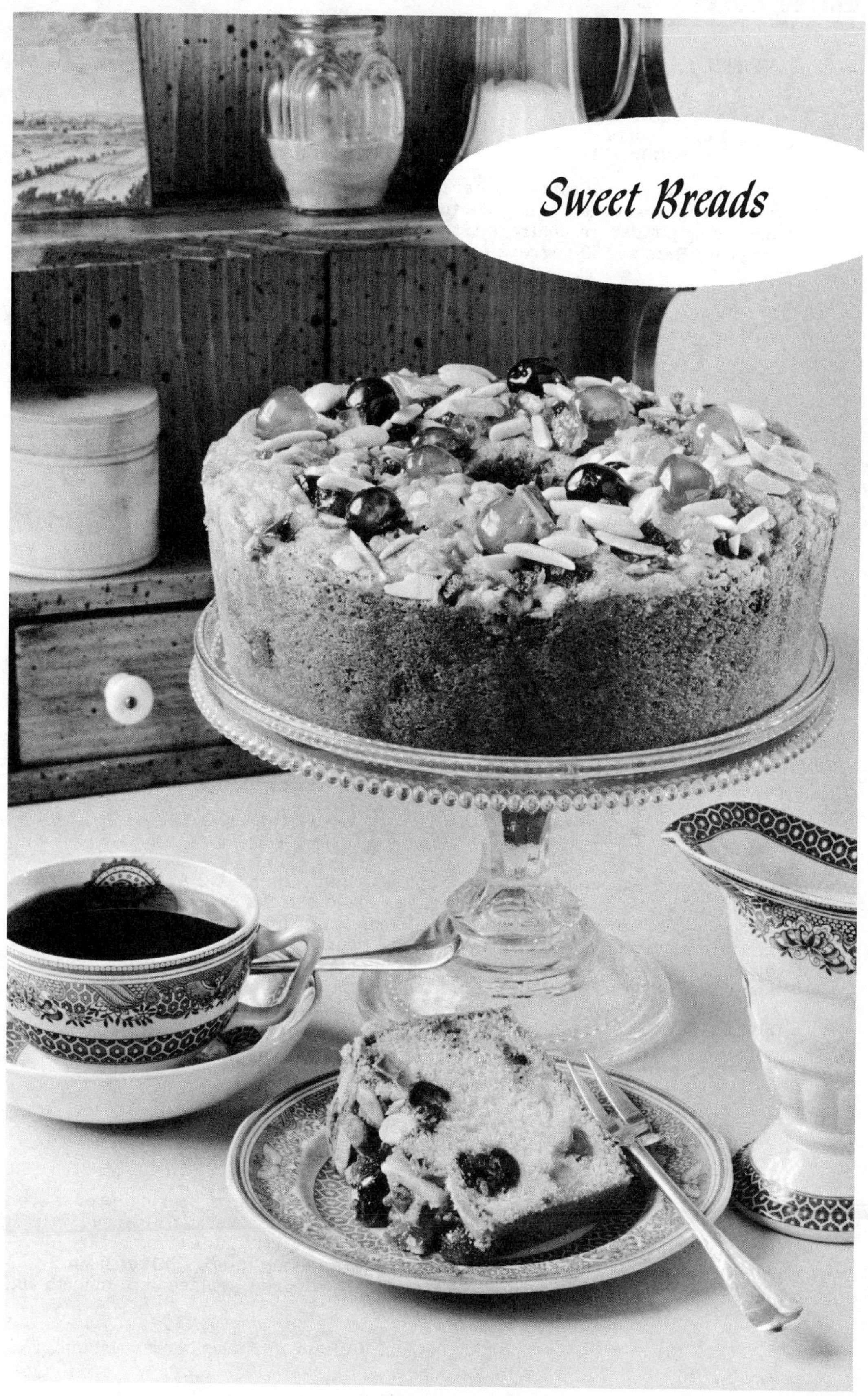

RECIPE FOR FRUITED SOUR CREAM COFFEE CAKE ON PAGE 298

APRICOT COFFEE CAKE

1 c. finely cut dried apricots
1 c. currants
1 c. butter
1 ½ c. sugar
4 eggs
2 ½ c. flour
1 tsp. baking powder

Soak apricots and currants in water for 1 hour; drain well in strainer. Cream butter and sugar well; add an egg at a time, beating well. Add fruits. Add sifted flour and baking powder gradually, stirring well. Pour into greased and floured 8 x 5-inch pan. Bake at 350 degrees for 1 hour or until done.

Mrs. Violet S. Seelhorst, Galveston, Tex.

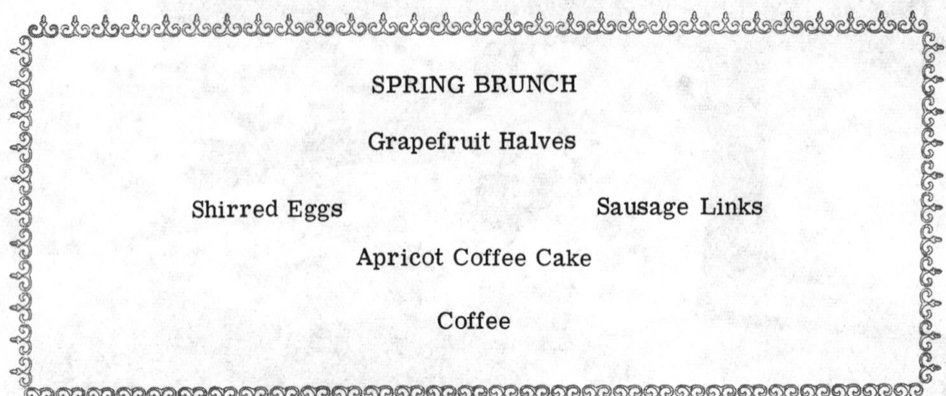

SPRING BRUNCH

Grapefruit Halves

Shirred Eggs   Sausage Links

Apricot Coffee Cake

Coffee

BUBBLE COFFEE RING

1 c. firmly packed brown sugar
2 tsp. cinnamon
Sweet Dough Recipe
½ c. butter or margarine, melted
1 c. toasted chopped filberts
¼ c. golden raisins

Mix brown sugar and cinnamon. Shape dough into 1-inch balls; dip in butter and coat with sugar and cinnamon mixture. Place half the balls in well-greased 9-inch tube pan; sprinkle with half the filberts and raisins. Repeat. Cover; let rise in warm place until doubled in bulk, about 1 hour. Bake at 375 degrees for 1 hour, or until cake tests done. Cool in pan 10 minutes. Invert pan on serving dish. Let stand several minutes before removing pan.

SWEET DOUGH:

½ c. milk
½ c. sugar
1 tsp. salt
½ c. butter or margarine, softened
2 pkg. active dry yeast
½ c. warm water
2 eggs, slightly beaten
1 tbsp. grated lemon peel
4 ½ c. sifted all-purpose flour

Scald milk; stir in sugar, salt and butter. Cool to lukewarm. Sprinkle yeast over warm water in large bowl; let stand 5 minutes. Stir yeast until blended. Stir in milk mixture, eggs, lemon peel and 2 cups flour; beat until smooth. Stir in remaining flour to make soft dough. Cover with damp towel. Chill at least 2 to 3 hours or overnight. Knead dough on lightly floured surface until smooth and elastic.

Mrs. William R. Eichenberger, Miami, Fla.

COBBLESTONE COFFEE CAKE

½ c. milk
½ c. shortening
½ c. sugar
½ tsp. salt
1 pkg. dry yeast
¼ c. warm water
3 to 3½ c. sifted flour
2 eggs, beaten
¼ c. melted butter or margarine
⅔ c. brown sugar
½ tsp. cinnamon
½ c. raisins
½ c. nuts, chopped
½ c. mixed candied fruit, chopped

Scald milk; add shortening, sugar and salt. Stir until sugar dissolves. Cool to lukewarm. Dissolve yeast in water and combine with milk mixture. Stir in half the flour; add eggs and beat well. Add enough remaining flour to make a soft dough. Turn out on lightly floured board; knead till smooth and elastic. Place in greased bowl and brush with shortening; cover and let rise in a warm place, 80 to 85 degrees until doubled in size, about 2 hours. Punch down and form into 1-inch balls. Roll each ball in butter; then in a mixture of brown sugar and cinnamon. Place a layer of balls in 9-inch pan and sprinkle with raisins, nuts and fruit. Cover with another layer of balls and repeat until all dough has been used. Cover and let rise until doubled in size. Bake at 350 degrees for 40 minutes. Yield: 24 pieces.

Mrs. Rogers Whittington, Van Buren, Ark.

CORNFLAKE COFFEE CAKE

1½ c. sifted flour
1 tsp. cinnamon
1 tsp. baking powder
½ tsp. soda
½ tsp. salt
½ c. butter or margarine
1 c. white sugar
2 eggs
2 c. cornflakes
1 c. sour cream
½ c. (packed) brown sugar
½ c. finely chopped pecans

Sift flour with cinnamon, baking powder, soda and salt. Cream butter; add white sugar and cream well. Add eggs and beat well. Crush cornflakes to make 1 cup crumbs. Add dry ingredients alternately with sour cream; stir in 1/2 cup cornflake crumbs. Combine remaining crumbs, brown sugar and pecans; mix. Spoon 1/2 of batter into greased 9 x 9 x 2-inch pan; sprinkle with 1/2 of crumb mixture. Bake at 350 degrees for 40 minutes or until done. Cut into squares to serve. Yield: 18-20 servings.

Mrs. Novella Shoaf, Hickory, N. C.

CRUNCHY COFFEE CAKE

⅔ c. brown sugar
2 tbsp. butter
1 c. chopped nuts
2 c. plus 2 tbsp. sifted flour
¾ c. white sugar
2 tsp. baking powder
½ tsp. salt
1 tsp. cinnamon
¼ tsp. nutmeg
⅓ c. shortening
1 c. milk
2 eggs

Combine brown sugar, butter, nuts and 2 tablespoonfuls flour; chill. Sift dry ingredients. Add shortening and milk; beat for 1 minute and 30 seconds. Add eggs; beat for 1 minute and 30 seconds. Pour 1/3 of batter into greased baking dish. Sprinkle 1/2 of chilled topping over batter. Cover with remaining batter; sprinkle with remaining topping. Bake at 350 degrees for 35 to 40 minutes. Yield: 6-8 servings.

Mrs. Cleo H. Lemons, Sandy Ridge, N. C.

FRUITED SOUR CREAM COFFEE CAKE

1 c. fruitcake fruit
½ c. chopped almonds
2 c. plus 1 tbsp. sifted all-purpose flour
1 ¼ c. sugar
1 tsp. cinnamon
1 tsp. baking powder
1 tsp. baking soda
1 tsp. salt
½ c. butter
1 tsp. almond extract
2 eggs
1 c. sour cream

In small mixing bowl, lightly toss candied fruit, almonds and 1 tablespoon flour until fruit is coated. Blend 1/4 cup sugar and cinnamon. Sift together 2 cups flour, baking powder, baking soda and salt. In large mixing bowl beat butter, sugar and almond extract until light and fluffy. Add 1 egg at a time, beating well after each addition. Stir in flour mixture alternately with sour cream, starting and ending with dry ingredients. Turn half the batter into greased 8-inch tube pan. Sprinkle half the fruit-nut mixture onto batter. Sprinkle on half the sugar, cinnamon mixture; repeat. With a twisting motion, pass a knife through the batter a few times to swirl in the flavorings. Bake in 350-degree oven until cake tester inserted in center comes out clean, about 50 minutes. Cool in pan, top side up, on a wire rack; remove cake from pan and finish cooling on wire rack.

Photograph for this recipe on page 295.

FRUIT ROLL

2 c. sifted plain flour
2 tbsp. sugar
3 tsp. baking powder
1 tsp. salt
6 tbsp. shortening
⅔ to ¾ c. milk
3 c. finely cut-up fruit
1 tbsp. butter
½ tsp. cinnamon

Sift dry ingredients together; cut shortening into mixture until fine. Stir in milk to make soft dough. Knead lightly; roll 1/3 inch thick into an oblong sheet. Spread with 3 cups fruit. Dot with butter and cinnamon. Roll into oblong roll as a jelly roll; place in greased 13 x 9-inch pan and lightly brown at 450 degrees. Reduce heat to 350 degrees and pour boiling syrup over roll. Cook approximately 30 minutes longer.

SYRUP:

1 ½ c. sugar
2 c. liquid (either juice left from fruit or water)
1 stick oleo

Combine ingredients. Yield: 8 servings.

Mrs. Marie R. Duggan, Kite, Ga.

LAURA'S COFFEE CAKE

1 ½ c. flour
1 tsp. baking powder
¼ lb. margarine
1 c. plus 2 tbsp. sugar
2 eggs
1 c. sour cream
1 tsp. soda
1 tsp. vanilla favoring
1 tbsp. cinnamon

Sift flour with baking powder. Cream margarine; gradually add 1 cup sugar. Blend in an egg at a time, beating well after each addition. Combine sour cream with soda. Add alternately with sifted dry ingredients to the creamed mixture. Blend in

(Continued on next page)

vanilla. Pour 1/2 of batter into greased 9-inch round springform pan. Sprinkle with mixture of remaining sugar and cinnamon. Cover with remaining batter. Combine flour and sugar; cut in margarine. Sprinkle over top of coffee cake. Bake at 350 degrees for 45 minutes. Yield: 16 servings.

Laura Whitcomb, Enterprise, Ala.

MORAVIAN SUGAR CAKE

1 pkg. yeast
½ c. lukewarm water
1 c. hot mashed potatoes
1 c. white sugar
4 tbsp. butter, softened
½ c. shortening
1 tsp. salt
1 c. potato water
2 eggs, beaten
Flour
Brown sugar
Ciinnamon

Soak yeast in water for a few minutes. Combine mashed potatoes, white sugar, soft butter, shortening and salt. Add yeast and potato water. Let rise in warm place until spongy. Add eggs and enough flour to make a soft dough. Let rise until doubled in bulk. Punch down and spread in pans. When light, make holes for pieces of additional butter and brown sugar; dust with cinnamon. Bake at 375 degrees for about 20 minutes.

Mrs. Carlton H. Dunlap, Walnut Cove, N. C.

SOUR CREAM COFFEE CAKE

½ lb. margarine
1 c. sugar
2 eggs
1 tsp. vanilla
2 c. flour
1 tsp. baking powder
1 tsp. baking soda
¼ tsp. salt
1 c. sour cream
Filling

Cream margarine and sugar; add eggs and vanilla. Sift dry ingredients together; add alternately with sour cream to mixture. Pour half of batter in greased tube pan; sprinkle with half of filling. Add remaining batter; sprinkle on topping. Bake at 350 degrees for 45 minutes.

FILLING:

¼ c. sugar
½ c. nuts, chopped
1 tbsp. cinnamon

Mix ingredients well.

Mrs. T. P. Adams, Matthews, N. C.

SOUR CREAM COFFEE CAKE

1 c. butter
1 ¼ c. sugar
2 eggs, lightly beaten
1 c. sour cream
1 tsp. vanilla
2 c. flour
½ tsp. baking soda
1 tsp. baking powder
¼ c. sugar
½ tsp. cinnamon

(Continued on next page)

Cream butter and sugar well. Add eggs, sour cream and vanilla; beat thoroughly. Sift together flour, soda and baking powder; gradually add to sour cream mixture. Pour half of batter into a greased 9 x 13-inch pan; sprinkle with half of mixed sugar and cinnamon. Add remaining batter; top with remaining sugar mixture. Bake at 350-degrees for 30 minutes. Yield: 12 servings.

Mrs. R. W. Menius, Asheboro, N. C.

SOUR CREAM COFFEE CAKE

Sugar
2 sticks margarine
2 eggs
½ pt. sour cream
2 c. flour
½ tsp. soda
1 ½ tsp. baking powder
1 tsp. vanilla flavoring
2 tsp. cinnamon
1 c. chopped nuts

Combine 1 1/4 cups sugar, margarine and eggs in mixing bowl; beat until fluffy. Blend in sour cream. Add flour, soda and baking powder to creamed mixture. Add vanilla; blend well. Spoon 1/2 of batter into buttered and floured tube pan. Mix 1/2 cup sugar, cinnamon and nuts; sprinkle 1/2 of mixture over batter. Repeat with a layer of batter and top with remaining nut mixture. Place in cold oven. Set temperature at 350 degrees. Bake for 55 minutes. Yield: 20 servings.

Mrs. John J. Marlow, Andrews, Tex.

SOUR CREAM COFFEE CAKE

2 c. sifted cake flour
1 tsp. baking powder
1 tsp. soda
¼ tsp. salt
½ c. butter
1 ¼ c. sugar
1 tsp. vanilla flavoring
2 eggs
1 c. sour cream
1 tbsp. cinnamon
¼ c. chopped pecans

Sift cake flour with baking powder, soda and salt on paper. Cream butter, 1 cup sugar and vanilla thoroughly in large bowl; beat in an egg at a time. Stir in sifted dry ingredients in four additions alternately with sour cream, beating just until smooth each time. Turn 1/2 the batter into greased and floured 9 x 3-inch angel food cake pan. Combine remaining sugar, cinnamon and pecans; sprinkle 1/2 the nut mixture over batter. Add remaining batter. Sprinkle with remaining nut mixture. Bake at 350 degrees for 40 minutes or until done. Yield: 6-8 servings.

Marilyn Truitt, Charleston, S. C.

STREUSEL-FILLED COFFEE CAKE

¾ c. sugar
¼ c. shortening
1 egg
½ c. milk
1 ½ c. sifted flour
2 tsp. baking powder
½ tsp. salt

Mix sugar, shortening and egg thoroughly. Stir in milk. Sift together dry ingredients; stir into mixture. Spread 1/2 of the batter in greased and floured 9-inch square pan.

(Continued on next page)

STREUSEL:

½ c. brown sugar
2 tbsp. flour
2 tsp. cinnamon
2 tbsp. butter, melted
½ c. chopped nuts

Mix all ingredients well; sprinkle batter with 1/2 of streusel mixture. Add remaining batter; sprinkle remaining streusel mixture over top. Bake at 375 degrees for 25 to 35 minutes.

Elgie Hurley, Randleman, N. C.

VIENNESE SWEET BREAD

Flour
Sugar
3 tsp. baking powder
1 tsp. soda
½ tsp. salt
3 eggs, slightly beaten
¾ c. oil
1 tsp. vanilla flavoring
¼ c. sour milk or sour cream
Cinnamon
Raisins
Chopped nuts

Sift 3 1/2 cups flour with 1 cup sugar, baking powder, soda and salt into large bowl. Add eggs, oil, flavoring and milk; mix well with rubber spatula or wooden spoon. Turn out onto a well-floured board. Knead dough until smooth, using 1/2 cup flour. Divide dough into four parts; pat each part out into 9 x 4-inch rectangle. Sprinkle with a sugar-cinnamon mixture; top with raisins and nuts. Roll up like jelly rolls and place on ungreased cookie sheets. Sprinkle rolls with sugar and a small amount of water. Bake in preheated 400-degree oven for 5 minutes; lower heat to 375 degrees and bake for 15 minutes longer. Cool on rack.

Mrs. Walter Bertsch, Andrews, Tex.

YAM ROLL

⅔ c. eggs (3 large)
1 c. sugar
5 tbsp. water
1 tsp. vanilla
1 c. flour
1 tsp. baking powder
¼ tsp. salt

Preheat oven to 375 degrees. Grease and flour 15 x 10 7/8-inch jelly roll pan. Beat eggs until thick; gradually beat in sugar. Beat in water, vanilla, flour, baking powder and salt all at one time. Beat until smooth; pour in prepared pan. Bake until it tests done about 12 to 15 minutes. Sprinkle powdered sugar on towel; turn cake onto cloth. Fold hem of towel over long edge; roll cake gently, rolling towel in it. Cool on wire rack, seam side down. If cake is warm, filling will melt.

FILLING:

¼ c. light brown sugar
2 eggs
⅛ tsp. salt
1 c. yams, mashed
¼ tsp. allspice
1 tbsp. butter
½ c. chopped nuts
½ tsp. vanilla
1 c. whipping cream

Cook sugar, eggs, salt and mashed yams in saucepan, stirring constantly until thick. When cooked turn heat off and add allspice, butter, chopped nuts and vanilla. Set aside to cool. When cool, add 1/2 cup whipped cream. Top with remaining

(Continued on next page)

whipping cream, 2 tablespoons additional sugar and 1 tablespoon additional vanilla, if desired. Yield: 10 servings.

Vivian J. Ryland, Effie, La.

CORNMEAL DOUGHNUTS

¾ c. sweet milk
1 ½ c. very fine white cornmeal
½ c. butter
¾ c. sugar
2 eggs
1 ½ c. white flour
2 tsp. baking powder
¼ tsp. cinnamon
1 tsp. salt

Heat milk; stir in cornmeal and let cook for 10 minutes. Add butter, sugar, eggs and flour sifted with baking powder, cinnamon and salt. Roll out on floured board; cut. Fry in deep hot cooking oil until browned. Drain well and roll in sugar.

Mrs. Samuel T. Smith, Huntsville, Ala.

YEAST DOUGHNUTS

⅔ c. milk, scalded
⅓ c. water
⅓ c. plus 1 tsp. sugar
1 pkg. yeast
½ c. shortening
2 eggs
1 c. mashed potatoes
1 tsp. salt
1 tsp. vanilla
4 c. flour

Combine all ingredients and mix well. Let rise until doubled in size; work down and roll out 1/4 inch thick. Cut with doughnut cutter; let rise until doubled in size. Fry in hot oil. Drain well. Yield: 3 dozen.

Mrs. Eugene Saling, Pindall, Ark.

RAISED DOUGHNUTS

1 c. milk
⅔ c. sugar
3 tbsp. shortening
1 tsp. salt
1 cake yeast or 1 pkg. dry yeast
2 tbsp. lukewarm water
5 c. flour
2 eggs, well beaten
1 tsp. nutmeg

Scald milk; add sugar, shortening and salt. Let cool to lukewarm. Add yeast to water. Add yeast mixture to milk. Add 2 cups flour or enough to make spongy; set in warm place to rise. When light, add eggs, nutmeg and remaining flour or enough to make a soft dough. Cover; let rise until double in bulk. Knead until free from large bubbles. Roll out on slightly floured board 1/2 inch thick. Cut with doughnut cutter; cover and set in warm place to rise again until double in bulk. Drop doughnuts topside down in deep hot fat, 370 degrees. Fry until puffy and brown on underside; turn and fry on other side. Drain on absorbent paper; sprinkle with powdered sugar while still warm. Yield: 30 doughnuts.

Mrs. Elsie S. Trader, Benson, N. C.

DOUGHNUTS

1 can biscuits
1 ½ c. cooking oil
1 c. powdered sugar
1 tsp. cinnamon

Cut centers out of biscuits; fry in deep fat until golden brown, turning once. Shake the doughnuts in sugar and cinnamon until covered. Serve while warm. Yield: 10 servings.

Mrs. Shelton Edge, Roseboro, N. C.

GRANDMOTHER'S DOUGHNUTS

½ c. mashed potatoes
¾ c. sugar
1 egg
½ c. milk
2 c. flour
2 ½ tsp. baking powder
½ tsp. salt
½ tsp. nutmeg

Combine potatoes, sugar, egg and milk; sift dry ingredients and add. Roll out dough and cut with doughnut cutter. Drop into deep fat; fry until golden brown. Roll in powdered sugar or granulated sugar. Yield: 3 dozen.

Mrs. Paul Katonak, Aiken, S. C.

APRICOT BREAD

3 c. flour
2 ¼ c. sugar
1 ½ t. salt
1 ½ tsp. soda
1 ½ tsp. cinnamon
4 eggs
1 ⅓ c. cooking oil
1 ½ c. cooked apricots
1 c. chopped pecans

Combine dry ingredients in mixing bowl; add eggs and oil. Beat until smooth, then add apricots. Mix thoroughly and add nuts. Prepare pan or pans by greasing and dusting with flour. Bake at 325 degrees for 1 hour and 15 minutes or until done. Yield: 18-20 servings.

Mrs. Carl Adams, Perryville, Ark.

APRICOT-NUT LOAF

2 c. flour
3 tsp. baking powder
¼ tsp. soda
½ tsp. salt
1 c. sugar
1 c. chopped dried apricots
½ c. orange juice
⅓ c. cold water
1 egg, beaten
3 tbsp. melted shortening
½ c. chopped nuts

Sift first 5 ingredients together; blend in remaining ingredients. Bake for 1 hour at 325 degrees in greased loaf pan.

Mrs. C. C. Weigle, Lubbock, Tex.

BANANA BREAD

1 ¾ c. sifted flour
2 tsp. baking powder
¼ tsp. soda
½ tsp. salt
⅓ c. shortening
⅔ c. sugar
2 eggs
1 c. mashed ripe bananas
½ c. chopped walnuts

Sift together flour, baking powder, soda and salt. Beat shortening until creamy in medium mixing bowl; add sugar gradually and continue beating until light and fluffy. Add eggs; beat well. Add flour mixture alternately with bananas. Stir in nuts. Turn into an 8 1/2 x 4 1/2 x 2 1/2-inch loaf pan. Bake in a 350-degree oven for 1 hour.

Mrs. Martha Wolfe, Tampa, Fla.

BANANA CORNMEAL LOAF

1 c. cornmeal
1 c. flour
3 tsp. baking powder
1 tsp. salt
⅔ c. sugar
2 eggs
1 c. mashed ripe bananas
½ c. melted shortening
1 c. chopped nuts

Sift together first 5 ingredients. Beat eggs well; add mashed bananas and melted shortening. Add dry mixture. Stir until well blended. Add chopped nuts. Stir lightly. Grease bottom of loaf pan. Sprinkle lightly with additional cornmeal. Pour batter into pan. Bake at 350 degrees 60 to 70 minutes or until bread is done. Cool in pan 20 to 30 minutes before turning out on rack. Cool thoroughly before slicing or wrapping for storage.

Mrs. Fred Gibbons, Houston, Tex.

BANANA-NUT BREAD

½ c. butter or margarine
1 c. sugar
2 eggs, well beaten
3 ripe bananas, crushed
1 tsp. soda
2 c. flour
¼ c. chopped nuts

Cream butter and sugar. Add eggs, then bananas. Sift soda and flour together; add to creamed mixture. Add nuts. Place in large greased and floured loaf pan. Bake in 350-degree oven for 45 minutes or until toothpick inserted comes out clean.

Mrs. Jack Rich, Oak Ridge, Tenn.

SAVANNAH BREAD

⅓ c. shortening
¾ c. chunk-style peanut butter
⅔ c. sugar
2 eggs
1 c. mashed ripe bananas
1 ¾ c. sifted flour
2 tsp. baking powder
½ tsp. salt
¼ tsp. soda
¼ c. buttermilk

(Continued on next page)

Cream shortening; add peanut butter. Gradually add sugar, creaming until light and fluffy. Add eggs, 1 at a time, beating well after each addition. Stir in mashed bananas. Sift together remaining dry ingredients; add alternately with buttermilk, mixing until well blended. Spoon batter into greased loaf pan. Bake at 350 degrees 1 hour or until center tests done. Cool on rack.

Mrs. Joe E. Deaton, Jackson, Tenn.

BANANA-CHERRY-NUT BREAD

1 stick margarine
1 c. sugar
3 eggs
3 or 4 mashed ripe bananas
1 c. raisins
½ c. pecans
2 c. flour
1 tsp. salt
½ tsp. soda
⅓ c. maraschino cherries
1 t. vanilla

Cream margarine until fluffy; add sugar and beat well. Add eggs, 1 at a time, beating after each addition. Add bananas, beating well. Dredge raisins and nuts in 1 cup flour. Add salt and soda to remaining flour; add this to butter mixture. Add raisins, nuts, cherries and vanilla to mixture. Pour into loaf pan lined with waxed paper. Bake at 325 degrees until straw emerges clean. Yield: 12 servings.

Joye Weaver, Leonard, Tex.

BISHOP'S BREAD

1 c. sugar
3 eggs
4 tbsp. baking powder
1 ½ tsp. salt
1 ½ c. flour
⅓ c. cherry juice
1 c. chopped dates
1 c. maraschino cherries
2 c. nuts
1 pkg. chocolate bits

Mix as for any loaf cake, using cherry juice instead of milk. If mixture seems to be too soft, add more flour; add chopped dates, cherries, nuts and chocolate bits last. Bake in a loaf or tube cake pan in a medium oven. Yield: 15 servings.

Mrs. Mildred Drinkard, Collinsville, Miss.

BOSTON BROWN BREAD

1 c. cornmeal
1 c. rye flour
1 c. graham flour
¾ tbsp. soda
1 tsp. salt
¾ c. molasses
2 c. sour milk or 1 ¾ c. sweet milk

Mix and sift all dry ingredients. Mix molasses and milk; add to dry ingredients and beat thoroughly. Turn into well-greased molds. Fill each about 2/3 full. Cover and steam for 3 hours. Remove covers and bake at 375 degrees long enough to dry bread.

Mrs. Edna Williams, Jacksonville, Ala.

BRUNCH CINNAMON BREAD

2 cakes yeast
¼ c. lukewarm water
1 c. milk
¼ c. shortening
½ c. sugar
1 tsp. salt
5 to 6 c. sifted all-purpose flour
2 eggs, beaten
2 tsp. melted butter
1 tbsp. cinnamon
1 c. spiced jelly beans or gum drops (opt.)

Soften yeast in water. Scald milk; add shortening, sugar and salt, stirring until shortening is melted. Stir in 2 cups flour; beat until smooth. Add yeast and eggs; combine thoroughly. Add enough flour to make a soft dough, about 3 cups. Toss onto a floured board and knead until satiny. Place in a greased bowl; brush top of dough lightly with melted fat. Cover and let rise in a warm place until doubled in bulk, about 2 hours. Divide dough in half and roll each half into a 6 x 16-inch rectangle about 1/2 inch thick. Spread very lightly with melted butter; sprinkle with cinnamon and jelly beans. Roll up as a jelly roll. Place each roll in a greased loaf pan; brush tops with melted butter. Let rise in a warm place until triple in bulk, about 1 hour and 30 minutes. Brush tops again with melted butter. Bake at 375 degrees for 50 minutes or until loaf is slightly browned and shrinks slightly from sides of pan. Place hot pans on cooling rack before turning out.

Mrs. John F. McCloskey, Sanford, Fla.

BUTTERMILK-NUT BREAD

1 egg
2 c. sugar
2 tbsp. melted shortening
2 c. sifted flour
¾ tsp. baking powder
1 tsp. soda
1 tsp. salt
1 c. buttermilk
1 c. chopped nuts

Beat eggs well. Beat in sugar and shortening until smooth and creamy. Sift flour; measure and sift again with baking powder, soda and salt. Add alternately with buttermilk to egg mixture. Fold in 3/4 cup nuts. Pour into oiled and floured pan; sprinkle remaining nuts on top. Bake at 350 degrees for 1 hour. Let set for 1 day before serving.

Mrs. W. G. Harper, Bessemer, Ala.

CARROT BREAD

2 c. flour
2 tsp soda
2 tsp. cinnamon
½ tsp. salt
1 ½ c. sugar
½ c. flaked coconut
½ c. chopped pecans
1 c. vegetable oil
2 tsp. vanilla extract
2 c. grated raw carrots
3 eggs

Mix dry ingredients together; add coconut and pecans. Mix in remaining ingredients. Pour into greased 9 x 5 x 3-inch loaf pan; let stand 20 minutes. Bake at 350 degrees about 1 hour. Cool slightly; remove from pan. When cold, wrap and refrigerate. Cut into slices to serve.

Mrs. C. E. Barnette, Johnson City, Tenn.

Abraham Lincoln's log cabin birthplace in Kentucky.

CARROT BREAD

- 1 c. sugar
- ⅔ c. cooking oil
- 2 eggs, beaten
- ¼ tsp. salt
- 1 tsp. baking powder
- 1 tsp. soda
- 1 tsp. nutmeg
- 1 tsp. cinnamon
- 1 ½ c. flour
- 2 c. grated carrots

Mix all ingredients. Pour into a greased or waxed paper-lined loaf pan. Bake at 325 degrees for 1 hour. Yield: 12 servings.

Mrs. John C. Edge, Hurst, Tex.

CRANBERRY-BANANA BREAD

- ¼ c. butter
- 1 c. sugar
- 1 egg
- 2 c. sifted flour
- 3 tsp. baking powder
- ½ tsp. salt
- ½ tsp. cinnamon
- 1 c. mashed bananas
- ¼ c. milk
- 1 tsp. grated orange rind
- 1 ½ c. diced cranberries
- 1 c. chopped pecans

Cream butter and sugar; add egg and beatwell. Add sifted dry ingredients alternately with mixture of bananas, milk and orange rind. Stir in cranberries and pecans. Turn into greased 9 x 5 x 3-inch loaf pan. Bake at 350 degrees for 1 hour and 5 minutes. Yield: 12 servings.

Mrs. M. D. Kenimer, Borger, Tex.

CRANBERRY BREAD

- 1 c. sugar
- 2 tbsp. vegetable oil
- 1 egg
- 2 c. sifted flour
- 2 tsp. baking powder
- 1 tsp. salt
- 1 tsp. soda
- ¾ c. orange juice
- Grated rind of 1 orange
- 1 c. cranberries, cut in halves
- ½ c. chopped nuts

(Continued on next page)

Cream sugar and oil; beat in egg. Sift dry ingredients together; add alternately to creamed mixture with orange juice. Fold in orange rind, cranberries and nuts. Pour into greased and floured loaf pan. Bake for 1 hour, or until done, in preheated 350-degree oven.

Mrs. Charles R. Owen, Memphis, Tenn.

CRANBERRY BREAD

3 c. sifted all-purpose flour
3 tsp. double-acting baking powder
1 ½ tsp. salt
½ tsp. soda
½ c. shortening
1 ½ c. sugar
2 eggs
¾ c. fresh orange juice
1 ½ tbsp. grated orange rind
¾ c. chopped nuts
2 ¼ c. fresh cranberries, coarsely chopped

Sift first 3 ingredients together and set aside. Add soda to shortening; mix well. Gradually blend in sugar. Beat in eggs, 1 at a time. Add flour mixture alternately with orange juice. Stir in orange rind, nuts and cranberries. Turn into well-greased, lightly floured 9 x 5 x 3 1/2-inch pan. Bake in 350-degree oven 1 hour and 30 minutes. Remove from pan and cool.

Mrs. Bill Adcock, Newbern, Tenn.

DATE-HONEY BREAD

1 ½ c. chopped dates
½ c. sugar
⅓ c. plus 2 tbsp. honey
2 tbsp. butter
1 c. boiling water
3 c. sifted flour
3 tsp. baking powder
½ tsp. salt
½ tsp. cinnamon
1 beaten egg
½ c. chopped walnuts
¼ c. confectioners' sugar
2 tbsp. grated orange rind

Combine dates, sugar, 1/3 cup honey, butter and water; cool thoroughly. Sift together dry ingredients. Add egg to cooled mixture; stir in dry ingredients just enough to mix well. Stir in walnuts. Bake in a well-greased 9 1/2 x 5 x 3-inch loaf pan at 350 degrees for 55 to 60 minutes or until loaf tests done. Remove from pan onto a wire rack. Blend confectioners' sugar with remaining honey. Spoon down center of bread; sprinkle with grated orange rind.

Mrs. John A. Fierro, Jr., Winter Haven, Fla.

DELICIOUS BRAN BREAD

1 c. All-Bran
1 c. sugar
1 c. raisins
1 c. milk
1 egg
1 c. self-rising flour
½ c. chopped nuts
¼ c. melted oleo

Combine first 4 ingredients; mix well and let stand, uncovered, overnight. Stir in remaining ingredients next morning. Pour into loaf pan. Bake at 325 degrees for 1 hour and 15 minutes.

Mrs. H. M. Williams, Savannah, Tenn.

DATE AND NUT LOAF

1 pkg. dates
1 ½ c. boiling water
1 stick butter
1 ½ c. sugar
1 tsp. salt
2 eggs, beaten
2 ⅔ to 3 c. flour
1 tsp. soda
1 tsp. cream of tartar
1 tsp. vanilla
1 c. nuts

Cut up dates; add boiling water, butter, sugar and salt. Set aside to cool. Add eggs when mixture is cool. Sift flour, soda and cream of tartar together; combine with date mixture. Add vanilla and nuts; mix together. Pour into greased and floured loaf pan. Bake at 325 degrees for 1 hour.

Della Woeford, Irvine, Ky.

HONEY-WHOLE WHEAT BREAD

1 c. milk
2 tbsp. sugar
1 tsp. salt
¼ c. butter
½ c. honey or molasses
2 pkg. active dry yeast
1 ½ c. warm water
3 ½ c. sifted all-purpose flour
4 c. unsifted whole wheat flour

Heat milk to a slow simmer; remove from heat. Add sugar, salt, butter and honey, stirring until butter melts. Cool to lukewarm. Sprinkle yeast over warm water in large bowl; stir until yeast dissolves. Stir in milk mixture. Add all-purpose flour and 2 1/2 cups whole wheat flour; beat until smooth, about 2 minutes. Gradually add remaining whole wheat flour. Mix with hands until dough leaves sides of bowl. Turn out onto lightly floured board; cover with bowl and let rest for 10 minutes. Knead about 10 minutes by folding down and away from you. Continue kneading until dough is smooth and elastic. Place in lightly greased bowl; turn dough to bring greased side to top. Cover with towel; let rise in warm place, away from draft, about 1 hour and 15 minutes or until doubled in bulk. Punch down dough; turn out onto floured pastry cloth and divide in half. Shape each half into smooth balls; cover with towel and let rest for 10 minutes. Shape each ball into a loaf; place in pan and brush with melted butter. Cover with towel; let rise until sides of dough reach top of pan. Bake at 400 degrees for 50 minutes. For variation add 1 cup finely chopped nuts or 1 1/2 cups seedless raisins with first addition of flour.

Mrs. F. C. Abraham, Tracy City, Tenn.

LEMON BREAD

1 c. margarine
2 c. sugar
4 eggs
½ tsp. salt
½ tsp. soda
3 c. flour
1 c. buttermilk
Grated rind of 1 lemon
1 c. chopped nuts
Juice of 3 lemons
1 c. confectioners' sugar

Cream margarine and sugar; blend in an egg at a time. Sift salt with soda and flour. Add to creamed mixture alternately with buttermilk. Fold in rind and nuts. Pour into 2 large greased loaf pans. Bake at 350 degrees for 40 minutes. Combine lemon juice and confectioners'sugar; let stand to allow sugar to dissolve. Turn bread out onto waxed paper or foil; spoon lemon juice and sugar mixture over hot bread. Yield: 12 servings.

Mrs. Dudley McCoy, Lake Charles, La.

LEMON GLAZED BREAD

⅓ c. melted margarine or butter
1 ¼ c. sugar
2 eggs
¼ tsp. almond extract
1 ½ c. sifted flour
1 tsp. salt
1 tsp. baking powder
½ c. milk
1 tsp. grated lemon peel
½ c. chopped nuts
3 tbsp. lemon juice

Preheat oven to 325 degrees. Grease ovenproof glass, loaf baking dish. Blend margarine and 1 cup sugar well; beat in an egg at a time and add extract. Sift dry ingredients together; add alternately with milk to egg mixture and blend just enough to mix. Fold in lemon peel and nuts. Pour into prepared baking dish. Bake for 70 minutes or until tests done in center. Mix lemon juice and remaining 1/4 cup sugar; stir until sugar dissolves. When bread is done spread with lemon sauce immediately. Cool in pan for 10 minutes before removing. Slices better after standing for a day. Freezes well.

Mrs. Ross Gutterrez, Hurst, Tex.

MAPLE-NUT BREAD

2 ½ c. flour
1 c. sugar
½ tsp. salt
3 tsp. baking powder
1 beaten egg
1 c. milk
¾ tsp. maple flavoring
1 c. chopped nuts

Combine all dry ingredients; stir in egg, milk and flavoring and mix well. Add chopped nuts. Pour into greased loaf pan. Bake at 350 degrees for 1 hour.

June Jones, Baton Rouge, La.

NEVER-FAIL GRAHAM BREAD

1 c. white flour
1 tsp. baking soda
½ tsp. salt
1 c. sugar
½ c. raisin-bran flakes
1 c. unsifted graham flour
1 c. milk

Sift white flour, soda and salt together; add sugar, bran flakes and graham flour. Mix all together well. Add milk. Pour into buttered loaf pan. Bake at 300 to 325 degrees for about 1 hour. Let cool about 10 minutes before removing from pan.

Mrs. Mable Rowland, Jacksonville, Fla.

NUT BREAD

1 c. graham flour
1 c. white flour
1 c. buttermilk
1 c. sugar
1 c. chopped nuts
1 c. raisins
1 tsp. baking powder
1 tsp. salt
½ tsp. soda

Mix all ingredients thoroughly. Pour in greased loaf pan. Bake at 325 degrees for 35 minutes.

Mrs. Wright King, Rome, Ga.

NEW-FASHIONED BOSTON BROWN BREAD

1 c. plus 1 tbsp. sifted all-purpose flour
1 c. white cornmeal
1 ½ tsp. baking powder
1 tsp. salt
¾ tsp. soda
1 c. whole wheat flour
1 egg, slightly beaten
2 tbsp. butter or margarine, melted
⅔ c. dark molasses
1 ⅔ c. buttermilk
1 c. shredded cheddar cheese
½ c. raisins

Sift together into mixing bowl, 1 cup all-purpose flour, cornmeal, baking powder, salt and soda; stir in wheat flour. Combine egg, butter or margarine, molasses and buttermilk; add to batter along with cheese. Stir only until blended. Toss raisins with remaining flour; stir into batter. Pour batter into well-greased loaf pan; cover top of pan with double thickness of foil. Place in shallow baking pan; surround loaf pan with water. Bake 2 hours in preheated 350-degree oven. Remove from oven; cool 10 minutes. Serve warm with butter.

Susan Toaz, Bradenton, Fla.

OATMEAL BREAD

1 cake yeast
¼ c. lukewarm water
½ c. shortening
2 c. oats
2 ½ c. boiling water
2 tsp. salt
¼ c. sugar
2 eggs, slightly beaten
⅓ c. instant milk crystals (opt.)
5 ½ c. flour

Dissolve yeast in lukewarm water. Mix shortening, oats, boiling water, salt and sugar; cool to lukewarm. Stir in eggs, yeast and milk; add flour. Cover; let rise for 45 minutes. Knead lightly on floured board; shape into two loaves. Let rise for 45 minutes. Bake at 350 degrees for 40 minutes. Remove from pan to cool. Yield: 2 loaves.

Elise Roach, Celina, Tenn.

ORANGE BREAD

4 oranges
1 ½ c. sugar
⅓ c. water
3 tbsp. butter
1 ⅓ c. orange juice
3 eggs, well beaten
4 c. sifted all-purpose flour
4 tsp. baking powder
½ tsp. soda
2 tsp. salt

Wash oranges; dry. Remove thin orange rind with a sharp knife, cutting around orange. Cut rind into very thin slivers with scissors or knife. Combine sugar and water. Add rind; stir constantly over low heat until sugar is dissolved. Cook slowly 5 minutes. The peel and syrup should measure 1 1/3 cups. Add butter; stir until melted. Add orange juice and beaten eggs. Sift flour, baking powder, soda and salt together into mixing bowl. Add orange mixture and mix just enough to moisten. Batter should be lumpy. Turn into waxed paper-lined and greased 9 x 5 x 3-inch loaf pan. Bake at 325 degrees 1 hour and 15 minutes. Turn out on rack to cool.

Mrs. Juanita S. Dorsey, Arkadelphia, Ark.

ORANGE BREAD

1 lge. thick-skinned orange, ground or grated
¼ c. sugar
1 ½ tsp. salt
¼ c. butter
1 cake yeast
1 egg, beaten
3 c. (about) flour

Add enough water to ground orange to make 1 cup. Combine orange mixture, sugar, salt and butter; bring to boil. Cool until lukewarm; add yeast, beating until smooth. Add egg and enough flour to make stiff dough. Knead for 5 minutes, adding flour to keep from sticking to board. Cover; let rise in a warm place until double in bulk. Knead for 1 minute on a floured board. Shape into loaf; put in 10 x 5 x 3 1/2-inch pan. Bake at 375 degrees until done.

Mrs. Charles B. Quade, Arlington, Va.

ORANGE-NUT BREAD

3 c. flour
4 tsp. baking powder
¼ tsp. salt
1 c. sugar
½ c. nuts
1 c. fresh orange juice
Grated rind of 1 orange
1 egg, slightly beaten
⅓ c. salad oil

Preheat oven to 325 degrees. Sift together dry ingredients; stir in nuts. Combine orange juice, orange rind, egg and oil. Blend into dry ingredients; do not beat. Pour in greased ovenproof glass baking pan. Bake for 45 minutes to 1 hour.

Mrs. Don Bolden, Burlington, N. C.

ORANGE-NUT BREAD

2 ¼ c. flour
¾ c. sugar
3 tsp. baking powder
1 tsp. salt
½ to 1 c. finely chopped orange peel
1 c. broken pecans
2 eggs, beaten
3 tbsp. melted butter or margarine

Sift first 4 ingredients; add orange peel and nuts. Combine eggs, milk and butter; stir into dry ingredients. Pour into greased loaf pan. Bake at 350 degrees for 55 minutes. Remove from pan. Cool on rack. Store for 1 to 2 days in airtight container. Slice thin.

Vida Butcher, Miami, Fla.

PEANUT BUTTER BREAD

2 c. flour
4 tsp. baking powder
1 tsp. salt
⅓ c. sugar
½ c. peanut butter
¾ c. evaporated milk, diluted with ¾ c. water

Sift together dry ingredients; cut in peanut butter. Add milk; beat thoroughly. Pour into a greased loaf pan. Bake at 350 degrees for about 1 hour.

Mrs. William E. Robbins, High Point, N. C.

PAWPAW-NUT BREAD

½ c. margarine
1 c. sugar
2 eggs
2 c. flour
1 tsp. soda
¼ tsp. salt
¼ c. nuts
1 c. pawpaw pulp
½ tsp. vanilla
¼ tsp. almond flavoring

Cream margarine and sugar; beat in eggs. Add dry ingredients. Stir in nuts, pawpaw pulp and flavoring. Pour into 9 x 9 x 2-inch pan. Bake at 350 degrees 30 minutes.

Mrs. Ray Colboch, Rogersville, Tenn.

PINEAPPLE QUICK BREAD

2 c. sifted flour
3 tsp. baking powder
½ tsp. soda
1 tsp. salt
¾ c. sugar
1 egg
1 8 ¾ -oz. can crushed pineapple
2 tbsp. melted butter, cooled
½ c. chopped walnuts

On a piece of waxed paper, sift flour, baking powder, soda, salt and sugar. In a medium mixing bowl, beat egg until thick; stir in undrained crushed pineapple and butter. Add sifted dry ingredients; stir until combined. Fold in walnuts. Turn into a greased ovenproof glass loaf dish. Bake at 325 degrees about 50 minutes or until cake tester comes out clean. Turn out on wire rack; turn right side up on rack. Cool. Loaf slices best after storing in tightly covered container overnight. If desired, fold in 1/2 cup medium fine grated sharp cheddar cheese into the batter with the walnuts.

Olive Manley, Pompano Beach, Fla.

POPPY SEED BREAD

1 tbsp. poppy seed
½ c. sweet milk
⅔ c. shortening
¾ c. sugar
2 eggs, beaten
2 c. flour
½ tsp. salt
2 tsp. baking powder
½ tsp. vanilla
1 tbsp. lemon rind

Soak poppy seed in milk. Cream shortening and sugar. Stir in eggs. Sift together flour, salt and baking powder. Add to creamed mixture alternately with milk-poppy seed mixture. Stir in vanilla and lemon rind. Place in greased and floured loaf pan. Bake at 325 degrees for 1 hour and 10 minutes. Cool for 5 minutes in pan.

Mrs. W. W. Jackson, Corpus Christi, Tex.

PUMPKIN BREAD

3 ⅓ c. flour
2 tsp. soda
1 to 1 ½ tsp. salt
1 to 3 tsp. cinnamon
1 to 2 tsp. nutmeg
3 c. sugar
4 eggs
2 c. pumpkin
1 c. cooking oil
⅔ c. cold water
1 c. raisins (opt.)
1 ½ c. pecans

Sift dry ingredients. Beat eggs until thick; add to dry ingredients. Add remaining ingredients except nuts; beat until blended. Fold in pecans. Turn into two greased 13 x 14-inch bread pans. Bake at 350 degrees for 1 hour. Bread may be baked in four 1-pound coffee cans. Bake at 325 degrees for 1 hour.

Mrs. R. H. Mackay, Hardy, Ark.

PUMPKIN BREAD

⅔ c. oleo
2 ⅔ c. sugar
4 eggs
1 1-lb. can pumpkin
⅔ c. water
3 ½ c. flour
½ tsp. baking powder
2 tsp. soda
1 ½ tsp. salt
½ tsp. nutmeg
1 tsp. cinnamon
⅔ c. chopped nuts
1 c. white raisins

Cream oleo and sugar together; add eggs, 1 at a time. Add pumpkin and water. Sift all dry ingredients together; stir in nuts and raisins. Mix pumpkin mixture and dry ingredients together. Grease pan and line with greased brown paper. Pour batter into pan. Bake at 350 degrees. Bake 1 large loaf for 1 hour and 20 minutes; 2 small loaves for 1 hour or until cracks in center.

Mrs. J. B. Francis, Marion, Va.

PUMPKIN BREAD

1 ½ c. sugar
¾ tsp. salt
¼ tsp. baking powder
1 tsp. soda
½ tsp. cinnamon
½ tsp. powdered cloves
½ tsp. nutmeg
½ c. water
½ c. salad oil
1 c. canned pumpkin
1 ⅔ c. flour
2 eggs, beaten
¾ c. raisins
¾ c. nuts, chopped

Combine all ingredients, except raisins and nuts; blend well. Stir in raisins and nuts. Bake in a greased pan for 1 hour at 350 degrees. Let cool 20 minutes before removing from pan.

Mrs. Robert F. Beyer, Sarasota, Fla.

RAISIN BREAD

2 pkg. yeast
1 c. lukewarm water
2 c. milk
1 c. sugar
1 tbsp. salt
½ c. salad oil
2 eggs, beaten
3 lb. flour
1 ½ 15-oz. boxes seedless raisins

(Continued on next page)

Dissolve yeast in lukewarm water. Heat milk to scalding; add sugar and salt and cool. Add oil to eggs; combine with yeast and sugar mixtures. Add flour to make stiff dough. Beat well with wooden spoon until dough slips from spoon. Place in warm place; let rise to double in bulk. Stir in raisins and more flour. Turn out onto floured board; knead. Place in bowl; let rise for 1 hour or double in bulk. Turn out; divide in three or four pieces according to pan size. Knead well until smooth; place in greased pan. Let rise to double in bulk. Bake in moderate oven for 40 minutes or until done. Yield: 40 servings.

Merle Turner, Springfield, Ga.

RAISIN BREAD

- 2/3 c. hot water
- 1/2 c. sugar
- 1 1/2 tsp. salt
- 1/4 c. shortening
- 2 pkg. active dry yeast
- 1/2 c. warm water
- 1 egg, beaten
- 3 1/4 c. sifted flour
- 1 c. seedless raisins

Combine hot water, sugar, salt and shortening; heat until shortening melts. Cool to lukewarm. Place yeast and warm water in a bowl; stir until yeast is dissolved. Add shortening mixture to yeast mixture and blend thoroughly. Add egg, flour and raisins; beat for 2 minutes. Cover bowl with a towel; let rise in warm place for 2 hours, until more than doubled. Pat down; beat for 30 seconds. Place in a greased 1 1/2-quart casserole. Bake at 400 degrees for 40 minutes. Cool in casserole.

Mrs. S. E. Reuter, Charleston, S. C.

RAISIN-GUMDROP BREAD

- 3 c. sifted flour
- 3 1/2 tsp. baking powder
- 1 tsp. salt
- 3/4 c. sugar
- 1/2 c. chopped pecans
- 1/2 c. dark raisins
- 1 c. cut-up colored gumdrops
- 2 eggs, beaten
- 4 tbsp. melted shortening
- 1 1/4 c. milk
- 1/2 tsp. almond extract

Sift dry ingredients into bowl; stir in nuts, raisins and gumdrops. Combine eggs, shortening, milk and extract. Add to dry ingredients. Mix only until dry ingredients are moistened. Bake in greased paper-lined 9 x 5 x 3-inch pan at 350 degrees for 1 hour or until center tests done. Cool. Wrap and store 24 hours before slicing. This bread can be wrapped and frozen for 2 to 3 months after cooling.

Mrs. Joe E. Deaton, Jackson, Tenn.

SHORT 'NIN' BREAD

- 4 c. flour
- 1 c. light brown sugar
- 1 lb. butter

Mix flour and sugar. Add butter. Place on floured surface and pat into desired shape. Bake at 325 to 350 degrees for 20 to 25 minutes.

Mrs. J. W. Hopkins, Abilene, Tex.

SPICE CORN BREAD

1 c. enriched flour
1 c. enriched cornmeal
½ c. sugar
1 tbsp. baking powder
½ tsp. cinnamon
½ tsp. nutmeg
½ tsp. salt
½ c. shredded coconut
½ c. ground nutmeats
⅓ c. shortening
¾ c. milk
1 egg yolk

Put all dry ingredients, coconut, nutmeats and shortening into a bowl; blend until the consistency of sand. Make a well in center of dry mixture; pour in liquid and stir until batter is moist. Batter will be quite thin. Pour in buttered pan. Bake at 500 degrees for 15 to 20 minutes. Yield: 12 servings.

Mrs. W. A. Jones, Americus, Ga.

WELSH BREAD

½ yeast cake
2 c. milk, scalded
1 c. sugar
½ c. melted butter
½ c. melted margarine
9 c. flour
½ lb. small white raisins
½ lb. currants
¼ lb. candied citron, cut small
¼ c. chopped candied lemon or orange peel
2 tsp. salt
½ c. grated raw carrots

Dissolve yeast in 1/4 cup warm water. Add cooled scalded milk and 1 cup warm water to the yeast. Add sugar, butter and margarine. Mix a little of the flour with fruits. Add salt, remainder of flour, fruits and carrots to yeast mixture. Knead a little. Put in a large bowl; cover and set in a warm spot to rise until doubled in size. Shape dough into 3 loaves. Let rise again until light, about 1 hour. Bake at 350 degrees for 1 hour. Allow to cool before serving in thin slices.

Mrs. Sherburne P. Sweetland, Laurel, Fla.

BANANA CORN BREAD MUFFINS

1 15-oz pkg. corn bread mix
½ c. sugar
¼ tsp. baking powder
3 med. bananas, mashed
¼ c. lukewarm water
1 egg

Combine the corn bread mix, sugar and baking powder in mixing bowl. Add bananas, water and egg; beat hard with spoon for 1 minute. Spoon into fluted paper muffin liners; place in large muffin pans. Bake at 425 degrees for 15 to 20 minutes. Yield: 12 large muffins.

Mrs. Charles R. Owen, Memphis, Tenn.

BANANA MUFFINS

½ c. shortening
1 c. sugar
1 c. bananas, mashed
2 eggs, lightly beaten
2 ½ c. flour
2 ½ tsp. soda
½ tsp. salt

(Continued on next page)

Cream shortening with sugar; add bananas. Add the lightly beaten eggs. Sift dry ingredients together; stir into batter. Pour into greased muffin pans. Bake at 350 degrees 20 to 25 minutes.

Mrs. Eric Brown, Tullos, La.

BANANA-NUT MUFFINS

1 c. flour
½ c. sugar
2 ½ tsp. baking powder
½ tsp. salt
¼ tsp. soda
¾ c. oats
1 egg, beaten
3 tbsp. fat, melted
½ c. milk
½ c. banana, mashed
⅓ c. nuts, chopped

Sift dry ingredients together; add oats. Add remaining ingredients; stir only until flour is moistened. Fill greased muffin cups 2/3 full. Bake at 400 degrees for 20 to 25 minutes. Yield: 12 servings.

Mrs. James Wagoner, Brevard, N. C.

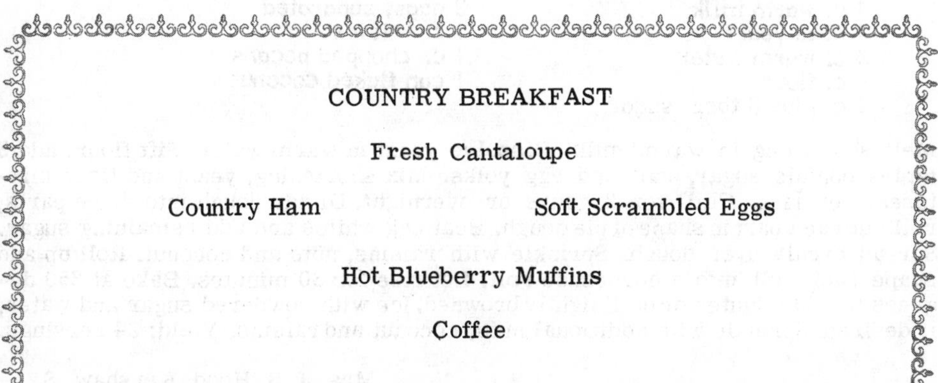

COUNTRY BREAKFAST

Fresh Cantaloupe

Country Ham

Soft Scrambled Eggs

Hot Blueberry Muffins

Coffee

BLUEBERRY MUFFINS

2 ⅔ c. flour
1 c. blueberries
¼ c. butter
¼ c. sugar
1 egg
½ tsp. salt
4 tsp. baking powder
1 c. milk

Mix 2/3 cup of flour with blueberries. Let stand 1 hour. Cream butter, sugar and egg. Sift remaining 2 cups flour with salt and baking powder. Add alternately with milk to creamed mixture. Add floured blueberries. Bake in greased muffin pans at 400 degrees for 25 minutes.

Gertrude Nichols, Eureka, Ark.

HOCUS-POCUS BUNS

1 pkg. dry yeast
¼ c. warm water
¾ c. lukewarm milk
¾ c. sugar
1 tsp. salt
1 egg
¼ c. soft shortening
3 ½ to 3 ¾ c. flour
24 marshmallows
½ c. melted butter
2 tsp. cinnamon

Dissolve yeast in water. Add milk, 1/4 cup sugar, salt, egg, shortening and one-half of flour. Mix with spoon until smooth. Add enough remaining flour to handle easily; mix by hand. Turn onto lightly floured board; knead for 2 minutes or until smooth and elastic. Place in greased bowl; turn greased side up. Cover with damp cloth; let rise in warm place until doubled, about 1 hour and 30 minutes. Punch down; let rise again until almost doubled, about 30 minutes. Divide dough in half; roll out to 1/4 inch thickness. Cut twelve 3 1/2-inch circles from each half. Dip marshmallows in butter, cinnamon and sugar mixture. Wrap piece of dough around each marshmallow; dip in butter mixture again. Place in large greased muffin tins with pinched side down. Let rise for 20 minutes. Bake at 375 degrees for 15 minutes. Remove immediately. Yield: 24 servings.

Mrs. Don Wottrich, Houston, Tex.

HORSESHOE ROLLS

1 c. shortening
1 c. warm milk
1 cake yeast
½ c. warm water
4 c. flour
1 c. plus 3 tbsp. sugar
1 tsp. salt
3 eggs, separated
1 c. raisins
1 c. chopped pecans
1 can flaked coconut

Melt shortening in warm milk. Dissolve yeast in warm water. Sift flour; add 3 tablespoonfuls sugar, salt and egg yolks. Mix shortening, yeast and flour mixtures; let rise. Chill for 2 hours or overnight. Divide dough into three parts; roll out each part in shape of pie dough. Beat egg whites and add remaining sugar. Spread evenly over dough. Sprinkle with raisins, nuts and coconut. Roll up and shape each roll into a horseshoe roll. Let rise for 30 minutes. Bake at 350 degrees for 30 minutes or until lightly browned. Ice with powdered sugar and water, if desired. Sprinkle with additional nuts, coconut and raisins. Yield: 24 servings.

Mrs. J. S. Hood, Kershaw, S. C.

MINCEMEAT ROLLS

1 box hot roll mix
1 pkg. mincemeat
½ c. plus 3 tbsp. water
½ c. sugar
1 lge. apple
1 c. confectioners' sugar

Prepare hot roll mix according to package directions. Let rise until doubled; punch down. Remove from bowl and knead until smooth. Divide dough in half; roll each half into a 10 x 15-inch rectangle. Cut mincemeat into pieces; cook with 1/2 cup water, sugar and apples. Cool. Spread dough with mincemeat mixture; roll like a jelly roll. Place in buttered round 9-inch cake pan. Make cuts with scissors 1 inch apart and almost through the roll; turn each slice on side. Let rise until doubled. Bake at 370 degrees for 20 minutes. Spread with glaze made of confectioners' sugar and enough water to make of spreading consistency.

Mrs. T. C. Stoudemayer, Greenville, S. C.

RECIPE FOR WAFFLES DIABLE ON PAGE 356

AVOCADO-NUT BREAD

2 c. flour
½ tsp. soda
¾ c. sugar
½ tsp. baking powder
¼ tsp. salt
1 egg, slightly beaten
½ c. sour milk
½ c. mashed avocado
1 c. nuts

In a large bowl, sift together flour, soda, sugar, baking powder and salt. Add egg, sour milk, mashed avocado and nuts, mixing only enough to moisten. Pour into a greased 9 x 5 x 3-inch loaf pan. Bake at 350 degrees for 1 hour.

Mrs. F. T. Black, El Paso, Tex.

BUTTERMILK BISCUITS

2 c. flour
1 tsp. baking powder
¼ tsp. soda
1 tsp. salt
2 tbsp. shortening
⅔ c. buttermilk

Mix all ingredients; roll out 1/3 to 1/2 inch thick. Cut with biscuit cutter. Bake at 450 degrees for 10 minutes.

Mrs. Vera Lineberger, Gastonia, N. C.

CHEESE BISCUITS

½ lb. sharp cheese, grated
½ lb. margarine
2 c. sifted flour
½ tsp. salt
½ tsp. cayenne pepper
1 tsp. Worcestershire sauce
1 c. chopped nuts

Have cheese and margarine at room temperature; combine. Add flour, salt, cayenne pepper and Worcestershire sauce. Add nuts. Drop from teaspoon onto ungreased cookie sheet. Bake at 400 degrees for 12 to 15 minutes.

Mrs. Charles R. Owen, Memphis, Tenn.

CORNMEAL ROLLS

1 ¼ c. flour
¾ c. cornmeal
½ tsp. salt
4 tsp. baking powder
1 tbsp. sugar
2 tbsp. shortening
1 egg, well beaten
½ c. milk
Melted butter or shortening

Sift together flour, cornmeal, salt, baking powder and sugar. Mix in shortening with fingers; add egg and milk. Roll out on floured board; cut into rounds with large cutter. Brush with melted butter; fold over as for parker house rolls. Brush tops with beaten egg or milk, if desired. Bake at 400 to 450 degrees for 10 minutes. Yield: 15 rolls.

Mrs. H. F. Dickenson, Harrogate, Tenn.

CORNMEAL BISCUITS

1 ½ c. self-rising flour
½ c. cornmeal
¼ c. shortening
¾ c. milk

Mix flour and meal; cut in shortening. Stir in milk to make a soft dough. Knead lightly; roll out 1/4 to 1/2-inch thickness. Cut out with floured knife; place on ungreased baking sheet. Bake at 450 degrees for 12 to 15 minutes or until golden brown. Yield: 1 dozen biscuits.

Mrs. D. B. Schoenberg, Cola, S. C.

EASY CORNMEAL ROLLS

1 ½ c. flour
¾ c. cornmeal
3 tsp. baking powder
¼ tsp. soda
1 tsp. salt
1 tbsp. sugar
4 tbsp. shortening
1 egg
½ c. buttermilk
Melted butter

Sift dry ingredients. Combine shortening, egg and buttermilk; add to dry ingredients. Mix well; roll on lightly floured board. Cut as for biscuits; brush with melted butter. Fold as for parker house rolls; place on greased baking sheet. Bake at 475 degrees for 12 to 15 minutes.

Mrs. A. M. Boom, Memphis, Tenn.

FIESTA BISCUITS

2 tbsp. margarine
2 c. biscuit mix
⅔ c. milk
2 tbsp. finely chopped green pepper
2 tbsp. finely chopped onion
2 tbsp. finely chopped pimento

Cut margarine into biscuit mix; stir in milk, green pepper, onion and pimento to make stiff dough. Roll out 1/2 inch thick; cut with small biscuit cutter. Place on ungreased cookie sheet with edges touching. Bake at 450 degrees for 8 to 10 minutes or until brown. Yield: 2 dozen biscuits.

Mrs. E. J. Zink, Dallas, Tex.

HOT BISCUITS

1 c. flour
1 ½ tsp. baking powder
½ tsp. salt
2 tbsp. shortening
½ c. milk

Sift dry ingredients together; cut in shortening with pastry blender. Add milk; mix well. Roll out approximately 3/4 inch thick; cut with biscuit cutter. Place on well-oiled baking pan, turning once to coat both sides with oil. Bake at 475 degrees for approximately 10 minutes. Yield: 4 servings.

Mrs. Hugh W. Sheffield, Dallas, Tex.

MARYLAND BEATEN BISCUITS

2 c. prepared biscuit mix
½ c. ice water

Combine biscuit mix and ice water with a fork; place on floured board. Knead for 15 minutes or until air bubbles blister surface. If desired, dough may be put through a meat grinder twice and kneaded for 3 to 5 minutes. Roll out 1/2 inch thick; cut out 24 biscuits with a 1 1/2-inch cutter. Prick with fork. Bake on ungreased pan for 15 minutes at 450 degrees. Yield: 2 dozen biscuits.

Mrs. Fern Coffield, Salem, Ky.

NEW-FASHIONED BISCUITS

2 c. flour
4 tsp. baking powder
1 tsp. salt
1 tbsp. sugar
¾ c. milk
½ c. mayonnaise
1 tsp. grated lemon rind

Sift dry ingredients together; stir in milk, mayonnaise and lemon rind. Knead for 1 minute. Roll and cut into desired size. Bake at 450 degrees for 12 minutes or until done. Serve hot. Yield: 12-15 servings.

Mrs. Flo Ponder, Ruston, La.

PINK BISCUITS

2 c. sifted flour
4 tsp. baking powder
½ tsp. salt
½ c. vegetable shortening
¾ c. tomato juice

Sift together flour, baking powder and salt; cut in shortening. Add tomato juice gradually until soft dough is formed; roll on slightly floured board. Cut with biscuit cutter. Bake at 400 degrees to 450 degrees for 15 minutes.

Mrs. Russell O. Behrens, Apalachicola, Fla.

SODA BISCUITS

1 c. sifted flour
½ tsp. baking soda
½ tsp. salt
4 tbsp. shortening
¾ c. (about) sour milk or buttermilk

Sift together flour. Sift again with the baking soda and salt; cut in shortening until mixture resembles coarse cornmeal. Add enough milk to make soft dough; turn onto floured board. Knead slightly; roll out 1/2 inch thick. Cut with floured biscuit cutter. Prick with fork; place on ungreased baking sheet. Bake at 475 degrees for 12 to 15 minutes. Yield: 12 biscuits.

Betty Simpson, Dobson, N. C.

SOUTHERN DROP BISCUITS

2 c. flour
1 tbsp. baking powder
½ tsp. cream of tartar
4 tbsp. shortening

(Continued on next page)

¾ tsp. salt
½ tsp. soda
1 c. buttermilk
1 stick butter or margarine

Sift dry ingredients together twice. Using two knives, cut shortening into flour mixture until well mixed. Add buttermilk; stir well. Drop level tablespoonfuls of dough onto greased aluminum foil or cookie sheet. Place a pat of butter on each biscuit. Bake 10 minutes at 450 degrees. Yield: 26 biscuits.

Mrs. James E. Shotts, Jasper, Ala.

SUNDAY SPECIAL

Crisp Fried Chicken with Gravy

Fresh String Beans | Stewed Tomatoes

Southern Drop Biscuits

Baked Apple

Coffee | Tea

CORNMEAL BREAD

½ c. shortening
½ c. sugar
2 eggs
1 ½ c. bran cereal
1 c. milk
1 c. flour
½ c. yellow cornmeal
3 tsp. baking powder
1 tsp. salt

Cream shortening; add sugar slowly, beating in well. Add well-beaten eggs until well blended. Add bran cereal and milk together and let stand 5 minutes before adding to mixture. Sift together flour, cornmeal, baking powder and salt. Add to first mixture with bran cereal mixture. Mix well. Bake in greased 10-inch square pan in 350-degree oven for 30 minutes. Cut and serve with butter.

Mrs. J. Robert Chrisman, Greensboro, N. C.

BISCUIT SKILLET BREAD

1 can mushroom soup
2 eggs, beaten
2 tbsp. oil
1 tsp. instant minced onion
2 c. prepared biscuit mix
¼ c. butter or oleo
¼ c. Parmesan cheese

(Continued on next page)

Blend soup, eggs and oil. Stir onion into biscuit mix. Make a well in biscuit mix; pour in soup mixture and blend. Melt butter in large iron skillet. Spoon batter into melted butter; sprinkle with cheese. Bake at 400 degrees for 25 minutes. Yield: 6-8 servings.

Mrs. James A. Fleming, Ocala, Fla.

CHEESE STRAWS

- 1 8-oz. wedge sharp cheddar cheese
- 1 stick oleo or butter
- 2 ½ c. flour
- ¾ tsp. red pepper
- 1 tsp. salt
- 1 tsp. sugar
- 2 tsp. water

Grate cheese; add remaining ingredients in order listed. Roll thin and cut into 3 x 1/2-inch strips. Place on greased cookie sheet. Bake 10 minutes at 400 degrees. Yield: 120 straws.

Mrs. W. W. Nance, Alexandria, Va.

CHEESE STRAWS

- 1 pkg. pastry mix
- ½ lb. cheddar cheese, grated
- 1 c. chopped pecans (opt.)
- ½ (or less) sm. can pimentos

Roll out the pastry mix. Sprinkle cheese, pecans and pimentos on top. Turn pastry over half and roll slightly. Cut into narrow strips. Bake in preheated 425 to 450-degree oven about 10 minutes or until slightly browned.

Mrs. R. F. Raiborn, San Angelo, Tex.

CHEESE WAFERS

- 1 stick butter
- 1 c. flour
- 1 tsp. salt
- ⅛ tsp. red pepper
- 1 sm. box Old English cheese
- Pecans

Cut butter into flour; add salt and pepper. Grate cheese into mixture. Form in a roll; chill. Slice and place a pecan on each wafer. Bake at 300 degrees for about 10 minutes.

Mrs. Reuben D. Baughn, Mayodan, N. C.

BACON CORN BREAD

- 1 c. sifted flour
- ¾ c. cornmeal
- 4 tsp. baking powder
- ¾ tsp. salt
- 4 tbsp. sugar
- 1 egg, beaten
- 1 c. milk
- 3 tbsp. melted shortening
- 1 tsp. Worcestershire sauce
- 8 strips bacon, minced

(Continued on next page)

Mix and sift flour, cornmeal, baking powder, salt and sugar in a bowl. In another bowl, beat egg; blend in milk, shortening and Worcestershire sauce. Add to dry ingredients, stirring just enough to moisten. Pour into a greased and floured 9-inch square pan. Bake in 425-degree oven 20 to 25 minutes. During the last 15 minutes of baking, sprinkle minced bacon on top. Bread is done when a toothpick inserted in center comes out clean. Place under broiler a few minutes until bacon is crisp. Remove to a rack. When ready to serve, cut into squares.

Mrs. Robbie Jo Brown, Sweetwater, Tenn.

BUTTERMILK CORN BREAD

1 c. cornmeal
1 c. sifted flour
1 tsp. baking soda
4 tsp. baking powder
1 tsp. salt
2 tbsp. sugar
1 egg
1 c. buttermilk
3 tbsp. melted shortening

Sift dry ingredients. Beat egg with buttermilk; add this to dry ingredients. Stir in shortening. Pour batter into hot greased 8 x 10-inch pan. Bake at 425 degrees for 30 minutes.

Mrs. E. Horman, Sr., Cocoa Beach, Fla.

CHEESE SWIRLS

1 c. sifted flour
2 tsp. baking powder
¼ tsp. salt
2 tbsp. shortening
⅓ c. milk
½ c. shredded sharp cheese

Sift dry ingredients together; cut in shortening till mixture is like coarse crumbs. Add milk all at once; stir just till dough follows fork around bowl. Turn out on lightly floured surface and knead 30 seconds. Roll in rectangle 1/4 inch thick. Sprinkle with cheese; roll as for jelly roll and seal edge. Cut into 1/2-inch slices. Bake at 425 degrees about 12 to 15 minutes. Yield: 8-10 swirls.

Mrs. W. W. Clay, Atlanta, Ga.

CHEDDAR CORN BREAD

1 c. flour
1 c. yellow cornmeal
1 tbsp. baking powder
2 tbsp. salt
2 eggs, beaten
1 c. milk
2 c. shredded sharp cheddar cheese

Sift together dry ingredients; add eggs, milk and cheese. Stir just until blended; pour into hot well-greased 1 1/2-quart ring mold. Bake at 425 degrees for 20 minutes. If desired, center of corn bread may be filled with meat stew or creamed vegetable. Yield: 6 servings.

Mrs. A. Frank Arnold, Spruce Pine, N. C.

CLOCKED CORN BREAD

12 cooked sausage links
1 c. buttermilk
1 egg, beaten
1 c. self-rising meal
2 tbsp. sausage grease

Line bottom of heavy iron skillet with greased heavy paper. Arrange sausage links like clock numerals. Mix together remaining ingredients; pour over sausage. Bake in 400-degree oven for 30 minutes. Turn upside down onto hot plate; cut into wedges.

Mrs. E. P. Pruitt, Jr., Birmingham, Ala.

CORN BREAD

1 ½ c. cornmeal
1 c. cream-style corn
1 c. buttermilk
⅔ c. cooking oil
2 eggs
3 tsp. baking powder
1 tsp. salt
1 med. onion, chopped (opt.)
3 hot chili peppers, chopped
2 tsp. chopped bell pepper
1 c. grated sharp cheddar cheese

Mix all ingredients except cheese; pour half the mixture into hot greased skillet. Sprinkle half the cheese over batter; pour remaining batter over cheese. Top with remaining cheese. Bake for 35 to 40 minutes at 450 degrees.

Mrs. W. F. Owen, Goodlettsville, Tenn.

CORN PONETTES

¾ c. cornmeal
½ c. flour
2 tsp. baking powder
¼ tsp. salt
1 med. onion, grated
1 egg
1 c. cream-style corn
Dash Tabasco

Sift meal, flour, baking powder and salt. Add onion to lightly beaten egg; stir into corn. Add Tabasco; stir corn mixture into dry ingredients. Batter will be very stiff. Drop by rounded teaspoonfuls into hot cooking oil. Cook until a golden brown; turn and brown evenly. Drain. Yield: 6-8 servings.

Mrs. B. R. Coley, Lithonia, Ga.

EASY MEXICAN CORN BREAD

1 c. cornmeal
1 8 ¾-oz. can cream-style corn
1 c. chopped onions
1 7-oz. jar pimentos, chopped
1 c. grated cheese
¼ c. shortening
3 eggs
1 tbsp. sugar

Mix all ingredients. Bake in 10-inch pie pan at 350 degrees for about 45 minutes.

Mrs. Laeta M. McMullen, Pensacola, Fla.

GREEN CHILI-CORN BREAD

1 c. yellow cornmeal
3 tsp. baking powder
1 c. canned cream-style corn
½ tsp. salt
⅓ c. salad oil
2 eggs
1 c. buttermilk or cream
1 sm. can green chilies
1 c. grated sharp cheese

Mix cornmeal, baking powder, corn, salt, oil, eggs and buttermilk. Grease 9-inch square baking pan or cast iron skillet. Pour in 1/2 mixture. Place chilies in strips on top. Sprinkle with 1/2 of the grated cheese. Pour in remaining batter and sprinkle with remaining cheese. Bake at 325 degrees for 1 hour.

Glenyth Herring, Midland, Tex.

HOT MEXICAN CORN BREAD

1 ½ c. cornmeal
1 tsp. salt
3 tsp. baking powder
1 c. milk
3 eggs
1 sm. can cream-style corn
⅔ c. oil
½ c. chopped bell pepper
1 c. grated American cheese
3 lge. jalapeno peppers, chopped

Sift dry ingredients together; add milk and eggs. Mix well. Stir in remaining ingredients. Bake in a 9 x 13 x 2-inch pan at 350 degrees for 45 minutes.

Mrs. Thomas M. Winfiele, Baton Rouge, La.

HOT MEXICAN CORN BREAD

1 c. cornmeal
1 tsp. baking powder
½ tsp. soda
½ tsp. salt
1 c. sweet milk
2 eggs
½ c. bacon grease
1 No. 2 can cream-style corn
2 tbsp. flour
3 sm. hot peppers, cut fine
½ lb. grated sharp cheese

Mix all ingredients except peppers and cheese. Pour half of mixture into hot greased skillet. Sprinkle with cheese and peppers. Add remaining batter. Bake at 400 degrees for 40 minutes or until done.

Mrs. W. T. Bowman, Bearden, Ark.

HOT PEPPER CORN BREAD

1 ½ c. yellow cornmeal
4 tbsp. all-purpose flour
1 tsp. soda
½ tsp. baking powder
1 c. cream-style corn
1 c. buttermilk
¼ c. oil
½ lb. grated cheddar cheese
3 jalapeno peppers, chopped
3 slices crisp fried bacon (opt.)

(Continued on next page)

Mix cornmeal, flour, soda and baking powder. Stir in corn. Add buttermilk and oil. Pour half of mixture into hot greased pan. Sprinkle cheese, peppers and crumbled bacon over mixture. Add remaining mixture. Bake in preheated oven at 400 degrees for about 30 minutes or until brown. Yield: 6-8 servings.

Mrs. Velma Mixon, Baton Rouge, La.

MEXICAN CORN BREAD

1 c. self-rising flour
1 c. milk
¼ c. oil
2 eggs
½ lb. sharp hoop cheese, grated
1 can cream-style corn
1 sm. onion, chopped

Mix all ingredients; pour in greased pan. Bake at 400 degrees until brown.

Mrs. Gene Gentry, Baldwyn, Miss.

MEXICAN CORN BREAD

1 c. cornmeal
1 c. cream-style corn
½ tsp. soda
½ tsp. salt
2 tbsp. bacon drippings
¾ c. buttermilk
2 eggs
1 c. grated mozzarella cheese
8 slices crisp bacon, crumbled finely
1 c. chopped hot jalapeno peppers

Mix all ingredients. Pour into greased skillet or pan. Bake in 400-degree oven for 35 minutes.

Mrs. James A. Dukes, Lubbock, Tex.

MEXICAN CORN BREAD

1 pkg. corn bread mix
1 can cream-style corn
1 can chili peppers
1 c. grated cheese

Combine corn bread mix and corn. Pour 1/2 of batter into a skillet or pan. Cover with the peppers and cheese. Pour on remaining corn bread mixture. Bake as directed on package.

Eleanor Vickers, Jackson, Miss.

MEXICAN CORN BREAD

2 eggs, beaten
1 c. cream-style corn
3 tsp. baking powder
1 c. sour cream
⅔ c. salad oil
1 c. yellow meal
1 ½ tsp. salt
Chopped hot peppers
1 c. grated cheddar cheese

(Continued on next page)

Combine first 7 ingredients for batter. Pour 1/2 of batter in greased pan; cover with peppers and 1/2 cheese. Repeat. Bake 1 hour at 350 degrees. Serve hot.

Mrs. A. T. Caldwell, Pocahontas, Ark.

HOT MEXICAN CORN BREAD

3 c. self-rising cornmeal
3 tsp. baking powder
1 tsp. salt
3 eggs, beaten
2 ½ c. sweet milk
½ c. cooking oil
3 tsp. sugar
1 lge. onion, chopped
1 No. 2 can cream-style corn
1 ½ c. grated cheese
2 canned jalapeno peppers, chopped
1 tsp. pepper liquid

Combine all ingredients; pour into 2 large baking pans. Bake at 450 degrees until brown.

Mrs. Irene H. Ferguson, Springville, Ala.

MEXICAN CORN BREAD, MISSISSIPPI-STYLE

1 c. plain cornmeal
1 c. self-rising cornmeal
1 c. easy-pour pancake mix
1 c. finely grated onion
1 ½ c. grated sharp cheddar cheese
1 tsp. soda
½ tsp. salt
3 tbsp. sugar
1 No. 303 can cream-style
½ c. cooking oil
1 tbsp. finely crushed red pepper or 1 tsp. powdered red pepper
2 c. sweet milk
2 eggs, beaten

Mix all ingredients, stirring in milk and eggs last. Bake in corn bread stick pans or muffin tins at 400 degrees or bake in baking pan at 375 degrees until lightly browned.

Mrs. John C. Zachary, Laurel, Miss.

MISSISSIPPI CORN BREAD

3 c. corn bread mix
3 eggs
2 ½ c. milk
½ c. grated cheese
2 tbsp. sugar
1 lge. onion
¼ lb. crumbled bacon
1 c. cream-style corn
¼ c. chopped pimento
¼ c. chopped cherry hot peppers

Combine all ingredients in order given; pour into greased 13 x 9 1/2 x 2-inch glass pan. Bake at 425 degrees until brown. Yield: 15 servings.

Mrs. Frank McCollum, Birmingham, Ala.

CORN BREAD

1 c. cornmeal
1 c. flour
2 tbsp. sugar
4 tsp. baking powder
1 ½ tsp. salt
1 ½ c. milk
2 tbsp. shortening
2 eggs, beaten

Sift dry ingredients; add milk, shortening and eggs. Beat well; pour into greased shallow pan. Bake at 400 degrees to 450 degrees for about 25 minutes.

Mrs. R. P. Smith, Victoria, Va.

CORN BREAD

½ c. flour
½ c. white cornmeal
1 tbsp. (scant) baking powder
1 tbsp. sugar (opt.)
½ tsp. salt
1 egg
½ c. plus 2 tbsp. milk
3 tbsp. hot melted shortening
or cooking oil

Sift together first 5 ingredients. Beat egg slightly; add milk and shortening. Add milk mixture to cornmeal mixture; pour into hot well-greased pans or muffin tins. Bake at 500 degrees until golden brown. Yield: 4 servings.

Mrs. Hugh W. Sheffield, Dallas, Tex.

CORN BREAD FOR BARBECUE

½ c. buttermilk
3 beaten eggs
1 c. yellow cornmeal
½ tsp. salt
1 to 3 jalapeno peppers,
finely chopped
1 No. 303 can cream-style
corn
2 lge. onions, finely chopped
3 cloves garlic, chopped
½ tsp. soda
¾ lb. sharp cheddar cheese,
grated
1 green pepper, cut in strips
1 can pimento, cut in strips

Combine buttermilk and eggs; add cornmeal, salt, jalapeno peppers, corn, onions, garlic and soda. Pour half the batter into hot greased iron skillet; add cheese. Add remaining batter; garnish with green pepper and pimento. Bake at 350 degrees for 45 minutes.

Mrs. Howard Lewis, Murfreesboro, Ark.

CORN PONE

1 ½ c. water-ground
cornmeal
¼ c. powdered milk
¼ tsp. salt
1 ½ c. water
Bacon grease

Mix all ingredients except bacon grease together; let stand for a few minutes. Shape into oblong pones; put on hot greased griddle. With the tip of a spoon, make 10 to 12 indentations in each pone; fill with bacon grease. Bake at 550 degrees for 15 to 20 minutes or till brown.

Elsa Henderson, Pensacola, Fla.

BRAN-CORNMEAL STICKS

2 tbsp. shortening
2 tbs. sugar
1 egg
1 c. milk
¾ c. prepared bran
½ c. cornmeal
1 c. flour
3 tbsp. baking powder
1 tsp. salt

Cream shortening. Add sugar; mix well. Add well-beaten egg, milk, bran and cornmeal. Sift flour; measure. Sift with baking powder and salt; add to cornmeal mixture, stirring only until well blended. Pour into well-oiled pans. Bake in 400-degree oven 20 minutes. Yield: 12 sticks.

Mrs. Leonard Jones, Jackson, Tenn.

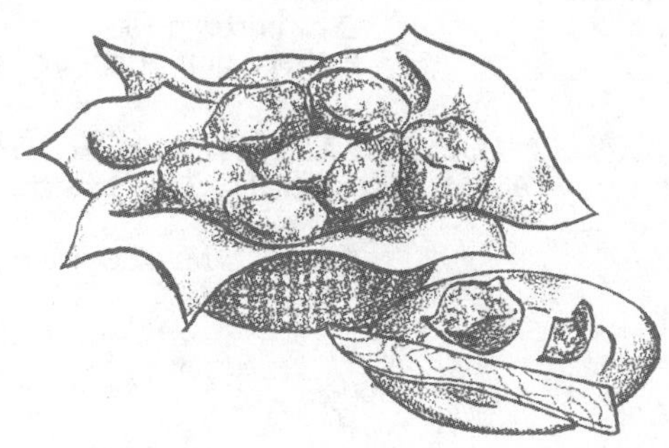

CHEESE CORN STICKS

1 ½ c. yellow cornmeal
½ c. flour
3 tbsp. sugar
1 tbsp. baking powder
½ tsp. salt
1 c. milk
1 egg, beaten
¼ c. butter, melted
¼ lb. cheddar cheese, cubed

Sift together cornmeal, flour, sugar, baking powder and salt. Blend milk, egg and butter; stir into dry ingredients just to moisten. Add cheddar cheese. Spoon into well-buttered corn stick pans. Bake 18 to 20 minutes in preheated 425-degree oven. Serve hot.

Mrs. G. C. Thompson, Franklin, Tenn.

CORN STICKS

2 c. cornmeal
1 c. milk
1 egg
1 tbsp. lard
2 tsp. baking powder
½ tsp. salt

Beat together all ingredients. Bake in greased tins the shape of sticks or ears of corn in 500-degree oven for 10 to 12 minutes.

Mrs. M. L. Orwin, McCall, S. C.

CORN STICKS

2 c. cornmeal
½ tsp. salt
1 tsp. soda
1 tsp. baking powder
2 eggs
2 c. buttermilk
½ c. pecans, chopped
4 tbsp. shortening

Mix dry ingredients; add beaten eggs. Slowly add milk and nuts. Add melted shortening last. Pour into greased stick mold. Bake in oven at 350 degrees about 25 minutes. Yield: 12 sticks.

Mrs. R. L. Anderson, Travelers Rest, S. C.

DIXIE CORN STICKS

1 ½ c. white cornmeal
3 tbsp. flour
1 tsp. salt
1 tsp. soda
1 egg
2 c. buttermilk
2 tbsp. drippings or butter

Mix dry ingredients; add egg and milk. Add melted butter; stir lightly. Bake in hot greased corn stick pan at 450 degrees until golden brown.

Mrs. Eunice Ricks, Jarratt, Va.

GOLDEN CORN STICKS

½ c. all-purpose flour
1 ¼ c. cornmeal
½ tsp. baking soda
1 ¼ tsp. double-acting baking powder
1 tsp. salt
1 tbsp. sugar
1 egg
1 ¼ c. buttermilk
¼ c. vegetable oil

Sift flour; measure. Resift 3 times with remaining dry ingredients. Beat egg; add buttermilk and oil. Add dry ingredients; beat quickly until well mixed. Grease corn stick or muffin pans generously with oil; heat for about 5 minutes in preheated oven. Remove from oven; immediately fill hot pans 2/3 full of batter. Bake in 425-degree oven 12 to 15 minutes until golden brown. Serve hot. Yield: 16 corn sticks.

Mrs. Donald Young, Ocean Springs, Miss.

TENNESSEE CORN STICKS

1 c. yellow cornmeal
1 ½ tsp. baking powder
½ c. flour
½ tsp. salt
2 tbsp. sugar
1 egg
¾ c. milk
1 tbsp. butter

Mix and sift dry ingredients. Add beaten egg and milk; add melted butter. Bake in corn stick pans or in a shallow pan 20 minutes at 400 degrees. This is a thin crisp bread when baked in a 7 x 11-inch pan. Yield: 6-8 servings.

Mrs. Charles L. Cummings, Charleston Heights, S. C.

HERB CORN STICKS

2 c. self-rising cornmeal
½ c. sifted self-rising flour
2 tbsp. sugar
1 tsp. celery seed
¼ tsp. nutmeg
1 egg, beaten
¼ c. melted shortening or oil
1 ¼ c. milk
3 tbsp. melted butter
4 tbsp. grated Parmesan cheese

Mix together cornmeal, flour and sugar. Stir in celery seed and nutmeg. Blend together beaten egg, shortening and milk. Add to dry ingredients; mix lightly only until dry ingredients are moistened. Fill greased corn stick pans to top. Bake in 425-degree oven for 20 to 25 minutes. Remove from pans. Brush 1/3 of each corn stick with melted butter. Sprinkle buttered end with cheese or roll in cheese to coat one end. Serve hot. Yield: 14 corn sticks.

Mrs. Thomas Chrestman, Cleveland, Miss.

PLANTATION CORN STICKS

1 ¼ c. cornmeal
½ tsp. salt
½ tsp. soda
1 ¼ c. buttermilk
2 tbsp. light brown unsulphured molasses
2 eggs, beaten until light
4 tbsp. melted shortening

Sift cornmeal, salt and soda together; add buttermilk, stirring well. Add molasses; fold in beaten eggs. Mix well. Add slightly cooled melted shortening. Bake in a well-greased corn stick iron at 425 degrees for 20 to 25 minutes. Yield: 8 corn sticks.
PERSONAL COMMENT: These are as Aunt Ellen Peak, our old colored mammy, made them.

Mrs. John C. Key, Mount Pleasant, S. C.

CORN ZEPHYRS

1 c. white cornmeal
1 tbsp. shortening
4 c. boiling water
1 ⅛ tsp. salt
4 egg whites

Combine cornmeal and shortening in top of double boiler; pour boiling water over cornmeal. Add 1 teaspoonful salt; cook for 30 minutes, stirring frequently. Cool. Beat egg whites until stiff with remaining salt; fold lightly into cornmeal mixture. Drop batter by spoonfuls onto greased baking sheet. Bake at 350 degrees for 30 minutes. Serve hot. If desired, 4 egg yolks may be added to batter before folding in egg whites; bake at 425 degrees for 20 to 25 minutes.

Bert H. Oglesby, Birmingham, Ala.

CRACKLING BREAD

2 c. cornmeal
½ tsp. soda
2 tsp. baking powder
2 tsp. salt
2 c. sour milk
2 eggs
1 c. chopped cracklings

(Continued on next page)

Sift dry ingredients together; add milk, well-beaten eggs and cracklings. Pour into a very hot well-greased pan. Bake from 40 to 50 minutes at 400 to 450 degrees.

Mrs. Roy McMurry, Sandy Hook, Miss.

CRACKLING BREAD

1 qt. cornmeal
1 tsp. soda
½ tsp. salt
Buttermilk
1 c. minced crisp cracklings

Sift dry ingredients together; add enough buttermilk to make into a soft dough. Add cracklings. Make into small pones. Bake at 400 degrees until brown.

Lucile Freese, Nashville, Tenn.

CRACKLING CORN BREAD

1 ½ c. cornmeal
¼ c. flour
1 tsp. soda
1 tsp. salt
2 c. buttermilk
1 egg
1 c. finely cut cracklings

Sift together dry ingredients. Add buttermilk and egg, stirring until well blended. Season cracklings with additional salt to taste and fold into batter. Pour batter into very hot greased skillet or muffin pan. Bake in 450-degree oven for about 25 minutes.

Mrs. Dollie Wilson, Smithdale, Miss.

OLD-DIXIE CRACKLING CORN

1 ½ c. cornmeal
¾ c. flour
½ tsp. soda
¼ tsp. salt
1 c. buttermilk
1 c. diced cracklings

Sift together the dry ingredients. Add milk; stir in cracklings. Form into cakes. Place on greased baking pan. Bake at 400 degrees about 30 minutes. Serve hot.

Hazel Wimer, Hightown, Va.

CUSTARD CORN BREAD

2 eggs
½ c. sugar
1 ½ c. sweet milk
1 ½ c. cornmeal
½ c. flour
1 c. buttermilk
1 tsp. soda
¼ tsp. salt
2 tbsp. melted oleo

(Continued on next page)

Beat eggs; add sugar, 1 cup sweet milk, cornmeal and flour. Mix buttermilk, soda and salt; add to cornmeal mixture. Pour batter into hot iron skillet with melted oleo; pour remaining sweet milk over batter. Do not stir. Bake for 30 minutes at 375 degrees.

Mrs. John S. Allen, Columbia, Tenn.

DELICIOUS CORN BREAD

- 2 eggs
- 2 c. buttermilk
- 4 tbsp. bacon drippings
- 2 c. water-ground cornmeal
- 2 tsp. baking powder
- 1 tsp. baking soda
- 1 ½ tsp. salt

Combine eggs, buttermilk and 2 tablespoons melted bacon drippings. Mix all dry ingredients; add to egg mixture. Melt remaining bacon drippings in 8-inch iron skillet; pour batter into skillet. Bake at 325 degrees for 20 minutes; turn corn bread and continue baking for 15 minutes. Yield: 6 servings.

Fannie F. Carden, Durham, N. C.

CUSTARD-TOPPED CORN BREAD

- 2 eggs
- 1 tbsp. sugar
- 2 c. sweet milk
- 1 c. buttermilk
- ½ tsp. soda
- 1 tsp. baking powder
- 1 ½ c. cornmeal
- ½ c. flour
- 1 tsp. salt
- 2 tbsp. cooking oil

Beat eggs until light; add sugar and beat again. Stir in 1 cup sweet milk and buttermilk. Combine dry ingredients; add to milk mixture. Add oil; pour into 9-inch square baking dish. Carefully pour remaining sweet milk over top of batter; do not stir. Bake at 400 degrees for about 30 minutes or until set. Yield: 9-10 servings.

Mrs. N. E. Barnes, Gadsden, Ala.

GRITS CORN BREAD

- 1 c. corn grits
- 1 c. flour
- 4 tsp. baking powder
- ¼ c. sugar
- ½ tsp. salt
- 1 c. less 2 tbsp. milk
- 2 eggs, beaten
- ¼ c. melted butter or margarine

Mix together all dry ingredients; add remaining ingredients. Stir just until moistened; pour into 8 x 8-inch greased baking pan. Bake at 400 degrees for 20 minutes or until brown.

Mrs. F. M. Caperton, Greenwood, Miss.

GOLDEN CORN CAKE

1 c. cornmeal
1 c. flour
¼ c. sugar
5 tsp. baking powder
1 c. milk
1 egg
2 tbsp. melted butter

Mix all ingredients in order given; pour into buttered shallow baking dish. Bake at 450 degrees for 15 to 20 minutes. Serve hot.

Mrs. J. A. Stansbury, Clinton, Miss.

GRITS BATTER BREAD

½ c. water-ground cornmeal
1 c. cooked grits
1 ½ c. milk
1 tsp. salt
2 eggs
2 tbsp. melted butter

Mix ingredients in order given; pour in baking dish. Bake at 350 degrees for 20 minutes.

Mrs. Thomas J. Craig, Petersburg, Va.

HERBED CORN GEMS

2 c. self-rising cornmeal
½ tsp. salt
¼ tsp. powdered thyme
½ tsp. celery seed
1 egg
2 tsp. grated onion
½ c. sour cream or evaporated milk
2 tbsp. melted fat

Sift first 4 ingredients together. Beat egg slightly; add onion. Blend sour cream into egg; stir into cornmeal mixture. Add fat, stirring only to moisten. Pinch off pieces of dough; shape into rough little balls about 1 1/2 inches in diameter. Place in lightly greased muffin pans or on greased cookie sheet. Bake at 450 degrees for 20 minutes. Serve hot.

Mrs. J. O. Honeycutt, Gardendale, Ala.

HOMINY GRITS BATTER BREAD

2 eggs, beaten
1 c. cold cooked grits
1 c. cornmeal
2 tsp. baking powder
2 tsp. salt
2 tsp. sugar
Milk
2 tbsp. bacon drippings

Mix eggs, grits, cornmeal, baking powder, salt and sugar. Add enough milk to make batter the consistency of custard. Heat bacon drippings in 9 or 10-inch skillet; pour batter into skillet. Bake about 40 minutes at 350 degrees. Yield: 8 servings.

Mrs. Wayne Miller, Poplarville, Miss.

Frozen formation in Mammoth Cave, Kentucky.

FRIED CORNMEAL MUSH

4 c. water
1 c. white cornmeal
1 tsp. salt

Heat 3 cups water to boiling. Mix cornmeal with remaining cold water and salt; stir into hot water. Cook until thickened, stirring frequently. Cover; continue to cook for 5 minutes. Pour into loaf pan; cool. Slice 1/2 inch thick; fry on lightly greased griddle or skillet until golden brown, turning once. Serve hot with syrup.

Mrs. Elsie Hart, Pocahontas, Ark.

HOT CHEESE CORN BREAD

1 c. yellow cornmeal
1 c. sifted flour
¼ c. sugar
½ tsp. salt
4 tsp. baking powder
1 ½ c. shredded sharp American cheese
1 egg
1 c. milk
¼ c. shortening

Sift together cornmeal, flour, sugar, salt and baking powder; add cheese. Add egg, milk and shortening; beat just until smooth. Pour into 8-inch square pan. Bake for 30 minutes at 375 degrees. Yield: 8 servings.

Mrs. W. T. Bowman, Bearden, Ark.

EASY HUSH PUPPIES

2 c. cornmeal
1 tbsp. flour
½ tsp. soda
1 tsp. baking powder
1 tsp. salt
3 tbsp. finely chopped onion
1 c. buttermilk
1 egg

(Continued on next page)

Mix all dry ingredients together; add onion, then milk. Add beaten egg last. Drop by spoonfuls into pan in which fish is fried. Fry to a golden brown; drain on paper. If a deep pan or kettle is used, hush puppy breads will float when done.

Mrs. John White, Dalton, Ga.

FAVORITE HUSH PUPPIES

¾ c. white cornmeal
¼ c. flour
½ tsp. salt
½ tsp. sugar
1 tbsp. baking powder
¼ c. milk
1 egg
1 lge. onion, chopped fine
1 tbsp. chili sauce

Sift dry ingredients together; add milk and unbeaten egg. Mix well. Add just enough water to make batter drop-thickness. Add onion and chili sauce; mix. Drop by small spoonfuls into deep 425 to 450-degree fat. Fry until golden brown; drain on paper napkins.

Mrs. Lyn High, Miami, Fla.

FLUFFY HUSH PUPPIES

1 c. flour
1 c. cornmeal
2 tsp. baking powder
1 tsp. salt
1 tsp. sugar
1 egg
1 c. (about) milk
1 med. onion, chopped
1 sm. potato, grated
Oil

Combine dry ingredients in bowl. Add egg and milk; beat until smooth. Stir in onion and potato. Heat oil in skillet, 1 inch deep, to about 375 degrees. Drop batter by spoonfuls into hot oil; fry until golden brown on both sides. Drain on paper towels. Do not use baking powder and salt if self-rising meal and flour are used. Yield: 24 hush puppies.

Mrs. William F. Cosby, Rockford, Tenn.

HOT WATER HUSH PUPPIES

1 c. cornmeal
½ c. flour
¼ tsp. soda
1 tsp. salt
2 tbsp. sugar

Mix the above ingredients thoroughly. Add 1 1/2 cups boiling water and stir quickly, letting boiling water cook the meal to a heavy batter consistency. Add more water if necessary. Drop batter by spoonfuls into hot bacon fat and press flat, about 1/2 inch thick. Brown on both sides. Serve hot.

Mrs. Fred Mika, Brownsville, Tex.

HUSH PUPPIES

1 c. self-rising cornmeal
3 tbsp. sugar
1 tsp. baking powder
½ c. sweet milk
1 egg
2 tbsp. grated onion

(Continued on next page)

Sift dry ingredients together. Add sweet milk; mix. Add egg and onion; stir well. Drop from tablespoon into deep hot fat; fry to a golden brown. Serve immediately with fish or vegetables.

Mrs. Hugh Moreland, Starkville, Miss.

HUSH PUPPIES

2 c. cornmeal
2 tsp. baking powder
1 tsp. salt
1 ½ c. sweet milk
½ c. water
1 lge. onion, chopped fine

Sift dry ingredients together; add milk and water. Stir in chopped onion. Add more milk or meal as necessary to form a soft workable dough. With hands, mold dough into oblong cakes about 5 inches long and 3 inches wide. Fry in deep hot fat or oil until well browned.

Mrs. J. A. Stansbury, Clinton, Miss.

HUSH PUPPIES

1 c. self-rising cornmeal
½ c. flour
1 med. onion, chopped or grated
1 egg, beaten
1 c. milk
¼ tsp. salt

Combine all ingredients. Drop by teaspoonfuls into fat; deep fry. Yield: 4 servings.

Mrs. Hubert Garrett, Bolivar, Tenn.

HUSH PUPPIES

1 c. self-rising cornmeal
1 sm. onion, diced
1 egg
½ tsp. salt
Buttermilk

Combine cornmeal, onion, egg and salt; add enough buttermilk to make a soupy batter. Spoon batter, 1 tablespoonful for each hush puppy, into rapidly boiling cooking oil. Turn hush puppies in oil until golden brown. Remove; drain well. Do not overcook.

Mrs. Joseph O. Johnston, Albany, Ga.

SPECIAL HUSH PUPPIES

1 c. cornmeal
½ c. flour
1 ½ tsp. baking powder
¾ tsp. salt
2 tbsp. minced onion
⅔ c. milk
1 egg

(Continued on next page)

Mix all dry ingredients; add minced onion, milk and egg. Mix thoroughly; do not beat. Drop by teaspoonfuls into hot oil; cook until golden brown. Serve hot.

Mrs. Donald Young, Ocean Springs, Miss.

TASTY HUSH PUPPIES

- 1 c. fine cornmeal
- 3 tbsp. flour
- 1 tsp. salt
- 1 tsp. baking powder
- 1 tsp. sugar (opt.)
- ⅛ tsp. baking soda
- 1 egg
- 1 tbsp. cooking oil or bacon drippings
- ½ c. thin buttermilk
- 1 grated onion

Mix dry ingredients. Stir in remaining ingredients all at once; mix well. Drop by teaspoonfuls in hot deep fat. Cook till brown. If buttermilk is very thick, use half water and half milk mixed together.

Mrs. Richard L. Fortner, Port St. Joe, Fla.

JOHNNYCAKE

- 1 c. cornmeal
- 2 tbsp.whole wheat flour
- ½ tsp. salt
- 1 tbsp. sugar
- 1 ½ tbsp. melted shortening
- 1 c. boiling milk
- 1 egg, separated

Sift cornmeal and flour together; spread thin on baking sheet. Brown lightly at 275 degrees; remove from oven. Add salt and sugar; add shortening. Add milk quickly. Beat egg white until stiff. Beat egg yolk; fold into egg white. Fold into cornmeal mixture; drop batter from spoon in rectangular shape into greased baking pan, leaving 1/2 inch between each cake. Bake at 400 degrees for 30 minutes.

Dorothy Ryan, The Plains, Va.

JOHNNIE CAKE

- ¾ tsp. soda
- 1 ¼ c. buttermilk
- 2 eggs, well beaten
- 1 ¼ c. flour
- 2 tsp. baking powder
- ½ tsp. salt
- 1 c. cornmeal
- 3 tbsp. shortening, melted

Add soda to buttermilk; add eggs. Sift dry ingredients. Add milk mixture to dry ingredients; add melted shortening. Bake at 425 degrees for 40 minutes.

Mrs. Z. L. Wynn, Knoxville, Tenn.

CORNMEAL MUFFINS

- 1 c. cornmeal
- ½ c. flour
- 1 tsp. baking powder
- ½ tsp. salt
- ½ tsp. soda
- 1 c. buttermilk
- 1 egg
- Liquid vegetable shortening

(Continued on next page)

Put cornmeal in mixing bowl. Sift flour, baking powder, salt, and soda on top of meal. Stir. Add buttermilk; beat well. Break in egg; beat well. Put about 1 teaspoon of vegetable shortening in each cup of an iron muffin pan. Place greased pan in oven until smoking hot. Pour batter into hot pan, filling each cup about 2/3 full. Bake at 475 degrees for 15 to 20 minutes. Yield: 8 or 9 large muffins.

Mrs. S. A. Wall, Fort Worth, Tex.

MISS LUCY'S CORN BREAD

1 c. cornmeal
1 tsp. soda
1 tsp. salt
1 tsp. sugar
1 c. cooked grits
2 eggs
2 c. buttermilk

Sift first 4 ingredients. Mash grits with fork; mix into dry ingredients. Beat eggs; add buttermilk. Add egg mixture to cornmeal mixture; pour into well-greased 10-inch pan. Bake at 400 degrees for 25 to 30 minutes or until brown.

Mrs. Karl N. Hill, Charlotte, N. C.

MUFFIN CORN BREAD

⅔ tsp. salt
2 tsp. sugar
1 c. all-purpose flour
1 c. cornmeal
3 tsp. baking powder
1 ¼ c. milk
2 eggs, beaten
3 tbsp. peanut oil or bacon drippings

Blend dry ingredients; add milk, eggs and shortening. Pour into greased pan, about 9 x 14 inches. Bake 30 minutes in preheated 425-degree oven.

Mrs. Alta Yelvington Forbess, Pineville, N. C.

BACON-CORN BREAD MUFFINS

1 ¾ c. cornmeal
1 tsp. salt
1 tsp. sugar
1 tsp. baking powder
½ tsp. soda
1 egg
1 ½ c. buttermilk
3 or 4 strips crisply cooked bacon

Preheat oven to 500 degrees. Mix dry ingredients; add beaten egg. Pour in buttermilk. Add bacon and stir enough to mix. Pour batter into greased pan until cups are 2/3 full. Bake 15 minutes or until muffins are golden brown on top.

Jane Hunt Clark, Lexington, Ky.

CORN MUFFINS

1 ½ c. sifted flour
3 tsp. baking powder
1 tsp. salt
¼ c. sugar
¾ c. yellow cornmeal
2 eggs, beaten
1 c. milk
¼ c. melted shortening

(Continued on next page)

Sift together flour, baking powder, salt, sugar; add cornmeal. Add eggs, milk and shortening. Stir well. Pour in greased muffins pans. Bake at 425 degrees for 20 minutes.

Eunice Kelley, Walhalla, S. C.

CORN MUFFINS

1 c. sifted flour
1 tsp. salt
3 tsp. baking powder
1 to 2 tbsp. sugar
¾ c. cornmeal
2 eggs, well beaten
1 c. milk
¼ c. vegetable oil

Mix and sift first 4 ingredients; add cornmeal. Combine well-beaten eggs, milk and vegetable oil. Add to dry ingredients. Mix just enough to dampen. Bake in greased muffin or cornstick pans at 425 degrees 25 minutes.

Brenda Warren, Andalusia, Ala.

CORNMEAL MUFFINS

⅓ c. shortening
1 c. sugar
2 eggs, well beaten
1 ¼ c. cornmeal
¾ c. sifted flour
2 ½ tsp. baking powder
¾ tsp. salt
½ c. raisins
1 c. milk

Preheat oven to 400 degrees. Cream shortening and sugar until light and fluffy; stir in eggs, then cornmeal. Mix and sift flour, baking powder, and salt. Stir raisins into flour mixture. Add to cornmeal mixture. Add milk; stir just enough to moisten. Spoon into greased muffin pans. Bake 25 minutes. Yield: 16 muffins.

Mrs. Jewel Thaggard, Parkton, N. C.

CORNMEAL MUFFINS

1 c. meal
¼ tsp. soda
1 tsp. (rounded) baking powder
½ tsp. salt
1 egg
Buttermilk

Sift dry ingredients together; add egg and enough buttermilk to make soft batter. Mix well. While mixing, heat muffin tins in hot oven with about 1/2 teaspoon fat in each tin. Pour fat into batter. Fill tins about 3/4 full. Bake for 30 minutes at 450 degrees. Yield: 6 muffins.

Mrs. H. M. Laney, Montgomery, Ala.

CORNBREAD MUFFIN OR STICKS

2 c. self-rising meal
1 ½ c. fresh buttermilk
1 tsp. sugar
1 or 2 well-beaten eggs
2 tbsp. melted shortening

(Continued on next page)

Combine all ingredients, adding melted shortening last. Put batter in a well-greased muffin or cornstick pan. Bake for 15 to 20 minutes at 425 to 450 degrees.

Mrs. Ruby Willis, Paris, Tenn.

CREOLE CORN MUFFINS

1 ½ c. sifted flour
3 tsp. baking powder
1 tsp. salt
3 tbsp. sugar
¾ c. cornmeal
1 egg, well beaten
1 c. milk
¼ c. melted shortening
1 tbsp. green pepper, chopped
1 tsp. onion, chopped fine
½ c. grated cheese

Sift flour with baking powder, salt and sugar; add cornmeal and mix. Combine beaten egg, milk and melted shortening. Add to dry ingredients; stir vigorously until all flour is dampened. Add green pepper, onion and cheese. Pour batter into muffin pans that have been greased with shortening. Bake at 400 degrees 25 to 30 minutes. Yield: 12 muffins.

Mrs. S. E. Luker, San Antonio, Tex.

DOUBLE CORN MUFFINS

1 c. sifted all-purpose flour
2 tbsp. sugar
2 tsp. baking powder
¾ tsp. salt
1 c. yellow cornmeal
1 beaten egg
1 8 ¾-oz. can cream-style corn
¾ c. milk
2 tbsp. cooking oil

Sift together flour, sugar, baking powder and salt; stir in cornmeal. Combine egg, corn, milk and cooking oil. Add to dry ingredients; stir just till moistened. Fill greased 2-inch muffin pans 2/3 full. Bake at 425 degrees for 30 minutes or till golden brown. Yield: 20 muffins.

Mrs. Hugh E. Miller, Bristol, Tennessee

GRITS-CORNMEAL MUFFINS

1 c. sweet milk
1 egg
1 c. cold, boiled enriched grits
1 tbsp. melted fat
½ tsp. salt
2 tsp. baking powder
1 ¼ c. cornmeal

(Continued on next page)

Beat milk and egg into grits; add melted fat and dry ingredients. Mix well. Bake in well-greased muffin pans for 30 minutes at 400 to 425 degrees. Yield: 12 muffins.

Mrs. Bill Jones, Americus, Ga.

MAPLE-CORN MUFFINS

1 egg
⅓ c. milk
2 tbsp. maple syrup
½ c. yellow cornmeal
¾ c. all-purpose flour
1 ½ tsp. baking powder
¼ tsp. salt
3 tbsp. butter, melted

Beat egg; add milk and syrup. Beat again. Mix cornmeal, flour, baking powder and salt. Gradually stir in syrup mixture. Add butter. Spoon into tiny well-greased preheated muffin cups, filling only 3/4 full. Bake at 425 degrees 15 minutes or until muffins are crisp and brown. Serve hot with butter and maple syrup. Yield: 1 dozen.

Hedy Laniar, San Antonio, Tex.

SOUTHERN CORN MUFFINS

1 c. boiling water
1 c. white cornmeal
½ c. milk
½ tsp. salt
2 tsp. baking powder
1 tbsp. soft butter
1 egg, well beaten

Pour boiling water over cornmeal. Mix well; beat in milk, salt, baking powder, butter and egg. Pour into very well-greased glass custard cups. Bake in a 475-degree oven for 25 to 30 minutes. Serve hot.

Mrs. Eddie A. Landry, Ponchatoula, La.

OLD-FASHIONED CORN BREAD

2 c. white cornmeal
1 tsp. soda
1 tsp. baking powder
1 tsp. salt
Buttermilk

Mix dry ingredients well; add enough buttermilk to make a very soft batter. Pour into well-greased and floured 8 or 9-inch pan. Bake at 450 degrees until brown.

Mrs. R. A. Aldridge, Gretna, Va.

OLD-FASHIONED QUICK CORN BREAD

1 ¾ c. cornmeal
½ c. flour
½ tsp. baking powder
½ c. sugar
½ tsp. soda
½ tsp. salt
2 c. buttermilk
Shortening the size of an egg

(Continued on next page)

Sift dry ingredients; stir in buttermilk. Place shortening in loaf pan; place in hot oven until melted. Pour shortening into batter; stir. Place batter in loaf pan. Bake for 45 minutes at 400 degrees.

Mrs. Craig McRody, Lewisburg, Tenn.

OVEN CORN BREAD

1 c. cornmeal
1 c. flour
½ tsp. salt
4 tsp. baking powder
¾ c. milk
1 egg, well beaten
¼ c. melted butter or shortening

Sift together cornmeal, flour, salt and baking powder; stir in milk. Add egg; beat briskly. Stir in melted butter. Bake at 350 degrees to 400 degrees 30 minutes.

Mrs. Iona C. O'Brian, St. Petersburg, Fla.

RICE CORN BREAD

1 c. cornmeal
1 c. cold cooked rice
1 tsp. baking powder
Butter size of an egg, melted
2 c. milk
1 egg
½ tsp. salt

Mix all ingredients; let stand for 20 minutes. Beat; pour into greased shallow pan. Bake for 40 minutes at 350 degrees. Yield: 4-6 servings.

Mrs. J. Ward McPherson, Houston, Tex.

SKILLET CORN BREAD

1 ½ c. flour
4 tsp. baking powder
2 tbsp. sugar
2 tbsp. salt
1 tsp. sage
½ tsp. thyme
1 ½ c. yellow cornmeal
1 ½ c. chopped celery
1 pkg. onion soup mix
¼ c. chopped pimento
3 eggs, beaten
1 ½ c. milk
⅓ c. salad oil

Sift flour, baking powder, sugar and salt; add sage, thyme, cornmeal, celery, soup mix and pimento. Stir to blend. Combine eggs, milk and oil; add to dry ingredients. Stir just enough to moisten; pour into oiled 10 or 11-inch skillet. Bake at 400 degrees for 35 to 40 minutes.

Mildred Moore, Hollywood, Fla.

SOUTH CAROLINA BATTER BREAD

4 eggs, beaten separately
2 ½ c. milk
1 c. cooked rice
4 tbsp. cornmeal
2 tsp. sugar
2 tsp. baking powder
1 tsp. salt
1 ½ tbsp. (heaping) butter

(Continued on next page)

Beat egg yolks 3 minutes; add milk slowly. Add rice and dry ingredients; fold in stiffly beaten egg whites. Pour into baking dish in which butter has been melted. Bake at 350 degrees for 45 minutes to 1 hour.

Mrs. James P. Thomas, Cape Charles, Va.

SOUTHERN SALMON CORN BREAD

1 7 ¾-oz. can salmon
1 c. sifted flour
1 c. cornmeal
4 tsp. baking powder
¼ c. sugar
½ tsp. salt
Milk
1 egg, beaten
¼ c. butter, melted

Drain salmon, reserving liquid; flake salmon. Sift together flour, cornmeal, baking powder, sugar and salt. Add enough milk to salmon liquid to make 1 cup liquid; combine liquid, egg and butter. Add to dry ingredients; mix just enough to moisten. Stir in salmon; place in well-greased 8 x 8 x 2-inch baking dish. Bake at 425 degrees for about 30 minutes. Yield: 6 servings.

Mrs. Corrine Weaver, Newcomb, Tenn.

BUTTERMILK SPOON BREAD

1 ½ c. boiling water
1 c. white cornmeal
1 tbsp. fat
1 ½ tsp. salt
¾ tsp. soda
2 eggs, separated
1 ½ c. buttermilk

Pour boiling water over cornmeal and fat; mix well. Cool slightly. Add salt, soda and egg yolks, mixing well. Add buttermilk; fold in stiffly beaten egg whites. Pour into 1 1/2-quart casserole. Bake in oven at 350 degrees for 1 hour or until firm. Spoon out; serve hot with butter.

Margaret Connelly, Arden, N. C.

CORNMEAL SPOON BREAD

1 c. cornmeal
2 c. cold water
1 tsp. salt
2 eggs, well beaten
1 c. sweet milk
1 tbsp. shortening, melted

Mix cornmeal, cold water and salt; boil until thick. Add eggs, milk and shortening. Bake in a well-greased pan 25 minutes at 450 degrees. Serve from dish. Yield: 6 servings.

Mrs. James Tresper, Covington, Tenn.

SOUTHERN SPOON BREAD

1 c. cornmeal
2 c. boiling water
½ tsp. salt
2 tbsp. butter or margarine
4 eggs, beaten
1 c. cold milk

(Continued on next page)

Stir cornmeal into boiling salted water. Stir for 1 minute; remove from heat. Add butter; beat well. Add eggs; beat in cold milk. Beat again; pour into hot buttered baking dish. Bake 25 minutes in 450-degree oven. Serve from baking dish. Yield: 8 servings.

Mrs. Earl H. Shelton, Arlington, Va.

OLD CHARLESTON SPOON BREAD

1 ½ tbsp. butter or margarine
1 c. cooked hominy or grits
½ tsp. salt
2 eggs, beaten
1 c. milk
1 ½ c. cornmeal
1 tsp. baking powder

Mix butter in warm grits; add salt. Add eggs and milk gradually. Mix in cornmeal and baking powder. Mixture should be consistency of thick boiled custard. Pour into well-greased baking dish. Bake in oven at 400 degrees until golden brown. Serve hot.

Mellison Smith, Mobile, Ala.

OLD VIRGINIA SPOON BREAD

1 ½ c. boiling water
1 c. self-rising cornmeal
1 tbsp. butter
3 egg yolks, beaten
1 c. buttermilk
1 tsp. sugar
¼ tsp. soda
3 egg whites, beaten only enough to hold soft peaks

Pour boiling water over cornmeal; stir to keep from lumping until cooled slightly. Add butter and egg yolks; stir until egg is thoroughly blended. Stir in buttermilk; blend in sugar and soda. Fold in egg whites. Pour into greased 2-quart casserole. Bake 45 to 50 minutes in 375-degree oven. Serve hot with butter. Yield: 4-6 servings.

Mrs. Emmett Crockett, Murfreesboro, Tenn.

SOUTHERN TOMATO SPOON BREAD

1 c. cornmeal
1 c. tomato juice
2 c. scalded milk
¼ c. butter or margarine
1 sm. or ½ med. onion, finely grated
1 tsp. baking powder
¾ tsp. salt
3 eggs, separated

Mix cornmeal with cold tomato juice. Slowly stir cornmeal mixture into scalded milk; cook until thick, stirring often. Remove from heat; add butter, onion, baking powder and salt. Beat yolks; gradually add hot mixture, stirring vigorously to blend. Beat egg whites until stiff, but not dry; fold into cornmeal mixture. Turn into a greased 1 1/2-quart baking dish. Bake in 375-degree oven for 40 to 50 minutes or until silver knife inserted in center comes out clean.

Mrs. G. B. Powell, Birmingham, Ala.

SOUTHERN SPOON BREAD

- 2 c. cornmeal
- 2 c. boiling water
- 3 tbsp. melted butter
- 1 tsp. salt
- 1 ½ c. sweet milk
- 3 eggs

Sift meal; stir into boiling water. Mix until smooth and free of lumps. Add melted butter and salt; thin with milk. Separate eggs; beat until light. Add yolks, then whites to mixture. Pour into a buttered baking dish. Bake in 350-degree oven about 30 minutes. Serve in the dish in which bread was baked.

Mrs. J. A. Stansbury, Clinton, Miss.

SOUTHERN SPOON BREAD

- 2 c. boiling water
- 1 c. white cornmeal
- 1 tbsp. melted butter
- 1 tsp. baking powder
- 3 egg yolks, beaten
- 3 egg whites, stiffly beaten

Pour boiling water over meal; boil 5 minutes, stirring constantly. Remove from heat; cool. Add remaining ingredients to cornmeal except egg whites; mix thoroughly. Fold in egg whites. Pour into greased 8 x 10 x 1-inch baking pan. Bake in preheated oven at 400 degrees for about 40 to 45 minutes.

Mrs. Richard Humphreys, Summerville, Ga.

SPOON BREAD

- 1 c. yellow cornmeal
- 1 ½ c. boiling water
- 1 ½ tbsp. butter or margarine
- 3 egg yolks
- 1 c. buttermilk
- 2 tsp. sugar
- 1 tsp. salt
- 1 tsp. baking powder
- ¼ tsp. soda
- 3 egg whites

Set oven at 375 degrees. Measure cornmeal into bowl. Pour boiling water onto cornmeal; stir until cool to keep free of lumps. Beat in butter and egg yolks. Stir in buttermilk; blend in sugar, salt, baking powder and soda. Beat egg whites only until soft peaks form; fold into cornmeal mixture. Bake in greased 2-quart casserole about 40 or 50 minutes until set. Serve with real butter.

Mrs. Joseph W. Hudgens, York, S. C.

SPOON BREAD AND BACON BITS

- 5 slices bacon, diced
- 2 tbsp. margarine, melted
- 1 lge. or 2 sm. eggs
- 2 tbsp. sugar
- ½ tpp. salt
- ½ tsp. soda
- 1 c. (scant) yellow cornmeal
- ¼ c. flour
- ½ c. sour cream
- ⅓ c. milk

Cook bacon until crisp. Put melted margarine in 1 1/2-quart casserole. Mix eggs, sugar, salt, soda, cornmeal, flour and sour cream; blend well. Stir in bacon bits. Pour mixture over melted butter. Slowly pour in milk; do not stir. Bake at 350 to 375 degrees for 30 minutes. Yield: 6 servings.

Mrs. Ruth E. Horman, Cocoa Beach, Fla.

SPOON BREAD

1 c. water
6 tbsp. grits
2 tbsp. butter or oleo
1 tbsp. sugar
1 tsp. salt
1 c. milk
2 eggs, well beaten
½ c. cornmeal

Bring water to a boil in a medium saucepan. Add grits; cook, stirring constantly, until thickened. Stir butter into grits; add sugar, salt, milk and eggs. Stir until well blended. Add cornmeal; stir until smooth. Turn into a well-buttered 1-quart casserole or baking dish. Bake in oven at 350 degrees for 1 hour or until firm. Yield: 4 servings.

Mrs. George H. Yenowine, Middletown, Ky.

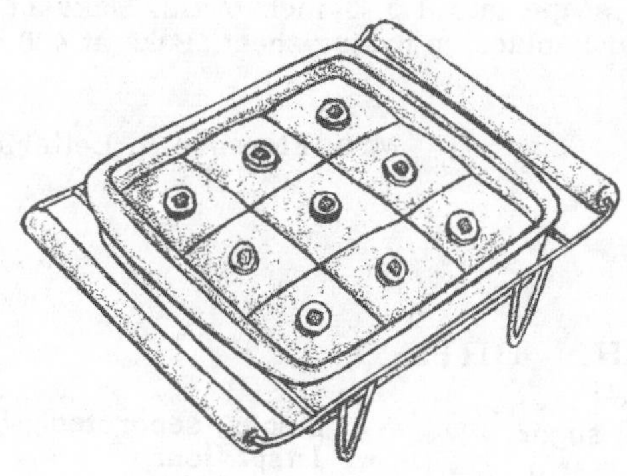

SPOON BREAD FOR TWO

2 tbsp. beaten egg or
  1 sm. egg
½ c. milk
¼ c. white cornmeal
1 tsp. baking powder
½ tsp. salt
2 tsp. butter

Beat egg well; add milk. Sift in cornmeal, baking powder and salt. Heat butter in a small 5 or 6-inch frying pan, buttering entire surface of pan. Pour butter into batter; stir in. Turn mixture into buttered pan. Bake in oven at 400 degrees for 30 minutes or until bread is firm and lightly brown.

Mrs. Blanche Coffin, Chester, Va.

UPSIDE-DOWN CORN BREAD

4 tbsp. butter or margarine
1 18-oz. can apple slices
1 1-lb. pkg. sausage
  links, cooked
½ c. sifted flour
1 tbsp. sugar
3 tsp. baking powder
1 c. cornmeal
½ tsp. salt
1 egg, slightly beaten
¾ c. milk
3 tbsp. sausage drippings
  or salad oil

(Continued on next page)

Melt butter in 9 x 9 x 2-inch pan; spread apple slices in pan. Arrange sausage over apples. Sift flour, sugar, baking powder, cornmeal and salt. Combine egg, milk and drippings; pour into a well in center of dry ingredients. Stir until smooth; pour batter over sausage and apples. Bake at 425 degrees for 25 minutes or until golden brown. Yield: 4-6 servings.

Mrs. Nell White, Miami, Fla.

VIRGINIA CORN PONE

2 c. water-ground cornmeal
1 tsp. salt
1 ½ tsp. lard
1 ½ tsp. butter
1 c. milk

Mix all ingredients; shape into 1 x 3-inch ovals. Make an indentation in top of each pone with fingers; place on baking sheet. Bake at 400 degrees for 25 minutes or until brown.

Mrs. Florence A. Detterich, Columbia, Tenn.

WALDORF CORN BREAD

1 c. cornmeal
1 tsp. (or more) sugar
1 tsp. salt
1 c. boiling water
2 eggs, separated
1 tsp. flour
1 tsp. baking powder

Combine cornmeal, sugar and salt. Pour boiling water over cornmeal mixture; let stand for 8 hours. Beat egg yolks; add to cornmeal mixture. Add flour and baking powder; mix well. Beat egg whites until stiff but not dry; fold into mixture. Bake in greased pan at 450 degrees until brown.

Mrs. James E. Dearborn, Bossier City, La.

FRENCH TOAST OR LOST BREAD

2 eggs
½ c. sugar
¼ tsp. cinnamon
4 to 6 slices bread

Beat eggs, sugar and cinnamon together. Dip bread in mixture and fry on buttered griddle. Yield: 4-6 servings.

Mrs. Harriet Lard, Maringoun, La.

IRISH SODA BREAD

4 c. sifted all-purpose flour
¼ c. granulated sugar
1 tsp. salt
1 tsp. baking powder
2 tbsp. caraway seed
¼ c. butter or margarine

(Continued on next page)

2 c. light or dark raisins
1 ⅓ c. buttermilk
1 egg, unbeaten
1 tsp. baking soda
1 egg yolk or a little cream

Preheat oven to 375 degrees. Grease 2-quart casserole. Sift flour, sugar, salt and baking powder into mixing bowl; stir in caraway seed. Cut in butter with pastry blender or 2 knives until consistency of coarse cornmeal; stir in raisins. Combine buttermilk, egg and soda; stir into flour mixture until just moistened. Turn dough onto lightly floured surface; knead lightly until smooth. Shape into ball. Place in casserole. Make 4-inch cross, 1/4-inch deep, in center. Brush with yolk, beaten with fork. Bake 1 hour and 10 minutes, or until done. Cool in pan 10 minutes; remove. Cool before slicing.

Mrs. Walter F. Stack, Lovettsville, Va.

HOMINY MUFFINS

1 c. cold cooked hominy grits
1 c. milk
1 c. flour
4 tsp. baking powder
½ tsp. salt
2 eggs, well beaten

Soften grits with milk. Sift flour, baking powder and salt; add to grits. Add eggs; pour into well-greased muffin tins. Bake at 400 degrees for 30 minutes.

Mrs. George S. Quillin, Fayetteville, N. C.

QUICKIE OATMEAL MUFFINS

1 c. quick-cooking oats
1 c. flour
2 ½ tsp. baking powder
1 tsp. salt
3 tbsp. sugar
½ c. evaporated milk
½ c. water
2 tbsp. melted shortening or oleo

Mix dry ingredients. Combine milk and water; add to dry ingredients. Add melted shortening; stir until blended. Pour into greased muffin tins. Bake at 350 degrees for about 20 minutes. Yield: 10 muffins.

Mrs. C. L. Fox, Amarillo, Tex.

RICE MUFFIN FRITTERS

1 egg
1 c. milk
1 c. cooked rice
1 ½ c. flour
4 tsp. baking powder
½ tsp. salt
3 strips cooked crisp bacon
Tart jelly

Beat egg; add milk and rice. Mix well; add flour that has been sifted with baking powder and salt. Line glass molds or muffin tins with crumbled bacon; pour batter over bacon. Bake at 425 degrees for 30 minutes. To serve, invert muffins and top each muffin with a spoonful of jelly.

Mrs. Otto Murphy, Springfield, Tenn.

RICE MUFFINS

1 c. flour
1 tbsp. sugar
½ tsp. salt
1 ½ tsp. baking powder
1 egg
⅔ c. milk
1 c. cold cooked rice
2 tbsp. melted shortening

Sift flour, sugar, salt and baking powder 3 times; set aside. Beat egg thoroughly; add milk and rice. Stir in shortening; immediately add flour mixture. Stir until dry ingredients are just dampened; batter should not be smooth. Spoon into buttered muffin pan, filling 2/3 full. Bake at 425 degrees for 20 minutes or until browned. Serve hot. Yield: 8-10 muffins.

Mrs. George Pecsek, Virginia Beach, Va.

BLUEBERRY-BUTTERMILK PANCAKES

2 c. sifted flour
½ tsp. salt
1 tbsp. baking powder
3 tbsp. sugar
2 eggs
2 c. buttermilk
2 tbsp. melted butter
2 c. fresh or frozen blueberries

Reserve 1/4 cup flour; set aside. Sift remaining flour, salt, baking powder and sugar. Beat eggs; stir in buttermilk and butter. Add dry ingredients all at once to buttermilk mixture. Toss blueberries with reserved flour; add to batter. Stir just until moistened. Cook on buttered hot griddle, turning once. Use a scant 1/4 cup batter for each pancake.

Mrs. R. L. Marcheasseau, Miami, Fla.

CORNMEAL GRIDDLE CAKES

1 c. sifted flour
4 tsp. baking powder
1 tsp. salt
1 c. cornmeal
1 egg, well-beaten
2 c. milk
2 tbsp. shortening, melted

Sift flour, baking powder and salt together; add cornmeal and mix well. Combine egg and milk; add to dry ingredients. Stir in shortening. Cook on hot griddle turning once. If a thinner batter is preferred, use more milk.

Mrs. Frank Cress, Salisbury, N. C.

CORNMEAL PANCAKES

1 c. cornmeal
1 c. sifted flour
1 tsp. salt
2 tsp. baking powder
½ tsp. baking soda
½ c. water
2 eggs, beaten
2 c. buttermilk

(Continued on next page)

Sift dry ingredients. Mix water, eggs and buttermilk; add to dry ingredients. Stir; add more water if necessary to make thin batter. Pour batter by tablespoonfuls onto hot greased griddle. Bake, turning once. Serve with butter and honey. Yield: 40 2-inch pancakes.

Mrs. Henry Hudson, Cocoa Beach, Fla.

CORNMEAL PANCAKES

- 1 ½ c. self-rising cornmeal
- 1 ½ c. pancake mix
- 3 eggs, slightly beaten
- 6 tbsp. oil, melted shortening or bacon drippings
- 3 c. (about) milk

Mix cornmeal and pancake mix; add eggs, oil and milk. Mix until large lumps disappear; do not beat until smooth. Bake on hot griddle or skillet, turning once. Yield: 24-30 pancakes.

Mrs. H. F. Glenn, Huntsville, Ala.

FLUFFY GRIDDLE CAKES

- 2 c. sifted flour
- 3 tsp. baking powder
- 1 tsp. salt
- 2 tbsp. sugar
- 1 egg
- 1 ½ c. milk
- 2 tbsp. melted butter or shortening
- 1 tsp. vanilla flavoring

Combine dry ingredients; add egg, milk, butter and vanilla. Bake on hot slightly greased griddle, turning once.

Eddie Chism, Coker, Ala.

LACY-EDGED CORN CAKES

- 1 c. white cornmeal
- ½ tsp. salt
- ½ tsp. soda
- 1 egg
- 1 ¼ c. buttermilk
- 1 tbsp. lard, bacon fat or shortening
- Old-Fashioned Brown Sugar Sauce

Mix cornmeal, salt and soda with fork; add egg. Add buttermilk slowly. Heat lard in 12-inch skillet; drop batter by tablespoonfuls into hot fat from a height, allowing 2 inches between cakes. Turn once. Serve immediately with hot Old-Fashioned Brown Sugar Sauce.

OLD-FASHIONED BROWN SUGAR SAUCE:

- 1 c. (packed) dark brown sugar
- ¼ c. water
- 1 tbsp. butter

Mix all ingredients in small saucepan; bring to boil. Boil, stirring occasionally, for 2 to 3 minutes or until the consistency of maple syrup.

Mrs. John R. Richards, Lookout Mountain, Tenn.

RIPE OLIVE SNACK BREAD

1 c. ripe olives
1 egg
⅓ c. melted margarine or butter
1 tbsp. instant minced onion or ¼ c. chopped onion
1 tsp. Worcestershire sauce
2 ½ c. grated sharp cheddar cheese
3 c. prepared biscuit mix
1 c. milk
1 tsp. caraway seed (opt.)

Cut olives into large pieces, removing seeds. Beat egg lightly; add margarine, onion, Worcestershire sauce, cheese and olives. Set aside. Combine biscuit mix and milk; stir into a soft dough. Spread very thin onto greased 10 x 15-inch pan, as for pizza dough. Spoon combined ingredients over dough evenly; sprinkle with caraway seed. Bake at 350 degrees 15 to 20 minutes until well browned. Serve hot. Yield: 2 dozen squares.

Martha C. Berry, Louisville, Ky.

SCONES

3 c. flour
4 tsp. baking powder
1 tbsp. sugar
¼ tsp. salt
¼ tsp. soda
3 tbsp. shortening
1 c. sour milk or buttermilk

Sift together dry ingredients; add shortening, mixing in with fork. Add liquid to make soft dough. Turn out on floured board; toss lightly until smooth. Cut into 4 equal parts. Shape each into a round about 1/2 inch thick. Cut into quarters to make triangular pieces. Place in greased baking pan. Bake at 425 degrees for 20 minutes. Split; butter and serve hot. Yield: 16 pieces.

Erline Rice, Florence, Ala.

TORTILLAS

1 c. boiling water
1 c. cornmeal
1 tsp. salt

Stir boiling water into cornmeal; add salt. Mix well; pat out into thin cakes. Bake on ungreased griddle, turning once.

Mrs. D. H. Wilson, Dodd City, Tex.

BUTTERMILK WAFFLES

1 c. cornmeal
1 ½ c. water
1 tsp. salt
1 tbsp. shortening
2 eggs, separated
1 c. wheat flour
¾ tsp. soda
½ c. sweet milk
½ c. buttermilk

(Continued on next page)

Cook cornmeal, water, salt and shortening together for 10 minutes, stirring constantly; cool. Beat egg yolks until very light; add to cooled mush. Sift together flour and soda; add to mush alternately with the sweet milk. Fold in beaten egg whites; add buttermilk. Bake in a hot waffle iron.

Mrs. Edna Williams, Jacksonville, Ala.

CORNMEAL WAFFLES

- 1 c. flour
- 3 tsp. baking powder
- 1 tsp. salt
- 2 tbsp. sugar
- 1 c. cornmeal
- 2 eggs
- 1 ⅓ c. milk
- ¼ c. fat, melted and cooled or cooking oil

Stir dry ingredients together. Beat eggs with milk; add dry ingredients and melted fat. Beat until just smooth. Bake on hot waffle iron. Yield: 5-6 waffles.

Mrs. H. H. Huddleston, Louisville, Ky.

CORNMEAL WAFFLES

- 1 ½ c. boiling water
- 1 c. cornmeal
- 1 tsp. salt
- 4 tbsp. fat
- 2 eggs, separated
- ½ c. sweet milk
- 1 c. sifted flour
- ½ tsp. soda
- 2 tsp. baking powder
- 1 tbsp. sugar
- ⅔ c. sour milk

Add boiling water to cornmeal; stir in salt and fat. Cook in top of double boiler for 10 minutes, stirring occasionally; cool. Beat egg yolks; add sweet milk. Add egg mixture to cornmeal mixture. Mix flour, soda, baking powder and sugar together; add to cornmeal mixture with sour milk. Fold in stiffly beaten egg whites. Bake in hot waffle iron. Yield: 6-8 single waffles.

Mrs. Thomas Chrestman, Cleveland, Miss.

CORNMEAL WAFFLES

- 1 tsp. salt
- 1 ¾ c. cornmeal
- 2 eggs
- 1 ½ c. buttermilk
- ⅓ c. melted butter
- ¼ c. flour
- ¼ tsp. soda
- 2 tsp. baking powder

Mix salt and cornmeal together. Beat eggs; add buttermilk and butter. Add egg mixture to cornmeal. Sift flour, soda and baking powder together; add. Cook immediately in hot waffle iron. Yield: 8-10 waffles.

Mrs. W. W. Mynatt, Gatlinburg, Tenn.

CORNMEAL WAFFLES

1 c. boiling water
1 c. yellow cornmeal
2 c. sifted flour
1 tsp. soda
1 tsp. salt
1 tbsp. sugar
1 c. melted shortening or oleo
2 c. sour milk
2 eggs, separated

Pour boiling water over cornmeal, being careful not to let mixture lump. Sift flour, soda, salt and sugar; add shortening. Mix slightly; add milk and beaten egg yolks. Blend; add cornmeal mixture. Mix until smooth; fold in beaten egg whites. Bake on waffle iron.

Grace L. Ferriday, Metairie, La.

CORNMEAL WAFFLES

2 c. white cornmeal
1 ½ c. boiling water
3 c. flour
3 tbsp. sugar
1 ¼ tbsp. baking powder
1 ½ tsp. salt
2 eggs, separated
1 ½ c. milk
4 tbsp. shortening, melted

Cook cornmeal and water together for 20 minutes. Sift remaining dry ingredients; add to cornmeal mixture. Add egg yolks and milk; add shortening. Beat egg whites until stiff; fold into batter. Bake on hot waffle iron.

Mrs. R. L. Anderson, Travelers Rest, S. C.

CRISP WAFFLES

2 tbsp. melted shortening or oil
1 c. (packed) pancake mix
1 egg
1 ¼ c. milk

Add melted shortening to mix; add egg and milk. Stir until smooth. Bake on waffle iron for 10 minutes at 300 degrees.

Clara Thompson, Abbeville, Miss.

WAFFLE DIABLE

2 eggs
1 ½ c. milk
2 tsp. salad oil or melted shortening
1 c. pancake mix
1 c. instant whole wheat cereal
2 4 ½-oz. cans deviled ham, drained

Preheat waffle iron. Beat eggs, milk and oil. Add pancake mix and cereal. Mix well. Stir in ham. Bake in hot iron using 1/2 cup batter for each waffle. Yield: 6 7-inch waffles.

Photograph for this recipe on page 319 .

RECIPE FOR POTATO AU GRATIN BREAD ON PAGE 374

Old-Fashioned Bread

Bread, the staff of life, is one of man's oldest foods. And it is one of the most memorable. Remember the old-fashioned aroma of bread baking in grandmother's oven drifting into every nook in the house? Nothing was quite as tempting.

These old-fashioned memories can be made modern day. The joy of making your own bread is unsurpassable. Too, making special breads for particular occasions can quickly become tradition in your home.

As a rule, protein-rich foods are expensive. Bread is not only an inexpensive source of protein and carbohydrates, but it contains important minerals and B vitamins.

Bread can be made from just flour, salt and water. But it becomes more valuable nutritionally when yeast, shortening, sugar and milk are added.

Too often, there is a tendency to cut out bread completely when you want to lose weight. Most physicians, however, suggest eliminating all sweets and cutting down, but not eliminating bread.

BEGIN RIGHT

Begin with good ingredients for really memorable bread. Although the amounts and flavorings in different breads may vary, the basic way of mixing them remains the same.

YEAST . . . is a living plant which makes doughs and batters rise. Compressed yeast comes in cake form and must be refrigerated. Fresh compressed yeast will keep about two weeks. If stored in the freezer, it will keep about two months.

Dry yeast is in granular form and if stored in a cool, dry place will keep for several months. It needs greater heat and more moisture to activate it than compressed yeast does.

Because yeast is a plant, it likes warm, even temperature. Too much heat can kill its action and too little can slow it down. To dissolve yeast, rinse a bowl in hot water and dry it thoroughly. Dissolve the yeast in the warm bowl in water that is comfortably warm on the inside of your wrist. Check the temperature with a candy thermometer if you want. It should read 105-115°F.

FLOUR . . . Wheat flour is used for bread making because it contains gluten, a special substance. When flour is stirred and kneaded with liquid, the gluten stretches to form an elastic framework. This framework holds the bubbles of gas produced by the yeast. Without gluten, a satisfactory yeast bread cannot be produced.

White wheat flour may be used successfully in making bread. So can rye flour, whole wheat, graham, buckwheat, and soy flours. But to produce airy light bread, these must be used carefully and usually mixed with other flours.

Rye flour most nearly resembles wheat flour except that it will not hold the leavening agent. Bread made entirely of rye flour is dark and heavy. Rye breads can be made lighter by making a sponge of wheat flour and letting it rise. This develops the yeast and mellows the wheat gluten. Then rye flour is added to make a dough.

Whole wheat and graham flours are usually combined with at least an equal amount of white flour. Otherwise, they are too sticky to knead.

Buckwheat flour is the heaviest, so a smaller amount is used. A mixture of 2 tablespoons of soy flour with each cup of wheat flour can be used in almost any recipe. A little more water and seasoning are usually necessary. Adding soy proteins adds to the nutritional value of the baked bread.

LIQUID . . . Water, milk, or water in which potatoes have been cooked are the liquids usually used for making yeast breads. If fresh or reconstituted dry milk is used, it is heated or scalded and then cooled before using. Water makes crusty breads with a good wheaty flavor. Milk makes breads with softer crusts and a velvety, creamy white crumb that browns easily in toasting.

SUGAR . . . Furnishes food for the yeast, so that it can form the gas which makes dough or batter rise. It adds flavor and helps the crust to brown as the bread bakes. White sugar is most often used. Some special breads, though, call for brown sugar, molasses or honey.

EGGS . . . Add food value, color and rich flavor to breads. They help make the crumb fine and the crust tender.

FAT . . . Such as margarine, salad or cooking oils, hydrogenated shortening, lard or butter are called shortening when used in baked foods. Shortening helps make baked goods tender, helps keep the baked item soft and in breads gives a soft, silky crumb.

SALT . . . Brings out the flavor. It also controls the action of the yeast, slowing its rate of gas formation.

OTHER INGREDIENTS . . . Such as spices and herbs give flavor to special breads. Many festive breads call for fruits, candied or grated fruit peel or nuts.

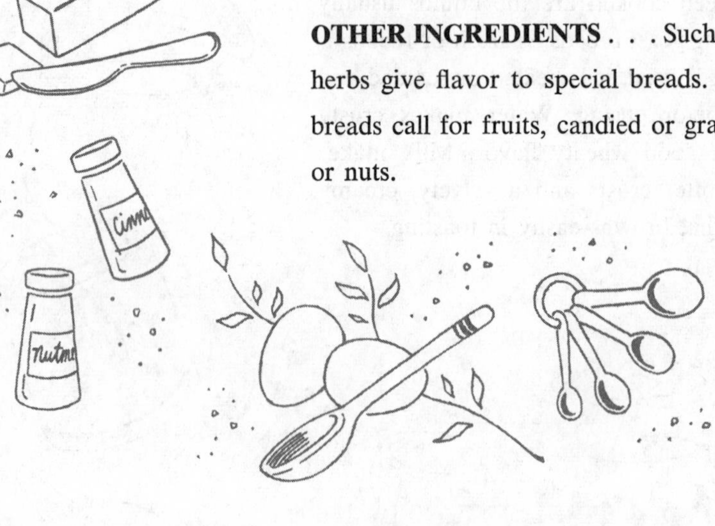

For Making Bread You Need . . .

A large glass or crockery bowl that holds at least 2 quarts. When warmed, it holds the dough at an even temperature. It also protects the dough from sudden temperature changes or chilling.

A set of standard measuring spoons.

A measuring cup to measure liquids. This kind of cup has a lip for pouring, like a pitcher, and a little space above the top of the measuring line.

A set of measuring cups for measuring dry ingredients.

A small saucepan, about 1 pint in size, for scalding milk and melting shortening.

A large wooden spoon for mixing.

A rubber or plastic bowl scraper.

A bread board.

A medium size spatula or plain knife.

A large sharp knife or kitchen scissors to cut dough or stiff batter.

Baking pans or cookie sheets.

THESE EXTRAS HELP

Egg beater
Electric mixer
Rolling pin
Pastry cloth
Pastry brush
Wire cooling racks

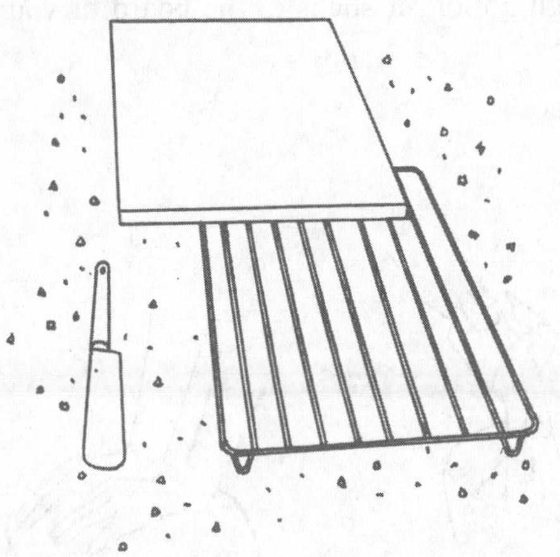

Successful Breadmaking

The tastiness of the bread that you serve your family is determined by several steps:

1. ADDING LIQUIDS—Once the yeast is dissolved, other liquids are added. They must be lukewarm or at room temperature before they are added. Otherwise, they will affect the action of the yeast. Test the liquid by dropping a small amount on the inside of your wrist. It should feel neither hot nor cold. If you use a thermometer, it should read 90-95°F.

2. ADDING FLOUR—Measure out the full amount of flour. Stir in half of it, or the amount called for in the recipe method, and blend it in. Then beat until smooth. Add enough of the remaining flour to make a rough-looking dough that pulls away from the sides of the bowl.

3. KNEADING—This is the important step that makes dough "come alive" and change from a rough, sticky, unresponsive mass into a satiny smooth, non-sticky, elastic ball. Turn the dough onto a lightly floured bread board or pastry cloth. If the dough seems sticky when you first turn it out, sprinkle it lightly with flour or fold the lightly floured cloth over it and press down; then smooth out the cloth and knead. Flour your hands, too.

Kneading is easy. Press the dough into a flat ball with the palms of your hands. Fold it over toward you, then with the heels of your hands, push it down and away. Turn it a quarter of the way around and repeat. Keep kneading until the dough looks very smooth and no longer feels sticky. As you knead, sprinkle extra flour little by little over the dough until the dough no longer sticks to the board or your hands.

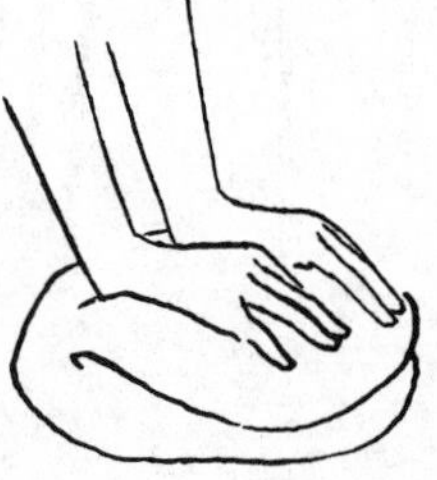

4. RISING—Cover the kneaded dough with a cloth while you wash the mixing bowl with warm water. Grease the inside of the bowl lightly. Press the top of the dough in the bowl, then turn the dough over. This greases the surface of the dough slightly so it stretches easily as it rises and does not dry out. Cover with a clean towel and set the bowl in a warm place (80-85°F.) for the dough to rise until doubled in bulk.

5. TESTING FOR DOUBLED IN BULK—Press the dough with the tip of your fingers, making a dent about ½ inch deep. If the dent disappears, let the dough rise a little longer and test again. If the dent remains, the dough has risen enough and is ready for the next step.

6. PUNCHING DOWN—When the dough has doubled, plunge your fist into the center, then fold the edges of the dough to the center and turn the dough over completely.

7. SHAPING—After punching the dough down, divide it into portions by cutting it with a large knife. Shape each piece into a ball. Cover and let dough "rest" for five minutes. This "rest" makes the dough easier to handle and causes the bread to hold its shape better.

8. TESTING FOR LIGHTNESS—After shaping, allow breads to rise until they are doubled in bulk. To tell if they have risen enough, press the bread lightly near the bottom or edge with your little finger. If the small dent remains, the bread is ready for baking.

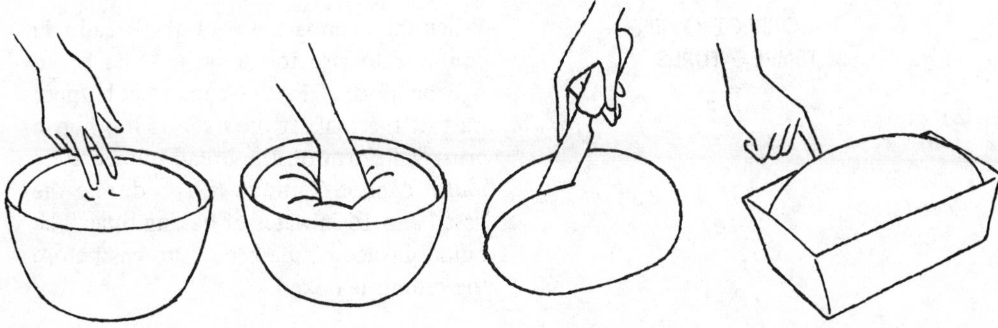

What Causes Inferior Bread

INFERIOR FLOUR

The homemaker who thinks she is saving money by buying a less expensive flour for bread making may find that her cheap flour is really expensive when her bread comes from the oven with a poor texture, color, flavor and volume.

TOO MUCH FLOUR

Dough that is too stiff results in a coarse-textured bread that is small in volume and has a dry crumb.

INACTIVE YEAST

If it acts at all, old yeast will act very slowly and will not give good results. Yeast plants that are dead cannot leaven bread.

OVER OR UNDER KNEADING

When dough is kneaded too much it becomes sticky and will not rise well in the oven. If dough is kneaded too little, the bread will be streaked and have an inferior texture which sometimes contains lumps.

OVER AND UNDER RISING

A small flat loaf which browns too quickly in the oven results from too little rising. The crumb will be compact and dull. If bread is allowed to rise too long, the loaf will be porous with little flavor and have a pale crust and a bad texture. The bread will crumble badly. The dough may become sour if the rising continues for too long a period.

INCORRECT OVEN TEMPERATURES

When the oven is too cool, the bread will continue to rise too long and the bread will be porous in the center and upper part of the loaf. If the oven is too hot, a crust will form on the bread immediately and it cannot continue to rise during the first 10 to 15 minutes of baking time. The outer surface of the bread browns before the crumb is baked.

Yeast Rolls

Shaping the dough for rolls is one of the most delightful steps in making yeast rolls. Try your hand at making each of these shapes.

PARKER HOUSE ROLLS

Roll dough in a circle until about ½ inch thick. Cut dough with a biscuit cutter. With the dull edge of a knife, crease the round of dough to one side of the center. Brush with melted butter and fold large side over small side. Seal edges. Place about 1 inch apart on greased baking sheet. Cover and let rise until doubled in bulk. Brush top with melted butter.

PAN ROLLS

Roll the dough into balls which are about one-third the size of a desired baked roll. Place balls about ¼ inch apart in a shallow baking pan. Cover and let rise. Brush with melted butter when doubled in bulk.

CLOVERLEAF ROLLS

Form dough into three small balls about the size of large marbles. Dip balls into melted butter. Place three balls in each greased cup of a muffin pan. Allow dough to rise.

CRESCENT ROLLS

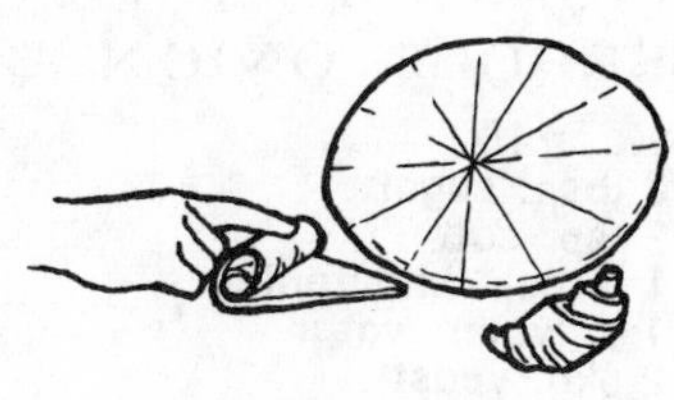

Divide dough into three equal parts and roll into a circle about 10 to 12 inches in diameter. Cut each circle into pie-shaped wedges. Roll each piece beginning with the larger end and sealing the small end. Place 2 inches apart on a baking sheet. Be sure the point of the dough is underneath. Curve each rolled piece to form a crescent. Cover and let rise, then brush with melted butter.

BUTTERFLAKE OR FAN ROLLS

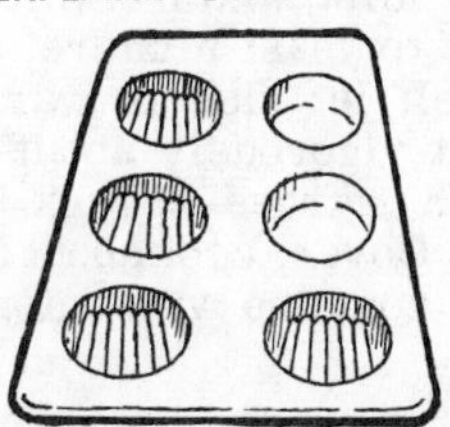

Roll dough into a thin rectangular sheet. Brush with melted butter and cut into strips about 1½ inches wide. Stack 5, 6 or 7 strips one on top of the other. Cut 1½ inches long and place end down in muffin pans. Allow dough to rise.

GOLDEN CHEESE STICKS

1 ¼ c. milk
1 tbsp. sugar
1 tsp. salt
½ tsp. butter or margarine
1 envelope or ½ cake yeast
1 tbsp. warm water
2 ¾ c. flour
1 ½ c. shredded American cheese
Melted butter or margarine

Scald milk; add sugar, salt and 1/2 tablespoon butter. Crumble the yeast into the warm water to soften and add to milk mixture. Add 2 cups flour and blend. Add cheese to remaining flour and blend again. Knead on a floured board 10 minutes. Place in a greased bowl; brush with melted butter. Cover; let rise in a warm place until doubled. Knead; roll in 8 x 10-inch rectangle. Cut in 5 crosswise strips 1 inch wide. Place on well greased cookie sheet. Bake in 375-degree oven for 20 to 25 minutes. Remove immediately and serve hot.

Mary K. Love, Pegram, Tenn.

BUTTERMILK BREAD

1 c. buttermilk
3 tbsp. sugar
2 ½ tsp. salt
⅓ c. shortening
1 pkg. yeast
1 c. warm water
5 ½ to 5 ¾ c. flour, unsifted
¼ tsp. soda

Scald buttermilk; stir in sugar, salt and shortening. Cool to lukewarm. Sprinkle yeast over warm water in mixing bowl; stir to dissolve. Add milk mixture. Add 3 cups flour and soda; beat until smooth. Add enough of remaining flour to handle dough easily. Turn onto lightly floured board; knead until smooth and elastic, about 10 minutes. Place in greased bowl; cover with cloth. Let rise until doubled, about 1 hour in warm place. Punch down; round up on lightly floured cloth. Let rest 15 minutes. Cut in half; flatten into 2 oblong pieces. Fold into loaf; put each in a separate loaf pan. Cover; let rise in warm place until center is slightly higher than pan, about 1 hour. Bake 35 to 45 minutes at 400 degrees.

Mrs. R. A. Aldridge, Gretna, Va.

CASSEROLE ONION BREAD

1 c. milk
3 tbsp. sugar
2 tsp. salt
1 ½ tbsp. shortening
1 c. warm water
2 pkg. yeast
4 ½ c. plain flour
1 tsp. onion salt
½ tsp. celery salt
2 tbsp. margarine
¾ c. coarsely chopped onion
1 egg yolk
1 tsp. water

Scald milk; add sugar, salt and shortening. Cool to lukewarm. Measure warm water into 2 1/2-quart bowl; sprinkle or crumble in yeast. Stir until dissolved; add cooled milk mixture. Sift flour; measure. Add onion salt and celery salt. Add all at once to yeast mixture; stir until well blended, about 2 minutes. Cover with clean towel; let rise in warm place until tripled in bulk, about 40 minutes. Stir down; beat vigorously about 30 seconds. Turn into greased 2-quart casserole; bake at 375 degrees on rack just below center of oven. Melt butter over low heat; add onion. Cover; cook about 5 minutes. Cool. Beat egg yolk until light; add water. Mix well; combine with onion. When bread is set, about 40 minutes, spoon onion

(Continued on next page)

mixture evenly over top. Bake 20 minutes more. Remove from oven; turn out and cool on rack.

Mrs. Warren P. Carson, Savannah, Ga.

CHEESE BREAD

1 c. hot water
¼ c. plus 1 tsp. sugar
1 ½ tsp. salt
2 tbsp. lukewarm water
1 pkg. dry or compressed yeast
1 egg, well beaten
½ lb. grated process American cheese
3 to 4 c. sifted all-purpose flour

Combine hot water, 1/4 cup sugar and salt in large bowl; cool to lukewarm. Stir remaining sugar into lukewarm water. Add yeast; let stand 5 to 10 minutes until thoroughly dissolved. Stir and add to first mixture. Stir in egg, cheese and flour to make stiff dough. Turn on lightly floured board; knead until smooth and elastic, about 2 to 3 minutes. Mold into loaf; place in greased 10 x 5 x 3-inch loaf pan. Brush with salad oil. Cover with towel; let rise in warm place, 80 to 85 degrees, until doubled in bulk. Bake at 375 degrees for 45 minutes or until done. Remove from pan; brush with oil. Cool on wire cake rack.

Mrs. Ted G. Tudor, Port Neches, Tex.

CORN BREAD

½ cake yeast
¼ c. lukewarm water
½ c. cornmeal
1 ¾ c. boiling water
1 ½ tsp. salt
2 tbsp. sugar
1 tbsp. shortening
2 ¾ to 3 c. sifted flour

Soften yeast in lukewarm water. Cook cornmeal in boiling water 10 minutes; add salt, sugar and shortening. Cool until lukewarm; stir occasionally to prevent film. When cool, add softened yeast; beat well. Add flour; mix well. Knead, using as little flour on board as possible. Put in greased bowl; grease top. Cover; let rise to double. Knead down; let rise again. Shape in loaves; place in pans and let rise again. Bake 10 minutes at 400 to 425 degrees. Reduce to 375 degrees for 35 to 40 minutes.

Mrs. E. G. Bright, Pasadena, Tex.

CORNMEAL BREAD

1 pkg. dry yeast
¼ c. warm water
½ c. milk
¼ c. shortening
¼ c. sugar
1 tsp. salt
¼ c. cold water
½ c. cornmeal
1 egg
2 c. flour
Butter

Dissolve yeast in warm water. Scald milk; pour over shortening, sugar and salt. Beat in yeast, cold water, cornmeal and egg; add enough flour to make a stiff dough. Turn out on floured board; knead until smooth, about 10 minutes. Put

(Continued on next page)

in lightly buttered bowl; brush top with butter. Let rise in warm place until light, about 1 to 2 hours. Turn out on board; let rest 10 minutes. Shape into loaf; place in buttered 9 x 5 x 3-inch pan. Let rise until almost doubled. Bake in preheated oven at 400 degrees for 15 minutes. Reduce heat to 350 degrees and bake 15 minutes longer. Brush with butter; cool on rack.

Mrs. C. R. Dougherty, Opelika, Ala.

CORNMEAL-RAISIN BREAD

2 pkg. dry yeast
½ c. warm water
1 ⅓ c. milk, scalded
¾ c. sugar
1 tbsp. salt
⅓ c. shortening
2 eggs, beaten
1 ½ c. cornmeal
6 c. sifted flour
1 ½ c. raisins

Soften yeast in warm water. Pour scalded milk over sugar, salt and shortening; stir occasionally until shortening melts. Cool to lukewarm. Stir in eggs and cornmeal; add yeast and 3 cups flour. Beat until smooth; stir in remaining flour and raisins. Beat until well blended, about 2 minutes. Batter will be stiff. Cover; let rise in warm place until doubled in size, about 1 hour. Stir batter down; beat vigorously about 30 seconds. Divide batter between two 8 1/2 x 4 1/2 x 2 1/2-inch loaf pans. With floured hands, pat to smooth tops of loaves. Cover; let rise about 45 minutes or until almost doubled. Bake at 375 degrees 45 to 50 minutes. Remove from pans; cool.

Mrs. F. W. Allain, Hammond, La.

COUNTY FAIR EGG BREAD

1 ½ c. scalded milk
½ c. butter
2 tsp. salt
½ c. sugar
2 cakes yeast
½ c. lukewarm water
2 beaten eggs
9 c. (about) flour, sifted

Pour scalded milk over butter, salt and sugar; cool. Dissolve yeast in lukewarm water; let stand until it bubbles, about 5 minutes. Add yeast and beaten eggs to cooled milk. Gradually add flour, beating in thoroughly. Do not add any more flour than is necessary to make an easily handled dough. Turn out onto floured board; knead until smooth and elastic. Place in greased bowl. Cover; let rise until doubled in size, about 1 hour and 30 minutes. Punch down; turn out onto a lightly floured board. Shape into 3 loaves; place in greased 8-inch loaf pan. Cover; let rise until dough is just to the top of the pans. Bake in 425-degree oven for 10 minutes, then lower heat to 350 degrees and bake 40 minutes longer or until bread is done.

Mrs. Charles Stirewalt, Old Fort, N. C.

DELICIOUS YEAST CORN BREAD

1 egg
4 tbsp. melted shortening
1 c. buttermilk
1 c. cornmeal
¼ tsp. soda
2 tbsp. sugar
1 tsp. salt
1 yeast cake dissolved in ¼ c. warm water
1 ½ c. (about) sifted all-purpose flour

(Continued on next page)

Beat egg in electric beater; add shortening, buttermilk, cornmeal, soda, sugar, salt and yeast mixture. Beat until light and fluffy. With a large spoon, add sifted flour to make a soft dough. Place on floured surface; knead until smooth and sticky. Place in greased bowl; grease top of dough. Cover with cloth; let rise again until doubled in bulk. Bake in 350-degree oven about 50 minutes to 1 hour. Remove from pan; wet top with cold water. Place on side; cover with cloth to cool.

Mrs. Florence A. DeHerich, Columbia, Tenn.

DILLY BREAD

- 1 pkg. active dry yeast
- ¼ c. warm water
- 1 c. cottage cheese
- 2 tbsp. sugar
- 1 tbsp. minced onion
- 1 tbsp. butter, melted
- 1 tsp. dill seed
- 1 tsp. salt
- ¼ tsp. soda
- 1 unbeaten egg
- 2 ¼ to 2 ½ c. flour

Soften yeast in water. Heat cottage cheese until lukewarm; add all ingredients except flour, adding yeast last. Mix well. Add flour to form a stiff dough. Let mixture rise in a warm place until doubled in size, 50 to 60 minutes. Stir down dough. Turn into a well-greased 1 1/2-quart casserole or 2 small loaf pans. Let rise in a warm place for 40 minutes. Bake until golden brown in a 350-degree oven for about 45 minutes for a large loaf or about 35 minutes for small loaves. Spread butter and salt over bread after removing from oven.

Bruce Keener, Jr., Louisville, Tenn.

DOUBLE-GOOD BREAD

- 4 tbsp. sugar
- 4 tsp. salt
- ½ stick butter
- 2 lge. eggs
- 2 c. water
- 3 tbsp. instant potatoes
- 1 pkg. yeast
- 6 c. flour
- 6 tbsp. wheat germ

Mix sugar, salt, butter and eggs in large bowl. Measure water in pan with potatoes; mix together. Heat until warm to touch. Add to egg mixture; mix well. Sprinkle yeast over all; mix well. Let stand. Measure flour; sift. Add wheat germ. When yeast has dissolved, add half of flour and wheat germ mixture;

(Continued on next page)

mix well. Add remaining flour. Cover; let rise until doubled in warm place. Place on floured surface; knead. Cut dough in half; place each half in bread pan. Press dough to fill pan. Cover; let rise almost to top of pan. Bake at 350 degrees for 30 to 35 minutes until brown.

Mrs. James J. Elder, North Miami, Fla.

DOUBLE-TRICK CHEESE BREAD

2 pkg. active dry yeast
½ c. warm water
1 11-oz. can cheddar cheese soup
1 packet dry garlic salad dressing mix
3 ½ to 3 ¾ c. all-purpose flour

Soften yeast in warm water in large mixing bowl. Add soup and salad dressing mix. Gradually add flour to form a stiff dough, beating well after each addition. Knead on floured surface until smooth and elastic, about 5 minutes. Place in greased bowl, turning dough to grease all sides. Cover; let rise in warm place until light and doubled in size, about 30 minutes. Shape dough into four 10-inch long loaves; place on greased cookie sheets. Cover; let rise again until light and doubled in size, about 30 minutes. Bake at 400 degrees for 30 to 40 minutes. Remove from cookie sheets immediately. Cool on wire racks. If desired, slice and toast in 250-degree oven for 10 minutes or in bread toaster set at lowest temperature.

Mrs. J. C. McLamb, Fort Lauderdale, Fla.

FRENCH BREAD

1 pkg. yeast
1 ½ c. hot water
1 ½ tsp. salt
1 tbsp. sugar
1 tbsp. shortening, softened
4 c. flour
Melted butter or margarine

Dissolve yeast in 1/2 cup of the water; set aside. In another bowl dissolve salt and sugar in remaining water. Add shortening and yeast mixture; mix well. Add a little flour at the time, mixing well. Work through dough with spoon at 10 minute intervals for 5 consecutive times. Turn dough onto lightly floured surface and divide into half. Shape into 2 balls; let rest 10 minutes. Roll each ball into a 12 x 9 rectangle. Then roll firmly as for jelly roll, starting with the long side. Seal edges. Place on baking sheet and score top 6 times diagonally. Cover with towel and let stand 1 hour and 30 minutes. Bake 30 to 35 minutes at 400 degrees. Brush top with melted butter while hot. Yield: 2 loaves.

Mrs. W. E. Fiorentini, Handsboro, Miss.

GOLDEN BATTER BREAD

1 c. milk
¼ c. margarine or butter
¼ c. sugar
2 tsp. salt
2 pkg. dry yeast
½ c. warm water
1 egg, beaten
4 ½ c. sifted flour
1 3 ½-oz. can French-fried onion rings

(Continued on next page)

Scald milk till it bubbles; remove from heat. Add butter, sugar and salt; cool to lukewarm. Sprinkle yeast in warm water; stir until dissolved. Add to milk mixture. Stir in beaten egg and 3 cups flour; spoon beat until smooth. Stir in remaining flour, making stiff batter. Turn in well-greased large bowl; let rise. Stir in onion rings; put in 2 well-greased 1 1/2-quart round casseroles or 2 loaf pans. Let rise. Bake at 350 degrees for 40 minutes.

Mrs. R. E. White, Starkville, Miss.

HERB BREAD

1 pkg. dry yeast
1 ¼ c. warm water
2 tbsp. soft shortening
2 tsp. salt
1 tsp. caraway seed
½ tsp. nutmeg
½ tsp. crumbled sage
3 c. sifted flour

Sprinkle yeast on water; add shortening and salt. Add caraway seed, nutmeg and sage to 1 1/2 cups flour; add to yeast mixture. Beat 2 minutes or 300 strokes by hand. Add remaining flour; blend with spoon until smooth. Cover; let rise in warm place 30 minutes. Stir down, beating 25 strokes. Spread evenly in greased 9 x 5 x 3-inch loaf pan. Let rise for 40 minutes. Bake 45 minutes at 350 degrees or until bread tests done. Brush top with melted butter.

Mrs. Joseph J. Shippen, Atlanta, Ga.

HERB-CHEESE BREAD

1 c. milk
¼ c. butter or margarine
1 ½ tbsp. sugar
1 ½ tsp. salt
1 egg, slightly beaten
1 ¼ -oz. pkg. active dry yeast
½ c. warm water
½ c. grated Parmesan and Romano cheese
½ tsp. dehydrated imported oregano
¼ tsp. whole marjoram
4 ½ c. sifted all-purpose flour

In medium saucepan, scald milk over low heat. Stir in butter, sugar and salt; continue to stir until melted. Remove from heat; cool to lukewarm. Stir in egg. Dissolve yeast in warm water. In medium mixing bowl, combine yeast and milk mixture. Stir in cheese, oregano and marjoram. Stir in 1 cup sifted flour; beat until mixture becomes smooth. Repeat 3 more times, beating well after each addition. Turn dough onto well-floured board; knead until sticky and all of the flour has disappeared. Knead in remaining 1/2 cup sifted flour. Ball of dough will be sticky and hard to handle. Place in large mixing bowl. Cover; set in warm place free from draft. Let rise about 1 hour or until doubled in bulk. Turn onto a well-floured board. With a floured rolling pin, roll out all air in dough. Fold into a smooth loaf; place in well-greased 9 x 5 x 3-inch loaf pan. Cover; let rise about 45 minutes in a warm place, free from draft, until all sides of dough reach pan top and is well rounded. Bake in 400-degree oven 50 minutes or until crust is dark golden brown. Remove from oven; turn out of pan immediately. Cool at room temperature.

Mrs. James F. Dorsey, Arkadelphia, Ark.

HOME-BAKED BREAD

1 pkg. dry yeast
2 c. warm milk
4 tbsp. butter or oleo
1 tsp. salt
⅓ c. sugar
1 egg, beaten
5 ½ c. presifted flour or enough to make a stiff dough

Dissolve yeast in warm milk; add butter, salt, sugar, beaten egg and flour. Mix thoroughly. Put in a warm place to rise until double in bulk. Stir down once or twice; divide into 2 loaves. Put in pans; let rise to top of pan. Bake in 350-degree oven 30 minutes or until done.

Mrs. Lelon Hopkins, Paducah, Ky.

LIGHT BREAD

½ c. shortening
¼ c. sugar
1 beaten egg
1 cake yeast or dry yeast
½ c. warm water
½ c. cold water
3 to 3 ½ c. flour
½ tsp. baking powder
½ tsp. soda
1 tsp. salt

Melt shortening; add sugar slowly. Add beaten egg. When cool, add yeast softened in warm water. Stir; add cold water. Sift in flour with baking powder, soda and salt; mix well. Cover tightly; refrigerate overnight. Remove from refrigerator; knead 5 minutes. Put in well-greased pan. Cover; let rise until double in bulk. Bake at 400 degrees for 50 minutes to 1 hour.

Mrs. Hobert Collins, Knoxville, Tenn.

LIGHT BREAD

2 pkg. yeast
4 c. water
1 c. sugar
2 tbsp. salt
2 beaten eggs
14 c. (or more) plain flour
6 tbsp. shortening, melted or oil

Add yeast to water; let stand 5 minutes. Add sugar, salt and egg. Add half the flour, shortening then more flour. Place on board; knead. Put back in clean bowl; let rise until doubled. Turn out on board; knead. Cut into pieces; knead each piece until firm. Have additional cooled melted shortening in pans. Place loaf in pan; roll to grease surface. Let rise. Bake in 350-degree oven for 40 minutes or more. Rub butter over loaves several times during baking. Recipe may also be used for icebox rolls. Dough may be refrigerated from 2 to 4 days if used for rolls. Yield: 6 loaves.

Mrs. Robert M. Johnson, Hixson, Tenn.

NO-KNEAD OAT BREAD

2 c. boiling water
1 c. rolled oats
1 tsp. salt
½ c. molasses or honey
3 tbsp. butter
2 pkg. yeast
⅓ c. warm water
6 c. flour

(Continued on next page)

Pour boiling water over oats; let stand 30 minutes. Add salt, molasses and butter. Stir in yeast that was softened in warm water. Add flour gradually, beating after each addition; mix well. Cover; let rise till doubled in bulk. Cut down with a knife. Shape into loaves. Place in greased pan; cover. Let rise again. Bake at 325 degrees about 50 minutes. Butter crust while warm.

Vivienne H. Coates, Union City, Tenn.

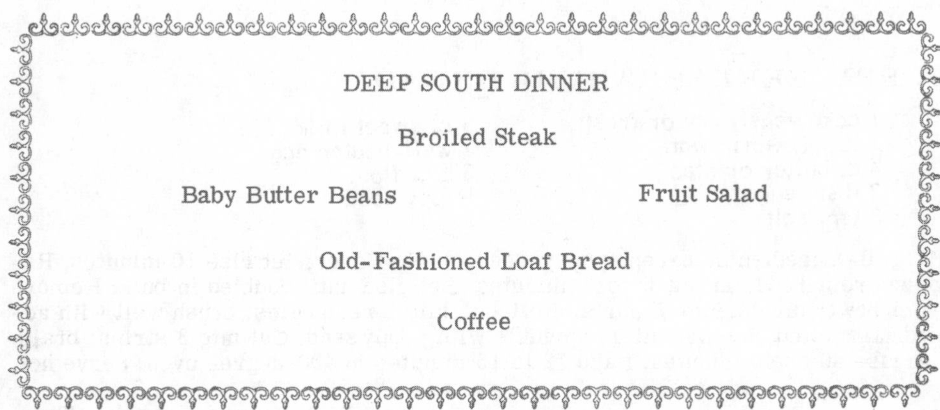

DEEP SOUTH DINNER

Broiled Steak

Baby Butter Beans

Fruit Salad

Old-Fashioned Loaf Bread

Coffee

OLD-FASHIONED LOAF BREAD

1 pkg. dry yeast
¼ c. warm water
2 c. milk, scalded
2 tsp. salt
2 tbsp. sugar
2 tbsp. butter
6 c. (about) flour

Sprinkle dry yeast over warm water; set aside for 5 minutes. Scald milk; pour into bowl containing salt, sugar and butter. When milk mixture is lukewarm, pour in dissolved yeast. Add 3 cups flour; beat 2 minutes with electric beater. Slowly add remaining flour, beating dough with spoon. Add flour until dough is too stiff to beat with spoon. Turn dough onto lightly floured board; cover with bowl for 20 minutes. Knead dough until it bubbles and crackles then looks smooth and elastic, 8 to 10 minutes. Put dough into bowl; butter top. Cover; set in warm place until doubled in bulk. Press dough down; knead a little, very lightly. Shape loaves. Place in buttered loaf pans. Cover; let rise until double. Bake in 375-degree oven for 45 to 50 minutes. Remove from pans; cool.

Mrs. Louise Reed, Big Rock, Tenn.

ORANGE VELVET BREAD

1 c. milk
2 tbsp. (scant) sugar
2 tbsp. shortening
2 tsp. salt
2 tbsp. grated orange rind
1 egg, well beaten
1 yeast cake
2 tbsp. warm water
2 ½ to 3 c. flour

Combine milk, sugar, shortening, salt and orange rind; place over low heat. Stir constantly until mixture is scalded. Remove from heat; cool slightly. Add egg;

(Continued on next page)

cool to lukewarm. Stir in yeast dissolved in warm water. Stir in enough flour to make firm dough. Knead lightly on floured board. Place in greased bowl; put in warm place, not over 70 to 74 degrees, to rise slowly until increased 3/4 in bulk. Knead down lightly. Divide dough in half; place in 2 greased 1-pound coffee cans. Let rise to 3/4 larger in bulk. Bake in 350-degree oven 20 to 25 minutes. Slice thick; serve warm.

Hattie Barringer, Charlotte, N. C.

POPPY SEED BRAIDED BREAD

1 cake yeast, dry or fresh
¼ c. lukewarm water
¼ c. butter or oleo
3 tbsp. sugar
2 tsp. salt
¾ c. sweet milk
1 well-beaten egg
3 ½ c. flour
Poppy seed

Mix all ingredients, except poppy seed, well. Cover; let rise 10 minutes. Remove from bowl; knead 5 to 7 minutes. Let rise until doubled in bulk. Remove from bowl; divide into 2 parts. Roll out into 2 rectangles; brush well with additional melted oleo or butter. Sprinkle with poppy seed. Cut into 3 strips; braid. Let rise 30 or 40 minutes. Bake 12 to 15 minutes in 400-degree oven. Serve hot.

Mrs. W. I. Kinsey, Franklin, Tenn.

POTATO BREAD

2 c. milk, scalded
1 pkg. active dry yeast
1 c. cold mashed potatoes
2 tsp. salt
1 tbsp. sugar
1 ½ tbsp. butter or margarine
6 c. sifted all-purpose flour

Pour milk into a large bowl; cool to lukewarm. Sprinkle yeast over milk; stir until dissolved. Blend in potatoes, salt, sugar and butter. Gradually add 4 cups flour, stirring vigorously with a wooden spoon as flour is added. Add enough of the remaining flour to handle easily. Turn dough onto a floured board; knead until smooth and elastic. Place in greased bowl; turn once to bring greased side up. Cover with damp cloth; let rise in a warm place until doubled in bulk, about 1 hour. Punch down with fist. Pull edges into center; turn dough over in bowl. Cover; let rise again until almost doubled, about 30 minutes. Divide dough into 2 equal portions; shape each into a loaf. Place in 2 greased 7 1/2 x 4 1/2 x 3-inch loaf pans. Cover; let rise until almost doubled in bulk, about 45 minutes. Bake loaves in 350-degree oven about 50 minutes. Remove bread from pans immediately; cool thoroughly on racks.

Mrs. Simon L. Blan, Clifton, Tex.

POTATO AU GRATIN BREAD

1 6-oz. box au gratin potato mix
4 c. boiling water
2 pkg. or cakes yeast
2 tbsp. sugar
1 tbsp. salt
¼ c. peanut oil
6 ½ c. unsifted flour
¼ c. warm water

(Continued on next page)

Soak au gratin potato slices in boiling water. Cool until warm, about 30 minutes. Drain, reserving 2 cups liquid. Place reserved potato liquid in large warm mixing bowl. Sprinkle or crumble in yeast; stir until dissolved. Add sugar, salt, 1/4 cup peanut oil and 3 cups flour. Beat until smooth. Mix in drained potato slices and enough additional flour to make soft dough. Turn out onto lightly floured board; knead until smooth and elastic, about 8 minutes. Place in greased bowl, turning to grease top. Cover; let rise in warm place free from draft until doubled in bulk, about 45 minutes. Punch down dough. Turn out onto lightly floured board. Divide in half. Flatten each half to an oblong 15 x 8 inches. Combine au gratin sauce mix with warm water. Spread each oblong with half this mixture. Roll up from 8 inch sides as for jelly rolls; seal edges. Place loaves in 2 greased 9 x 5 x 3-inch loaf pans. Brush tops of loaves with peanut oil. Cover; let rise in warm place, free from draft, until doubled in bulk, about 1 hour. Bake in 375-degree oven for 45 minutes or until done.

Photograph for this recipe on page 357.

PUMPERNICKEL BREAD

1 ½ c. warm water
3 pkg. active dry yeast
½ c. molasses
4 tsp. salt
1 to 3 tsp. caraway seed
2 ¾ c. sifted rye flour
2 tbsp. shortening
3 ½ to 4 c. sifted flour
Cornmeal

Measure water into bowl; add yeast, stirring to dissolve. Stir in molasses, salt and caraway seed. Mix rye flour in with spoon until smooth; mix in shortening with hands and enough sifted flour to handle easily. Turn onto lightly floured board; knead until smooth. Place in greased bowl, turning to grease top. Cover; let rise in warm place until double in bulk. Punch down; shape into 2 round loaves, slightly flattened. Place on greased baking sheet sprinkled with cornmeal. Cover with damp cloth; let rise 1 hour. Bake 30 to 35 minutes in 350-degree oven.

Trudy Dickerson, Midland, Tex.

QUICK SUNDAY BREAD

1 pkg. or cake dry yeast
¼ c. warm water
1 c. water
2 tbsp. sugar
2 tbsp. lard or butter
1 tsp. salt
3 c. flour

Dissolve yeast in warm water. Add remaining ingredients; mix well. Pour in well-greased loaf pan. Let rise in warm place for 1 hour. Bake in preheated oven at 450 degrees for 15 minutes. Reduce heat to 300 degrees; bake 30 minutes or until done.

Dr. Robert H. Harvey, Erwin, Tenn.

RAISIN CASSEROLE BREAD

⅔ c. hot water
½ c. sugar
1½ tsp. salt
¼ c. shortening
½ c. warm water
2 pkg. active dry or compressed yeast
1 egg, beaten
3 ¼ c. sifted flour
1 c. seedless raisins

(Continued on next page)

Mix together hot water, sugar, salt and shortening; cool to lukewarm. Measure warm water in a bowl; sprinkle or crumble in yeast. Stir until dissolved; stir in sugar mixture. Add egg, flour and raisins. Stir until well blended, about 2 minutes. Let rise in warm place, free from draft, about 50 minutes or until more than doubled in bulk. Stir down; beat vigorously about 30 seconds. Turn into greased 1 1/2-quart casserole. Bake, uncovered, in preheated 400-degree oven about 45 minutes.

Mrs. A. J. Richards, Louisville, Ky.

SALLY LUNN BREAD

1 pkg. active dry
or compressed yeast
¼ c. lukewarm water
¾ c. milk
½ c. butter
⅓ c. sugar
3 eggs
1 tsp. salt
4 c. flour

Soften yeast in lukewarm water. Heat milk to lukewarm; combine with yeast. Cream butter and sugar together; add well-beaten eggs and mix well. Add salt to flour; stir flour into butter-sugar mixture alternately with milk-yeast mixture. Beat well with a wooden spoon. Turn into a buttered bowl; let rise in a warm place until doubled in bulk, 1 hour and 30 minutes. Beat again; pour into a well-buttered 3 1/2 x 10-inch ring mold or angel cake pan. Let rise again until doubled in bulk, about 40 minutes. Bake in 350-degree oven for 45 minutes. Unmold; serve warm. Yield: 6 servings.

Mrs. R. D. Bailey, Paducah, Ky.

ALABAMA BISCUITS

2 ½ c. flour
1 tbsp. sugar
2 tsp. baking powder
1 tsp. salt
4 tbsp. shortening
1 ½ pkg. dry yeast
dissolved in ⅓ c.
lukewarm water
¾ c. sweet milk
Oleo

Sift dry ingredients together. Cut shortening in with pastry blender. Add yeast, water and milk; work into soft dough. Roll 1/8 inch thick; cut with 2 different size cutters. Dip each in melted oleo. Place smaller biscuits on top; arrange on an ungreased cookie sheet. Let rise until double in size. Partially bake at 400 degrees. When ready to serve, finish browning and serve very hot. Yield: 35 biscuits.

May Read, Monroe, La.

ANGEL BISCUITS

4 c. flour
1 c. lard
2 c. buttermilk
1 pkg. yeast, dissolved in
warm water
1 tsp. soda
1 tsp. salt
3 tsp. baking powder

Mix all ingredients as for biscuits. Bake in oven at 450 degrees for about 10 to 15 minutes. Do not let rise.

Mrs. Allen Ozbirn, Ripley, Miss.

Nation's tallest lighthouse at Cape Hatteras, North Carolina.

CORNMEAL ICEBOX ROLLS

1 cake yeast or 1 pkg. dry yeast
Flour
1 c. white cornmeal
1 tbsp. salt
1 c. melted shortening
½ c. sugar
2 c. potato water

Make a sponge of the yeast, 1/2 cup lukewarm water and 3 tablespoons flour. Cover; allow to stand until light. Sift cornmeal slowly into 4 cups boiling water; add salt. Stir constantly until thick. Cook over hot water 30 minutes. Add shortening, sugar and potato water. Stir until well blended; cool. Add the sponge. Add sufficient flour to make a dough stiff enough to knead. Turn onto lightly floured board; knead until smooth and elastic. Cover with a damp cloth; allow dough to double in bulk. Knead down. Cover closely; place in refrigerator. Remove portion of dough required from refrigerator 2 hours or more before rolls are needed. Allow dough to warm to room temperature. Form into rolls; place in well-oiled pans. Cover; let rise until triple in bulk. Bake in oven at 450 degrees about 15 minutes. The unused portion of the dough should be worked down, covered closely with waxed paper and returned to refrigerator until needed. Dough will keep in refrigerator for a week. Boil 1 cup diced potatoes in 2 cups water to make potato water. Yield: 6 dozen rolls.

Lyn Lynes, Mountain Home, Ark.

ICEBOX ROLLS

1 pkg. dry yeast
¼ c. sugar
1 tsp. salt
1 ½ tbsp. shortening
1 egg, beaten
4 c. flour

Dissolve yeast in 1/4 cup lukewarm water with 1/2 teaspoon sugar. Add yeast mixture, remaining sugar, salt, shortening and egg to 1 cup warm water in large container. Beat in 2 cups flour, then beat in remaining flour. Place in icebox. When ready to use, shape; let rise until double in bulk, 1 hour and 30 minutes to 3 hours. Bake in 400 to 450-degree oven until browned. Yield: 18 rolls.

Mrs. Willie Chance, Elizabeth, La.

REFRIGERATOR BISCUITS

5 c. sifted flour
3 tsp. baking powder
1 tsp. salt
3 tbsp. sugar
¾ c. shortening
2 c. buttermilk
1 pkg. yeast, dissolved in ½ c. warm water

Sift dry ingredients together; cut in shortening until well mixed. Add buttermilk and dissolved yeast; work together with large spoon until all flour is moistened. Cover bowl; refrigerate until ready to use. Take out as much dough as needed; roll out on floured board 1/2 inch thick. Let biscuits rise about 45 minutes before baking. Bake in shallow pan or cookie sheet in 400-degree oven about 12 minutes or until golden brown. This dough will keep several days in refrigerator. Yield: 6 dozen rolls.

Mrs. Homer Hooks, Leesburg, Fla.

REFRIGERATOR ROLLS

2 c. boiling water
½ c. plus 1 tsp. sugar
1 tbsp. salt
2 tbsp. shortening
2 cakes quick-acting yeast
¼ c. lukewarm water
2 eggs, beaten
8 c. flour, sifted before measuring

Mix boiling water, 1/2 cup sugar, salt and shortening; cool to lukewarm. Soften yeast in lukewarm water; add remaining sugar. Stir into shortening mixture. Add beaten eggs; stir in 4 cups flour. Beat thoroughly; stir in remaining flour. Mix thoroughly; it is not necessary to knead dough. Place in greased bowl; grease surface lightly with melted butter. Cover tightly; store in refrigerator till ready to use. About 1 hour and 30 minutes to 2 hours before serving time, shape on floured surface. Let rise in warm place till double in bulk. Bake 15 to 20 minutes at 425 degrees.

Mrs. Marvin Ramey, Jr., Maryville, Tenn.

WHOLE WHEAT ROLLS

3 tbsp. molasses
2 tbsp. sugar
2 ½ tsp. salt
¼ c. margarine
1 c. milk, scalded
2 pkg. yeast
½ c. warm water
2 ¼ c. unsifted whole wheat flour
2 ¼ c. unsifted plain flour

Stir molasses, sugar, salt and margarine into milk; cool to lukewarm. Dissolve yeast in warm water; add milk mixture. Add enough of each kind of remaining flour to make a soft dough. Knead on lightly floured board until smooth and elastic. Place in greased bowl; turning to grease top. Cover; let rise in warm place until doubled in bulk. Punch down; shape into rolls. Cover; let rise 30 minutes. Bake at 400 degrees 15 minutes. Yield: 24 servings.

Mrs. Bill Hyde, Robbinsville, N. C.

WHOLE WHEAT ROLLS

¾ c. milk, scalded
¼ c. sugar
3 tbsp. shortening
1 tsp. salt
1 pkg. yeast
¼ c. lukewarm water
1 egg, slightly beaten
1 ½ to 2 c. plain flour
1 ½ to 2 c. whole wheat flour

Pour hot milk over sugar, shortening and salt; cool to lukewarm. Soften yeast in water; add egg and beat well. Add yeast to milk mixture; add half of flours. Beat with rotary beater until mixture is smooth and bubbles appear. Add enough of remaining flours to form a soft dough. Knead on floured board until smooth. Place in a greased bowl; cover and let rise in a warm place until doubled in bulk. Knead lightly; shape into rolls. Let rise until doubled. Bake at 400 degrees for 20 minutes. Yield: 6-8 servings.

Mrs. Bernard D. Black, Liberty, N. C.

YEAST BISCUITS

1 pkg. yeast
Warmed buttermilk
2 c. sifted flour
¼ tsp. salt
¼ tsp. soda
1 tbsp. sugar
2 tbsp. melted shortening

Dissolve yeast in 1/4 cup warm water; add enough warmed buttermilk to equal 1 cup. Sift all dry ingredients in bowl; add shortening and yeast mixture. Roll thin; cut. Brush with melted butter; put 2 biscuits together. Brush top with butter. Let rise on cookie sheet 30 to 45 minutes. Bake in 450-degree oven. Yield: 12 large biscuits.

Mrs. Carol Ann Young, Swannanoa, N. C.

YEAST ROLLS

2 pkg. yeast
1 c. warm water
1 c. shortening
1 pt. boiling water
2 qt. plain flour
1 tsp. salt
½ c. sugar
2 eggs

Dissolve yeast in warm water; let stand about 30 minutes. Melt fat in boiling water; cool. Sift flour, salt and sugar in large bowl; make a well in center. Pour in dissolved yeast, melted fat and water and beaten eggs; mix well. Let rise about 1 hour in warm place; knead and shape into rolls. Put in warm place; cover and let rise until double in size. Bake in oven at 400 degrees until browned. Yield: 4 dozen large rolls.

Mrs. Charles Hyatt, Roebuck, S. C.

INDEX

ACKNOWLEDGMENTS

We wish to thank the many women who submitted their favorite recipes for inclusion in this book. We regret that lack of space made it impossible for us to include all of them.

We wish also to express our appreciation for the use of photographs supplied us by the following: Cover—National Association of Frozen Food Packers (recipes on pages 29, 83, 106 and 197); and Frontispiece—Duranel-Stainless-Clad Aluminum (recipe on page 122).

Title page photographs were supplied by the following: American Dairy Association; National Kraut Packers Association; Best Foods Division, Corn Products Company; International Packers Limited; National Association of Frozen Food Packers; National Dairy Council; Evaporated Milk Association; National Macaroni Institute; The Ruth Lundgren Company; The Borden Company; Ralston Purina Company; and Fleischmann's Yeast.